Omar Amer

Veterinary Parasitology Questions

AF792050

Omar Amer

Veterinary Parasitology Questions

Noor Publishing

Imprint

Cover image: www.ingimage.com

Publisher:
Noor Publishing
is a trademark of
Dodo Books Indian Ocean Ltd. and OmniScriptum S.R.L publishing group

120 High Road, East Finchley, London, N2 9ED, United Kingdom
Str. Armeneasca 28/1, office 1, Chisinau MD-2012, Republic of Moldova, Europe
Managing Directors: Ieva Konstantinova, Victoria Ursu
info@omniscriptum.com

Printed at: see last page
ISBN: 978-620-9-40305-7

Veterinary Parasitology Questions

Prof. Omar H. Amer

2026

AUTHORS

Prof. Omar Hassan Amer

Doctor of Veterinary Medicine specializing in Parasitology at Zagazig University, Egypt.

He obtained his PhD in Parasitology with a focus on filariasis in dogs, and completed postdoctoral studies from 1993 to 1994 at the University of Giessen, Germany.

His postdoctoral research investigated the effect of chemotherapy on specific antibody levels (IgM, IgG1, IgG2, and IgA) in *Brugia malayi*-infected *Mastomys coucha*.

His primary research interests include the diagnosis and treatment of parasitic infections in domestic and wild animals, as well as the epidemiology of fish-borne parasitic diseases.

From 2009 to 2019, he spent ten years teaching and conducting research in Medical Parasitology at the University of Hail, Saudi Arabia, within the Faculty of Medicine, where he also served as Vice Dean for the Faculty of Applied Medical Sciences.

Contents

CHAPTER	TITLE	PAGE
-----	PREFACE	4
CHAPTER: ONE	RUMINANT PARASITES QUESTIONS	6
CHAPTER : TWO	EQUINE PARASITES QUESTIONS	73
CHAPTER : THREE	PET ANIMAL PARASITE QUESTIONS	183
CHAPTER:FOUR	POULTRY PARASITES QUESTIONS	250
CHAPTER:FIVE	RABBIT PARASITES QUESTIONS	377
CHAPTER:SIX	FISH PARASITES QUESTIONS	438
CHAPTER:SEVEN	PARASITOLOGY DIAGNOSTIC QUESTIONS	495
CHAPTER:EIGHT	CASE STUDIES IN VET.PARASITOLOGY	529
CHAPTER:NINE	REFRENCES	

Preface

This book has been designed as a comprehensive question-based guide in the field of **Veterinary Parasitology**, aiming to support undergraduate and postgraduate veterinary students, as well as practicing veterinarians. It provides a structured and practical approach to understanding parasitic diseases affecting different animal species of veterinary importance.

The content includes carefully prepared questions on **ruminant parasites**, **equine parasites**, **pet animal parasites**, **poultry parasites**, **rabbit parasites**, and **fish parasites**, covering major internal and external parasites, their life cycles, pathogenic effects, diagnosis, control, and prevention.

In addition, a dedicated section on **Parasitology Diagnostic Questions** has been included to enhance students' skills in laboratory diagnosis, parasite identification, and interpretation of diagnostic findings. This section emphasizes practical knowledge essential for clinical and field applications.

The book also features **case studies in veterinary parasitology**, which are intended to bridge the gap between theoretical knowledge and real-life clinical situations. These case studies encourage critical thinking, problem-solving, and application of parasitological principles in veterinary practice.

This compilation of questions and case studies is intended to serve as a valuable revision tool, examination aid, and reference resource, contributing to a deeper understanding of parasitic diseases and their impact on animal health, productivity, and public health

Dr. Omar Hassan Amer
Prof. of Parasitology, Zagazig University

2026

Introduction

Veterinary parasitology constitutes a core discipline within veterinary medical sciences, providing essential knowledge for understanding the epidemiology, pathology, diagnosis, and control of parasitic diseases affecting animals. Parasitic infections remain a major cause of economic loss in animal production systems and pose significant health challenges in companion animals and aquatic species. Therefore, a thorough and systematic approach to parasitology is indispensable for veterinary education and professional practice.

This book is structured as a comprehensive **question-based academic resource** designed to support the learning and assessment needs of veterinary students and professionals. It encompasses a wide spectrum of parasitological topics, with an emphasis on host-specific parasite biology and clinically relevant diagnostic approaches.

The book includes carefully formulated questions covering:

- Ruminant parasitology
- Equine parasitology
- Pet animal parasitology
- Poultry parasitology
- Rabbit parasitology
- Fish parasitology
- Diagnostic techniques in parasitology
- Case studies in veterinary parasitology

By combining foundational theoretical concepts with applied diagnostic and case-based questions, this book promotes analytical thinking and problem-solving skills. It is intended to reinforce core parasitological principles, facilitate examination preparation, and enhance the reader's ability to interpret laboratory findings and clinical presentations.

This work is designed to serve as an academic reference for undergraduate and postgraduate veterinary students, as well as a revision and teaching aid for veterinarians and educators, contributing to the development of competency in the diagnosis and management of parasitic diseases across diverse animal species.

CHAPTER ONE :RUMINANT PARASITES QUESTIONS

1- TrematodesParasites of Ruminant Animals MCQs on Rumen Flukes (Paramphistomes)

1. What is the scientific name of the common rumen fluke found in cattle?
A. *Fasciola hepatica*
B. *Paramphistomum cervi*
C. *Schistosoma bovis*
D. *Dicrocoelium dendriticum*
Answer: B

2. Where do adult Paramphistomes primarily reside in ruminants?
A. Liver
B. Small intestine
C. Rumen and reticulum
D. Lungs
Answer: C

3. Which stage of the Paramphistome life cycle is responsible for clinical signs in young animals?
A. Egg
B. Adult fluke
C. Metacercaria
D. Immature fluke (in the duodenum)
Answer: D

4. What is the intermediate host for Paramphistomum spp.?
A. Earthworm
B. Snail
C. Ant
D. Mosquito
Answer: B

5. How are Paramphistome infections most commonly diagnosed in live animals?
A. Blood smear
B. Baermann technique
C. Fecal sedimentation
D. Skin scraping
Answer: C

6. Which of the following drugs is effective against immature Paramphistomes?
A. Albendazole
B. Closantel
C. Oxyclozanide
D. Ivermectin
Answer: C

7. What type of eggs are produced by Paramphistomes?
A. Operculated, yellowish eggs
B. Thick-shelled, segmented eggs
C. Thin-shelled, larvated eggs
D. Non-operculated, clear eggs
Answer: A

8. Clinical signs of acute Paramphistomosis include:
A. Weight gain and lethargy
B. Diarrhea, dehydration, and anorexia
C. Constipation and jaundice
D. Respiratory distress
Answer: B

9. What environmental condition promotes the life cycle of Paramphistomes?
A. Dry and cold weather
B. High altitude and snow
C. Warm and moist environment
D. Arid desert conditions
Answer: C

10. Which control strategy is best for reducing Paramphistome infection in grazing animals?
A. Use of insecticides
B. Avoiding grazing in snail-infested areas
C. Vaccination
D. Restricting protein supplements
Answer: B

Fasciola sp. Questions :

MCQs on ***Fasciola*** sp.

1. Which of the following is the primary site of infection for *Fasciola hepatica* in the definitive host?
A. Intestine
B. Lungs
C. Liver
D. Kidneys
Answer: C. Liver

2. The intermediate host for *Fasciola* species is usually:
A. Freshwater fish
B. Snail
C. Mosquito
D. Tick
Answer: B. Snail

3. The infective stage of *Fasciola hepatica* for humans is:
A. Miracidium
B. Cercaria
C. Metacercaria
D. Sporocyst
Answer: C. Metacercaria

4. Humans become infected with *Fasciola hepatica* by ingesting:
A. Undercooked liver
B. Contaminated water
C. Raw aquatic vegetation
D. Infected meat
Answer: C. Raw aquatic vegetation

5. Which of the following is a common diagnostic method for fascioliasis?
A. Blood smear
B. Sputum analysis
C. Stool examination for eggs
D. Skin biopsy
Answer: C. Stool examination for eggs

6. Fascioliasis is primarily classified as a:
A. Bacterial infection
B. Viral infection
C. Protozoan infection
D. Helminthic infection
Answer: D. Helminthic infection

7. Which drug is most effective in treating fascioliasis?
A. Metronidazole
B. Albendazole
C. Praziquantel
D. Triclabendazole
Answer: D. Triclabendazole

8. *Fasciola gigantica* differs from *Fasciola hepatica* primarily in:
A. Host species
B. Life cycle
C. Geographic distribution and size
D. Morphology of eggs
Answer: C. Geographic distribution and size

9-During the life-cycle, Fasciola hepatica (liver-fluke) infects its intermediate host and primary host at the following larval stages respectively.

A. Radiae and miracidium
B. Cercaria and rediae
C. Metacercaria and cercaria
D. Miracidium and metacercaria
Answer: D

10-The metacercaria's cyst of liver fluke survives the actions of gastric juices of host because
A. it produces multiple larval forms
B. cyst wall is multiple larval forms
C. it secretes an additional tough coat around it
D. it undergoes segmentation
Answer: B

MCQ in D. dendriticum

1. What is the definitive host of *Dicrocoelium dendriticum***?**

A. Snail
B. Ant
C. Sheep
D. Cow

Answer: C. Sheep

2. What type of parasite is *Dicrocoelium dendriticum***?**

A. Nematode
B. Cestode
C. Trematode
D. Protozoan

Answer: C. Trematode

3. What is the first intermediate host of *D. dendriticum*?

A. Cow
B. Ant
C. Freshwater snail
D. Land snail

Answer: D. Land snail

4. Which of the following is the second intermediate host for *D. dendriticum*?

A. Slug
B. Mosquito
C. Ant
D. Earthworm

Answer: C. Ant

5. Where in the definitive host does *D. dendriticum* primarily reside?

A. Small intestine
B. Large intestine
C. Gall bladder
D. Bile ducts

Answer: D. Bile ducts

6. How does the definitive host get infected with ***D. dendriticum***?

A. Ingesting contaminated water
B. Eating raw meat
C. Ingesting infected ants
D. Skin penetration

Answer: C. Ingesting infected ants

7. What is a key behavioral change in ants infected with *D. dendriticum*?

A. Aggressive behavior
B. Climbing vegetation and clamping onto grass
C. Avoidance of sunlight
D. Increased reproduction

Answer: B. Climbing vegetation and clamping onto grass

8. What is the main pathological effect of *D. dendriticum* in livestock?

A. Intestinal blockage
B. Anemia
C. Liver cirrhosis and bile duct inflammation
D. Lung congestion

Answer: C. Liver cirrhosis and bile duct inflammation

9. What diagnostic method is commonly used to identify *D. dendriticum* infection?

A. Blood smear
B. ELISA
C. Fecal egg examination
D. Skin scraping

Answer: C. Fecal egg examination

10. Which of the following is a preventive measure against *D. dendriticum* infection in livestock?

A. Vaccination
B. Keeping livestock away from wet pastures
C. Deworming only in winter
D. Feeding only during night

Answer: B. Keeping livestock away from wet pastures

2-Cestode parasites

MCQs on ***Moniezia expansa*** and ***Moniezia benedeni***

1. What type of organism is *Moniezia expansa*?
A. Bacterium
B. Protozoan
C. Cestode
D. Nematode
Answer: C. Cestode

2. ***Moniezia benedeni* commonly infects which of the following animals?**
A. Pigs
B. Cattle
C. Horses
D. Dogs
Answer: B. Cattle

3. **What is the intermediate host for *Moniezia* species?**
A. Mosquito
B. Snail
C. Mite
D. Flea
Answer: C. Mite (specifically oribatid mites)

4. **How are sheep typically infected with *Moniezia expansa*?**
A. Ingestion of contaminated water
B. Skin penetration
C. Eating oribatid mites on pasture
D. Through wounds
Answer: C. Eating oribatid mites on pasture

5. ***Moniezia expansa* is most commonly found in which part of the host's body?**
A. Liver
B. Lungs
C. Small intestine
D. Rumen
Answer: C. Small intestine

6. **Which of the following is a distinguishing morphological feature of *Moniezia expansa*?**
A. Cylindrical body
B. Scolex with suckers and rostellum
C. Broad, short proglottids with bilateral genital pores
D. Hooks on the scolex
Answer: C. Broad, short proglottids with bilateral genital pores

7. **Which drug is commonly used to treat *Moniezia* infections in ruminants?**
A. Ivermectin
B. Albendazole
C. Levamisole
D. Amprolium
Answer: B. Albendazole

8. **What is the main difference between *Moniezia expansa* and *Moniezia benedeni*?**
A. Shape of scolex
B. Host specificity
C. Mode of transmission
D. Intermediate host
Answer: B. Host specificity (*M. expansa* mainly in sheep/goats; *M. benedeni* in cattle)

9. **Which age group of animals is more susceptible to *Moniezia* infections?**
A. Newborns
B. Adults
C. Young animals (less than 1 year)
D. Aged animals
Answer: C. Young animals (less than 1 year)

10. **Which clinical sign is least likely associated with heavy *Moniezia* infection?**
A. Diarrhea
B. Bloat
C. Neurological symptoms
D. Poor growth
Answer: C. Neurological symptoms

Answer: D

MCQs on *Avitellina centripunctata*

1. Avitellina   is primarily found in which host?*
A. Humans
B. Pigs
C. Sheep and goats
D. Dogs
Answer: C. Sheep and goats

2. What type of parasite is *Avitellina centripunctata*?
A. Trematode
B. Nematode
C. Cestode
D. Protozoa
Answer: C. Cestode

3. Where in the host is *Avitellina centripunctata* usually located?
A. Liver
B. Lungs
C. Small intestine
D. Stomach
Answer: C. Small intestine

4. What is a characteristic morphological feature of *Avitellina centripunctata*?
A. Armed scolex with suckers
B. Unsegmented body
C. Scolex without hooks
D. Presence of a pseudocoelom
Answer: C. Scolex without hooks

5. The intermediate host of *Avitellina centripunctata* is usually:
A. Mosquito
B. Snail
C. Oribatid mite
D. Earthworm
Answer: C. Oribatid mite

6. What type of lifecycle does *Avitellina centripunctata* follow?
A. Direct
B. Indirect
C. Both
D. None
Answer: B. Indirect

7. Which diagnostic method is commonly used to detect *Avitellina centripunctata* infection?
A. Blood smear
B. Skin scraping
C. Fecal examination
D. X-ray
Answer: C. Fecal examination

8. Which class does *Avitellina centripunctata* belong to?
A. Monogenea
B. Trematoda
C. Cestoda
D. Nematoda
Answer: C. Cestoda

9. What is the shape of the proglottids in *Avitellina centripunctata*?
A. Long and slender
B. Fan-shaped
C. Triangular
D. Square
Answer: B. Fan-shaped

10. Control of *Avitellina centripunctata* involves:
A. Antiviral drugs
B. Use of anthelmintics and pasture management
C. Vaccination
D. Use of antibiotics
Answer: B. Use of anthelmintics and pasture management

Multiple-choice questions (MCQs) related to **cestode larval stages in sheep and goats**, with a focus on parasitology:

1. Which of the following is the larval stage of *Taenia hydatigena* **found in sheep and goats?**

A. Cysticercus ovis
B. Cysticercus tenuicollis
C. Coenurus cerebralis
D. Hydatid cyst
Answer: B. Cysticercus tenuicollis

2. The larval stage of *Taenia multiceps* **in sheep is known as:**

A. Cysticercus cellulosae
B. Coenurus cerebralis
C. Cysticercus tenuicollis
D. Hydatid cyst
Answer: B. Coenurus cerebralis

3. Which larval stage causes "gid" or "staggers" in sheep?

A. Cysticercus ovis
B. Coenurus cerebralis
C. Hydatid cyst
D. Cysticercus tenuicollis
Answer: B. Coenurus cerebralis

4. ***Echinococcus granulosus*** causes what type of larval stage in sheep and goats?

A. Cysticercus
B. Hydatid cyst
C. Coenurus
D. Tetrathyridium
Answer: B. Hydatid cyst

5. Which organ is most commonly affected by *Cysticercus tenuicollis* in small ruminants?

A. Brain
B. Heart
C. Liver
D. Lungs
Answer: C. Liver

6. The larval stage of *Taenia ovis* in sheep is known as:

A. Coenurus cerebralis
B. Cysticercus tenuicollis
C. Cysticercus ovis
D. Hydatid cyst
Answer: C. Cysticercus ovis

7. Which larval stage develops in the brain of sheep, causing neurological signs?

A. Cysticercus ovis
B. Cysticercus tenuicollis
C. Coenurus cerebralis
D. Hydatid cyst
Answer: C. Coenurus cerebralis

8. The intermediate host for *Echinococcus granulosus* includes:

A. Dog
B. Sheep and goats
C. Humans
D. A and C only
Answer: B. Sheep and goats

9. Which cestode larval stage is zoonotic and can affect humans severely?

A. Cysticercus ovis
B. Coenurus cerebralis
C. Hydatid cyst
D. Cysticercus tenuicollis
Answer: C. Hydatid cyst

10. What is the definitive host for most cestodes affecting sheep and goats?

A. Cow
B. Pig
C. Dog
D. Sheep
Answer: C. Dog

Common nematode worms in sheep

MCQs on ***Haemonchus contortus***:

1. **What is the common name for *Haemonchus contortus*?**
   A. Liver fluke
   B. Barber's pole worm
   C. Lungworm
   D. Threadworm
   Answer: B. Barber's pole worm
2. ***Haemonchus contortus* primarily infects which organ in ruminants?**
   A. Liver
   B. Small intestine
   C. Abomasum
   D. Lungs
   Answer: C. Abomasum
3. **What is the primary mode of transmission for *H. contortus*?**
   A. Direct skin penetration
   B. Ingestion of infective larvae
   C. Transplacental
   D. Through insect vectors
   Answer: B. Ingestion of infective larvae
4. **Which stage of *H. contortus* is infective to the host?**
   A. Egg
   B. L1
   C. L2
   D. L3
   Answer: D. L3
5. **What is a common clinical sign of *Haemonchus contortus* infection?**
   A. Diarrhea
   B. Coughing
   C. Pale mucous membranes
   D. Jaundice
   Answer: C. Pale mucous membranes

6. **The "barber's pole" appearance of *H. contortus* is due to:**
   A. Its segmented body
   B. Spiraled red gut and white ovaries
   C. External striping
   D. Parasite pigmentation
   Answer: B. Spiraled red gut and white ovaries
7. **What diagnostic method is commonly used to detect *H. contortus* infection?**
   A. Blood smear
   B. ELISA
   C. Fecal egg count (FEC)
   D. PCR
   Answer: C. Fecal egg count (FEC)
8. **Which of the following is a major concern in the control of *H. contortus*?**
   A. Resistance to antibiotics
   B. Resistance to anthelmintics
   C. Vaccine development
   D. Difficulty in culturing in lab
   Answer: B. Resistance to anthelmintics
9. **What management strategy can help reduce *H. contortus* burden on pasture?**
   A. Increase stocking rate
   B. Continuous grazing
   C. Rotational grazing
   D. Overgrazing
   Answer: C. Rotational grazing
10. **Which tool is often used in the field to assess anemia caused by *H. contortus*?**
   A. McMaster chamber
   B. Hematocrit centrifuge
   C. FAMACHA chart
   D. PCR test
   Answer: C. FAMACHA chart

MCQ on Ostertagia

1. **What type of organism is *Ostertagia ostertagi*?**
A. Protozoa
B. Trematode
C. Nematode
D. Cestode
Answer: C. Nematode

2. ***Ostertagia ostertagi* primarily infects which part of the host?**
A. Small intestine
B. Large intestine
C. Rumen
D. Abomasum
Answer: D. Abomasum

3. **Which of the following animals is the primary host for *Ostertagia ostertagi*?**
A. Sheep
B. Cattle
C. Goats
D. Pigs
Answer: B. Cattle

4. **The main pathological effect of *Ostertagia* is due to**:
A. Blood loss
B. Mucosal damage in the abomasum
C. Liver damage
D. Blockage of bile ducts
Answer: B. Mucosal damage in the abomasum

5. **What is the infective stage of *Ostertagia ostertagi*?**
A. L1
B. L2
C. L3
D. L4
Answer: C. L3

6. What term is used to describe the disease caused by *Ostertagia*?
A. Fascioliasis
B. Ostertagiosis
C. Haemonchosis
D. Coccidiosis
Answer: B. Ostertagiosis

7. What is the characteristic clinical sign of ostertagiosis?
A. Diarrhea and weight loss
B. Jaundice
C. Anemia and bottle jaw
D. Constipation
Answer: A. Diarrhea and weight loss

8. Which type of ostertagiosis is associated with hypobiosis (arrested larval development)?
A. Type I
B. Type II
C. Chronic
D. None of the above
Answer: B. Type II

9. Type I ostertagiosis typically affects:
A. Adult cattle in winter
B. Young cattle in their first grazing season
C. Calves before weaning
D. Sheep during lambing
Answer: B. Young cattle in their first grazing season

10. Which diagnostic method is commonly used to confirm ostertagiosis?
A. Blood smear
B. Urine analysis
C. Fecal egg count and abomasal histology
D. Skin scraping
Answer: C. Fecal egg count and abomasal histology

MCQ in *Trichostrongylus*

1Trichostrongylus species are primarily found in which part of the host's body?
A. Lungs
B. Liver
C. Small intestine
D. Skin
Answer: C. Small intestine

2. What is the most common route of transmission of Trichostrongylus in animals?
A. Direct skin penetration
B. Ingestion of contaminated food or water
C. Vector-borne
D. Transplacental
Answer: B. Ingestion of contaminated food or water

3. Which of the following is a characteristic feature of Trichostrongylus eggs?
A. Operculated
B. Thick-shelled with polar plugs
C. Thin-shelled and oval
D. Barrel-shaped
Answer: C. Thin-shelled and oval

4. In ruminants, heavy Trichostrongylus infection can lead to which clinical sign?
A. Hematuria
B. Diarrhea and weight loss
C. Convulsions
D. Pneumonia
Answer: B. Diarrhea and weight loss

5. Trichostrongylus species are typically:
A. Dioecious with indirect lifecycle
B. Hermaphroditic with indirect lifecycle
C. Dioecious with direct lifecycle
D. Hermaphroditic with direct lifecycle
Answer: C. Dioecious with direct lifecycle

6. Which diagnostic method is commonly used to identify Trichostrongylus infections?
A. Blood smear
B. Baermann technique
C. Fecal flotation or McMaster egg count
D. Skin scraping
Answer: C. Fecal flotation or McMaster egg count

7. Trichostrongylus infections are more common during:
A. Winter
B. Dry season
C. Wet and warm seasons
D. During host hibernation
Answer: C. Wet and warm seasons

8. Which of the following is a major difference between Trichostrongylus and hookworms?
A. Trichostrongylus has teeth in the buccal capsule
B. Trichostrongylus larvae cannot penetrate skin
C. Trichostrongylus has an indirect lifecycle
D. Hookworms are found in the stomach
Answer: B. Trichostrongylus larvae cannot penetrate skin

9. In humans, Trichostrongylus infection is often associated with:
A. Consumption of raw or undercooked fish
B. Walking barefoot in contaminated soil
C. Eating contaminated vegetables
D. Drinking unpasteurized milk
Answer: C. Eating contaminated vegetables

10. Control of Trichostrongylus in livestock primarily involves:
A. Vaccination
B. Use of antibiotics
C. Anthelmintic treatment and pasture management
D. Surgical removal of worms
Answer: C. Anthelmintic treatment and pasture management

MCQ in *Nematodirus battus*

1. What is the primary host of *Nematodirus battus*?
A. Cattle
B. Horses
C. Sheep
D. Pigs
Answer: C. Sheep

2. What age group of sheep is most commonly affected by *Nematodirus battus*?

A. Adult sheep
B. Newborn lambs
C. Lambs aged 6–12 weeks
D. Yearlings
Answer: C. Lambs aged 6–12 weeks

3. Where in the body does *Nematodirus battus* reside?

A. Rumen
B. Small intestine
C. Large intestine
D. Liver
Answer: B. Small intestine

4. Which feature is unique to *Nematodirus battus* eggs compared to other nematodes?

A. Oval-shaped
B. Large with multiple blastomeres
C. Extremely small and thin-shelled
D. Found only in blood
Answer: B. Large with multiple blastomeres

5. How is *Nematodirus battus* infection typically transmitted?

A. Transplacental
B. Direct contact
C. Ingestion of L3 larvae on pasture
D. Through skin penetration
Answer: C. Ingestion of L3 larvae on pasture

6. What is unusual about the development of *Nematodirus battus* larvae compared to most nematodes?

A. Eggs hatch in the host
B. Eggs hatch immediately after being laid
C. All larval stages develop inside the egg
D. They require a secondary host
Answer: C. All larval stages develop inside the egg

7. What environmental condition typically triggers mass hatching of *Nematodirus battus* eggs?

A. High humidity
B. Sudden drop in temperature
C. Cold period followed by a warm spell
D. Continuous rainfall
Answer: C. Cold period followed by a warm spell

8. Which of the following is a key clinical sign of *Nematodirus battus* infection in lambs?

A. Coughing
B. Constipation
C. Diarrhea (often profuse and watery)
D. Lameness
Answer: C. Diarrhea (often profuse and watery)

9. What is the primary method of diagnosing *Nematodirus battus* infection?

A. Blood smear
B. Skin scraping
C. Fecal egg count
D. Liver biopsy
Answer: C. Fecal egg count

10. Which of the following is a common anthelmintic used to treat *Nematodirus battus* infections?

A. Ivermectin
B. Levamisole
C. Benzimidazoles
D. All of the above
Answer: D. All of the above

MCQ in Oesophagostomum

1. Oesophagostomum species are commonly known as:

A. Barber's pole worm
B. Nodular worm
C. Whipworm
D. Threadworm
Answer: B. Nodular worm

2. The characteristic lesions caused by Oesophagostomum in the intestines are:

A. Ulcers
B. Granulomas
C. Nodules
D. Polyps
Answer: C. Nodules

3. Oesophagostomum primarily infects which part of the host's gastrointestinal tract?

A. Stomach
B. Small intestine
C. Large intestine
D. Esophagus
Answer: C. Large intestine

4. Which of the following hosts are *not* commonly infected by Oesophagostomum spp.?

A. Cattle
B. Sheep
C. Goats
D. Horses
Answer: D. Horses

5. The infective stage of Oesophagostomum is:

A. L1
B. L2
C. L3
D. L4
Answer: C. L3

6. What is the mode of transmission of Oesophagostomum spp.?

A. Transplacental
B. Ingestion of infective larvae from contaminated soil or forage
C. Skin penetration
D. Vector-borne
Answer: B. Ingestion of infective larvae from contaminated soil or forage

7. Which Oesophagostomum species is known to occasionally infect humans?

A. O. dentatum
B. O. radiatum
C. O. bifurcum
D. O. columbianum
Answer: C. O. bifurcum

8. Diagnosis of Oesophagostomum infection is best confirmed by:

A. Blood smear
B. Skin scraping
C. Fecal flotation
D. Radiography
Answer: C. Fecal flotation

9. What type of life cycle does Oesophagostomum have?

A. Direct
B. Indirect with arthropod intermediate host
C. Indirect with snail host
D. Complex with multiple intermediate hosts
Answer: A. Direct

10. A common clinical sign in ruminants heavily infected with Oesophagostomum is:

A. Respiratory distress
B. Lameness
C. Diarrhea
D. Jaundice
Answer: C. Diarrhea

MCQs on Chabertia

***1.Chabertia ovina* primarily infects which type of animals?**
A. Dogs
B. Horses
C. Ruminants
D. Pigs
Answer: C. Ruminan

2. What is the common name of *Chabertia ovina*?
A. Barber pole worm
B. Large-mouthed bowel worm
C. Wire worm
D. Lungworm

Answer: B. Large-mouthed bowel worm

3. Where in the host is *Chabertia ovina* typically found?
A. Small intestine
B. Lungs
C. Large intestine
D. Liver
Answer: C. Large intestine

4. What type of lifecycle does *Chabertia ovina* have?
A. Direct
B. Indirect
C. Transovarial
D. Complex with intermediate host
Answer: A. Direct

5. The infective stage of *Chabertia ovina* is:
A. Egg
B. L1 larva
C. L2 larva
D. L3 larva
Answer: D. L3 larva

6. How does *Chabertia ovina* cause damage to the host?
A. Blood sucking in the lungs
B. Mucosal scraping in the large intestine
C. Blocking bile ducts
D. Damaging liver tissue
Answer: B. Mucosal scraping in the large intestine

7. Which clinical sign is commonly associated with *Chabertia ovina* infection?
A. Coughing
B. Diarrhea
C. Blindness
D. Lameness
Answer: B. Diarrhea

8. Which diagnostic method is used to detect *Chabertia ovina*?
A. Skin scraping
B. Blood smear
C. Fecal egg count
D. Nasal swab
Answer: C. Fecal egg count

9. Chabertia eggs can be confused with:
A. Strongyle-type eggs
B. Trichuris eggs
C. Fasciola eggs
D. Taenia eggs
Answer: A. Strongyle-type eggs

10. Control of *Chabertia ovina* primarily involves:
A. Antibiotics
B. Vaccination
C. Strategic deworming
D. Isolation of infected animals
Answer: C. Strategic deworming

Trichuris ovis* and *Trichuris globulosa *(* Whipworm) MCQ

1. Trichuris ovis is most commonly found in which animal?

A) Dog
B) Sheep and goats
C) Pig
D) Cat
Answer: B) Sheep and goats

*2. **Trichuris globulosa** primarily infects:*

A) Swine
B) Cattle
C) Dogs
D) Horses
Answer: B) Cattle

3. The whipworm resides in which part of the host's body?

A) Stomach
B) Small intestine
C) Cecum and colon
D) Liver
Answer: C) Cecum and colon

4. What is the characteristic shape of Trichuris eggs?

A) Oval with a rough shell
B) Lemon-shaped with bipolar plugs
C) Spherical and thick-shelled
D) Barrel-shaped with operculum
Answer: B) Lemon-shaped with bipolar plugs

5. Mode of transmission of Trichuris species is:

A) Skin penetration
B) Ingestion of embryonated eggs
C) Transplacental
D) Vector-borne
Answer: B) Ingestion of embryonated eggs

6. What is the prepatent period (time from infection to egg shedding) of Trichuris spp.?

A) 5–10 days
B) 1–2 weeks
C) 6–8 weeks
D) 1 year
Answer: C) 6–8 weeks

7. Which structure is characteristic of the anterior end of Trichuris?

A) Scolex with suckers
B) Blunt and wide
C) Long, slender and hair-like
D) Coiled
Answer: C) Long, slender and hair-like

8. Trichuris species cause the most damage to the:

A) Nervous system
B) Muscular system
C) Intestinal mucosa
D) Respiratory tract
Answer: C) Intestinal mucosa

9. Diagnosis of Trichuris infection is primarily through:

A) Blood smear
B) Baermann technique
C) Fecal flotation for eggs
D) Skin scraping
Answer: C) Fecal flotation for eggs

10. Heavy infections with Trichuris ovis/globulosa may result in:

A) Coughing and dyspnea
B) Diarrhea and weight loss
C) Lameness
D) Photosensitization
Answer: B) Diarrhea and weight loss

Trichuris ovis **and** ***Trichuris globulosa*** *(* Whipworm) MCQ

1. Trichuris ovis is most commonly found in which animal?

A) Dog
B) Sheep and goats
C) Pig
D) Cat
Answer: B) Sheep and goats

2. ***Trichuris globulosa*** *primarily infects:*

A) Swine
B) Cattle
C) Dogs
D) Horses
Answer: B) Cattle

3. The whipworm resides in which part of the host's body?

A) Stomach
B) Small intestine
C) Cecum and colon
D) Liver
Answer: C) Cecum and colon

4. What is the characteristic shape of Trichuris eggs?

A) Oval with a rough shell
B) Lemon-shaped with bipolar plugs
C) Spherical and thick-shelled
D) Barrel-shaped with operculum
Answer: B) Lemon-shaped with bipolar plugs

5. Mode of transmission of Trichuris species is:

A) Skin penetration
B) Ingestion of embryonated eggs
C) Transplacental
D) Vector-borne
Answer: B) Ingestion of embryonated eggs

6. What is the prepatent period (time from infection to egg shedding) of Trichuris spp.?

A) 5–10 days
B) 1–2 weeks
C) 6–8 weeks
D) 1 year
Answer: C) 6–8 weeks

7. Which structure is characteristic of the anterior end of Trichuris?

A) Scolex with suckers
B) Blunt and wide
C) Long, slender and hair-like
D) Coiled
Answer: C) Long, slender and hair-like

8. Trichuris species cause the most damage to the:

A) Nervous system
B) Muscular system
C) Intestinal mucosa
D) Respiratory tract
Answer: C) Intestinal mucosa

9. Diagnosis of Trichuris infection is primarily through:

A) Blood smear
B) Baermann technique
C) Fecal flotation for eggs
D) Skin scraping
Answer: C) Fecal flotation for eggs

10. Heavy infections with Trichuris ovis/globulosa may result in:

A) Coughing and dyspnea
B) Diarrhea and weight loss
C) Lameness
D) Photosensitization
Answer: B) Diarrhea and weight loss

ITESTINAL PROTOZOA OF SHEEP AND GOATS
Sheep and goats coccidiosis MCQ

1. What is the primary causative agent of coccidiosis in sheep and goats?

A. *Eimeria* spp.
B. *Cryptosporidium* spp.
C. *Giardia* spp.
D. *Toxoplasma* spp.
Answer: A. *Eimeria* spp.

2. How is coccidiosis primarily transmitted among sheep and goats?

A. Through respiratory droplets
B. By tick bites
C. Ingestion of sporulated oocysts from contaminated feed or water
D. Vertical transmission from dam to offspring
Answer: C. Ingestion of sporulated oocysts from contaminated feed or water

3. Which age group is most susceptible to clinical coccidiosis?

A. Adult animals
B. Newborns (0-3 days)
C. Young animals (3 weeks to 6 months)
D. Pregnant females only
Answer: C. Young animals (3 weeks to 6 months)

4. Which of the following is NOT a common clinical sign of coccidiosis in goats or sheep?

A. Diarrhea (sometimes bloody)
B. Weight gain
C. Dehydration
D. Anorexia
Answer: B. Weight gain

5. What environmental condition promotes the sporulation of *Eimeria* oocysts?

A. Cold and dry
B. Hot and dry
C. Warm and moist
D. Freezing temperatures
Answer: C. Warm and moist

6. What is the primary method of diagnosing coccidiosis in small ruminants?

A. Serological test
B. Fecal flotation to detect oocysts
C. PCR test
D. Skin scraping
Answer: B. Fecal flotation to detect oocysts

7. Which of the following anticoccidial drugs is commonly used in treatment?

A. Tylosin
B. Amprolium
C. Penicillin
D. Ivermectin
Answer: B. Amprolium

8. What is the main goal of preventive management for coccidiosis?

A. Eradicate all parasites
B. Eliminate all sheep and goats
C. Minimize oocyst buildup and reduce exposure
D. Rely solely on vaccination
Answer: C. Minimize oocyst buildup and reduce exposure

9. Which *Eimeria* species is considered highly pathogenic in goats?

A. *Eimeria alabamensis*
B. *Eimeria ninakohlyakimovae*
C. *Eimeria tenella*
D. *Eimeria zuernii*
Answer: B. *Eimeria ninakohlyakimovae*

10. Which of the following management practices helps control coccidiosis outbreaks?

A. Overcrowding animals
B. Keeping pens wet and muddy
C. Providing clean, dry bedding and regular sanitation
D. Feeding raw meat
Answer: C. Providing clean, dry bedding and regular sanitation

Sheep and goats coccidiosis MCQ

1. What is the primary causative agent of coccidiosis in sheep and goats?

A. *Eimeria* spp.
B. *Cryptosporidium* spp.
C. *Giardia* spp.
D. *Toxoplasma* spp.
Answer: A. *Eimeria* spp.

2. How is coccidiosis primarily transmitted among sheep and goats?

A. Through respiratory droplets
B. By tick bites
C. Ingestion of sporulated oocysts from contaminated feed or water
D. Vertical transmission from dam to offspring
Answer: C. Ingestion of sporulated oocysts from contaminated feed or water

3. Which age group is most susceptible to clinical coccidiosis?

A. Adult animals
B. Newborns (0-3 days)
C. Young animals (3 weeks to 6 months)
D. Pregnant females only
Answer: C. Young animals (3 weeks to 6 months)

4. Which of the following is NOT a common clinical sign of coccidiosis in goats or sheep?

A. Diarrhea (sometimes bloody)
B. Weight gain
C. Dehydration
D. Anorexia
Answer: B. Weight gain

5. What environmental condition promotes the sporulation of *Eimeria* oocysts?

A. Cold and dry
B. Hot and dry
C. Warm and moist
D. Freezing temperatures
Answer: C. Warm and moist

6. What is the primary method of diagnosing coccidiosis in small ruminants?

A. Serological test
B. Fecal flotation to detect oocysts
C. PCR test
D. Skin scraping
Answer: B. Fecal flotation to detect oocysts

7. Which of the following anticoccidial drugs is commonly used in treatment?

A. Tylosin
B. Amprolium
C. Penicillin
D. Ivermectin
Answer: B. Amprolium

8. What is the main goal of preventive management for coccidiosis?

A. Eradicate all parasites
B. Eliminate all sheep and goats
C. Minimize oocyst buildup and reduce exposure

D. Rely solely on vaccination
Answer: C. Minimize oocyst buildup and reduce exposure

9. Which *Eimeria* species is considered highly pathogenic in goats?

A. *Eimeria alabamensis*
B. *Eimeria ninakohlyakimovae*
C. *Eimeria tenella*
D. *Eimeria zuernii*
Answer: B. *Eimeria ninakohlyakimovae*

10. Which of the following management practices helps control coccidiosis outbreaks?

A. Overcrowding animals
B. Keeping pens wet and muddy
C. Providing clean, dry bedding and regular sanitation
D. Feeding raw meat
Answer: C. Providing clean, dry bedding and regular sanitation

Sheep and goats coccidiosis MCQ

1. What is the primary causative agent of coccidiosis in sheep and goats?

A. *Eimeria* spp.
B. *Cryptosporidium* spp.
C. *Giardia* spp.
D. *Toxoplasma* spp.
Answer: A. *Eimeria* spp.

2. How is coccidiosis primarily transmitted among sheep and goats?

A. Through respiratory droplets
B. By tick bites
C. Ingestion of sporulated oocysts from contaminated feed or water
D. Vertical transmission from dam to offspring
Answer: C. Ingestion of sporulated oocysts from contaminated feed or water

3. Which age group is most susceptible to clinical coccidiosis?

A. Adult animals
B. Newborns (0-3 days)
C. Young animals (3 weeks to 6 months)
D. Pregnant females only
Answer: C. Young animals (3 weeks to 6 months)

4. Which of the following is NOT a common clinical sign of coccidiosis in goats or sheep?

A. Diarrhea (sometimes bloody)
B. Weight gain
C. Dehydration
D. Anorexia
Answer: B. Weight gain

5. What environmental condition promotes the sporulation of *Eimeria* oocysts?

A. Cold and dry
B. Hot and dry
C. Warm and moist
D. Freezing temperatures
Answer: C. Warm and moist

6. What is the primary method of diagnosing coccidiosis in small ruminants?

A. Serological test
B. Fecal flotation to detect oocysts
C. PCR test
D. Skin scraping
Answer: B. Fecal flotation to detect oocysts

7. Which of the following anticoccidial drugs is commonly used in treatment?

A. Tylosin
B. Amprolium
C. Penicillin
D. Ivermectin
Answer: B. Amprolium

8. What is the main goal of preventive management for coccidiosis?

A. Eradicate all parasites
B. Eliminate all sheep and goats
C. Minimize oocyst buildup and reduce exposure
D. Rely solely on vaccination
Answer: C. Minimize oocyst buildup and reduce exposure

9. Which *Eimeria* species is considered highly pathogenic in goats?

A. *Eimeria alabamensis*
B. *Eimeria ninakohlyakimovae*
C. *Eimeria tenella*
D. *Eimeria zuernii*
Answer: B. *Eimeria ninakohlyakimovae*

10. Which of the following management practices helps control coccidiosis outbreaks?

A. Overcrowding animals
B. Keeping pens wet and muddy
C. Providing clean, dry bedding and regular sanitation
D. Feeding raw meat
Answer: C. Providing clean, dry bedding and regular sanitation

Giardiasis in Sheep & Goats MCQ

1.What is the causative agent of Giardiasis in sheep and goats?
A. Eimeria spp.
B. Giardia duodenalis
C. Cryptosporidium parvum
D. Trichostrongylus spp
Answer: B. Giardia duodenalis

2. How is Giardiasis primarily transmitted in small ruminants?
A. Through insect bites
B. Inhalation of spores
C. Fecal-oral route via contaminated water or feed
D. Vertical transmission from mother to fetus
Answer: C. Fecal-oral route via contaminated water or feed

3. Which age group of sheep and goats is most commonly affected by Giardiasis?
A. Adults over 3 years
B. Neonates under 1 week
C. Young animals, especially weanlings
D. Pregnant females
Answer: C. Young animals, especially weanlings

4. Which of the following is a common clinical sign of Giardiasis in goats?
A. Coughing
B. Diarrhea
C. Lameness
D. Nasal discharge
Answer: B. Diarrhea

5. What type of diarrhea is typically associated with Giardia infection in small ruminants?
A. Bloody diarrhea
B. Frothy, malodorous, and greasy diarrhea
C. Watery with mucus
D. Constipation followed by explosive diarrhea
Answer: B. Frothy, malodorous, and greasy diarrhea

6. What diagnostic test is commonly used to confirm Giardia infection?
A. Fecal flotation with zinc sulfate
B. ELISA blood test
C. Nasal swab culture
D. Radiography
Answer: A. Fecal flotation with zinc sulfate

7. Which of the following medications is commonly used to treat Giardiasis in sheep and goats?
A. Amprolium
B. Albendazole
C. Ivermectin
D. Oxytetracycline
Answer: B. Albendazole

8. How can Giardiasis in a flock be prevented or controlled?
A. Regular deworming for liver flukes
B. Isolation of coughing animals
C. Ensuring clean water and sanitation
D. Supplementing diet with minerals
Answer: C. Ensuring clean water and sanitation

9. Is Giardia zoonotic (can be transmitted to humans)?
A. No
B. Yes, particularly certain genotypes
C. Only through meat consumption
D. Only in immunocompromised individuals
Answer: B. Yes, particularly certain genotypes

10. Which environmental factor most favors the survival of Giardia cysts?
A. Direct sunlight
B. High temperatures
C. Cold, moist environments
D. Dry and windy climates
Answer: C. Cold, moist environments

Toxoplasmosis in Sheep and Goats MCQ

1. What is the causative agent of toxoplasmosis in sheep and goats?
A. *Neospora caninum*
B. *Toxoplasma gondii*
C. *Eimeria spp.*
D. *Babesia ovis*
Correct Answer: B

2. What is the primary mode of transmission of *Toxoplasma gondii* to sheep and goats?
A. Tick bites
B. Vertical transmission
C. Ingestion of oocysts from contaminated feed or water
D. Aerosol inhalation
Correct Answer: C

3. Which definitive host is responsible for shedding *T. gondii* oocysts in the environment?
A. Rodents
B. Cattle
C. Dogs
D. Cats
Correct Answer: D

4. What is a common clinical sign of toxoplasmosis in pregnant ewes or does?
A. Mastitis
B. Diarrhea
C. Abortion
D. Lameness
Correct Answer: C

5. At what stage of gestation is *T. gondii* infection most likely to cause abortion in sheep?
A. Early gestation
B. Mid gestation
C. Late gestation
D. Postpartum
Correct Answer: B

6. Which fetal lesion is commonly associated with toxoplasmosis in sheep and goats?
A. Encephalomalacia
B. White necrotic foci in the cotyledons of the placenta
C. Hydronephrosis
D. Joint swelling
Correct Answer: B

7. What is the most reliable diagnostic method for confirming toxoplasmosis in sheep and goats?
A. Blood culture
B. Fecal flotation
C. Serology (e.g., ELISA, IFAT)
D. Skin scraping
Correct Answer: C

8. Which of the following management strategies helps prevent toxoplasmosis in small ruminants?
A. Feeding raw meat
B. Allowing cats in feed storage areas
C. Controlling cat access to feed and water
D. Administering broad-spectrum antibiotics regularly
Correct Answer: C

9. Is there a vaccine available for toxoplasmosis in sheep?
A. No
B. Yes, a live attenuated vaccine
C. Yes, a killed vaccine
D. Yes, a recombinant DNA vaccine
Correct Answer: B

10. What is the zoonotic importance of *Toxoplasma gondii*?
A. It causes flu-like illness in humans
B. It causes no disease in humans
C. It is only dangerous to livestock
D. It causes rabies-like symptoms
Correct Answer: A

Anaplasma ovis MCQ

1. What type of organism is *Anaplasma ovis*?

A) Virus
B) Bacterium
C) Protozoan
D) Fungus
Answer C) Protozoan

2. *Anaplasma ovis* **primarily infects which type of animal?**

A) Cattle
B) Horses
C) Sheep and goats
D) Dogs
Answer: C) Sheep and goats

3. What is the main target cell of *Anaplasma ovis* **in the host?**

A) Neutrophils
B) Lymphocytes
C) Erythrocytes
D) Platelets
Answer: C) Erythrocytes

4. How is *Anaplasma ovis* **primarily transmitted?**

A) Direct contact
B) Inhalation
C) Tick bites
D) Ingestion of contaminated water
Answer: C) Tick bites

5. Which clinical sign is most commonly associated with *Anaplasma ovis* infection?

A) Lameness
B) Hemolytic anemia
C) Respiratory distress
D) Diarrhea
Answer: B) Hemolytic anemia

6. What type of pathogen is *Anaplasma ovis* in terms of Gram staining?

A) Gram-positive cocci
B) Gram-positive bacilli
C) Gram-negative coccobacilli
D) Acid-fast bacilli
Answer: C) Gram-negative coccobacilli

7. Which diagnostic technique is commonly used to detect *Anaplasma ovis*?

A) Culture on blood agar
B) ELISA for antibodies
C) Blood smear microscopy
D) Fecal flotation
Answer: C) Blood smear microscopy

8. What is a common histological finding in *Anaplasma ovis* infection?

A) Inclusion bodies in lymphocytes
B) Basophilic stippling in red blood cells
C) Morulae in neutrophils
D) Small round bodies in erythrocytes
Answer: D) Small round bodies in erythrocytes

9. Which of the following is a common vector of *Anaplasma ovis*?

A) *Rhipicephalus* spp.
B) *Ixodes* spp.
C) *Amblyomma* spp.
D) *Ctenocephalides* spp.
Answer: A) *Rhipicephalus* spp.

10. Which of the following antibiotics is most effective in treating *Anaplasma ovis*?

A) Penicillin
B) Tetracycline
C) Enrofloxacin
D) Metronidazole
Answer: B) Tetracycline

***Babesia ovis* MCQ**

1. What is the primary vector for *Babesia ovis*?

A. Tabanid flies
B. Rhipicephalus ticks
C. Ixodes ticks
D. Anopheles mosquitoes

Answer: B. *Rhipicephalus* ticks

2. *Babesia ovis* **primarily infects which type of host cell?**

A. Hepatocytes
B. Neutrophils
C. Erythrocytes
D. Lymphocytes

Answer: C. Erythrocytes

3. Which of the following is a common clinical sign of *Babesia ovis* infection in sheep?

A. Coughing
B. Diarrhea
C. Hemoglobinuria
D. Neurological symptoms

Answer: C. Hemoglobinuria

4. What is a common method used for the laboratory diagnosis of *Babesia ovis*?

A. Fecal flotation
B. Blood smear with Giemsa stain
C. ELISA for antibodies
D. PCR for viral RNA

Answer: B. Blood smear with Giemsa stain

5. Which of the following drugs is commonly used to treat *Babesia ovis* infections?

A. Albendazole
B. Oxytetracycline
C. Imidocarb dipropionate
D. Metronidazole

Answer: C. Imidocarb dipropionate

Babesia motasi MCQ

1. What is the primary host of *Babesia motasi*?

A) Cattle
B) Sheep and goats
C) Horses
D) Dogs

Answer: B) Sheep and goats

2. Which vector is responsible for transmitting *Babesia motasi*?

A) *Ixodes ricinus*
B) *Rhipicephalus sanguineus*
C) *Haemaphysalis* spp.
D) *Anopheles* mosquitoes

Answer: C) *Haemaphysalis* spp.

3. What is a common clinical sign of *Babesia motasi* infection in sheep?

A) Neurological tremors
B) Severe diarrhea
C) Hemolytic anemia and fever
D) Chronic wasting

Answer: C) Hemolytic anemia and fever

4. How is *Babesia motasi* typically diagnosed in the laboratory?

A) Urinalysis
B) Fecal flotation
C) Blood smear and PCR
D) ELISA for antibodies against bacteria

Answer: C) Blood smear and PCR

5. Which control method is most effective in preventing *Babesia motasi* infections?

A) Vaccination
B) Regular deworming
C) Vector control (tick management)
D) Antibiotic prophylaxis

Answer: C) Vector control (tick management)

Theileria ovis MCQ

1. What type of organism is *Theileria ovis*?

A) Bacteria
B) Virus
C) Protozoan
D) Fungus

Answer: C) Protozoan

2. *Theileria ovis* is primarily transmitted by which vector?

A) Tsetse flies
B) Ticks
C) Mosquitoes
D) Fleas

Answer: B) Ticks

3. Which animal species are the main hosts of *Theileria ovis*?

A) Cattle
B) Dogs
C) Sheep and goats
D) Horses

Answer: C) Sheep and goats

4. What is the typical clinical presentation of *Theileria ovis* infection in small ruminants?

A) Severe anemia and jaundice
B) Often subclinical or mild symptoms
C) Neurological signs
D) Severe respiratory distress

Answer: B) Often subclinical or mild symptoms

5. Which of the following diagnostic techniques is commonly used to detect *Theileria ovis*?

A) Urinalysis
B) Fecal flotation
C) Blood smear and PCR
D) Skin scraping

Answer: C) Blood smear and PCR

1. What is the primary host of *Theileria lestoquardi*?
A. Cattle
B. Dogs
C. Sheep
D. Horses

Answer: C. Sheep

2. Which tick genus is the primary vector for *Theileria lestoquardi*?
A. Rhipicephalus
B. Ixodes
C. Hyalomma
D. Dermacentor

Answer: C. Hyalomma

3. Which of the following is a major clinical sign of *Theileria lestoquardi* infection in sheep?
A. Coughing
B. Neurological symptoms
C. High fever and lymphadenopathy
D. Lameness

Answer: C. High fever and lymphadenopathy

4. What type of organism is *Theileria lestoquardi*?
A. Bacterium
B. Virus
C. Protozoan
D. Fungus

Answer: C. Protozoan

5. Which diagnostic method is commonly used for detecting *Theileria lestoquardi*?
A. Skin scraping
B. ELISA
C. PCR and blood smear examination
D. Fecal flotation

Answer: C. PCR and blood smear examination

Trypanosoma vivax *and* ***Trypanosoma evansi in sheep & Goats***

1. Which of the following vectors primarily transmits ***Trypanosoma vivax*** in Africa?

A. Tabanid flies
B. Glossina spp. (tsetse fly)
C. Sandflies
D. Mosquitoes

Answer: B. Glossina spp. (tsetse fly)

2. What is the common mode of transmission of *Trypanosoma evansi* **in sheep and goats?**

A. Oral ingestion
B. Tick bite
C. Mechanical transmission by biting flies
D. Transovarial transmission

Answer: C. Mechanical transmission by biting flies

3. Which clinical sign is most commonly associated with *Trypanosoma evansi* infection (Surra) in small ruminants?

A. Diarrhea
B. Progressive anemia and weight loss
C. Dermatitis
D. Polydipsia

Answer: B. Progressive anemia and weight loss

4. What diagnostic method is commonly used to detect *Trypanosoma* species in sheep and goats?

A. ELISA for FMD
B. Blood smear with Giemsa stain
C. Fecal flotation
D. Skin scraping

Answer: B. Blood smear with Giemsa stain

5. Which of the following drugs is commonly used in the treatment of trypanosomiasis in sheep and goats?

A. Albendazole
B. Diminazene aceturate
C. Tylosin
D. Enrofloxacin

Answer: B. Diminazene aceturate

ECTOPARASITES OF SHEEP AND GOATS

Common Ticks affecting sheep and goats MCQ

1. Which of the following tick species is most commonly associated with sheep and goats in tropical regions?

A. *Ixodes scapularis*
B. *Rhipicephalus (Boophilus) microplus*
C. *Rhipicephalus appendiculatus*
D. *Amblyomma variegatum*
Answer: D. *Amblyomma variegatum*

2. What is the main economic impact of tick infestation in sheep and goats?

A. Reduced wool quality
B. Decreased milk yield
C. Transmission of tick-borne diseases
D. All of the above
Answer: D. All of the abov

3. Which tick-borne disease is commonly transmitted to sheep by *Rhipicephalus* species?

A. Heartwater
B. Babesiosis
C. Theileriosis
D. Nairobi Sheep Disease
Answer: B. Babesiosis

4. The tick *Hyalomma anatolicum* primarily transmits which disease in small ruminants?

A. Anaplasmosis
B. Theileriosis
C. Q fever
D. Brucellosis
Answer: B. Theileriosis

5. What is the preferred habitat of *Amblyomma* ticks that infest goats and sheep?

A. Cold mountainous areas
B. Dry deserts
C. Warm, humid grasslands
D. High-altitude rocky terrains
Answer: C. Warm, humid grasslands

6. Which tick control method is most effective for large herds of sheep and goats?

A. Manual removal
B. Dipping or spraying with acaricides
C. Herbal remedies
D. Vaccination
Answer: B. Dipping or spraying with acaricides

7. Which stage of the tick life cycle is parasitic on animals?

A. Egg
B. Larva
C. Nymph and adult
D. Both B and C
Answer: D. Both B and C

8. How often should sheep and goats be treated with acaricides in tick-endemic areas?

A. Once a year
B. Every 3–4 months
C. Weekly
D. Every 2–4 weeks
Answer: D. Every 2–4 weeks

9. Which of the following is a clinical sign of heavy tick infestation in goats?

A. Excessive salivation
B. Anemia and skin irritation
C. Coughing
D. Diarrhea
Answer: B. Anemia and skin irritation

10. Which tick species is known to transmit *Ehrlichia ruminantium*, **the causative agent of heartwater disease?**

A. *Ixodes ricinus*
B. *Amblyomma variegatum*
C. *Rhipicephalus sanguineus*
D. *Dermacentor andersoni*
Answer: B. *Amblyomma variegatum*

Common mites affecting sheep and goatsMCQ

1. Which mite is the most common cause of mange in sheep and goats?

A. *Sarcoptes scabiei*
B. *Psoroptes ovis*
C. *Demodex caprae*
D. *Otodectes cynotis*
Answer: B. *Psoroptes ovis*

2. What is the primary clinical sign of *Sarcoptes scabiei* **infestation in goats?**

A. Hair loss on the back
B. Crusting and intense itching on ears and face
C. Limping
D. Nasal discharge
Answer: B. Crusting and intense itching on ears and face

3. *Chorioptes* **mites primarily infest which part of the body?**

A. Face
B. Ears
C. Lower limbs and tail area
D. Neck
Answer: C. Lower limbs and tail area

4. Which of the following mites is burrowing in nature?

A. *Psoroptes*
B. *Sarcoptes*
C. *Chorioptes*
D. *Otodectes*
Answer: B. *Sarcoptes*

5. How is mange typically transmitted among sheep and goats?

A. Inhalation
B. Through contaminated water
C. Direct contact with infested animals
D. Via insect bites
Answer: C. Direct contact with infested animals

6. *Demodex* **mites live primarily in:**

A. The respiratory tract
B. The gastrointestinal tract
C. Hair follicles and sebaceous glands
D. Bloodstream
Answer: C. Hair follicles and sebaceous glands

7. Which mange mite infestation is non-pruritic (less itchy) and often subclinical in goats?

A. *Psoroptes*
B. *Sarcoptes*
C. *Chorioptes*
D. *Demodex*
Answer: D. *Demodex*

8. Which mite infestation can be confirmed by a deep skin scraping?

A. *Psoroptes*
B. *Chorioptes*
C. *Sarcoptes*
D. *Otodectes*
Answer: C. *Sarcoptes*

9. What is a common treatment for mange mites in sheep and goats?

A. Amoxicillin
B. Ivermectin
C. Penicillin
D. Furosemide
Answer: B. Ivermectin

10. What environmental factor often increases the spread of mange mites in flocks?

A. Dry, hot weather
B. Isolation of animals
C. Overcrowding and poor hygiene
D. Cold water access
Answer: C. Overcrowding and poor hygiene

Common Lice Affecting Sheep and GoatsMCQ

1. Which of the following is a common biting louse of sheep?

A) *Linognathus ovillus*
B) *Damalinia ovis*
C) *Linognathus pedalis*
D) *Haematopinus suis*

Answer: B) *Damalinia ovis*

2. What type of lice are *Linognathus ovillus* and *Linognathus pedalis*?

A) Biting lice
B) Chewing lice
C) Sucking lice
D) Burrowing lice

Answer: C) Sucking lice

3. Which louse species primarily affects the face and neck of sheep?

A) *Damalinia ovis*
B) *Linognathus pedalis*
C) *Linognathus ovillus*
D) *Melophagus ovinus*

Answer: C) *Linognathus ovillus*

4. Which of the following is a chewing louse that affects goats?

A) *Haematopinus eurysternus*
B) *Linognathus africanus*
C) *Bovicola caprae*
D) *Melophagus ovinus*

Answer: C) *Bovicola caprae*

5. Lice infestations in sheep and goats are more common in which season?

A) Summer
B) Winter
C) Rainy
D) Monsoon

Answer: B) Winter

6. Which clinical sign is most commonly associated with lice infestation in small ruminants?

A) Diarrhea
B) Weight gain
C) Intense itching and wool loss
D) Nasal discharge

Answer: C) Intense itching and wool loss

7. Which control measure is most effective against lice infestations in sheep and goats?

A) Oral antibiotics
B) Topical insecticides (e.g., pour-on or sprays)
C) Anthelmintics
D) Vaccination

Answer: B) Topical insecticides (e.g., pour-on or sprays)

8. The life cycle of lice in sheep and goats is approximately how long?

A) 3–5 days
B) 2–3 weeks
C) 4–6 weeks
D) 2 months

Answer: B) 2–3 weeks

9. Which of the following is not a common method of lice transmission in goats and sheep?

A) Direct contact
B) Shared bedding
C) Insect bites
D) Grooming tools

Answer: C) Insect bites

10. Heavy lice infestations in small ruminants may lead to:

A) Improved wool quality
B) Severe anemia in the case of sucking lice
C) Resistance to dewormers
D) Increased reproduction

Answer: B) Severe anemia in the case of sucking lice

Common flies affecting sheep and goatsMCQ

1. Which of the following is a primary cause of myiasis (fly strike) in sheep?

A. Tabanus spp.
B. Musca domestica
C. *Lucilia sericata*
D. Stomoxys calcitrans
Answer: C. *Lucilia sericata*

2. The sheep ked (*Melophagus ovinus*) is classified as a:

A. Louse
B. Tick
C. Wingless fly
D. Mite
Answer: C. Wingless fly

3. Which fly is responsible for transmitting *Trypanosoma* spp. in goats?

A. Tsetse fly (*Glossina* spp.)
B. Horn fly (*Haematobia irritans*)
C. Stable fly (*Stomoxys calcitrans*)
D. Deer fly (*Chrysops* spp.)
Answer: A. Tsetse fly (*Glossina* spp.)

4. What is the common name for the parasitic condition caused by fly larvae in sheep wounds?

A. Scabies
B. Mange
C. Myiasis
D. Dermatitis
Answer: C. Myiasis

5. Which of the following flies is a blood-sucking fly affecting both sheep and goats?

A. *Lucilia sericata*
B. *Musca domestica*
C. *Stomoxys calcitrans*
D. *Fannia canicularis*
Answer: C. *Stomoxys calcitrans*

6. What is the lifecycle stage of the fly that causes damage in fly strike?

A. Adult
B. Egg
C. Pupa
D. Larva
Answer: D. Larva

7. Which environmental condition promotes fly strike in sheep the most?

A. Dry and cool climate
B. Wet and windy weather
C. Warm and humid conditions
D. Snowy and icy conditions
Answer: C. Warm and humid conditions

8. What is a major sign of fly strike in sheep?

A. Increased wool production
B. Bleeding from hooves
C. Foul smell and wool discoloration
D. Sudden weight gain
Answer: C. Foul smell and wool discoloration

9. Which fly lays eggs in open wounds, causing secondary infections in sheep and goats?

A. *Lucilia cuprina*
B. *Musca domestica*
C. *Tabanus* spp.
D. *Simulium* spp.
Answer: A. *Lucilia cuprina*

10. Which control measure is most effective against fly strike in sheep?

A. Feeding supplements
B. Routine tail docking and crutching
C. Increasing shade
D. Vaccination
Answer: B. Routine tail docking and crutching

ZOONOTIC PARASITES TRANSMITTED FROM SHEEP AND GOATS

1. Which of the following zoonotic helminths is commonly transmitted from sheep and goats to humans?

A. *Taenia saginata*
B. *Echinococcus granulosus*
C. *Ascaris lumbricoides*
D. *Trichuris trichiura*

Answer: B. *Echinococcus granulosus*

2. The larval stage of *Echinococcus granulosus* **in humans causes which disease?**

A. Ascariasis
B. Hydatid disease
C. Trichinellosis
D. Strongyloidiasis

Answer: B. Hydatid disease

3. How do humans typically get infected with *Echinococcus granulosus*?

A. Eating undercooked goat meat
B. Ingestion of eggs from contaminated dog feces
C. Drinking unboiled goat milk
D. Contact with infected goat skin

Answer: B. Ingestion of eggs from contaminated dog feces

4. Which of the following is a zoonotic nematode that can be transmitted from sheep/goats to humans through ingestion of larvae in raw liver?

A. *Trichinella spiralis*
B. *Fasciola hepatica*
C. *Dicrocoelium dendriticum*
D. *Capillaria hepatica*

Answer: B. *Fasciola hepatica*

5. What is the intermediate host of *Fasciola hepatica*?

A. Dog
B. Cattle
C. Freshwater snail
D. Human

Answer: C. Freshwater snail

6. Which zoonotic cestode is associated with goats and causes coenurosis in intermediate hosts and can occasionally infect humans?

A. *Taenia solium*
B. *Taenia hydatigena*
C. *Taenia multiceps*
D. *Hymenolepis nana*

Answer: C. *Taenia multiceps*

7. What is the definitive host of *Taenia multiceps*, which transmits the infection to intermediate hosts like sheep and goats?

A. Sheep
B. Human
C. Dog
D. Cow

Answer: C. Dog

8. Which of the following best describes the transmission route of zoonotic *Trichostrongylus* species from goats to humans?

A. Biting insects
B. Direct skin penetration
C. Ingestion of larvae in contaminated vegetables
D. Sexual contact

Answer: C. Ingestion of larvae in contaminated vegetables

9. What clinical symptom is most commonly seen in humans infected with *Trichostrongylus* species?

A. Severe anemia
B. Liver abscess
C. Diarrhea and abdominal pain
D. Skin ulcers

Answer: C. Diarrhea and abdominal pain

10. Which preventive measure is most effective in reducing zoonotic helminth infections from sheep and goats?

A. Avoiding goat milk
B. Deworming livestock and controlling dogs
C. Wearing gloves while cooking
D. Avoiding all contact with sheep

Answer: B. Deworming livestock and controlling dogs

ZOONOTIC PROTOZOA PARASITES TRANSMITTED FROM SHEEP AND GOATS MCQ

1. Which of the following protozoan parasites is commonly transmitted from sheep and goats to humans via contaminated water?
A. *Giardia lamblia*
B. *Toxoplasma gondii*
C. *Cryptosporidium parvum*
D. *Entamoeba histolytica*
Answer: C

2. What is the primary route of human infection with *Toxoplasma gondii* from small ruminants?
A. Inhalation of oocysts
B. Ingestion of undercooked meat
C. Skin contact with infected wool
D. Bites from infected insects
Answer: B

3. Which zoonotic protozoan is associated with neonatal diarrhea in lambs and kids and is transmissible to humans?

A. *Sarcocystis capracanis*

B. *Cryptosporidium parvum*

C. *Trypanosoma brucei*

D. *Giardia lamblia*

Answer: B

4. *Toxoplasma gondii* oocysts are shed primarily by which host?

A. Sheep

B. Humans

C. Cats

D. Goats

Answer: C

5. Humans can acquire *Giardia duodenalis* from sheep and goats through:

A. Mosquito bites

B. Inhalation of spores

C. Drinking contaminated water

D. Eating unwashed fruits only

Answer: C

6. Which of the following protozoa is *not* typically considered zoonotic from sheep and goats?

A. *Cryptosporidium parvum*

B. *Toxoplasma gondii*

C. *Giardia duodenalis*

D. *Eimeria spp.*

Answer: D

7. What stage of *Toxoplasma gondii* is infective to humans via consumption of meat?

A. Tachyzoite

B. Oocyst

C. Bradyzoite

D. Sporozoite

Answer: C

8. Which environmental condition favors survival of *Cryptosporidium* oocysts?
A. Dry heat
B. Freezing
C. High humidity and moderate temperature
D. Strong sunlight
Answer: C

9. Which of the following clinical signs in humans might suggest zoonotic protozoan infection from goats?
A. Jaundice
B. Diarrhea
C. Pneumonia
D. Skin rash
Answer: B

10. Which personal protective measure is most effective to prevent zoonotic protozoa transmission when handling sheep or goats?
A. Wearing woolen clothing
B. Avoiding eye contact
C. Practicing good hand hygiene
D. Administering antibiotics
Answer: C

CHAPTER TWO : EQUINE PARASITES QUESTIONS

HELMINTHES OF EQUINES QUESTIONS

Gastrodiscus aegyptiacus (Equine intestinal fluke)

1. What is the primary host of *Gastrodiscus aegyptiacus*?

A. Cattle
B. Dogs
C. Horses and donkeys
D. Sheep

Answer: C. Horses and donkeys

2. Where in the host does *Gastrodiscus aegyptiacus* primarily reside?

A. Stomach
B. Liver
C. Large intestine and cecum
D. Small intestine

Answer: C. Large intestine and cecum

3. What is the intermediate host for *Gastrodiscus aegyptiacus*?

A. Ticks
B. Snails (aquatic)
C. Mosquitoes
D. Earthworms

Answer: B. Snails (aquatic)

4. What is the common method of transmission of *Gastrodiscus aegyptiacus* to the definitive host?

A. Ingestion of contaminated water with metacercaria
B. Inhalation of parasite eggs
C. Skin penetration by larvae
D. Direct contact with infected animals

Answer: A. Ingestion of contaminated water with metacercaria

5. What is a common clinical sign in horses heavily infected with *Gastrodiscus aegyptiacus*?

A. Respiratory distress
B. Severe anemia
C. Colic and diarrhea
D. Skin lesions

Answer: C. Colic and diarrhea.

Case Study :

A 6-year-old Horse in a tropical region presents with intermittent diarrhea, weight loss despite good appetite, and signs of colic.

Fecal examination reveals operculated eggs suggestive of a trematode infection.

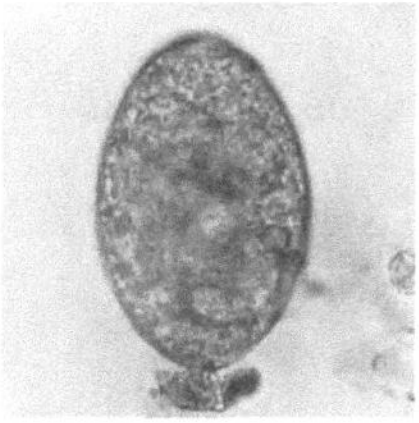

The horse is kept in a pasture with a freshwater stream, and there are frequent sightings of snails near the water source.

□ **Case Study Questions:**

Diagnosis & Identification

1. **What morphological features help identify *Gastrodiscus aegyptiacus* eggs in fecal samples?**
2. **Which diagnostic techniques are most effective for detecting *Gastrodiscus aegyptiacus* infections in horses?**
3. **How would you confirm that the eggs found in the feces belong to *Gastrodiscus aegyptiacus* and not other trematodes?**

Life Cycle & Transmission

4. **Describe the life cycle of *Gastrodiscus aegyptiacus*. What is the role of the intermediate host?**
5. **What environmental conditions favor the transmission of *G. aegyptiacus*?**
6. **How do horses typically become infected with this fluke?**

Clinical Signs & Pathology

7. **What clinical signs are associated with *G. aegyptiacus* infection in equines?**

8. **What pathological lesions might be observed in the intestine of an infected horse?**
9. **Why might heavily infected horses show signs of colic or diarrhea?**

Treatment & Control

10. **What are the recommended anthelmintics for treating *G. aegyptiacus* infections in horses?**
11. **How can infection with this parasite be prevented on a pasture with water sources?**
12. **What role do snail populations play in managing the risk of *G. aegyptiacus* infection?**

Epidemiology & Public Health

13. **In which regions is *Gastrodiscus aegyptiacus* most commonly found?**
14. **Are there any zoonotic concerns associated with *G. aegyptiacus*?**
15. **How can knowledge of the epidemiology help in planning a control strategy for this parasite on a farm?**

Fasciola hepatica

1. What is the primary site of infection for *Fasciola hepatica* in the horse?

A. Lungs
B. Small intestine
C. Liver
D. Kidneys

Answer: C. Liver

Fasciola hepatica, the liver fluke, primarily infects the liver and bile ducts.

2. What is the intermediate host for *Fasciola hepatica*?

A. Mosquito
B. Ant
C. Freshwater snail
D. Earthworm

Answer: C. Freshwater snail

The fluke requires a freshwater snail (e.g., *Lymnaea* species) as an intermediate host in its life cycle.

3. Which clinical sign is LEAST likely in equine fascioliasis?

A. Icterus (jaundice)
B. Weight loss
C. Colic
D. Coughing

Answer: D. Coughing

Respiratory signs like coughing are not typical. Liver-related signs such as weight loss and jaundice are more common.

4. How do horses typically become infected with *Fasciola hepatica*?

A. Inhalation of larval stages
B. Ingestion of contaminated water or vegetation
C. Bites from infected vectors
D. Skin penetration by larvae

Answer: B. Ingestion of contaminated water or vegetation

Horses ingest the metacercariae (infective stage) while grazing on contaminated vegetation near water bodies.

5. Which diagnostic method is most reliable for confirming *Fasciola hepatica* infection in horses?

A. Blood glucose test
B. Fecal egg count (sedimentation technique)
C. Skin scraping
D. Radiography

Answer: B. Fecal egg count (sedimentation technique)

Sedimentation is the preferred fecal test for detecting the large, heavy eggs of *F. hepatica*.

Case Study Question: Fasciola hepatica in a Horse

Case:

A 6-year-old Thoroughbred gelding presents with signs of chronic weight loss, intermittent colic, poor coat condition, and mild anemia.

The horse is kept on a farm with sheep and cattle, and has access to wet, marshy pastures with slow-draining water sources.

On physical exam, the horse is dull but responsive, has a body condition score of 3/9, and mild ventral edema.

Bloodwork reveals mild anemia, elevated liver enzymes (GGT and AST), and a slight eosinophilia. Fecal sedimentation reveals operculated eggs consistent with *Fasciola hepatica.*

Question:

Discuss the pathogenesis, diagnosis, and control of *Fasciola hepatica* infection in horses. Include in your answer the relevance of the horse's environment and the challenges associated with diagnosis and treatment.

Answer Guide (Summary)

1. Pathogenesis:

- *Fasciola hepatica* is a trematode (fluke) affecting mainly ruminants, but horses are accidental hosts.
- Lifecycle involves snails as intermediate hosts (usually *Galba truncatula*) in wet, marshy areas.
- Horses ingest metacercariae on contaminated vegetation.
- Immature flukes migrate through the liver parenchyma → chronic inflammation, fibrosis → bile duct damage.
- In horses, clinical disease is rare but can occur, especially with heavy infection or concurrent stress/poor management.

2. Clinical Signs in Horses:

- Often subclinical or mild signs.

- Chronic weight loss, colic, anemia, poor condition.
- Occasionally jaundice or edema.
- Liver enzyme elevation on biochemistry.

3. Diagnosis:

- Fecal sedimentation (not flotation) can detect operculated eggs.
- Serology may be useful but not always available or validated for horses.
- Liver biopsy or ultrasound can aid diagnosis, but invasive.
- Diagnosis often presumptive based on signs, history, and environment.

4. Environmental Relevance:

- Wet, poorly drained pastures favor snail populations.
- Presence of sheep and cattle increases contamination risk.
- Horses grazing in these areas can be exposed even if not typical hosts.

5. Treatment and Control:

- Triclabendazole is the drug of choice in ruminants, but **not licensed for horses**.
- Off-label use may be considered under veterinary supervision.
- Control: restrict access to wet pastures, snail control (drainage, fencing), co-grazing management.
- Monitor liver enzymes and fecal exams.

6. Challenges:

- Underdiagnosed in horses due to low prevalence and non-specific signs.
- Difficult to confirm diagnosis without post-mortem or advanced diagnostics.
- Limited treatment options for equines.

Anoplocephala magna Equine tapeworm

1. Which of the following statements correctly describes *Anoplocephala magna*?

A. It is a roundworm found in the small intestine of horses.
B. It is a large tapeworm that inhabits the small intestine of equines.
C. It is a protozoan parasite of the liver in horses.
D. It is a fluke found in the large intestine of horses.

Answer: B
Explanation: *Anoplocephala magna* is a large tapeworm (cestode) found mainly in the small intestine of horses and donkeys.

2. What is the intermediate host of *Anoplocephala magna*?

A. Housefly (*Musca domestica*)
B. Oribatid mite
C. Mosquito
D. Snail

Answer: B
Explanation: The life cycle of *A. magna* involves **oribatid mites** that live in soil or pasture. Horses become infected when they ingest these mites while grazing.

3. The infective stage of *Anoplocephala magna* for the horse is the:

A. Cysticercoid larva
B. Embryonated egg
C. Oncosphere
D. Proglottid

Answer: A
Explanation: Horses are infected by ingesting **cysticercoid larvae** within oribatid mites.

4. Which of the following clinical signs is *most commonly associated* with *Anoplocephala magna* infection in horses?

A. Severe anemia and jaundice
B. Colic and intestinal obstruction
C. Coughing and nasal discharge
D. Liver damage and icterus

Answer: B
Explanation: Heavy infections of *A. magna* can cause **colic, intestinal obstruction**, and **weight loss** due to irritation and blockage of the intestinal lumen.

5. How can *Anoplocephala magna* infection be diagnosed in horses?

A. Blood smear examination
B. Detection of eggs in feces by flotation
C. Skin scraping
D. Serological test for antibodies

Answer: B
Explanation: Diagnosis is commonly made by detecting **characteristic triangular or D-shaped eggs** in the feces using a **flotation technique**, though eggs may be shed intermittently.

Case Study : Equine Tapeworm Infection

A 7-year-old gelding used for trail riding presents with intermittent colic signs, mild weight loss, and reduced performance.

The owner mentions that the horse has not been dewormed in over a year.

On physical examination, the horse shows mild abdominal discomfort but no fever.

A fecal egg count reveals the presence of cestode eggs.

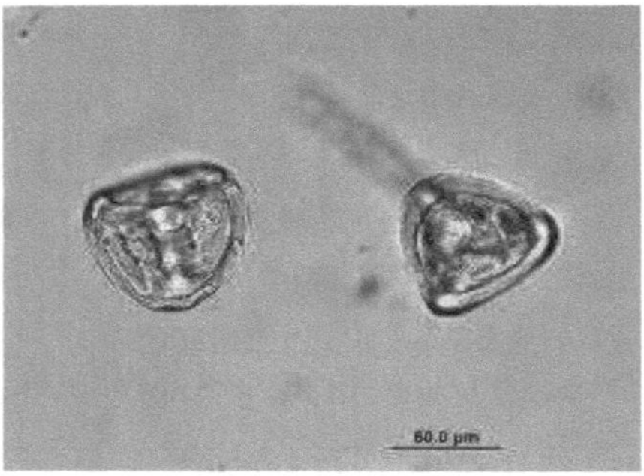

Additional background:

- ❖ The horse is kept on pasture with access to hay.
- ❖ The pasture is known to harbor oribatid mites.
- ❖ The fecal sample reveals eggs that are D-shaped with a pyriform apparatus.

Case Study Questions:

1. What is the most likely parasitic species responsible for the clinical signs in this horse?
2. What is the intermediate host of this parasite, and how is the life cycle completed?
3. How can you differentiate *Anoplocephala magna* from *Anoplocephala perfoliata* in terms of location in the host and morphology?
4. What are appropriate diagnostic techniques for detecting this parasite in horses?
5. Which anthelmintic treatments are effective against *Anoplocephala magna*?
6. What preventive measures can be taken to reduce the risk of reinfection?

Echinococcus equinus

1. What type of organism is *Echinococcus equinus*?

A. Bacteria
B. Protozoa
C. Cestode (tapeworm)
D. Nematode

Correct Answer: C. Cestode (tapeworm)
Explanation: *Echinococcus equinus* is a type of tapeworm belonging to the class Cestoda. It primarily affects equines as intermediate hosts.

2. What is the primary site of infection in horses by *Echinococcus equinus* larvae?

A. Lungs
B. Intestines
C. Liver
D. Kidneys

Correct Answer: C. Liver
Explanation: In horses, the larval stage (hydatid cyst) of *Echinococcus equinus* most commonly develops in the liver.

3. What form of *Echinococcus equinus* is found in the intermediate host (horse)?

A. Adult worm
B. Egg
C. Cystic larva (hydatid cyst)
D. Scolex

Correct Answer: C. Cystic larva (hydatid cyst)
Explanation: Horses act as intermediate hosts, harboring the hydatid cysts in organs like the liver.

4. What is the definitive host of *Echinococcus equinus*?

A. Horse
B. Cow
C. Dog
D. Pig

Correct Answer: C. Dog
Explanation: Dogs and other canids are definitive hosts where the adult tapeworm lives in the intestine.

5. What is the significance of *Echinococcus equinus* in terms of zoonosis (human health risk)?

A. High zoonotic risk
B. Moderate zoonotic risk
C. Low zoonotic risk
D. Not zoonotic

Correct Answer: D. Not zoonotic
Explanation: *Echinococcus equinus* is **not considered zoonotic**, unlike *E. granulosus*, meaning it does not typically infect humans.

Case Study Question: Echinococcus equinus in a Horse

Background:
A 10-year-old gelding was presented with progressive weight loss and intermittent colic over several weeks. On clinical examination, the horse showed signs of abdominal discomfort but no fever or abnormal bloodwork. An abdominal ultrasound revealed cystic lesions in the liver.

Question:

1. What is the likely parasitic cause of the hepatic cysts observed in this horse?
2. Describe the life cycle of *Echinococcus equinus* and the role of the horse in it.
3. How can *Echinococcus equinus* infection be diagnosed in horses?
4. What are the implications of this infection for public health and animal management?

Sample Answers:

1. **Likely Cause:**
   The most likely cause is *Echinococcus equinus* (formerly *E. granulosus* equine strain), which forms hydatid cysts in the liver and lungs of intermediate hosts like horses.
2. **Life Cycle of *Echinococcus equinus*:**
   - Definitive host: Usually dogs (especially those with access to horse carcasses).
   - Intermediate host: Horses ingest eggs shed in dog feces.
   - The oncospheres hatch, migrate through the bloodstream, and form hydatid cysts, especially in the liver or lungs.
   - Dogs become infected by eating infected horse organs containing fertile cysts.
3. **Diagnosis:**
   - Often incidental or post-mortem.
   - Imaging (ultrasound, radiography) may reveal cysts.
   - Serology is not always reliable in horses.
   - Confirmation typically requires histopathology or identification of cysts at necropsy.
4. **Public Health and Management Implications:**
   - Unlike *Echinococcus granulosus sensu stricto*, *E. equinus* is not known to be zoonotic (does not infect humans).
   - Still important for controlling the dog-horse life cycle to prevent spread.
   - Carcass disposal and deworming of dogs are key control measures.

***Gongylonema pulchrnm* Gullet worm**

1. What is the common name of *Gongylonema pulchrum* in horses?

A. Lungworm
B. Pinworm
C. Gullet worm
D. Stomach worm

Answer: C. Gullet worm

2. What is the primary location of *Gongylonema pulchrum* in the horse's body?

A. Small intestine
B. Gullet and esophagus
C. Lungs
D. Cecum and colon

Answer: B. Gullet and esophagus

3. Which of the following is the intermediate host for *Gongylonema pulchrum*?

A. Mosquito
B. Earthworm
C. Dung beetle
D. Cockroach

Answer: D. Cockroach

4. What is the main clinical significance of *Gongylonema pulchrum* infection in horses?

A. Severe colic
B. Respiratory distress
C. Usually asymptomatic
D. Acute diarrhea

Answer: C. Usually asymptomatic

5. How is *Gongylonema pulchrum* diagnosed in horses?

A. Fecal flotation
B. Endoscopy
C. Skin scraping
D. Blood smear

Answer: B. Endoscopy

Case Study Question: *Gongylonema pulchrum* in a Horse

Case study:

A 6-year-old mare presents with intermittent signs of discomfort around the mouth and throat.

The owner reports excessive salivation, head shaking, and a tendency to rub the face on objects.

The horse's appetite is normal, and there is no evidence of colic.

On oral examination, the veterinarian notices serpentine, thread-like movements in the mucosa of the mouth and esophagus.

A small biopsy sample from the buccal mucosa is taken and examined under the microscope, revealing slender nematodes embedded in the tissue.

Question:

1. **What is the most likely parasite involved in this case?**
2. **What is the life cycle of this parasite, and how does the horse become infected?**
3. **What diagnostic methods can be used to confirm the infection?**
4. **How should this condition be treated and managed?**

Answer:

1. Most Likely Parasite:

The most likely parasite is ***Gongylonema pulchrum***, commonly known as the "gullet worm."

It is known to infect the **mucosa of the esophagus, pharynx, and oral cavity** of various mammals, including horses.

2. Life Cycle and Transmission:

Gongylonema pulchrum has an **indirect life cycle**:

- **Intermediate hosts**: dung beetles or cockroaches ingest the eggs containing L1 larvae.

- The larvae develop into infective L3 stage in the beetle.
- The horse becomes infected by **ingesting the beetle or cockroach** containing the L3 larvae (e.g., while grazing or feeding).
- The larvae migrate to the **oral or esophageal mucosa**, where they embed and mature.

3. Diagnosis:

Clinical signs: facial rubbing, oral discomfort, excessive salivation.

Direct visualization: worms may be seen in the mucosa of the lips, buccal cavity, or esophagus as **serpentine, submucosal tracts**.

Biopsy or histopathology: confirms presence of embedded nematodes.

Fecal exams are usually **not useful**, as eggs are rarely passed in feces.

4. Treatment and Management:

Treatment may include **anthelmintics** such as:

- **Ivermectin** or **fenbendazole**, although efficacy can be variable due to the tissue-embedded nature of the worm.

In some cases, **mechanical removal** of worms from the mucosa (especially visible ones) may be required.

Environmental control: reduce exposure to intermediate hosts by:

- Proper feed storage
- Reducing beetle/cockroach populations in barns or feed areas

Threadworms – *Strongyloides westeri*

1. What is the primary route of transmission of *Strongyloides westeri* to foals?

A. Ingestion of contaminated feed
B. Transplacental transmission
C. Skin penetration
D. Lactogenic transmission (through mare's milk)

Correct Answer: D. Lactogenic transmission (through mare's milk)
Explanation: The primary mode of infection in foals is via the **mare's milk**, especially within the first weeks of life.

2. At what age are foals most commonly affected by *Strongyloides westeri*?

A. 1–2 days
B. 1–2 weeks
C. 4–6 weeks
D. 3–4 months

Correct Answer: B. 1–2 weeks
Explanation: Clinical signs typically appear around **1–2 weeks** of age, following infection shortly after birth via milk.

3. Which of the following is a typical clinical sign of *Strongyloides westeri* infection in foals?

A. Colic
B. Nasal discharge
C. Diarrhea
D. Laminitis

Correct Answer: C. Diarrhea
Explanation: The main clinical sign in infected foals is **mild to moderate diarrhea**. In severe cases, dehydration and weight loss may occur.

4. What is the best method for diagnosing *Strongyloides westeri* infection?

A. Blood culture
B. Fecal flotation test
C. PCR from nasal swab
D. Skin scraping

Correct Answer: B. Fecal flotation test
Explanation: Diagnosis is typically made by identifying **larvated eggs or larvae** in a **fecal flotation** sample.

5. Which of the following anthelmintics is effective against *Strongyloides westeri*?

A. Praziquantel
B. Fenbendazole
C. Ivermectin
D. Both B and C

Correct Answer: D. Both B and C
Explanation: Ivermectin and **Fenbendazole** are commonly used and effective against *Strongyloides westeri*.

Case Study: Strongyloides westeri in a Foal

Case Presentation:

A 10-day-old Thoroughbred foal presents with **watery diarrhea**, dehydration, and mild weakness.

The foal was born on a breeding farm with good hygiene practices.

The mare is healthy and was dewormed before foaling.

The foal has been nursing normally but recently became lethargic. No other foals on the farm are currently ill.

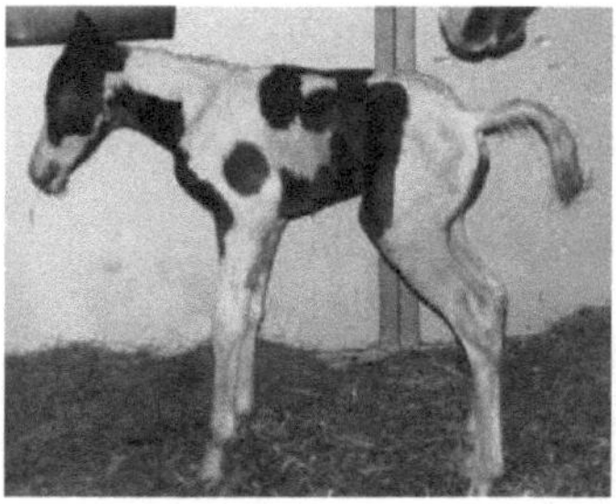

On physical exam:

- ❖ Temperature: 39.5°C (mild fever)
- ❖ Mucous membranes: tacky
- ❖ Capillary refill time: 2.5 seconds
- ❖ Body condition: fair
- ❖ Mild abdominal discomfort

A fecal flotation was performed, revealing **larvated eggs**.

Question:

1. What is the most likely diagnosis?
2. What is the most probable route of transmission in this case?
3. What life stage of the parasite is typically found in the feces?
4. What is the recommended treatment?
5. How can this condition be prevented in future foals?

Answer Key:

1. **Most likely diagnosis:**
    - **Strongyloides westeri** infection
2. **Most probable route of transmission:**
    - **Transmammary transmission** from the dam's milk. The larvae migrate to the mammary gland and are ingested during nursing.
3. **Life stage found in feces:**
    - **Larvated eggs** (eggs containing first-stage larvae). These are typical for Strongyloides species.
4. **Recommended treatment:**
    - **Ivermectin** (0.2 mg/kg PO once) or **oxibendazole** or **fenbendazole**.

- Supportive therapy: fluid and electrolyte replacement as needed.

5. **Prevention strategies:**
   - **Deworm mares 2–3 weeks before foaling** with ivermectin to reduce transmammary transmission.
   - Good hygiene and regular fecal monitoring in breeding farms.
   - Isolate and monitor newborn foals for early signs of diarrhea.

Parascaris *(Parascaris equorum)*

1. What is the primary route of transmission for *Parascaris equorum* in horses?

A. Skin penetration
B. Ingestion of infected larvae
C. Vector-borne via flies
D. Transplacental transmission

Correct Answer: B. Ingestion of infected larvae

2. Which age group of horses is most commonly affected by *Parascaris equorum*?

A. Newborn foals
B. Horses older than 5 years
C. Yearlings and foals (under 2 years old)
D. Mature broodmares

Correct Answer: C. Yearlings and foals (under 2 years old)

3. What is a common clinical sign of a heavy *Parascaris equorum* infection in foals?

A. Coughing and nasal discharge
B. Sudden death
C. Colic and poor growth
D. Laminitis

Correct Answer: C. Colic and poor growth

4. Which diagnostic method is typically used to detect *Parascaris equorum* infection?

A. Blood culture
B. Skin scraping
C. Fecal flotation for eggs
D. PCR test on saliva

Correct Answer: C. Fecal flotation for eggs

5. What is a major concern in treating *Parascaris equorum* in young horses?

A. Vaccine resistance
B. Drug-induced hypersensitivity
C. Resistance to commonly used anthelmintics
D. High cost of treatment

Correct Answer: C. Resistance to commonly used anthelmintics

Case Study: Parascaris equorum in a Young Horse

Case :

A 6-month-old Thoroughbred colt is presented with poor growth, a rough hair coat, intermittent coughing, and a pot-bellied appearance.

The foal is kept on a pasture with several other young horses and has not been dewormed in the past three months.

The owner reports that the foal has a decreased appetite and has recently passed worms in the feces.

On physical examination, the colt is underweight with mild nasal discharge and signs of abdominal discomfort. A fecal flotation reveals the presence of ascarid eggs.

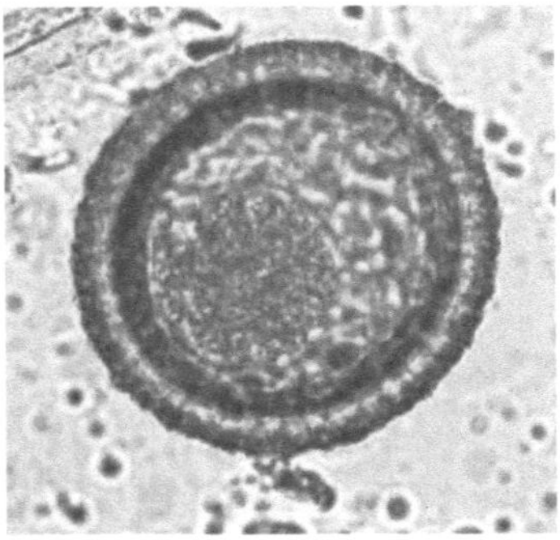

Ascarid eggs.

Case Study Questions & Answers

Q1: What is the most likely diagnosis?
A: The most likely diagnosis is **Parascaris equorum infection** (equine roundworm infestation), common in foals and young horses.

Q2: Describe the life cycle of *Parascaris equorum*.
A:

Ingestion of eggs containing infective larvae (L2) from contaminated environment (e.g., pasture, feed).

Larvae hatch in the small intestine, penetrate the intestinal wall, and migrate via the **liver to the lungs** (hepatotracheal migration).

Larvae are coughed up, swallowed, and **mature into adult worms in the small intestine**.

Eggs are passed in feces, becoming infective in the environment within 10-14 days.

Entire cycle takes about **10–12 weeks**.

Q3: What clinical signs are associated with *Parascaris equorum* infection?
A:

- Poor weight gain or weight loss
- Pot-bellied appearance
- Rough hair coat
- Intermittent coughing and nasal discharge (due to pulmonary migration)
- Colic or intestinal blockage (in heavy infestations)
- Lethargy and poor appetite
- Worms visible in feces or vomit

Q4: How is *Parascaris equorum* diagnosed?
A:

- **Fecal flotation** to detect characteristic ascarid eggs (thick shell, round).
- History and clinical signs (esp. in foals <1 year).
- In severe cases, **visualization of adult worms** in feces or vomit.
- **Ultrasound** may reveal intestinal obstruction in severe infestations.

Q5: What is the treatment and control strategy?
A:

Anthelmintics:

- Benzimidazoles (e.g., fenbendazole)
- Pyrantel pamoate
- Ivermectin or moxidectin (be cautious due to resistance concerns)

In heavy infestations, **use milder dewormers first (e.g., fenbendazole)** to avoid impaction from sudden worm die-off.

Deworm foals starting at **8 weeks of age**, then every 6–8 weeks until 1 year old.

Rotate drug classes to avoid resistance.

Pasture management: Regular removal of manure, avoid overstocking.

Keep young horses separated from adults if possible.

Q6: What complications can arise from heavy *Parascaris equorum* infections?
A:

Intestinal impaction or rupture due to large worm burdens (life-threatening).

Liver and lung damage from larval migration.

Secondary bacterial pneumonia due to pulmonary migration.

Reduced growth and performance.

Q7: Why is *Parascaris equorum* primarily a concern in young horses and not adults?
A:

Adult horses develop **immunity** to *Parascaris equorum.*

Infections are rare and typically subclinical in mature horses.

Foals and yearlings lack sufficient immunity and are more vulnerable to clinical disease.

***Oxyuris equi* Equine pinworm**

1. What is the most common clinical sign of Oxyuris equi infection in horses?

A. Diarrhea
B. Colic
C. Intense itching around the tail (pruritus ani)
D. Weight loss

Answer: C. Intense itching around the tail (pruritus ani)
□ **Explanation:** The female pinworm lays eggs around the anus, causing irritation and tail rubbing.

2. How is Oxyuris equi infection most commonly diagnosed?

A. Blood test
B. Urinalysis
C. Skin scraping
D. Tape impression from the perianal area

Answer: D. Tape impression from the perianal area
□ **Explanation:** Eggs are laid around the anus, and using clear adhesive tape to collect and examine them under a microscope is a common diagnostic method.

3. What is the life cycle type of Oxyuris equi?

A. Indirect with an intermediate host
B. Direct with no intermediate host
C. Requires an insect vector
D. Requires aquatic snails as intermediate hosts

Answer: B. Direct with no intermediate host
□ **Explanation:** Oxyuris equi has a **direct life cycle**; eggs are ingested from the environment and develop within the horse.

4. Where do the adult Oxyuris equi worms reside in the horse?

A. Stomach
B. Small intestine
C. Cecum and colon
D. Lungs

Answer: C. Cecum and colon
□ **Explanation:** Adult pinworms inhabit the large intestine, especially the cecum, colon, and rectum.

5. Which of the following dewormers is effective against Oxyuris equi?

A. Ivermectin
B. Praziquantel
C. Metronidazole
D. Tylosin

Answer: A. Ivermectin
□ **Explanation:** Ivermectin, along with others like pyrantel and fenbendazole, is effective against Oxyuris equi.

Case Study Question: Oxyuris equi (Equine Pinworm)

Case :

A 6-year-old mare is presented to your veterinary clinic with the owner's complaint that the horse has been frequently rubbing its tail against fences and stall walls.

The owner also noticed some yellowish-white, sticky material around the perineal region and tail head. The horse's appetite and general condition are otherwise normal.

On physical examination, the horse is alert and in good body condition, but there is evidence of hair loss and skin irritation near the tail head.

No other abnormalities are found. A cellophane tape test from the perianal region reveals oval eggs with an operculum under the microscope.

Question:

1. What is the **most likely diagnosis**?
2. What is the **causative agent**?
3. Describe the **life cycle** of the parasite.
4. What are the **clinical signs** associated with this infection?
5. How is the **diagnosis** confirmed?
6. What are the **treatment and control** strategies?

Answers:

1. **Most Likely Diagnosis:**
    - **Oxyuris equi infection** (Equine pinworm infestation)
2. **Causative Agent:**
    - *Oxyuris equi*, a large pinworm that infects the large intestine of horses.
3. **Life Cycle of Oxyuris equi:**
    - **Direct life cycle** (no intermediate host).
    - Adult worms live in the **colon and rectum.**

- Gravid females migrate to the **perianal area** and lay eggs in a sticky substance on the skin.
- Eggs fall into the environment or are rubbed off and contaminate surfaces (feed, water, grooming tools).
- Eggs become infective in **3–5 days**.
- Horse ingests infective eggs.
- Larvae hatch in the small intestine, migrate to the large intestine, and mature into adults.
- **Prepatent period**: ~5 months.

4. **Clinical Signs:**
   - Intense **pruritus (itchiness)** of the tail and perineum.
   - **Hair loss** and **skin excoriation** around the tail head ("rat tail" appearance).
   - Restlessness, rubbing against objects.
   - Occasionally mild colic or digestive disturbances.
5. **Diagnosis:**
   - **Cellophane tape test** (Scotch tape method) applied to the perianal area to detect eggs.
   - Fecal flotation is often **negative**, as eggs are laid outside the anus.
   - Observation of adult worms in feces (rare).
6. **Treatment and Control:**
   - **Anthelmintics** effective against pinworms:
     - **Ivermectin**, **moxidectin**, **pyrantel pamoate**, **fenbendazole**.
   - **Clean the perianal region** regularly to remove eggs.
   - Disinfect stalls, fences, grooming tools.
   - Rotate pastures and implement good **manure management**.
   - Treat all horses on the premises to prevent reinfection.

Stomach worms
Habronema muscae
H. *majus* (syn. H. *microstoma)* and *Draschia megastoma* (syn. H. *megastoma)*
Equine stomach worms, summer sores.

1. What is the intermediate host for Habronema species in horses?

A) Mosquitoes
B) Houseflies and Stable flies
C) Ticks
D) Fleas

Answer: B) Houseflies and Stable flies

Houseflies (Musca domestica) and *stable flies (Stomoxys calcitrans)* serve as intermediate hosts for Habronema spp.

2. What is the most common clinical manifestation of cutaneous habronemiasis (summer sores) in horses?

A) Diarrhea
B) Respiratory distress
C) Ulcerated, non-healing skin lesions
D) Convulsions

Answer: C) Ulcerated, non-healing skin lesions

Summer sores are caused when Habronema larvae are deposited onto skin wounds, leading to granulomatous lesions that do not heal easily.

3. Which species is most associated with tumor-like lesions in the stomach wall of horses?

A) Habronema muscae
B) Draschia megastoma
C) Habronema majus
D) Strongylus vulgaris

Answer: B) Draschia megastoma

Draschia megastoma is known to cause large nodular or tumor-like lesions in the stomach wall due to larval development within granulomatous nodules.

4. How do horses become infected with stomach worms like Habronema spp.?

A) Ingestion of contaminated water
B) Ingestion of intermediate host (flies) carrying infective larvae
C) Direct skin penetration
D) Vertical transmission from mare to foal

Answer: B) Ingestion of intermediate host (flies) carrying infective larvae

Horses ingest the infective larvae when they lick or consume feed/water contaminated by flies carrying L3 larvae.

5. Which diagnostic method is most useful for detecting adult Habronema spp. in the horse's stomach?

A) Skin scraping
B) Fecal flotation
C) Endoscopic examination or necropsy
D) PCR from blood

Answer: C) Endoscopic examination or necropsy

Adult Habronema worms are difficult to detect in feces due to larvated eggs and degradation; visualization via **endoscopy** or **necropsy** provides definitive diagnosis.

Case Study: Habronema muscae in a Horse

Case :

A 5-year-old gelding is presented in early summer with a non-healing, ulcerated skin lesion on the medial canthus of the left eye.

The lesion is raised, moist, and has yellowish granules with some pruritus.

The horse frequently rubs the area on fences.

The lesion has not responded to standard wound care and topical antibiotics. The owner reports the horse lives in a pasture with high fly activity.

□ **Questions & Answers**

Q1: What is the most likely diagnosis?

Answer:
The most likely diagnosis is **cutaneous habronemiasis** caused by **Habronema muscae** larvae.

Q2: What is the causative agent and its life cycle?

Answer:
Causative Agent: *Habronema muscae*, a parasitic nematode.

Life Cycle Overview:

1. Adult worms live in the horse's stomach.
2. Eggs or larvae are passed in the feces.
3. Fly larvae (especially *Musca domestica*, the housefly) ingest the larvae.
4. Larvae develop to the infective stage within the fly.
5. When flies feed on moist areas (e.g. wounds, eyes, genitalia), they deposit infective larvae.
6. If larvae are deposited on **intact skin or mucous membranes**, they **do not complete the life cycle**, but cause **cutaneous or ocular lesions** instead.

Q3: What are the clinical signs of cutaneous habronemiasis?

Answer:

Non-healing, ulcerated skin lesions ("summer sores")

Granulomatous, itchy, moist lesions

Presence of yellowish necrotic granules ("sulfur granules")

Common sites: eyes, prepuce, medial canthus, wounds, limbs

Q4: How is the diagnosis confirmed?

Answer:

Clinical history and **appearance of lesion** in summer

Cytology or **histopathology** of lesion showing eosinophilic granulomas and larvae

Response to therapy can also support diagnosis

Fecal exam may detect eggs (if adult worms are present in the stomach), but not in cutaneous cases

Q5: What is the treatment for Habronema muscae infection?

Answer:

Anthelmintic therapy: Ivermectin or moxidectin (systemic treatment to kill larvae)

Anti-inflammatory therapy: Corticosteroids to reduce inflammation

Topical therapy: Antiseptics, antibiotics if secondary infection present

Fly control: Essential to prevent reinfection

Surgical removal or cryotherapy in chronic or large granulomatous lesions

Q6: How can this condition be prevented?

Answer:

Fly control: Use of repellents, fly masks, and environmental management

Prompt wound care: Avoid attracting flies to open lesions

Strategic deworming: To eliminate adult *Habronema* in the stomach

Stable hygiene: Manure removal and fly breeding site reduction

□ **Summary:**

Habronema muscae causes **cutaneous lesions** when larvae are deposited by flies on wounds or mucous membranes. These **non-healing granulomatous lesions**, typically in summer, are managed by systemic dewormers and fly control, along with symptomatic treatment of the wounds.

Large strongyles

Strongylus vulgaris, Strongylus equinus and *Strongylus edentatus* Large Strongyles

MCQ 1

Which species of large strongyles is most commonly associated with verminous arteritis in horses?

A) Strongylus vulgaris
B) Strongylus equinus
C) Strongylus edentatus
D) Cyathostomes

Answer: A) Strongylus vulgaris

MCQ 2

Which large strongyle larva migrates through the liver and peritoneum in horses?

A) Strongylus vulgaris
B) Strongylus equinus
C) Strongylus edentatus
D) Strongyloides westeri

Answer: C) Strongylus edentates

MCQ 3

The adult Strongylus equinus is primarily found in which part of the horse's body?
A) Cecum and colon
B) Small intestine
C) Liver parenchyma
D) Mesenteric arteries

Answer: A) Cecum and colon

MCQ 4

Which of the following is the main pathogenic mechanism of Strongylus vulgaris in horses?
A) Larval migration through mesenteric arteries causing thrombosis
B) Intestinal wall ulceration by adult worms
C) Larval migration through liver causing fibrosis
D) Larval encystment in muscle tissue

Answer: A) Larval migration through mesenteric arteries causing thrombosis

MCQ 5

Which large strongyle species lacks teeth in its buccal capsule?
A) Strongylus vulgaris
B) Strongylus equinus
C) Strongylus edentatus
D) Strongyloides ransomi

Answer: C) Strongylus edentatus

Questions & Answers:

1. What is the life cycle of *Strongylus vulgaris*?

- ❖ Eggs are passed in the feces, hatch into larvae on pasture.
- ❖ Infective larvae (L3) are ingested by horses during grazing.
- ❖ Larvae penetrate the intestinal mucosa and migrate to the cranial mesenteric artery (around 2-3 weeks).

- ❖ They mature in the artery walls, causing inflammation and thrombus formation over several months.
- ❖ Larvae then return to the intestine to mature into adults and lay eggs.
- ❖ The entire cycle takes about 6-7 months.

2. What clinical signs are commonly associated with *Strongylus vulgaris* infection?

- ❖ Intermittent to severe colic due to intestinal ischemia.
- ❖ Weight loss and poor body condition.
- ❖ Diarrhea or loose stools.
- ❖ Lethargy and decreased appetite.
- ❖ Signs of systemic inflammation (fever, tachycardia).

3. How is the infection diagnosed?

- ❖ Fecal egg counts can detect strongyle eggs but cannot differentiate *S. vulgaris* from other strongyles.
- ❖ Serologic tests (ELISA) can detect antibodies against migrating larvae (less commonly used).
- ❖ Blood tests showing inflammation and anemia support diagnosis.
- ❖ Clinical signs and history of colic.
- ❖ Imaging (ultrasound) may reveal intestinal wall changes.

- ❖ Definitive diagnosis often involves response to treatment.

4. What treatment options are available?

- ❖ Anthelmintics effective against *S. vulgaris* include ivermectin, moxidectin, and fenbendazole (in some protocols).
- ❖ Careful treatment is needed because killing larvae in arteries can worsen thrombosis temporarily.
- ❖ Supportive care for colic (fluids, pain relief).
- ❖ Regular deworming schedules should be implemented post-treatment.

5. How can *Strongylus vulgaris* infection be prevented?

- ❖ Regular fecal egg count monitoring and targeted deworming.
- ❖ Pasture management: avoid overgrazing, rotate pastures, remove feces regularly.
- ❖ Deworming with effective drugs based on FEC results.

- ❖ Avoid deworming too frequently to prevent resistance but also not too infrequently to allow dangerous parasite build-up.

Small strongyles
Triodontophorus spp., *Trichonema* spp., *Cyathostomum* spp., *Cylicocyclus* spp.,
Cylicostephanus spp., *Cylicodontophorus* spp., *Gyalocephalus* spp., *Oesophagodontus* spp. and *Craterostomum* spp

MCQ 1:
Which of the following genera belong to small strongyles (cyathostomins) in horses?
A) Triodontophorus spp.
B) Trichonema spp.
C) Cyathostomum spp.
D) All of the above
Answer: D) All of the above

MCQ 2:
Which genus is NOT considered a small strongyle (cyathostomin)?
A) Cylicocyclus spp.
B) Cylicostephanus spp.
C) Gyalocephalus spp.
D) Strongylus vulgaris
Answer: D) Strongylus vulgaris

MCQ 3:
Which genus among the following is classified under small strongyles?
A) Oesophagodontus spp.
B) Trichonema spp.
C) Craterostomum spp.
D) All of the above
Answer: D) All of the above

MCQ 4:
Small strongyles primarily affect which species?
A) Cattle
B) Sheep
C) Horses
D) Pigs
Answer: C) Horses

MCQ 5:
Which of the following genera of small strongyles is known for causing larval cyathostominosis due to mass emergence of larvae?
A) Cyathostomum spp.
B) Trichonema spp.
C) Cylicostephanus spp.
D) All of the above
Answer: D) All of the above

Case Study: Small Strongyles Infection in a Horse

Background:
A 6-year-old Thoroughbred gelding used for competitive riding presents with intermittent diarrhea, weight loss, and a dull coat despite a normal appetite.

The horse is housed with several others on pasture.

Fecal egg counts have shown a moderate number of strongyle-type eggs. The owner reports that deworming was last done 6 months ago.

Clinical Examination:

- Mild anemia
- Mild colic signs
- Mild ventral edema
- Loss of body condition over the past 2 months

Diagnostic Workup:

Fecal egg count: 500 eggs per gram (EPG) of strongyle eggs

Fecal culture identified larvae consistent with small strongyles (*Cyathostominae*).

Bloodwork showed mild hypoalbuminemia.

Management history:
Previous deworming with ivermectin alone.

Questions:

1. **What is the significance of the small strongyles in this horse?**
2. **Why is this infection hard to treat?**
3. **What is the life cycle of small strongyles (Cyathostominae)?**
4. **What clinical syndrome is associated with larval cyathostominosis?**
5. **What treatment strategy should be recommended?**
6. **What prevention measures can be implemented?**

Answers:

1. **Significance of Small Strongyles:**
   Small strongyles (*Cyathostominae*) are the most common and important intestinal parasites of horses worldwide. They include genera such as *Triodontophorus*, *Trichonema*, *Cyathostomum*, and *Cylicocyclus*. Adult worms attach to the large intestinal mucosa, feeding and causing inflammation and damage. The larvae, especially the encysted stages, can cause severe disease. The clinical signs of weight loss, diarrhea, and poor coat suggest larval cyathostominosis.

2. **Why is this Infection Hard to Treat?**
   Small strongyles have a unique life cycle feature: their larvae can encyst in the large intestinal wall and remain dormant for months or even years (hypobiosis). During encysted stages, they are less susceptible to many common anthelmintics, making eradication difficult. When they emerge en masse, they cause mucosal damage and inflammation, leading to clinical

disease. There is also growing resistance to some anthelmintics (like benzimidazoles and pyrantel) complicating treatment.

3. **Life Cycle of Small Strongyles:**

- Eggs passed in feces hatch into larvae on pasture.
- Infective L3 larvae are ingested by the horse while grazing.
- L3 larvae penetrate the mucosa of the large intestine and encyst as L4 larvae.
- They may remain encysted for months (hypobiotic phase).
- Eventually, larvae emerge from the mucosa to mature into adults in the large intestine.
- Adults produce eggs passed in feces, completing the cycle.

4. **Clinical Syndrome Associated with Larval Cyathostominosis:**
   Larval cyathostominosis occurs when large numbers of encysted larvae emerge simultaneously from the intestinal mucosa, causing severe inflammation, mucosal ulceration, protein-losing enteropathy, diarrhea, weight loss, colic, and sometimes ventral edema due to hypoproteinemia. This syndrome is often acute and can be fatal if untreated.
5. **Treatment Strategy:**

- Use anthelmintics effective against encysted larvae, such as a five-day course of fenbendazole (10 mg/kg daily) or a single dose of moxidectin.
- Supportive care for diarrhea and protein loss (fluids, anti-inflammatories).
- Repeat fecal egg counts to monitor response.
- Avoid abrupt mass larval emergence by strategic deworming.

6. **Prevention Measures:**

- Implement targeted deworming based on fecal egg counts to reduce selection for resistance.
- Rotate anthelmintics but use those effective against encysted larvae when necessary.
- Pasture management: regular manure removal, avoid overcrowding.
- Avoid deworming during peak larval emergence times to prevent larval cyathostominosis.

Onchocerca cervicalis, *Onchocerca raillieti, Onchocerca reticulata*
Nuehal ligament worm

1. Which species of Onchocerca is commonly referred to as the "nuchal ligament worm"?

A) Onchocerca raillieti
B) Onchocerca cervicalis
C) Onchocerca reticulata
D) Onchocerca volvulus

Answer: B) Onchocerca cervicalis

2. What is the primary site of infection of *Onchocerca cervicalis* in horses?

A) Skin of the belly
B) Nuchal ligament
C) Lymph nodes
D) Joints

Answer: B) Nuchal ligament

3. Which of the following is true regarding *Onchocerca reticulata*?

A) It is primarily found in the nuchal ligament of horses
B) It commonly affects the flexor tendons and suspensory ligament
C) It causes river blindness in humans
D) It is transmitted by the blackfly (Simulium species)

Answer: B) It commonly affects the flexor tendons and suspensory ligament

4. What is the common vector for the transmission of Onchocerca species in horses?

A) Mosquito
B) Blackfly (Simulium species)
C) Horsefly (Tabanid species)
D) Tick

Answer: C) Horsefly (Tabanid species)

5. *Onchocerca raillieti* is primarily found in which host?

A) Humans
B) Cattle
C) Horses
D) Dogs

Answer: B) Cattle

Case Study Question:

A 7-year-old horse presents with areas of hair loss, scaling, and intense itching along the neck and shoulders. The owner reports that the horse has been rubbing itself against fence posts and appears uncomfortable. On physical examination, you notice dermatitis with some nodules under the skin in the cervical region. The horse has been stabled near a marshy area where black flies and biting midges are common.

1. What is the most likely cause of this condition?
2. How is this parasite transmitted?
3. What diagnostic methods would confirm the diagnosis?
4. What treatment options are available?
5. How can this condition be prevented?

Answer:

1. Most likely cause:
The clinical signs and location are typical of **Onchocerca cervicalis** infection, a filarial nematode parasite in horses. The dermatitis and pruritus (itching) are

caused by an immune reaction to microfilariae migrating through the skin, especially around the neck and shoulders.

2. Transmission:
Onchocerca cervicalis is transmitted by **biting midges** (genus *Culicoides*), which act as intermediate hosts. The larvae develop inside the midge and are transmitted to the horse during a bite.

3. Diagnostic methods:

Skin biopsy: Can reveal microfilariae in the skin.

Skin snip test: Small skin samples placed in saline can release microfilariae visible under a microscope.

Histopathology: Identification of adult worms in the ligamentum nuchae (neck ligament) during necropsy or biopsy confirms the diagnosis.

4. Treatment options:

Ivermectin or moxidectin: These macrocyclic lactones are effective in killing microfilariae and some adult worms.

Anti-inflammatory therapy: To control dermatitis and itching.

Management: Reducing exposure to biting midges by stabling horses during peak vector activity and using insect repellents.

5. Prevention:

Minimize exposure to biting midges by stabling horses at dawn and dusk when vectors are most active.

Use insect repellents and fly sheets.

Regular treatment with ivermectin/moxidectin to reduce microfilarial load and interrupt the parasite life cycle.

***Dictyocaulus arnfieldi* (Equine lungworm)**

1. What is the primary host of *Dictyocaulus arnfieldi*?

A) Cattle
B) Sheep
C) Donkeys
D) Horses

Answer: C) Donkeys

2. Which species is most commonly affected by clinical disease caused by *Dictyocaulus arnfieldi*?

A) Donkeys
B) Horses
C) Cattle
D) Goats

Answer: B) Horses

3. What is the main clinical sign in horses infected with *Dictyocaulus arnfieldi*?

A) Diarrhea
B) Severe coughing and respiratory distress
C) Lameness
D) Weight gain

Answer: B) Severe coughing and respiratory distress

4. How is *Dictyocaulus arnfieldi* primarily diagnosed?

A) Blood smear
B) Fecal flotation for eggs
C) Identification of larvae in feces via Baermann technique
D) Skin biopsy

Answer: C) Identification of larvae in feces via Baermann technique

5. What is the most effective way to control *Dictyocaulus arnfieldi* infection in a mixed herd of donkeys and horses?

A) Vaccination of horses
B) Deworming donkeys regularly
C) Feeding horses high-protein diet
D) Isolating horses only

Answer: B) Deworming donkeys regularly

Case Study Question:

A 5-year-old donkey and a 7-year-old horse share the same pasture. The donkey shows no signs of respiratory disease, but the horse develops a persistent cough, nasal discharge, and increased respiratory effort. On clinical examination, the horse has harsh lung sounds and occasionally coughs up mucus. Fecal examination of the horse reveals larvae consistent with Dictyocaulus species.

1. What is the most likely diagnosis for the horse?
2. Explain why the donkey is asymptomatic but the horse shows clinical signs.
3. How is Dictyocaulus arnfieldi transmitted?
4. What treatment and control measures would you recommend?

Answer:

1. **Diagnosis:**
   The horse is most likely suffering from **dictyocaulosis caused by Dictyocaulus arnfieldi (equine lungworm)** infection.
2. **Asymptomatic donkey, symptomatic horse:**
   Donkeys are the natural hosts of Dictyocaulus arnfieldi and usually harbor the parasite without clinical signs due to acquired immunity or tolerance.

Horses, however, are aberrant hosts and tend to develop clinical respiratory disease when infected because they have less effective immunity to the parasite.

3. **Transmission:**
   The parasite is transmitted via ingestion of infective larvae (L3) from contaminated pasture, water, or feed. Larvae are shed in the feces of infected donkeys, contaminate the environment, and then are ingested by horses grazing on the same pasture.
4. **Treatment and control:**
   - **Treatment:** Use anthelmintics effective against lungworms, such as ivermectin or fenbendazole, to treat infected horses.
   - **Control:** Avoid co-grazing horses with donkeys or regularly treat donkeys to reduce larval shedding. Maintain pasture hygiene, and rotate grazing areas if possible. Monitor horses regularly for clinical signs and perform fecal larval examinations.

Setaria equina **(Equine abdominal worm)**

1. What is the primary host of *Setaria equina*?

a) Cattle
b) Horses
c) Sheep
d) Pigs

Answer: b) Horses

2. *Setaria equina* primarily inhabits which part of the horse's body?

a) Intestines
b) Lungs
c) Abdominal cavity
d) Heart

Answer: c) Abdominal cavity

3. What is the main mode of transmission of *Setaria equina*?

a) Ingestion of contaminated water
b) Skin penetration by larvae
c) Bite of mosquito vectors
d) Direct contact with infected animals

Answer: c) Bite of mosquito vectors

4. Which of the following mosquitoes is commonly involved in the transmission of *Setaria equina*?

a) Anopheles
b) Aedes
c) Culex
d) Mansonia

Answer: c) Culex

5. The clinical signs of *Setaria equina* infection in horses are often:

a) Severe diarrhea
b) Respiratory distress
c) Usually asymptomatic or mild abdominal discomfort
d) Neurological signs

Answer: c) Usually asymptomatic or mild abdominal discomfort

Case Study Question:

A 7-year-old gelding horse is presented with intermittent neurological signs including hind limb weakness, ataxia, and occasional muscle tremors. The horse has been kept in a marshy area with abundant mosquito populations. On clinical examination, mild inflammation is observed along the spinal cord. Blood tests show eosinophilia. Based on these findings, what is the likely parasitic infection? Describe the life cycle, pathogenesis, clinical signs, diagnosis, and treatment of this parasite in horses.

Answer:

Likely Parasite:
Setaria equina, a filarial nematode that commonly infects horses.

Life Cycle:

- Adult *Setaria equina* worms reside in the peritoneal cavity of horses.
- Female worms release microfilariae into the bloodstream.
- Mosquitoes (intermediate hosts) ingest microfilariae during blood meals.
- Microfilariae develop into infective larvae inside mosquitoes.
- Infective larvae are transmitted to horses during subsequent mosquito bites, migrating to the peritoneal cavity to mature.

Pathogenesis:

- Usually, adult worms in the peritoneal cavity cause minimal pathology.
- Aberrant migration of larvae or adult worms into the central nervous system (CNS) can cause neurological signs.
- The inflammation and mechanical damage caused by migrating larvae/adults lead to hind limb weakness, ataxia, and tremors.
- Eosinophilia results from the host immune response to migrating parasites.

Clinical Signs:

- Hind limb weakness and ataxia.
- Muscle tremors.
- Occasionally signs of meningitis or encephalitis if CNS is involved.
- Mild fever and malaise.

Diagnosis:

- Detection of microfilariae in peripheral blood smear (may require concentration techniques).
- Clinical signs in conjunction with history of mosquito exposure.
- Response to antiparasitic treatment supports diagnosis.

Treatment:

- Ivermectin or moxidectin is effective against microfilariae and some larval stages.
- Corticosteroids may be used to reduce CNS inflammation if neurological signs are severe.
- Supportive care for neurological symptoms.
- Control of mosquito populations and minimizing exposure helps prevent infection.

Parafilaria multipapillosa
"summer bleeding"

1. What is the causative agent of "summer bleeding" in horses?

a) Onchocerca cervicalis
b) Parafilaria multipapillosa
c) Habronema muscae
d) Draschia megastoma

Answer: b) Parafilaria multipapillosa

2. What is the primary clinical sign of infection with Parafilaria multipapillosa in horses?

a) Diarrhea
b) Skin nodules with bleeding
c) Respiratory distress
d) Lameness

Answer: b) Skin nodules with bleeding

3. How is Parafilaria multipapillosa transmitted?

a) Direct contact with infected horses
b) Ingestion of contaminated feed
c) Through blood-feeding flies
d) Through contaminated water

Answer: c) Through blood-feeding flies

4. In which season is "summer bleeding" most commonly observed?

a) Winter
b) Spring
c) Summer
d) Autumn

Answer: c) Summer

5. What is the typical treatment used for Parafilaria multipapillosa infections?

a) Antibiotics
b) Anthelmintics such as ivermectin or moxidectin
c) Antifungal medications
d) Corticosteroids

Answer: b) Anthelmintics such as ivermectin or moxidectin

Case Study: Parafilaria multipapillosa and Summer Bleeding

Background:
A horse owner reports that during the summer months, their horses develop

bleeding nodules on the skin, primarily on the ventral abdomen and chest. The bleeding tends to be intermittent but recurrent each summer. The affected horses show no signs of systemic illness.

Question 1:

What is the likely cause of the bleeding nodules observed in the horses?

Answer:
The likely cause is infection with the parasite *Parafilaria multipapillosa*. This nematode causes subcutaneous nodules that bleed intermittently, particularly during warm months, a condition commonly known as "summer bleeding."

Question 2:

What is the life cycle and transmission method of *Parafilaria multipapillosa*?

Answer:
Parafilaria multipapillosa is transmitted by blood-feeding flies (usually *Musca* spp.). The adult worms live in subcutaneous nodules in the horse's skin and release microfilariae into the skin, which then attract flies. The flies pick up the microfilariae while feeding and transmit them to other horses when they bite, perpetuating the cycle.

Question 3:

What clinical signs and lesions are typically seen with *Parafilaria multipapillosa* infection?

Answer:

- Subcutaneous nodules, often on the ventral abdomen, chest, or shoulders
- Nodules may rupture, causing characteristic bleeding from the skin ("summer bleeding")
- Lesions may be pruritic and cause local irritation
- Systemic illness is rare, and horses generally remain otherwise healthy

Question 4:

How is *Parafilaria multipapillosa* infection diagnosed?

Answer:

- Clinical diagnosis based on characteristic seasonal bleeding nodules
- Detection of microfilariae in skin scrapings or biopsy samples from nodules
- Sometimes, parasitic identification through histopathology

Question 5:

What are the treatment and control measures for *Parafilaria multipapillosa* infection?

Answer:

- Treatment typically involves administration of ivermectin or other macrocyclic lactones, which are effective against adult worms and microfilariae
- Control measures include reducing exposure to biting flies through insecticides, fly repellents, and environmental management
- Avoiding overcrowding and improving stable hygiene can help minimize fly populations

***Thelazia lacrymalis* Eyeworm**

1. What is the primary site of infection of *Thelazia lacrymalis* in horses?

A) Stomach
B) Intestines
C) Lacrimal sac and conjunctival sac
D) Lungs

Answer: C) Lacrimal sac and conjunctival sac

2. What is the main vector responsible for transmitting *Thelazia lacrymalis* to horses?

A) Horsefly (Tabanus spp.)
B) Stable fly (Stomoxys calcitrans)
C) Housefly (Musca autumnalis)
D) Mosquito

Answer: C) Housefly (*Musca autumnalis*)

3. Which of the following clinical signs is most commonly associated with *Thelazia lacrymalis* infection in horses?

A) Diarrhea
B) Conjunctivitis and excessive lacrimation
C) Coughing and nasal discharge
D) Skin lesions

Answer: B) Conjunctivitis and excessive lacrimation

4. What is the characteristic appearance of *Thelazia lacrymalis* adult worms?

A) Thin, thread-like worms in the intestines
B) Small, white, thread-like worms in the eye
C) Large, segmented worms in the stomach
D) Flatworms in the liver

Answer: B) Small, white, thread-like worms in the eye

5. What is the most effective method to p

revent *Thelazia lacrymalis* infection in horses?

A) Deworming with broad-spectrum anthelmintics monthly
B) Controlling the vector (fly) population around horses
C) Vaccination against *Thelazia lacrymalis*
D) Regular hoof trimming

Answer: B) Controlling the vector (fly) population around horses

Case Study Question:

A 5-year-old horse presents with excessive tearing (epiphora), conjunctivitis, and mild irritation of the eyes. On examination, thin, white nematode worms are observed in the conjunctival sac and lacrimal ducts. The horse has access to pasture and is frequently around flies.

1. What is the likely diagnosis?
2. Describe the life cycle of the causative organism.
3. How is the infection transmitted?
4. What are the clinical signs typically associated with this infection?
5. What treatment and control measures should be taken?

Answer:

1. **Likely Diagnosis:**
   The horse is infected with *Thelazia lacrymalis*, commonly known as the eyeworm.
2. **Life Cycle:**
   - Adult worms live in the conjunctival sac and lacrimal ducts of horses.
   - Female worms release embryonated eggs or first-stage larvae (L1) into the tears.
   - These larvae are ingested by intermediate hosts, typically face flies (e.g., *Musca* spp.), when they feed on the horse's tears.
   - Inside the fly, larvae develop into infective third-stage larvae (L3).
   - Infective larvae migrate to the fly's mouthparts and are transmitted to another horse's eye when the fly feeds again, completing the cycle.

3. **Transmission:**
   Transmission occurs via mechanical transfer by face flies feeding on the eye secretions of infected horses and then onto uninfected horses.
4. **Clinical Signs:**
   - Excessive lacrimation (tearing)
   - Conjunctivitis and blepharospasm (eye irritation, blinking)
   - Photophobia
   - Corneal ulcers or keratitis in severe cases
   - Presence of visible worms in the conjunctival sac
5. **Treatment and Control:**
   - Mechanical removal of worms using forceps or flushing the eyes with saline.
   - Systemic or topical administration of anthelmintics effective against nematodes, such as ivermectin or moxidectin.
   - Control of face flies using insecticides or fly repellents to break the transmission cycle.
   - Maintain good stable hygiene and fly control measures to prevent reinfection.

INTERNAL PROTOZOA OF HORSES

Eimeria leuekarti **(syn.** ***Globidium leuckarti)***

E. leuckarti **is the only species known to infect the horse.**

MCQ 1:

Which species is the only known Eimeria species to infect horses?
A) Eimeria bovis
B) Eimeria leuckarti
C) Eimeria tenella
D) Eimeria maxima

Answer: B) Eimeria leuckarti

MCQ 2:

Eimeria leuckarti primarily infects which part of the horse's body?
A) Liver
B) Intestines
C) Lungs
D) Kidneys

Answer: B) Intestines

MCQ 3:

What type of organism is Eimeria leuckarti?
A) Bacteria
B) Virus
C) Protozoan parasite
D) Fungi

Answer: C) Protozoan parasite

MCQ 4:

The disease caused by Eimeria leuckarti in horses is generally known as:
A) Coccidiosis
B) Tetanus
C) Strangles
D) Lyme disease

Answer: A) Coccidiosis

MCQ 5:

Which of the following is a typical method for diagnosing Eimeria leuckarti infection in horses?
A) Blood culture
B) Fecal examination for oocysts
C) Skin biopsy
D) Nasal swab

Answer: B) Fecal examination for oocysts

Case Study Question:

A 2-month-old foal presents with intermittent diarrhea and poor growth despite normal nursing behavior. The foal's environment is a barn with several other young horses. On fecal examination, you notice oocysts approximately 70 µm in size with a smooth wall.

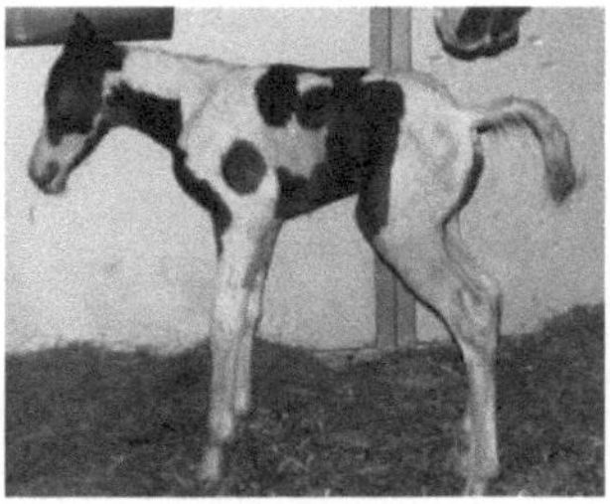

1. What is the most likely causative organism?
2. Describe the lifecycle and transmission of this organism.
3. What clinical signs are typically associated with infection?
4. How would you confirm the diagnosis?
5. What treatment and management strategies would you recommend?

Case Study Answer:

1. **Most likely causative organism:**
   Eimeria leuckarti (formerly *Globidium leuckarti*) is the most common coccidian parasite infecting horses, particularly young foals.
2. **Lifecycle and transmission:**

- *Eimeria leuckarti* has a direct lifecycle.
- Foals ingest sporulated oocysts from contaminated feed, water, or environment.
- In the intestine, sporozoites emerge, invade intestinal epithelial cells, and undergo asexual (schizogony) and sexual (gametogony) stages.
- Oocysts are shed unsporulated in feces and sporulate in the environment to become infective.

3. **Clinical signs:**
   - Often subclinical in most cases.
   - When clinical, signs include intermittent diarrhea, mild colic, poor weight gain, and occasionally dehydration in young foals.
   - Adult horses are usually resistant.
4. **Diagnosis:**
   - Identification of characteristic large, ellipsoidal oocysts (~70 μm) in fecal flotation.
   - Clinical history and age of the animal support diagnosis.
5. **Treatment and management:**
   - Treatment is rarely required as infections are often self-limiting.
   - Supportive care: fluids and nutrition if diarrhea is severe.
   - Anticoccidial drugs such as toltrazuril or sulfadimethoxine can be used if necessary.
   - Good hygiene and manure management reduce environmental contamination.
   - Avoid overcrowding and keep feeding areas clean.

Cryptosporidium parvum in Equine

1. What is the primary clinical sign of Cryptosporidium parvum infection in foals?

A. Colic
B. Diarrhea
C. Coughing
D. Lameness

Answer: ✅ B. Diarrhea

2. Cryptosporidium parvum primarily affects which age group in horses?

A. Adult horses
B. Geriatric horses
C. Neonatal and young foals
D. Pregnant mares

Answer: ✅ C. Neonatal and young foals

3. How is Cryptosporidium parvum most commonly transmitted in equines?

A. Vector-borne (through ticks)
B. Airborne droplets
C. Fecal-oral route
D. Transplacental transmission

Answer: ✅ C. Fecal-oral route

4. What is the best method for diagnosing Cryptosporidium parvum in foals?

A. Blood smear
B. Fecal flotation

C. Acid-fast staining of feces or PCR
D. Radiographs

Answer: ✅ C. Acid-fast staining of feces or PCR

5. Which of the following statements about Cryptosporidium parvum in equines is TRUE?

A. It is usually fatal in adult horses.
B. There is a highly effective vaccine available.
C. It is a self-limiting infection in immunocompetent foals.
D. Antibiotics are the primary treatment.

Answer: ✅ C. It is a self-limiting infection in immunocompetent foals.

Case Study:

A **3-week-old foal** presents with **watery diarrhea**, lethargy, and mild dehydration. The owner reports that the foal has been nursing normally but became progressively weaker over the past 48 hours. The mare is healthy, and there are several other foals on the premises showing similar signs.

On physical examination:

- Temperature: 39.5°C (mild fever)

- Heart rate: 80 bpm
- Mucous membranes: pink and moist
- Capillary refill time: <2 seconds

Fecal sample analysis using **acid-fast staining** reveals **small, round, red-staining oocysts**, approximately 4–6 μm in diameter.

Question:

1. What is the **most likely diagnosis**?
2. What is the **causative agent**?
3. Describe the **pathogenesis** of this organism.
4. What **diagnostic techniques** are used to confirm infection?
5. What is the **treatment and management** protocol?
6. What are the **zoonotic implications** of this pathogen?

✅ Answer:

1. Most likely diagnosis:

- **Cryptosporidiosis** caused by **Cryptosporidium parvum**.

2. Causative Agent:

- **Cryptosporidium parvum**, a **protozoan parasite** that infects the gastrointestinal tract.

3. Pathogenesis:

- Cryptosporidium parvum infects and colonizes the **microvillus border** of epithelial cells in the small intestine.
- It causes **villous atrophy**, **malabsorption**, and **secretory diarrhea**.
- Oocysts are shed in feces and are **immediately infectious**, leading to rapid environmental contamination and spread among foals.

- The infection is often **self-limiting** in immunocompetent animals but can be severe in neonates or immunocompromised individuals.

4. Diagnostic Techniques:

- **Fecal examination** using:
    - **Acid-fast staining** (detects oocysts)
    - **Fluorescent antibody test (IFA)**
    - **PCR** for species-level identification
- **ELISA** to detect antigen in feces

5. Treatment and Management:

- No specific anti-cryptosporidial treatment approved in horses, but supportive care is critical:
    - **Fluid therapy** to correct dehydration and electrolyte imbalances
    - **Nutritional support**
    - Maintain **clean, dry, hygienic environment**
    - **Halter management** and **isolation** of affected foals
- Some off-label use of drugs like **nitazoxanide** may be considered under veterinary guidance (though efficacy varies).

6. Zoonotic Implications:

- **Cryptosporidium parvum is zoonotic**.
- Humans, especially immunocompromised individuals (e.g., HIV/AIDS patients), are at risk of infection.
- Infection in humans causes **self-limiting watery diarrhea**, but can be life-threatening in immunocompromised people.
- Proper hygiene and use of **protective gloves/clothing** are essential when handling infected animals or their feces.

Giardia duodenalis in Equine

1. What is the primary route of transmission of *Giardia duodenalis* in horses?

A. Inhalation of cysts
B. Skin contact with infected animals
C. Ingestion of contaminated food or water
D. Blood-feeding arthropods

Answer: ✅ C. Ingestion of contaminated food or water
Explanation: *Giardia* is primarily transmitted via the fecal-oral route, usually through ingestion of cysts in contaminated water or feed.

2. What stage of *Giardia duodenalis* is infectious to horses?

A. Trophozoite
B. Merozoite
C. Cyst
D. Sporozoite

Answer: ✅ C. Cyst
Explanation: The cyst stage is the environmentally resistant and infectious stage. Horses become infected by ingesting these cysts.

3. Which of the following clinical signs is most commonly associated with *Giardia duodenalis* infection in foals?

A. Coughing and nasal discharge
B. Lameness
C. Diarrhea and weight loss
D. Colic with gas accumulation

Answer: ✅ C. Diarrhea and weight loss
Explanation: In foals, giardiasis can cause chronic diarrhea, weight loss, and poor growth, especially in cases of heavy infection.

4. What is the most appropriate diagnostic method for detecting *Giardia duodenalis* in horse feces?

A. Blood culture
B. Skin scraping
C. Fecal flotation with zinc sulfate
D. Radiography

Answer: ✅ C. Fecal flotation with zinc sulfate
Explanation: Giardia cysts can be detected using fecal flotation, particularly with zinc sulfate solution. ELISA or PCR can also be used for more sensitivity.

5. Which of the following statements about *Giardia duodenalis* in horses is TRUE?

A. It is a common cause of respiratory disease in adult horses
B. It only affects horses over 5 years of age
C. It is a zoonotic parasite with potential transmission to humans
D. It cannot be treated with any known antiparasitic agents

Answer: ✅ C. It is a zoonotic parasite with potential transmission to humans
Explanation: *Giardia duodenalis* is a zoonotic protozoan; transmission from animals to humans is possible, especially with certain assemblages (A and B).

Case Study

Background

A 3-year-old Arabian gelding kept at a riding stable starts showing intermittent loose feces (soft, occasionally watery), mild weight loss (loss of condition), dull hair coat, and mildly decreased appetite. There are several young foals in the stable, mixed ages of horses, shared water troughs and pastures. No recent deworming beyond regular strongyle control; hygiene is standard but pasture tended to be heavily grazed and not always free of fecal contamination.

A fecal exam of the affected horse is done; trophozoites or cysts of *Giardia duodenalis* are found. No other parasites (strongyles, etc.) in meaningful numbers; bacterial culture negative; feed and management unchanged recently.

Epidemiology & Genotyping

- Studies show that *Giardia duodenalis* infects horses worldwide; a meta-analysis estimated pooled prevalence ~ **8.9%** globally
- Younger horses (<3 years) have significantly higher prevalence.
- Molecular typing of isolates from horses often reveals assemblages **A**, **B**, and sometimes **E**—all having zoonotic potential (i.e. can infect humans).

Pathogenesis & Clinical Signs

- *G. duodenalis* infects (after ingestion of cysts) the small intestine; trophozoites attach to the small intestinal mucosa (especially duodenum, jejunum). This can lead to malabsorption, steatorrhea, damage to microvilli, impaired nutrient absorption, water loss.
- In many cases horses may be asymptomatic or have mild signs; but under stress, young age, poor nutrition, co-infection or high parasite load, clinical disease (diarrhea, weight loss, poor condition) may result. (From veterinary parasitology literature)

Diagnosis

- Fecal examination: detection of *Giardia* cysts or trophozoites. Conventional microscopy (smear, flotation) may detect cysts but sensitivity low.
- Antigen detection tests (e.g. ELISA, immunofluorescence) are better.
- Molecular methods (PCR targeting *β-giardin, glutamate dehydrogenase* (gdh), *triose phosphate isomerase* (tpi), SSU rRNA) used for species/assemblage/genotype typing. Useful for epidemiology and zoonotic risk. PubMed+2Astrophysics Data System+2

Treatment & Management

- There is less published data specifically for horses, but treatments effective in other species (calves, lambs, etc.) often work. Drugs used include metronidazole, fenbendazole, possibly others.
- Supportive care: improving nutrition, avoiding stress, clean water and hygiene.
- Regular cleaning of pastures, removal of feces, ensuring water troughs are clean and not contaminated.
- There are few controlled trials for equines; anecdotal or small sample reports suggest treatment may reduce shedding and clinical signs.

Case Resolution (Hypothetical)

In our case, the gelding is treated with **metronidazole** at a dose of e.g. 15 mg/kg orally twice daily for 5 days. Pasture hygiene is improved, water troughs cleaned daily, feces removed. After treatment, fecal exams are repeated on days 3, 7, 14: cyst shedding drops significantly; clinical signs improve: feces become more formed, weight gain, better coat.

Discussion Questions & Model Answers

Question	Model Answer / Key Points
1. What are the zoonotic implications of *Giardia duodenalis* in horses?	Horses can carry assemblages of *G. duodenalis* (A, B, E) that are infectious to humans. Shared water sources, or environmental contamination (pastures, troughs) may allow spillover. Therefore control in horses also helps public health. PubMed+2PubMed+2
2. Why might younger horses (foals, <3 years) be more susceptible?	Immune system is less developed; nutritional demands higher; more exposure to contaminated pastures; possibly less efficient hygiene or care in younger animals. Also may have higher parasite burdens. Evidence shows prevalence higher in younger horses. PubMed+1

Question	Model Answer / Key Points
3. What diagnostic approach is best?	Use a combination: initial screening by fecal flotation or microscopy; antigen detection to increase sensitivity; for epidemiological / zoonotic assessment, PCR and genotyping. Also multiple fecal samples on different days because cyst shedding can be intermittent.
4. What treatment options are available, and what are challenges?	Options: metronidazole (commonly used protozoal treatment), possibly fenbendazole, and other anti-protozoal/anti-giardial agents. Challenges: drug availability, cost, potential adverse effects, ensuring full courses; risk of relapse; hygiene and environmental contamination; asymptomatic carriers. Also resistance or reduced efficacy may occur.
5. How to control spread in a stable / farm environment?	Good pasture management: remove fecal material, thorough cleaning; clean water supply; avoid overcrowding; isolate or treat affected animals; ensure good nutrition; monitor neighboring livestock/wildlife; possibly periodic screening.

Key References & Data

- Colombian study: 17.4% of 195 horses positive; Assemblages A & B identified. PubMed
- Ahvaz, Iran: prevalence 35.7% among Arabian horses; assemblages AI and E. DOAJ+2Archives of Razi Institute+2
- Turkey: 16.6% of 150 healthy horses positive; all in assemblage A. PubMed
- Meta-analysis: global pooled prevalence ~8.93%; assemblage B most common, then A, E. PubMed

Sarcocystis neurona/Neospora hughesi:

1. Which of the following protozoan parasites is most commonly associated with Equine Protozoal Myeloencephalitis (EPM) in horses?

A. Toxoplasma gondii
B. Sarcocystis neurona
C. Neospora caninum
D. Giardia lamblia

Answer: B. **Sarcocystis neurona**

2. What is the definitive host for Sarcocystis neurona, the primary cause of EPM in horses?

A. Horse
B. Opossum
C. Dog
D. Cat

Answer: B. **Opossum**
(Specifically, Didelphis virginiana in North America.)

3. Neospora hughesi differs from Sarcocystis neurona in that:

A. It is not associated with EPM.
B. Its definitive host is known to be the opossum.
C. It can also cause disease in cattle.
D. Its definitive host remains unknown.

Answer: D. **Its definitive host remains unknown**

4. A horse presents with ataxia, muscle atrophy, and asymmetrical neurologic signs. Which diagnostic test is most helpful in confirming EPM?

A. Blood culture
B. Fecal floatation
C. Serum:CSF antibody ratio (SnSAG ELISA or IFAT)
D. Skin scraping

Answer: C. **Serum:CSF antibody ratio (SnSAG ELISA or IFAT)**

5. Which of the following best describes the pathogenesis of EPM caused by Sarcocystis neurona or Neospora hughesi?

A. Direct parasitism of the gastrointestinal tract
B. Production of neurotoxins that damage neurons
C. Protozoal migration and replication in the central nervous system
D. Hemolysis caused by intracellular replication

Answer: C. **Protozoal migration and replication in the central nervous system**

Equine Case Study: EPM (Sarcocystis neurona / Neospora hughesi)

Case Study:

A 7-year-old Thoroughbred gelding presents with a **2-week history of incoordination**, particularly in the hind limbs. The owner reports the horse sometimes stands with a wide stance and occasionally stumbles. There is **muscle atrophy** observed over the gluteal muscles. The horse is still eating and drinking normally, but has shown some **behavioral changes**, such as increased anxiety and irritability.

Neurological examination reveals:

- **Asymmetrical ataxia**, worse on the left hind
- **Muscle fasciculations** on the left shoulder
- **Cranial nerve function** is normal
- Negative for lameness on flexion tests

The veterinarian suspects **Equine Protozoal Myeloencephalitis (EPM)** and begins diagnostic workup.

Questions & Answers:

Q1: What is the most likely diagnosis?

Answer:
Equine Protozoal Myeloencephalitis (EPM), most likely caused by **Sarcocystis neurona**, though **Neospora hughesi** is also a potential causative agent.

Q2: What are the primary causative agents of EPM in horses?

Answer:

- **Sarcocystis neurona** (most common cause in North America)
- **Neospora hughesi** (less common)

Q3: How is EPM transmitted to horses?

Answer:

- **Sarcocystis neurona**: Horses become infected by ingesting **sporocysts** shed in the feces of the **definitive host**, the **opossum**.
- **Neospora hughesi**: Transmission is less well understood; vertical transmission (from mare to foal) is possible.

Note: Horses are considered aberrant hosts and do not shed the parasite.

Q4: What diagnostic tests can confirm EPM?

Answer:

- **Serum and CSF antibody testing**:
    - **Western blot**
    - **Indirect Fluorescent Antibody Test (IFAT)**
    - **ELISA**
- **CSF: serum antibody ratio** (SAG1 or SnSAG ELISAs) helps distinguish between exposure and active CNS infection.
- **PCR of CSF** (less commonly used)

A high antibody titer in serum alone is not diagnostic—CSF testing is critical.

Q5: What other diseases should be considered in the differential diagnosis?

Answer:

- Cervical vertebral stenotic myelopathy (Wobbler's)
- Equine Herpesvirus-1 (EHV-1) myeloencephalopathy
- Equine degenerative myeloencephalopathy (EDM)
- Trauma
- Rabies
- West Nile Virus

Q6: What is the recommended treatment for EPM?

Answer:

- **Antiprotozoal medications**:
    - **Ponazuril** (Marquis)
    - **Diclazuril**
    - **Sulfadiazine + pyrimethamine**
- **Anti-inflammatory therapy**:
    - NSAIDs (e.g., flunixin)
    - Corticosteroids (use with caution)
- **Vitamin E supplementation** (antioxidant support)

Treatment duration is typically 28–90 days, depending on drug and response.

Q7: What is the prognosis for horses with EPM?

Answer:

- Prognosis is **variable**:
  - ~60–70% improve with treatment
  - Some return to full athletic function
  - Others may have residual deficits
- Early diagnosis and treatment improve the prognosis.

Q8: How can EPM be prevented?

Answer:

- **Prevent opossum access** to feed and water
- **Good biosecurity and hygiene**
- **Properly store grain and hay**
- There is currently **no vaccine** available.

TRYPANOSOMA EQUIPERDUM

1. What disease is caused by *Trypanosoma equiperdum*?

A) Sleeping sickness
B) Surra
C) Dourine
D) Nagana

Correct Answer: ✅ C) Dourine
Explanation: *Trypanosoma equiperdum* causes **Dourine**, a venereal disease in equids.

2. What is the primary mode of transmission of *Trypanosoma equiperdum*?

A) Tsetse fly bite
B) Sexual contact
C) Contaminated water
D) Tick bite

Correct Answer: ✅ B) Sexual contact
Explanation: Unlike most trypanosomes, *T. equiperdum* is transmitted **sexually**, not by insect vectors.

3. Which species are primarily affected by *Trypanosoma equiperdum*?

A) Cattle
B) Dogs
C) Horses and donkeys
D) Pigs

Correct Answer: ✅ C) Horses and donkeys
Explanation: The parasite primarily affects **equids**—horses, donkeys, and mules.

4. Which of the following is a common clinical sign of Dourine?

A) Severe diarrhea
B) Facial paralysis
C) Edematous patches on the genitalia
D) Hair loss on the back

Correct Answer: ✅ C) Edematous patches on the genitalia
Explanation: One hallmark of Dourine is **genital swelling and edema**, especially in mares and stallions.

5. How is *Trypanosoma equiperdum* diagnosed in the laboratory?

A) Skin scraping
B) Microscopy of blood smear
C) Serological tests (e.g., CFT)
D) Fecal flotation

Correct Answer: ✅ C) Serological tests (e.g., CFT)
Explanation: Serological tests like the **Complement Fixation Test (CFT)** are commonly used for diagnosis because the parasite may not be easily found in blood.

Case Study: Trypanosoma equiperdum Infection in a Mare

Case Scenario:

A 5-year-old mare is presented to a veterinary clinic with a history of progressive weight loss, genital swelling, and incoordination in the hind limbs over the past few weeks. The owner reports that the mare was recently bred with a stallion from a neighboring farm. On examination, the mare shows edematous swelling of the vulva and perineal area, mucopurulent discharge, and patchy depigmentation around the genitals. Neurological examination reveals mild ataxia and paresis of the hind limbs.

Laboratory tests including serology and microscopic examination of vaginal secretions are performed. Trypanosomes are observed under the microscope, and serological tests confirm the presence of **Trypanosoma equiperdum** antibodies.

□ **Questions and Answers:**

Q1. What is the most likely diagnosis?

A1. Dourine caused by **Trypanosoma equiperdum**.

Q2. What is the mode of transmission of Trypanosoma equiperdum?

A2. Sexual transmission. It is transmitted through **coitus** between infected and healthy equids.

Q3. What are the key clinical signs of dourine?

A3.

- Genital swelling (vulva in mares, penis and prepuce in stallions)
- Mucopurulent genital discharge
- Cutaneous plaques or "silver dollar" lesions (hypopigmented)
- Hindlimb weakness or incoordination (ataxia, paresis)
- Progressive emaciation
- Intermittent fever

Q4. How is Trypanosoma equiperdum diagnosed?

A4.

- **Clinical signs** and history of recent breeding
- **Microscopy**: Identification of trypanosomes in vaginal or penile secretions
- **Serological tests**:
    - Complement Fixation Test (CFT) – standard test for dourine
    - ELISA or PCR (in more advanced settings)

Q5. What is the treatment and prognosis?

A5.

- No fully effective treatment is currently available. Some trypanocidal drugs (e.g., **diminazene aceturate**, **suramin**) may suppress clinical signs, but **do not eliminate the parasite**.
- Due to the **chronic nature and risk of transmission**, infected animals are often **culled** in many countries.
- **Prognosis**: Poor. Chronic disease often ends fatally or leads to euthanasia due to animal health policies.

Q6. What measures can be taken to prevent dourine?

A6.

- **Quarantine and testing** of all breeding animals before introduction to herds
- **Avoid breeding with unknown or untested animals**
- **Report and cull infected animals** (mandatory in many countries)
- **Surveillance and control programs** in endemic areas

***Trypanosoma brucei evansi*inEquine**

MCQ 1:

What disease is caused by *Trypanosoma brucei evansi* in equines?

A. Nagana
B. Surra
C. Dourine
D. Sleeping sickness

Answer: ✅ B. Surra

MCQ 2:

What is the primary mode of transmission of *T. brucei evansi* in equines?

A. Tsetse fly
B. Tick bite
C. Mechanical transmission by biting flies (e.g., Tabanus)
D. Contaminated water

Answer: ✅ C. Mechanical transmission by biting flies (e.g., Tabanus)

MCQ 3:

Which of the following is a common clinical sign of *T. brucei evansi* infection in horses?

A. Severe diarrhea
B. Hindlimb paralysis
C. Intermittent fever and anemia
D. Coughing and nasal discharge

Answer: ✅ C. Intermittent fever and anemia

MCQ 4:

Which diagnostic method is most commonly used for confirming *T. brucei evansi* infection?

A. Skin scraping
B. Blood smear microscopy
C. ELISA for viral antigen
D. Radiography

Answer: ✅ B. Blood smear microscopy

MCQ 5:

Which of the following drugs is commonly used for treating *T. brucei evansi* in equines?

A. Oxytetracycline
B. Suramin
C. Diminazene aceturate
D. Metronidazole

Answer: ✅ C. Diminazene aceturate

Equine Case Study: Trypanosoma brucei evansi (Surra)

📓 *Case Study Question:*

A 5-year-old male horse in a tropical region presents with progressive weight loss, intermittent fever, edema of the lower limbs, weakness, and anemia. The animal also shows signs of incoordination and reluctance to move. On examination, the mucous membranes are pale, and there is mild icterus. Blood smear reveals the presence of motile trypanosomes.

Based on clinical signs and lab findings:

1. What is the most likely diagnosis?
2. What is the etiological agent?
3. What are the primary modes of transmission for this pathogen?
4. Describe the pathogenesis of the disease.
5. How would you confirm the diagnosis?
6. Outline the treatment and control measures.

✅ *Answers:*

1. **Most likely diagnosis:**
   Surra – a trypanosomiasis caused by *Trypanosoma brucei evansi.*
2. **Etiological agent:**
   Trypanosoma brucei evansi, a protozoan parasite from the genus *Trypanosoma*.
3. **Modes of transmission:**
   - Mechanically transmitted by biting flies (especially **Tabanus** and **Stomoxys** spp.).
   - No cyclical development in vectors (unlike *T. brucei brucei*).
   - Iatrogenic transmission (via contaminated instruments) is also possible.
4. **Pathogenesis:**
   - Parasites multiply in blood and tissue fluids.
   - Cause anemia through hemolysis and bone marrow suppression.
   - Immune complexes and parasite toxins cause organ damage.
   - Chronic inflammation leads to wasting and neurological signs in some cases.

5. **Diagnosis confirmation:**
   - **Microscopy:** Giemsa-stained blood smear (detects trypomastigotes).
   - **Buffy coat method** or **microhematocrit centrifugation** (concentrates parasites).
   - **PCR** or **ELISA** for specific detection.
   - **CATT/T. evansi** (Card Agglutination Test for *T. evansi*) – a field diagnostic tool.
6. **Treatment and control:**
   - **Treatment:**
     - *Suramin* or *Diminazene aceturate* (depends on availability and resistance).
     - *Melarsomine* or *Quinapyramine* may also be used.
     - Supportive therapy: fluids, hematinics, anti-inflammatory drugs.
   - **Control:**
     - Vector control (fly repellents, insecticide sprays, proper stable management).
     - Quarantine and regular screening of animals.
     - Avoid sharing needles or surgical instruments.
     - Prophylactic treatment in endemic areas.

***Babesia caballi/Theileria equi*:**

Here are 5 multiple-choice questions (MCQs) on **Babesia caballi** and **Theileria equi**, along with their answers:

MCQ 1:

What is the primary host affected by Babesia caballi and Theileria equi?
A) Cattle
B) Horses
C) Sheep
D) Pigs

Answer: B) Horses

MCQ 2:

Which vector is primarily responsible for transmitting Babesia caballi and Theileria equi?
A) Ticks
B) Mosquitoes
C) Flies
D) Lice

Answer: A) Ticks

MCQ 3:

Babesia caballi and Theileria equi primarily cause which disease in horses?
A) Equine influenza
B) Equine piroplasmosis
C) Strangles
D) Equine infectious anemia

Answer: B) Equine piroplasmosis

MCQ 4:

Which stage of Babesia caballi and Theileria equi is typically found inside red blood cells?
A) Sporozoite
B) Merozoite
C) Gametocyte
D) Oocyst

Answer: B) Merozoite

MCQ 5:

Which diagnostic method is most commonly used to confirm infection with Babesia caballi or Theileria equi?
A) Blood smear microscopy
B) Urinalysis
C) Radiography
D) Skin biopsy

Answer: A) Blood smear microscopy

Study Questions & Answers: Babesia caballi / Theileria equi

Q1: What diseases do Babesia caballi and Theileria equi cause in horses?
A1: Both Babesia caballi and Theileria equi cause **equine piroplasmosis**, a tick-borne protozoan disease characterized by hemolytic anemia, fever, and jaundice in horses.

Q2: What is the main vector responsible for transmission of Babesia caballi and Theileria equi?
A2: The primary vectors are **ticks** from the genera *Dermacentor*, *Rhipicephalus*, and *Hyalomma*. Transmission occurs through tick bites.

Q3: How do Babesia caballi and Theileria equi differ in their lifecycle or pathology?
A3:

- *Babesia caballi* undergoes development primarily inside red blood cells and has a shorter incubation period. It generally causes less persistent infections.
- *Theileria equi* also infects red blood cells but can infect lymphocytes during early stages. It tends to cause more severe disease and can persist for years in carrier horses.

Q4: What diagnostic methods are commonly used to detect Babesia caballi and Theileria equi?
A4:

- **Microscopic examination** of stained blood smears to identify parasites inside red blood cells.
- **Serological tests** such as indirect fluorescent antibody test (IFAT) or ELISA.
- **PCR (Polymerase Chain Reaction)** for detection of parasite DNA, which is highly sensitive and specific.

Q5: What are common clinical signs of equine piroplasmosis?
A5:

- Fever
- Anemia and jaundice (due to hemolysis)
- Depression and lethargy
- Swelling of lymph nodes
- Petechiae and hemorrhages in severe cases

Q6: How is equine piroplasmosis treated?
A6: Treatment usually involves **antiprotozoal drugs** such as **Imidocarb dipropionate**. Supportive care may be necessary in severe cases.

Q7: How can equine piroplasmosis be controlled or prevented?
A7:

- Tick control through acaricides and pasture management.
- Screening and quarantining imported horses to prevent disease spread.
- Avoiding movement of infected horses to non-endemic areas

EQUINE PIROPLASMOSIS

1. What are the causative agents of Equine Piroplasmosis?

A) *Babesia caballi* and *Theileria equi*
B) *Trypanosoma evansi* and *Babesia bovis*
C) *Anaplasma marginale* and *Ehrlichia ruminantium*
D) *Leishmania donovani* and *Plasmodium falciparum*

Answer: A) *Babesia caballi* and *Theileria equi*

2. Which of the following is the primary mode of transmission for Equine Piroplasmosis?

A) Direct contact with infected horses
B) Ingestion of contaminated feed
C) Tick bites
D) Aerosol droplets

Answer: C) Tick bites

3. What is the common clinical sign seen in horses infected with Equine Piroplasmosis?

A) Neurological paralysis
B) Anemia and fever
C) Diarrhea
D) Severe cough

Answer: B) Anemia and fever

4. Which diagnostic test is most commonly used for detecting Equine Piroplasmosis?

A) ELISA and PCR
B) Skin scraping
C) Fecal flotation
D) Urine culture

Answer: A) ELISA and PCR

5. Which treatment is typically used for Equine Piroplasmosis?

A) Ivermectin
B) Imidocarb dipropionate
C) Penicillin
D) Metronidazole

Answer: B) Imidocarb dipropionate

Case Study Question:

A 5-year-old Thoroughbred gelding presents with intermittent fever, lethargy, jaundice, and anemia. The owner reports that the horse recently traveled to a region where tick infestations are common. On physical exam, mucous membranes appear pale and icteric, and the horse has a mildly elevated heart rate and respiratory rate. Blood smears reveal intraerythrocytic piroplasms.

Questions:

1. What is the most likely diagnosis?
2. What is the causative agent of this disease?
3. How is this disease transmitted?
4. What diagnostic methods can confirm the disease?
5. What treatment options are available?
6. How can this disease be prevented?

Case Study Answer:

1. **Most likely diagnosis:**
   Equine Piroplasmosis (EP)
2. **Causative agent:**
   Equine Piroplasmosis is caused by protozoan parasites of the genus *Theileria* (formerly *Babesia*), primarily *Theileria equi* and *Babesia caballi.*
3. **Transmission:**
   The disease is transmitted mainly via tick vectors, particularly species of the genera *Dermacentor*, *Rhipicephalus*, and *Amblyomma*. It can also be transmitted iatrogenically through contaminated needles or blood transfusions.
4. **Diagnostic methods:**
   - Microscopic examination of blood smears to identify intraerythrocytic piroplasms.
   - Serological tests such as ELISA or complement fixation test (CFT).
   - PCR assays for detecting parasite DNA with higher sensitivity.
5. **Treatment options:**
   - Antiprotozoal drugs such as imidocarb dipropionate are commonly used to treat infected horses.
   - Supportive therapy including fluids, blood transfusions if severe anemia is present, and management of secondary infections.
6. **Prevention:**
   - Control of tick populations through acaricides and environmental management.
   - Use of tick repellents on horses.
   - Screening and quarantine of imported horses to prevent disease spread.
   - Avoid sharing needles and equipment between horses.

Equine babesiosis is caused by B equi or B caballi.

1. What is the causative agent of Equine Babesiosis?

A) Trypanosoma evansi
B) Babesia caballi
C) Theileria parva

D) Anaplasma marginale

✅ **Correct answer: B) Babesia caballi**

2. Equine babesiosis is primarily transmitted by:

A) Mosquitoes
B) Tabanid flies
C) Ticks
D) Fleas

✅ **Correct answer: C) Ticks**

3. Which of the following parasites can cause Equine Babesiosis?

A) Babesia bigemina
B) Babesia equi
C) Plasmodium equinum
D) Leishmania equi

✅ **Correct answer: B) Babesia equi**

*(Note: "Babesia equi" is now classified as **Theileria equi**, but both terms are still used in literature.)*

4. A major clinical sign of Equine Babesiosis is:

A) Diarrhea
B) Hematuria
C) Neurological signs
D) Skin lesions

✅ **Correct answer: B) Hematuria**

5. Which of the following best describes Equine Babesiosis?

A) A viral disease affecting horses
B) A fungal infection of the hooves
C) A protozoan disease of red blood cells in horses
D) A bacterial respiratory disease in equines
✅ **Correct answer: C) A protozoan disease of red blood cells in horses**

Case Study Question: Equine Babesiosis

Case:
A 7-year-old Thoroughbred gelding recently imported from a tropical region presents with fever, lethargy, pale mucous membranes, and jaundice. The owner reports that the horse has not been eating well and seems weak. On clinical examination, the veterinarian notes elevated respiratory and heart rates, and mild colic symptoms. Bloodwork shows anemia and elevated bilirubin levels. A Giemsa-stained blood smear reveals intraerythrocytic piroplasms.

Question:

1. What is the most likely diagnosis?
2. What are the causative agents of this condition?
3. How is this disease transmitted?
4. What diagnostic tests can confirm the diagnosis?
5. What treatment and management strategies should be implemented?

✅ **Answers:**

1. **Most likely diagnosis:**
   The horse is most likely suffering from **equine babesiosis**, also known as **piroplasmosis**.
2. **Causative agents:**
   - *Babesia caballi*
   - *Theileria equi* (formerly *Babesia equi*)
3. **Transmission:**
   - The disease is **vector-borne**, primarily transmitted by **ticks** such as *Dermacentor*, *Rhipicephalus*, and *Hyalomma* species.

- It can also be transmitted iatrogenically (via contaminated instruments or blood transfusions).

4. **Diagnostic tests:**
    - **Microscopic examination** of Giemsa-stained blood smears to detect piroplasms in erythrocytes.
    - **Polymerase Chain Reaction (PCR)** for definitive identification and differentiation between *B. caballi* and *T. equi*.
    - **Serological tests** like **Indirect Fluorescent Antibody Test (IFAT)** or **competitive ELISA** to detect antibodies.
    - **Complete Blood Count (CBC)** may reveal anemia and thrombocytopenia.
5. **Treatment and management:**
    - **Imidocarb dipropionate** is the drug of choice:
        - For *B. caballi*: 2 mg/kg IM, may require 1–2 doses.
        - For *T. equi*: higher dose (4 mg/kg) and possibly repeated treatments.
    - Supportive therapy:
        - IV fluids, anti-inflammatories, and blood transfusion if anemia is severe.
    - **Tick control**: Use of acaricides and management to prevent reinfection.
    - Quarantine and testing of imported horses to prevent spread.

Surra (*Trypanosoma evansi* in equine)

1. What is the causative agent of Surra in equines?

A. *Trypanosoma cruzi*
B. *Trypanosoma brucei*
C. *Trypanosoma evansi*
D. *Trypanosoma equiperdum*

✅ **Answer: C. *Trypanosoma evansi***

2. What is the main mode of transmission of *Trypanosoma evansi* in horses?

A. Ingestion of contaminated water
B. Ticks
C. Biting flies (e.g., Tabanus and Stomoxys)
D. Direct contact with infected animals

✅ **Answer: C. Biting flies (e.g., Tabanus and Stomoxys)**

3. Which of the following is a common clinical sign of Surra in equines?

A. Diarrhea
B. Swelling of joints
C. Progressive emaciation and anemia
D. Pruritus

✅ **Answer: C. Progressive emaciation and anemia**

4. Which diagnostic method is commonly used to detect *Trypanosoma evansi* infection in horses?

A. Skin scraping
B. Blood smear microscopy
C. Fecal flotation
D. Radiography

✅ **Answer: B. Blood smear microscopy**

5. Which drug is commonly used to treat Surra in equines?

A. Ivermectin
B. Oxytetracycline
C. Quinapyramine
D. Enrofloxacin

✅ **Answer: C. Quinapyramine**

Case Study: Surra (Trypanosoma evansi in Equines)

Case Scenario:

A 5-year-old male horse from a tropical region presents with progressive weight loss, fever, incoordination, edema in the lower limbs and under the abdomen, and intermittent anemia.

The owner reports that the horse has become dull, shows poor performance, and has occasional episodes of staggering gait. The condition has been worsening over the past two weeks. The horse is kept near cattle and buffaloes, and tsetse and biting flies are common in the area.

Questions & Answers:

Q1: What is the most likely diagnosis?

Answer:
The most likely diagnosis is **Surra**, caused by the protozoan **Trypanosoma evansi**.

Q2: What is the etiological agent and its mode of transmission?

Answer:

- **Etiological agent:** *Trypanosoma evansi* (a protozoan parasite).
- **Mode of transmission:**
  - Mechanical transmission by **biting flies** (especially *Tabanus*, *Stomoxys* species).
  - No biological vector is needed—flies transmit the parasite by contaminated mouthparts.

Q3: What are the clinical signs commonly seen in equine Surra?

Answer:

- Intermittent fever
- Progressive emaciation
- Anemia
- Edema (legs, abdomen, sheath)
- Incoordination, hind limb weakness
- Nervous signs (e.g., ataxia, in severe cases)
- Reduced performance
- Death if untreated (especially in horses and mules)

Q4: What diagnostic methods can confirm the infection?

Answer:

- **Blood smear microscopy** (Giemsa-stained): detection of *T. evansi* trypomastigotes.
- **Buffy coat technique**: enhances detection sensitivity.
- **Card Agglutination Test for Trypanosomiasis (CATT/T. evansi)**
- **PCR**: highly sensitive and specific.
- **ELISA**: useful for serodiagnosis.
- Clinical signs and endemic location also support the diagnosis.

Q5: What is the treatment of choice for equine Surra?

Answer:

- **Suramin**: 3.3–5.0 mg/kg IV slowly (Repeat after 7–10 days)
- **Quinapyramine** (e.g., Quinapyramine sulfate & chloride):
    - Curative dose: 3–5 mg/kg SC (quinapyramine sulfate)
    - Prophylactic/long-acting form (quinapyramine chloride/sulfate combination)
- Treatment should be combined with supportive therapy.

Note: Suramin is generally more effective in horses.

Q6: What are some preventive and control measures?

Answer:

- Vector control: Reduce exposure to biting flies using repellents, nets, and fly traps.
- Isolation or separate housing of infected animals.
- Regular chemoprophylaxis in endemic areas.
- Screening and culling or treating carrier animals.
- Avoid keeping equines near cattle/buffaloes that may act as reservoirs.

Q7: What is the prognosis for equine Surra?

Answer:

- **Prognosis is guarded to poor** if treatment is delayed, especially in advanced neurological cases.
- Early diagnosis and proper treatment can result in recovery.
- Chronic cases or those with CNS involvement often have a poorer outcome.

***Gasterophilus* spp.**

1. What is the common name for Gasterophilus spp.?

A. Horse lice
B. Horse botfly
C. Stable fly
D. Tabanid fly

Answer: ✅ B. Horse botfly

2. Where do Gasterophilus spp. larvae typically develop inside the host?

A. Nasal passages
B. Lungs
C. Stomach and intestines
D. Liver

Answer: ✅ C. Stomach and intestines

3. How do Gasterophilus spp. eggs typically reach the horse's mouth?

A. Through contaminated feed
B. The horse licks or bites the area where eggs are laid
C. Flies inject eggs directly into the mouth
D. Eggs are inhaled during breathing

Answer: ✅ B. The horse licks or bites the area where eggs are laid

4. What is a common sign of a Gasterophilus spp. infestation in horses?

A. Bloody diarrhea
B. Excessive coughing
C. Stomach ulcers or colic symptoms
D. Hair loss

Answer: ✅ C. Stomach ulcers or colic symptoms

5. Which control method is most effective against Gasterophilus spp.?

A. Insecticidal sprays alone
B. Regular grooming and brushing only
C. Strategic deworming with ivermectin or moxidectin
D. Isolation of infected horses

Answer: ✅ C. Strategic deworming with ivermectin or moxidectin

Case Study: Gasterophilus spp. Infection in Horses

Question:

A 5-year-old Thoroughbred gelding is presented during a routine veterinary examination in late autumn. The owner reports the horse has been rubbing its face and lips frequently and sometimes appears uncomfortable when eating. On close inspection, you find small yellowish eggs adhered to the hairs on the horse's forelegs and shoulders. Oral examination reveals small red ulcers on the tongue and gums. Fecal flotation is negative for parasite eggs.

Based on the history and clinical findings:

1. What is the most likely diagnosis?
2. What is the life cycle of the suspected parasite?
3. How does this parasite affect the horse?
4. Why might fecal flotation be negative?
5. What is the recommended treatment and control strategy?

✅ Answer:

1. Most likely diagnosis:

- **Gasterophilus spp. infestation** (bot fly larvae, commonly *Gasterophilus intestinalis*).

2. Life cycle of Gasterophilus spp.:

- Adult bot flies lay eggs on the horse's hair (e.g., legs, shoulders, face).
- The horse licks or bites at the site, and the eggs hatch.
- First-stage larvae (L1) migrate into the oral cavity and embed in the mucosa.
- After about a month, L1s molt to second-stage larvae (L2) and migrate to the stomach.
- In the stomach, they develop into third-stage larvae (L3), attach to the gastric mucosa, and mature over several months.
- Mature larvae detach, are passed in feces, pupate in the soil, and emerge as adult flies.

3. How the parasite affects the horse:

- **Oral lesions**: From L1 migration and attachment (ulcers, irritation).
- **Gastric issues**: L3s attach to the stomach lining and may cause:
  - Gastritis
  - Ulcers
  - Interference with digestion or appetite
- **Behavioral signs**: Itching, rubbing, or oral discomfort.
- In severe cases: weight loss or colic.

4. Why fecal flotation is negative:

- Gasterophilus spp. do **not produce eggs** that are shed in feces.
- The larvae are passed as mature bots in the feces, and fecal flotation doesn't detect them.
- Diagnosis is based on **visual detection of eggs on hair** or larvae in mouth/stomach.

5. Recommended treatment and control:

- **Treatment:**
  - Administer a macrocyclic lactone:
    - **Ivermectin** or **Moxidectin** (kills migrating and gastric larvae)
  - Best time to treat: **late autumn**, after the first frost, to kill all internal larvae before they mature.
- **Control:**
  - Manually remove eggs with a bot knife or grooming stone daily during bot fly season.
  - Practice pasture hygiene and minimize fly populations.
  - Deworm regularly based on veterinarian recommendations.

Haematopinus equi & Damalinia) equi

1. Which of the following best describes *Haematopinus equi*?

A) Biting louse of horses
B) Sucking louse of horses
C) Flea of horses
D) Mite of horses

✅ **Correct Answer: B) Sucking louse of horses**

2. What is the primary difference between *Haematopinus equi* and *Damalinia equi*?

A) Color
B) Host preference
C) Mouthparts and feeding habits
D) Number of legs

✅ **Correct Answer: C) Mouthparts and feeding habits**
(*Haematopinus equi* is a sucking louse, while *Damalinia equi* is a chewing or biting louse.)

3. Where on the horse is *Damalinia equi* most commonly found?

A) Inside the ears
B) Around the mane, shoulders, and tail
C) Under the hooves
D) In the nasal cavity

✅ **Correct Answer: B) Around the mane, shoulders, and tail**

4. What clinical sign is commonly associated with infestation by either *Haematopinus equi* or *Damalinia equi*?

A) Vomiting
B) Hair loss and pruritus (itching)
C) Sneezing
D) Diarrhea

✅ **Correct Answer: B) Hair loss and pruritus (itching)**

5. Which stage of the lice life cycle is typically found glued to the horse's hair?

A) Larva
B) Nymph
C) Adult
D) Egg (Nit)

✅ **Correct Answer: D) Egg (Nit)**

Case Study: Lice Infestation in Horses

Case Description:

A 6-year-old gelding is presented to a veterinary clinic in early winter with complaints of intense itching, restlessness, and patchy hair loss. The owner reports that the horse frequently rubs itself against fences and walls. On physical examination, the horse shows signs of alopecia, excoriation, and scabbing, especially around the neck, shoulders, and flanks.

Close inspection reveals small, flat, yellowish parasites and their eggs (nits) attached to the hair shafts. Some parasites are seen moving slowly near the base of the mane and tail. Microscopic examination confirms the presence of **two types of lice**: **Haematopinus equi** and **Damalinia equi**.

? Question:

a. Identify the type of lice and classify them.

b. Discuss the life cycle of both lice.

c. Describe clinical signs and transmission.

d. Outline the diagnosis, treatment, and control strategies for managing this condition.

✅ Answer:

a. Identification & Classification:

Parasite	Common Name	Type	Classification
Haematopinus equi	Horse sucking louse	Sucking louse	Order: Anoplura
Damalinia equi	Horse biting louse	Biting louse	Order: Mallophaga (or Phthiraptera)

b. Life Cycle (Both are *incomplete metamorphosis*, host-specific lice):

- **Eggs (nits)** are laid on hair shafts.
- Hatch into **nymphs** → pass through 3 nymphal stages.
- Develop into **adults** on the host.
- **Entire life cycle (approx. 3-4 weeks)** is spent on the host.

Species	Feeding method	Location on host
Haematopinus equi	Blood-sucking	Mane, base of tail
Damalinia equi	Skin & debris	Neck, flanks, shoulders

c. Clinical Signs & Transmission:

Clinical Signs:

- Pruritus (intense itching)
- Alopecia (hair loss)
- Excoriation, scabs
- Restlessness, poor body condition (in heavy infestations)
- Anemia (in severe *Haematopinus equi* infestations)

Transmission:

- **Direct contact** between horses
- **Indirect contact** via grooming tools, tack, blankets
- More common in **winter months** due to thicker coats and close housing

d. Diagnosis, Treatment, and Control:

Diagnosis:

- Visual inspection of lice and nits
- Microscopy to differentiate between species

Treatment:

- **Topical insecticides:** e.g. Permethrin, Pyrethroids, Coumaphos
- **Systemic treatments:** Ivermectin (effective against *Haematopinus* only, not *Damalinia*)
- Repeat treatment in 2 weeks to kill newly hatched lice

Control:

- Treat all in-contact horses
- Clean and disinfect grooming equipment, tack, bedding
- Improve hygiene and reduce overcrowding
- Regular grooming, especially in winter

TICKS in equine

1. Which of the following is the most common tick species found on horses?

A. Rhipicephalus sanguineus
B. Ixodes scapularis
C. **Dermacentor variabilis**
D. Amblyomma americanum

Answer: C. Dermacentor variabilis

2. What is a major concern associated with tick infestation in horses?

A. Increased appetite
B. Overheating
C. **Transmission of diseases such as equine piroplasmosis**
D. Improved coat quality

Answer: C. Transmission of diseases such as equine piroplasmosis

3. Ticks can transmit which protozoan parasites that cause equine piroplasmosis?

A. **Babesia caballi and Theileria equi**
B. Trypanosoma evansi and Leishmania spp.
C. Plasmodium spp. and Eimeria spp.
D. Giardia and Cryptosporidium

Answer: A. Babesia caballi and Theileria equi

4. Which is a recommended method to control tick infestation in horses?

A. Increasing carbohydrate intake
B. **Regular grooming and use of acaricides**
C. Feeding raw meat
D. Daily washing with cold water

Answer: B. Regular grooming and use of acaricides

5. Where are ticks most commonly found on a horse's body?

A. Hooves and nostrils
B. **Under the tail, around ears, mane, and between the legs**
C. On the tongue and gums
D. Inside the stomach

Answer: B. Under the tail, around ears, mane, and between the legs

Equine Case Study: TICKS

Case Study Question:

A 7-year-old gelding Thoroughbred horse presents with signs of restlessness, frequent tail swishing, and occasional stamping of the hind legs. On close examination, the veterinarian observes multiple engorged ticks around the perineum, inner thighs, ears, and mane regions. The horse has mild anemia and patchy hair loss at tick attachment sites. The owner reports recent travel to a pasture area known for high tick infestation.

Question:

1. What are the likely species of ticks affecting this horse?
2. What are the clinical implications of tick infestation in equines?
3. What diagnostic approach should be taken in such a case?
4. Outline the treatment and control strategies for tick infestation in horses.
5. What tick-borne diseases should be considered in equines?

✅ **Answer:**

1. Likely Species of Ticks:

- **Rhipicephalus (Boophilus) spp.**
- **Hyalomma spp.**
- **Amblyomma spp.**
- **Dermacentor spp.**
  These are common hard ticks found on horses, depending on geographic location.

2. Clinical Implications of Tick Infestation:

- **Local effects:**
    - Irritation, itching, discomfort
    - Hair loss and skin damage at bite sites
    - Secondary bacterial infections
- **Systemic effects:**
    - Anemia (especially with heavy infestations)
    - Hypersensitivity reactions
- **Transmission of tick-borne diseases:**
    - Equine piroplasmosis (Babesia caballi, Theileria equi)
    - Lyme disease (Borrelia burgdorferi – in some regions)
    - Ehrlichiosis (rare in horses but possible)

3. Diagnostic Approach:

- **Physical examination:**
    - Look for visible ticks in common hiding spots: mane, tail base, ears, under jaw, between legs.
- **Tick identification:**
    - Morphologic ID under microscope to determine species.
- **Blood tests:**
    - Complete blood count (CBC) for anemia or signs of infection
    - Blood smears or PCR to detect piroplasmosis or other tick-borne pathogens

4. Treatment and Control Strategies:

Treatment:

- **Manual removal** of visible ticks using forceps.
- **Topical acaricides:**
    - Permethrin sprays or spot-on treatments
    - Fipronil (note: some products are off-label for horses – use vet guidance)
- **Systemic treatment** if secondary infection or tick-borne disease is diagnosed:
    - Antiprotozoals (e.g., imidocarb for piroplasmosis)
    - Antibiotics (if secondary bacterial infections)

Control:

- **Environmental management:**
  - Pasture rotation
  - Clearing brush and tall grass
- **Prophylactic treatments:**
  - Regular grooming and tick checks
  - Routine application of repellents or acaricides, especially before turnout in infested areas
- **Stable hygiene:**
  - Clean bedding, avoid contact with tick-infested animals

5. Tick-Borne Diseases to Consider:

- **Equine Piroplasmosis (Babesia caballi, Theileria equi)**
- **Lyme disease** (in endemic areas)
- **Ehrlichiosis (Anaplasma phagocytophilum)**
- **Tick Paralysis** (rare in equines, but possible with heavy infestation by certain species)

Sarcoptes scabei* var. *equi

1. What is Sarcoptes scabiei var. equi primarily responsible for in horses?

A) Respiratory infections
B) Mange (skin disease)
C) Gastrointestinal upset
D) Neurological disorders

Answer: B) Mange (skin disease)

2. What type of parasite is Sarcoptes scabiei var. equi?

A) Nematode
B) Protozoa
C) Mite
D) Bacteria

Answer: C) Mite

3. What is the main clinical sign of infestation by Sarcoptes scabiei var. equi?

A) Diarrhea
B) Intense itching and skin crusting
C) Coughing
D) Fever

Answer: B) Intense itching and skin crusting

4. How is Sarcoptes scabiei var. equi usually transmitted among horses?

A) Ingestion of contaminated feed
B) Direct skin-to-skin contact
C) Aerosol droplets
D) Contaminated water

Answer: B) Direct skin-to-skin contact

5. Which of the following is the most effective treatment for Sarcoptes scabiei var. equi infestation?

A) Antibiotics
B) Antifungal creams
C) Acaricides (e.g., ivermectin)
D) Antiviral drugs

Answer: C) Acaricides (e.g., ivermectin)

Case Study Question:

A 5-year-old horse presents with intense itching, hair loss, and thickened, crusty skin primarily around the head, neck, and shoulders. The owner reports that these symptoms have progressively worsened over several weeks. On physical examination, you notice erythema, scaling, and crust formation. Skin scrapings reveal the presence of a mite identified as *Sarcoptes scabiei* var. *equi.*

Questions:

1. What is the causative agent of the horse's condition, and how is it transmitted?
2. Describe the pathogenesis of the disease.
3. What are the clinical signs of sarcoptic mange in horses?
4. How is the diagnosis confirmed?
5. What treatment options are recommended for this condition?
6. What preventive measures can be taken to avoid spread and recurrence?

Case Study Answer:

1. **Causative agent and transmission:**
   The causative agent is *Sarcoptes scabiei* var. *equi*, a burrowing mite specific to horses. It is transmitted primarily through direct contact with infested animals or contaminated environments such as tack and grooming tools.
2. **Pathogenesis:**
   The mite burrows into the superficial layers of the skin, causing intense irritation and hypersensitivity reactions. This leads to inflammation, pruritus, and secondary bacterial infections from self-trauma.
3. **Clinical signs:**
   - Intense pruritus (itching)
   - Alopecia (hair loss)
   - Thickened, crusty, and scaly skin lesions
   - Erythema (redness) and sometimes lichenification (thickened skin)
     Lesions are often localized around the head, neck, shoulders, and legs.
4. **Diagnosis:**
   Diagnosis is confirmed by microscopic examination of skin scrapings revealing mites, eggs, or fecal pellets. Sometimes repeated scrapings are necessary due to low mite numbers.
5. **Treatment:**
   - Topical acaricides such as lime sulfur dips or amitraz
   - Systemic treatments like ivermectin or moxidectin administered according to veterinary guidance
   - Symptomatic care including anti-inflammatory drugs and treatment of secondary infections if present
6. **Prevention:**
   - Isolation and treatment of affected horses

- Regular cleaning and disinfection of equipment and environment
- Avoiding close contact between infected and healthy horses
- Routine monitoring for early signs of infestation

Chorioptic Mange in equine

1. What is the causative agent of Chorioptic mange in horses?

A) *Sarcoptes scabiei*
B) *Chorioptes bovis*
C) *Psoroptes ovis*
D) *Demodex* spp.

Answer: B) *Chorioptes bovis*

2. Which area of the horse's body is most commonly affected by Chorioptic mange?

A) Mane and tail
B) Hooves and legs
C) Head and neck
D) Abdomen and flanks

Answer: B) Hooves and legs

3. What is the primary clinical sign of Chorioptic mange in horses?

A) Severe alopecia all over the body
B) Intense pruritus and crusty lesions around the distal limbs
C) Respiratory distress
D) Diarrhea

Answer: B) Intense pruritus and crusty lesions around the distal limbs

4. Which diagnostic method is most commonly used to confirm Chorioptic mange in horses?

A) Blood test
B) Skin scraping and microscopic examination
C) Radiography
D) Urinalysis

Answer: B) Skin scraping and microscopic examination

5. What is the most effective treatment for Chorioptic mange in equines?

A) Oral antibiotics
B) Topical antifungal cream
C) Systemic and topical acaricides (e.g., ivermectin or lime sulfur dips)
D) Corticosteroids

Answer: C) Systemic and topical acaricides (e.g., ivermectin or lime sulfur dips)

Case Study Question:

A 5-year-old Thoroughbred gelding presents with intense pruritus, especially around the lower limbs and tail base. On examination, there is crusting, scaling, and hair loss primarily on the hind legs and tail region. The horse frequently stomps its feet and bites at the affected areas. Skin scrapings reveal the presence of mites.

1. What is the most likely diagnosis?
2. What is the causative agent?
3. Describe the pathogenesis of this condition.
4. What are the clinical signs commonly seen?
5. How would you confirm the diagnosis?
6. What treatment options are available?
7. What management practices would you recommend to prevent the spread?

Answer:

1. **Most likely diagnosis:**
   Chorioptic mange (also called leg mange or foot mange).
2. **Causative agent:**
   Chorioptes equi — a non-burrowing mite that infests the skin of horses, especially around the lower limbs and tail.
3. **Pathogenesis:**
   The mites feed on skin debris and cause irritation, leading to pruritus and self-trauma. Their presence triggers a hypersensitivity reaction, resulting in inflammation, scaling, crusting, and alopecia.
4. **Clinical signs:**
   - Intense pruritus, especially around the hind limbs, pasterns, and tail base
   - Crusting, scaling, and thickened skin
   - Alopecia from scratching and biting
   - Stomping or licking feet
   - Secondary bacterial infections may develop due to skin damage
5. **Diagnosis:**
   - Clinical signs and distribution of lesions
   - Microscopic examination of deep skin scrapings to identify *Chorioptes* mites or their eggs
   - Sometimes skin biopsy can help confirm the diagnosis
6. **Treatment:**
   - Topical acaricides such as lime sulfur dips, amitraz, or permethrin
   - Systemic treatment with ivermectin or moxidectin if necessary
   - Repeated treatments are usually required to eliminate all mites
   - Treat secondary infections with appropriate antibiotics or antiseptics
7. **Management and prevention:**
   - Isolate affected horses to prevent spread
   - Regular grooming and inspection for early detection
   - Maintain clean and dry bedding and environment
   - Treat all in-contact animals simultaneously to avoid reinfestation

Demodex caballi

1. What is Demodex caballi?

A) A bacterial infection affecting horses
B) A type of mite that infests horse hair follicles
C) A viral disease in horses
D) A fungal infection of the skin

Answer: B) A type of mite that infests horse hair follicles

2. Where is Demodex caballi typically found on horses?

A) Hooves
B) Respiratory tract
C) Hair follicles and sebaceous glands
D) Digestive tract

Answer: C) Hair follicles and sebaceous glands

3. What is the primary clinical sign of Demodex caballi infestation in horses?

A) Severe coughing
B) Hair loss and skin lesions
C) Colic
D) Lameness

Answer: B) Hair loss and skin lesions

4. How is Demodex caballi most commonly diagnosed?

A) Blood test
B) Skin biopsy or microscopic examination of skin scrapings
C) Urinalysis
D) Radiography

Answer: B) Skin biopsy or microscopic examination of skin scrapings

5. What is the usual treatment for Demodex caballi infestation in horses?

A) Antibiotics
B) Antiparasitic medications like ivermectin or amitraz
C) Antifungal cream
D) Surgical removal

Answer: B) Antiparasitic medications like ivermectin or amitraz

Case Study Question:

A 5-year-old horse presents with multiple hairless, crusty, and thickened skin lesions primarily around the face, neck, and shoulders. The owner reports mild itching and occasional scratching. On closer examination, you find follicular papules and nodules. A skin scraping reveals cigar-shaped mites under the microscope.

1. What is the most likely diagnosis?
2. What is the causative organism?
3. How is this condition transmitted?
4. What is the typical treatment and prognosis?

Case Study Answer:

1. **Most likely diagnosis:**
   Demodicosis (demodectic mange) in horses.
2. **Causative organism:**
   Demodex caballi — a species of Demodex mite that specifically affects horses.
3. **Transmission:**
   Transmission occurs primarily through direct contact between horses, especially from dam to foal. The mites live within hair follicles and sebaceous glands and multiply in cases of immune compromise or underlying disease.

4. **Treatment and prognosis:**
   Treatment often includes topical acaricides such as lime sulfur dips or amitraz, and systemic treatment with ivermectin or moxidectin. Supportive care includes managing secondary bacterial infections with antibiotics if necessary. Prognosis is generally good with appropriate treatment, but chronic or severe cases may require prolonged therapy. Immune status plays a role in recovery.

1. Which of the following parasites commonly transmitted from horses to humans can cause cutaneous larva migrans?

A) *Strongyloides westeri*
B) *Strongylus vulgaris*
C) *Draschia megastoma*
D) *Onchocerca cervicalis*

2. Which parasite, transmitted from equines, is known to cause glanders in humans?

A) *Trypanosoma equiperdum*
B) *Burkholderia mallei*
C) *Anaplasma phagocytophilum*
D) *Eimeria leuckarti*

3. What zoonotic parasite found in horses is primarily transmitted via the bite of infected flies and can cause "summer sores" in humans?

A) *Habronema spp.*
B) *Theileria equi*
C) *Babesia caballi*
D) *Parascaris equorum*

4. Which parasite larvae from horses are responsible for causing "equine strongyles" and can sometimes cause human infection through accidental ingestion?

A) *Cyathostomins*
B) *Strongylus vulgaris*
C) *Dictyocaulus arnfieldi*
D) *Gasterophilus intestinalis*

5. Which of the following zoonotic diseases is caused by a protozoan parasite transmitted from horses via ticks?

A) Babesiosis
B) Leptospirosis
C) Tetanus
D) Anthrax

CHAPTER THREE : PET ANIMAL PARASITE QUESTIONS

PART ONE : HELMITHES OF DOGS & CATS

TREMATODES

1- *Heterophyes heterophyes*

1. What is the definitive host of Heterophyes heterophyes?

A. Snail
B. Fish
C. Human
D. Mosquito
Answer: C. Human

2.Which organ does Heterophyes heterophyes primarily infect in humans?

A. Liver
B. Lungs
C. Small intestine
D. Kidneys
Answer: C. Small intestine

3. What is the mode of transmission for Heterophyes heterophyes?

A. Inhalation of spores
B. Skin penetration
C. Ingestion of raw or undercooked fish
D. Insect bite
Answer: C. Ingestion of raw or undercooked fish

4.What is the second intermediate host of Heterophyes heterophyes?

A. Bird
B. Fish
C. Dog
D. Snail
Answer: B. Fish

5. What is the typical symptom of heavy Heterophyes heterophyes infection?

A. Chronic cough
B. Abdominal pain and diarrhea
C. Jaundice
D. Skin rash
Answer: B. Abdominal pain and diarrhea

Alaria alata

1. What type of parasite is *Alaria alata*?

A. Cestode
B. Trematode
C. Nematode
D. Protozoan

Answer: ✅ B. Trematode
(*Alaria alata* is a fluke, which is a type of trematode.)

2. How do dogs and cats typically become infected with *Alaria alata*?

A. Inhalation of eggs
B. Contact with infected soil
C. Ingestion of paratenic hosts (e.g., frogs, snakes, rodents)
D. Through the skin

Answer: ✅ C. Ingestion of paratenic hosts
(*Alaria alata* larvae can be transmitted when carnivores eat infected paratenic hosts.)

3. Where in the body does *Alaria alata* mature in dogs and cats?

A. Liver
B. Lungs
C. Small intestine
D. Large intestine

Answer: ✅ C. Small intestine
(Adult *Alaria alata* flukes reside in the small intestine of the definitive host.)

4. What is a potential risk of *Alaria alata* to humans?

A. Causes severe neurological disease
B. It is zoonotic and can infect humans through undercooked meat
C. It causes hair loss
D. It leads to chronic kidney disease

Answer: ✅ B. It is zoonotic and can infect humans through undercooked meat
(Humans can be accidental hosts by consuming undercooked meat from infected wild animals.)

5. Which of the following is a typical diagnostic method for detecting *Alaria alata* in dogs and cats?

A. Blood smear
B. Skin scraping
C. Fecal flotation/sedimentation
D. Radiographs

Answer: ✅ C. Fecal flotation/sedimentation
(Eggs of *Alaria alata* may be found in feces using sedimentation techniques.)

Nanophyetus salmincola

1. What is the primary clinical significance of *Nanophyetus salmincola* infection in dogs?

A) Causes fatal anemia
B) Transmits *Neorickettsia helminthoeca*, the agent of salmon poisoning disease
C) Causes severe liver damage
D) Leads to chronic kidney disease

✅ Answer: B) Transmits *Neorickettsia helminthoeca*, the agent of salmon poisoning disease

2. How do dogs typically become infected with *Nanophyetus salmincola*?

A) Ingestion of contaminated water
B) Inhalation of eggs
C) Ingestion of raw or undercooked fish
D) Contact with infected feces

✅ Answer: C) Ingestion of raw or undercooked fish

3. What is a common clinical sign of salmon poisoning disease in dogs?

A) Polyuria and polydipsia
B) Vomiting and diarrhea
C) Seizures
D) Limping

✅ Answer: B) Vomiting and diarrhea

4. Which of the following regions is most commonly associated with *Nanophyetus salmincola* infections in dogs?

A) Northeastern United States
B) Pacific Northwest (USA)
C) Midwest (USA)
D) Southeast Asia

✅ Answer: B) Pacific Northwest (USA)

5. What is the most effective treatment for salmon poisoning disease in dogs?

A) Anthelmintics only
B) Supportive fluids and antiemetics
C) Tetracycline or doxycycline with praziquantel
D) Corticosteroids

✅ Answer: C) Tetracycline or doxycycline with praziquantel

Clonorchis sinensis

1. What is the definitive host of Clonorchis sinensis?

A. Snail
B. Fish
C. Dog
D. Mosquito

Answer: ✅ C. Dog

Dogs (along with humans and cats) can serve as definitive hosts for Clonorchis sinensis.

2. How do dogs become infected with Clonorchis sinensis?

A. Inhalation of eggs
B. Direct skin contact
C. Eating raw or undercooked infected fish
D. Drinking contaminated water

Answer: ✅ C. Eating raw or undercooked infected fish

Infection occurs when dogs ingest metacercariae encysted in fish tissue.

3. Which organ is primarily affected by Clonorchis sinensis in dogs?

A. Kidney
B. Heart
C. Liver
D. Lungs

Answer: ✅ C. Liver

The adult flukes reside in the bile ducts of the liver.

4. Which clinical sign might be seen in a dog with a heavy Clonorchis sinensis infection?

A. Coughing
B. Jaundice
C. Diarrhea
D. Sneezing

Answer: ✅ B. Jaundice

Liver damage from fluke infestation can lead to bile duct obstruction and jaundice.

5. What is the best method to diagnose Clonorchis sinensis in dogs?

A. Blood test
B. Urinalysis
C. Fecal examination for eggs
D. X-ray

Answer: ✅ C. Fecal examination for eggs

Paragonomus westermani & P. Kalikoti

1. What is the primary mode of transmission of *Paragonimus westermani* and *Paragonimus kellicotti* in dogs?

A. Inhalation of eggs from the environment
B. Skin penetration by cercariae
C. Ingestion of infected crustaceans (crabs or crayfish)
D. Transplacental transmission

✅ Answer: C. Ingestion of infected crustaceans (crabs or crayfish)

2. In dogs, where do adult *Paragonimus* species typically localize and cause pathology?

A. Intestines
B. Liver
C. Lungs
D. Kidneys

✅ Answer: C. Lungs

3. Which clinical signs are most commonly associated with *Paragonimus* infection in dogs?

A. Diarrhea and weight loss
B. Coughing and respiratory distress
C. Excessive salivation and vomiting
D. Neurological symptoms

✅ Answer: B. Coughing and respiratory distress

4. Which diagnostic method is commonly used to confirm *Paragonimus* infection in dogs?

A. Skin scraping
B. ELISA blood test
C. Fecal sedimentation or flotation to detect eggs
D. Urinalysis

✅ **Answer: C. Fecal sedimentation or flotation to detect eggs**

5. Which anthelmintic is commonly used to treat *Paragonimus* infections in dogs?

A. Ivermectin
B. Fenbendazole
C. Praziquantel
D. Metronidazole

✅ **Answer: C. Praziquantel**

CESTODES

Dipylidium caninum

1. What is the common mode of transmission of Dipylidium caninum in dogs and cats?

A) Direct contact with infected animals
B) Ingestion of contaminated water
C) Ingestion of infected fleas
D) Biting from ticks

Answer: ✅ C) Ingestion of infected fleas

2. What is the most common clinical sign of Dipylidium caninum infection in pets?

A) Vomiting
B) Coughing
C) Scooting or dragging the rear end
D) Excessive salivation

Answer: ✅ C) Scooting or dragging the rear end

3. What type of parasite is Dipylidium caninum?

A) Nematode
B) Trematode
C) Cestode
D) Protozoa

Answer: ✅ C) Cestode

4. Which intermediate host is essential for the life cycle of Dipylidium caninum?

A) Mosquito
B) Flea (Ctenocephalides spp.)
C) Snail
D) Rodent

Answer: ✅ B) Flea (Ctenocephalides spp.)

5. What is the best method to prevent Dipylidium caninum infection in pets?

A) Regular deworming with praziquantel only
B) Feeding cooked meat
C) Controlling fleas on the pet and in the environment
D) Keeping pets indoors only

Answer: ✅ C) Controlling fleas on the pet and in the environment

Diphyllobothrium latum

1. What type of parasite is *Diphyllobothrium latum*?

A. Nematode
B. Trematode
C. Cestode
D. Protozoa

Answer: ✅ C. Cestode
(*Diphyllobothrium latum* is a tapeworm, which is a type of cestode.)

2. What is the most likely route of *Diphyllobothrium latum* infection in dogs?

A. Ingestion of raw or undercooked freshwater fish
B. Inhalation of parasite eggs
C. Skin penetration by larvae
D. Biting insects

Answer: ✅ A. Ingestion of raw or undercooked freshwater fish
(Dogs become infected by eating raw fish containing plerocercoid larvae.)

3. Which of the following clinical signs may be observed in dogs infected with *Diphyllobothrium latum*?

A. Seizures
B. Coughing and sneezing
C. Vomiting and diarrhea
D. Often asymptomatic, but may show weight loss or diarrhea

Answer: ✅ D. Often asymptomatic, but may show weight loss or diarrhea
(Infections can be subclinical, but gastrointestinal signs can occur.)

4. What is the diagnostic method commonly used to identify *Diphyllobothrium latum* in dogs?

A. Blood smear
B. Skin scraping
C. Fecal flotation or sedimentation
D. Radiography

Answer: ✅ C. Fecal flotation or sedimentation
(Eggs or proglottids can be detected in feces.)

5. Which drug is commonly used to treat *Diphyllobothrium latum* infection in dogs?

A. Albendazole
B. Praziquantel
C. Metronidazole
D. Ivermectin

Answer: ✅ B. Praziquantel
(Praziquantel is effective against cestodes like *D. latum*.)

Spirometra mansoni

1. What is the common mode of transmission of *Spirometra mansoni* to dogs?

A) Inhalation of spores
B) Ingestion of infected intermediate hosts
C) Skin penetration by larvae
D) Contact with infected animals

Answer: ✅ B) Ingestion of infected intermediate hosts
Explanation: Dogs get infected by ingesting intermediate hosts like frogs, snakes, or birds containing plerocercoid larvae.

2. Which larval stage of *Spirometra mansoni* is infective to dogs?

A) Miracidium
B) Coracidium
C) Procercoid
D) Plerocercoid

Answer: ✅ D) Plerocercoid
Explanation: The plerocercoid (sparganum) is the infective stage for dogs and other definitive hosts.

3. Where in the dog's body does the adult *Spirometra mansoni* reside?

A) Small intestine
B) Lungs
C) Liver
D) Stomach

Answer: ✅ A) Small intestine
Explanation: The adult tapeworm resides in the small intestine of the definitive host.

4. What clinical sign is *most commonly associated* with *Spirometra mansoni* infection in dogs?

A) Coughing
B) Severe pruritus
C) Diarrhea or asymptomatic
D) Jaundice

Answer: ✅ C) Diarrhea or asymptomatic
Explanation: Infections are often subclinical but may cause mild gastrointestinal signs like diarrhea.

5. What is the diagnostic method of choice for detecting *Spirometra mansoni* infection in dogs?

A) Blood smear
B) Urinalysis
C) Fecal examination for eggs
D) Skin scraping

Answer: ✅ C) Fecal examination for eggs
Explanation: Diagnosis is typically made by identifying characteristic *Spirometra* eggs in feces using fecal flotation.

Taenia hydatigena

1. What is the definitive host of *Taenia hydatigena*?

A. Sheep
B. Pig
C. Dog
D. Cow

Answer: ✅ C. Dog
Explanation: Dogs (and other canids) are the definitive hosts where the adult tapeworm lives in the intestines.

2. What is the intermediate host for *Taenia hydatigena*?

A. Dog
B. Sheep
C. Cat
D. Human

Answer: ✅ B. Sheep
Explanation: Sheep (and other herbivores like goats, pigs, and cattle) are intermediate hosts, where the larval stage (Cysticercus tenuicollis) develops in the liver and peritoneal cavity.

3. Where in the dog does the adult *Taenia hydatigena* reside?

A. Stomach
B. Small intestine
C. Large intestine
D. Liver

Answer: ✅ B. Small intestine
Explanation: Adult *T. hydatigena* lives in the small intestine of the dog, where it attaches to the mucosa.

4. What is the mode of transmission of *Taenia hydatigena* to dogs?

A. Ingestion of contaminated water
B. Skin penetration by larvae
C. Ingestion of raw viscera from infected intermediate hosts
D. Inhalation of eggs

Answer: ✅ C. Ingestion of raw viscera from infected intermediate hosts
Explanation: Dogs get infected by eating raw organs (especially liver) of infected intermediate hosts containing cysticerci.

5. Which of the following best describes the larval stage of *Taenia hydatigena*?

A. Hydatid cyst
B. Cysticercus tenuicollis
C. Coenurus
D. Toxocara larva

Answer: ✅ B. Cysticercus tenuicollis
Explanation: The larval form of *T. hydatigena* is called *Cysticercus tenuicollis*, found mainly in the peritoneal cavity or on the liver surface of intermediate hosts.

Taenia multiceps

1. What is the definitive host of *Taenia multiceps*?

A) Sheep
B) Cattle
C) Dog
D) Pig

Answer: ✅ C) Dog

2. What is the intermediate host of *Taenia multiceps*?

A) Dog
B) Cat
C) Goat or sheep
D) Horse

Answer: ✅ C) Goat or sheep
(*Taenia multiceps* forms **coenurus cysts** in the brain of intermediate hosts like sheep.)

3. What form of the parasite is found in the intermediate host?

A) Adult worm
B) Egg
C) Coenurus
D) Cysticercus

Answer: ✅ C) Coenurus
(Coenurus cerebralis is the larval stage causing neurological signs in sheep.)

4. How is a dog infected with *Taenia multiceps*?

A) By ingesting contaminated water
B) By eating raw or undercooked meat
C) By ingesting coenurus cysts from infected sheep brain
D) Through the bite of a vector

Answer: ✅ C) By ingesting coenurus cysts from infected sheep brain

5. What is a common clinical sign in sheep infected with *Coenurus cerebralis* (larval stage)?

A) Diarrhea
B) Blindness and circling
C) Coughing
D) Lameness

Answer: ✅ B) Blindness and circling
(*"Gid" or "Sturdy" is the name of the disease caused by coenurus cysts in the brain.)

Taenia ovis

1. What is the definitive host of *Taenia ovis*?

A) Sheep
B) Dog
C) Human
D) Cattle

Answer: B) Dog

2. The intermediate host of *Taenia ovis* is:

A) Dog
B) Sheep
C) Pig
D) Cat

Answer: B) Sheep

3. What form of *Taenia ovis* is found in the intermediate host?

A) Adult tapeworm
B) Egg
C) Larval cyst (Cysticercus ovis)
D) Proglottid

Answer: C) Larval cyst (Cysticercus ovis)

4. The primary site of larval cysts (Cysticercus ovis) in sheep is:

A) Brain
B) Heart and skeletal muscles
C) Liver
D) Lungs

Answer: B) Heart and skeletal muscles

5. How is *Taenia ovis* transmitted to dogs?

A) By ingesting infected sheep meat or offal
B) By direct contact with infected sheep
C) Through mosquito bites
D) By contaminated water

Answer: A) By ingesting infected sheep meat or offal

Taenia pisiformis

1. What is the definitive host of *Taenia pisiformis*?
A) Rabbit
B) Dog
C) Sheep
D) Cat

Answer: B) Dog

2. What is the intermediate host of *Taenia pisiformis*?
A) Rabbit
B) Rat
C) Cow
D) Pig

Answer: A) Rabbit

3. How do dogs usually get infected with *Taenia pisiformis*?
A) By drinking contaminated water
B) By eating infected rabbit viscera
C) By flea bites
D) By inhaling eggs

Answer: B) By eating infected rabbit viscera

4. What is the main clinical sign seen in dogs infected with *Taenia pisiformis*?
A) Severe diarrhea
B) Neurological symptoms
C) Usually asymptomatic or mild digestive upset
D) Skin lesions

Answer: C) Usually asymptomatic or mild digestive upset

5. Which of the following drugs is commonly used to treat *Taenia pisiformis* in dogs?
A) Ivermectin
B) Praziquantel
C) Amoxicillin
D) Metronidazole

Answer: B) Praziquantel

Taenia serialis

1. What is the definitive host of *Taenia serialis*?

A) Sheep
B) Dog
C) Rabbit
D) Human

Answer: ✅ B) Dog
Explanation: Dogs are the definitive host where the adult tapeworm resides in the intestine.

2. What is the typical intermediate host for *Taenia serialis*?

A) Cow
B) Pig
C) Rabbit or hare
D) Goat

Answer: ✅ C) Rabbit or hare
Explanation: Rabbits and hares serve as intermediate hosts, where the larval stage (coenurus) develops in subcutaneous tissues or muscles.

3. How do dogs typically become infected with *Taenia serialis*?

A) Drinking contaminated water
B) Ingesting infected intermediate hosts
C) Inhalation of eggs
D) Direct contact with infected dogs

Answer: ✅ B) Ingesting infected intermediate hosts
Explanation: Dogs acquire infection by eating tissues of infected intermediate hosts containing coenurus cysts.

4. What form of *Taenia serialis* is found in the intermediate host?

A) Cysticercus
B) Hydatid cyst
C) Coenurus
D) Trophozoite

Answer: ✅ C) Coenurus
Explanation: The larval form of *T. serialis* is a coenurus, typically found in the subcutaneous tissues of intermediate hosts.

5. What is a common method for diagnosing *Taenia serialis* infection in dogs?

A) Blood smear
B) Skin biopsy
C) Fecal flotation for eggs
D) PCR of saliva

Answer: ✅ C) Fecal flotation for eggs
Explanation: Eggs of *T. serialis* may be detected in the feces of infected dogs using fecal flotation techniques.

Echinococcus granulosus

1. What is the definitive host of *Echinococcus granulosus*?

A. Sheep
B. Human
C. Dog
D. Cattle

Answer: ✅ C. Dog
Explanation: Dogs are the definitive hosts where the adult tapeworm resides in the small intestine.

2. How do dogs become infected with *Echinococcus granulosus*?

A. Ingesting contaminated water
B. Ingesting hydatid cysts in infected offal (organs)
C. Through skin contact with infected animals
D. Mosquito bite

Answer: ✅ **B. Ingesting hydatid cysts in infected offal (organs)**
Explanation: Dogs get infected by eating raw organs (especially liver/lungs) of intermediate hosts like sheep that contain hydatid cysts.

3. What is the primary zoonotic concern of *Echinococcus granulosus* infection?

A. Causes severe diarrhea in dogs
B. Leads to blindness in humans
C. Transmission to humans causing hydatid disease
D. Causes rabies-like symptoms in humans

Answer: ✅ **C. Transmission to humans causing hydatid disease**
Explanation: Humans can become accidental intermediate hosts and develop hydatid cysts in vital organs.

4. Which diagnostic method is most commonly used to detect *Echinococcus granulosus* in dogs?

A. Blood culture
B. Fecal flotation for eggs
C. Skin scraping
D. Urinalysis

Answer: ✅ **B. Fecal flotation for eggs**
Explanation: Eggs of *Echinococcus* can be detected in the feces of infected dogs using flotation techniques, although eggs resemble other taeniid eggs.

5. What is the best preventive measure to control *Echinococcus granulosus* infection in dogs?

A. Vaccinate dogs annually
B. Feed dogs raw liver and lungs from sheep
C. Regular deworming and preventing dogs from eating raw offal
D. Isolate dogs permanently

Answer: ✅ **C. Regular deworming and preventing dogs from eating raw offal**
Explanation: Regular treatment with praziquantel and preventing access to infected organs breaks the transmission cycle.

NEMATODES

Strongyloides stercoralis

1. What is the primary mode of transmission of *Strongyloides stercoralis* in dogs and cats?

A. Ingestion of eggs from the environment
B. Skin penetration by infective larvae
C. Bite from an infected insect
D. Transplacental transmission

Answer: ✅ B. Skin penetration by infective larvae

2. Which life stage of *Strongyloides stercoralis* is infective to the host?

A. Egg
B. Rhabditiform larva
C. Filiform (filariform) larva
D. Adult worm

Answer: ✅ C. Filiform (filariform) larva

3. Which of the following clinical signs is commonly associated with *Strongyloides stercoralis* infection in dogs and cats?

A. Hyperactivity
B. Severe vomiting only
C. Intermittent diarrhea and skin lesions
D. Excessive salivation

Answer: ✅ C. Intermittent diarrhea and skin lesions

4. What is the best diagnostic method for detecting *Strongyloides stercoralis* in feces?

A. Direct smear
B. Fecal flotation
C. Baermann technique
D. ELISA test

Answer: ✅ C. Baermann technique

5. Which of the following is an effective treatment for *Strongyloides stercoralis* in dogs and cats?

A. Amoxicillin
B. Praziquantel
C. Ivermectin or Fenbendazole
D. Metronidazole

Answer: ✅ C. Ivermectin or Fenbendazole

Toxascaris leonine

1. What type of parasite is Toxascaris leonina?

A. Cestode
B. Trematode
C. Nematode
D. Protozoan

Answer: ✅ C. Nematode

2. How is Toxascaris leonina most commonly transmitted to dogs and cats?

A. Transplacental transmission
B. Ingestion of infective eggs or paratenic hosts
C. Skin penetration
D. Through blood-sucking arthropods

Answer: ✅ B. Ingestion of infective eggs or paratenic hosts

3. Which of the following is least likely a clinical sign of Toxascaris leonina infection in adult animals?

A. Vomiting
B. Diarrhea
C. Intestinal blockage
D. Weight loss

Answer: ✅ C. Intestinal blockage
(*This is more common with Toxocara canis/cati than Toxascaris leonina.*)

4. What is the prepatent period of Toxascaris leonina?

A. 2–4 weeks
B. 6–10 days
C. 10–12 weeks
D. 1–2 days

Answer: ✅ A. 2–4 weeks

5. Which diagnostic method is most commonly used to detect Toxascaris leonina?

A. Blood smear
B. Fecal flotation
C. Skin scraping
D. Urinalysis

Answer: ✅ B. Fecal flotation

Toxocara canis

1. What type of parasite is *Toxocara canis*?

A) Cestode
B) Trematode
C) Nematode
D) Protozoa

Answer: ✅ C) Nematode

2. How is *Toxocara canis* primarily transmitted to puppies?

A) Through contaminated water
B) Through flea bites
C) Transplacental transmission
D) Through grooming

Answer: ✅ C) Transplacental transmission

3. What is a common clinical sign of *Toxocara canis* infection in puppies?

A) Hair loss
B) Bloody diarrhea
C) Pot-bellied appearance
D) Seizures

Answer: ✅ C) Pot-bellied appearance

4. Which diagnostic method is commonly used to detect *Toxocara canis* eggs in dogs or cats?

A) Skin scraping
B) Blood smear
C) Fecal flotation
D) ELISA

Answer: ✅ C) Fecal flotation

5. What zoonotic condition can be caused by *Toxocara canis* in humans?

A) Visceral larva migrans
B) Cutaneous larva migrans
C) Toxoplasmosis
D) Ringworm

Answer: ✅ A) Visceral larva migrans

Ancylostoma caninum

1. What type of parasite is *Ancylostoma caninum*?

A. Tapeworm
B. Roundworm
C. Hookworm
D. Fluke

✅ **Correct Answer:** C. Hookworm

2. How is *Ancylostoma caninum* most commonly transmitted to dogs?

A. Ingestion of contaminated food
B. Skin penetration by infective larvae
C. Inhalation of eggs
D. Biting insects

✅ **Correct Answer:** B. Skin penetration by infective larvae

3. Which of the following is a common clinical sign of *Ancylostoma caninum* infection in puppies?

A. Constipation
B. Seizures
C. Severe anemia
D. Hair loss

✅ **Correct Answer:** C. Severe anemia

4. Which diagnostic method is most commonly used to detect *Ancylostoma caninum* infection?

A. Blood smear
B. Radiography
C. Fecal flotation
D. Skin scraping

✅ **Correct Answer:** C. Fecal flotation

5. Can *Ancylostoma caninum* infect humans?

A. No, it is species-specific
B. Yes, it can cause cutaneous larva migrans
C. Yes, it can cause intestinal infection
D. Only through direct ingestion of adult worms

✅ **Correct Answer:** B. Yes, it can cause cutaneous larva migrans

Filaroides osleri

1. What is the primary host for *Filaroides osleri*?

A. Cat
B. Dog
C. Rabbit
D. Human

✅ **Answer:** B. Dog

Filaroides osleri primarily infects dogs, especially young ones. It is rare in cats.

2. What is the main clinical sign of *Filaroides osleri* infection in dogs?

A. Vomiting
B. Chronic cough
C. Diarrhea
D. Seizures

✅ **Answer:** B. Chronic cough

The parasite forms nodules in the trachea and bronchi, causing a persistent dry cough.

3. How is *Filaroides osleri* transmitted between dogs?

A. Mosquito bite
B. Inhalation of eggs
C. Ingestion of L1 larvae in saliva or feces
D. Skin penetration by L3 larvae

✅ **Answer:** C. Ingestion of L1 larvae in saliva or feces

Transmission occurs through direct contact with infected saliva or feces containing L1 larvae.

4. Which diagnostic method is most effective for identifying *Filaroides osleri* infection?

A. Blood smear
B. Urine analysis
C. Fecal flotation with Baermann technique
D. Chest radiograph only

✅ **Answer:** C. Fecal flotation with Baermann technique

The Baermann technique is effective in detecting the L1 larvae in feces. Bronchoscopy may also help.

5. Which treatment is commonly used for *Filaroides osleri* infection in dogs?

A. Ivermectin
B. Metronidazole
C. Amoxicillin
D. Furosemide

✅ **Answer:** A. Ivermectin

Anthelmintics like ivermectin or fenbendazole are used to treat *Filaroides osleri* infection.

Spirocerca lupi

1. What is the primary mode of transmission of *Spirocerca lupi* in dogs?

A. Direct contact with infected dogs
B. Ingestion of infective larvae from contaminated water
C. Ingestion of intermediate or paratenic hosts (e.g., beetles or reptiles)
D. Inhalation of larvae from the environment

Answer: ✅ C. Ingestion of intermediate or paratenic hosts (e.g., beetles or reptiles)

2. Where are the adult *Spirocerca lupi* worms typically found in infected dogs?

A. Lungs
B. Small intestine
C. Stomach lining
D. Esophageal wall and aorta

Answer: ✅ D. Esophageal wall and aorta

3. Which of the following is a common clinical sign of *Spirocerca lupi* infection in dogs?

A. Sneezing
B. Vomiting and regurgitation
C. Excessive salivation
D. Hind limb paralysis

Answer: ✅ B. Vomiting and regurgitation

4. Which diagnostic method is most commonly used to detect *Spirocerca lupi* infection?

A. Skin scraping
B. Urinalysis
C. Fecal flotation to detect eggs
D. Joint fluid analysis

Answer: ✅ C. Fecal flotation to detect eggs

5. What severe complication can *Spirocerca lupi* cause in chronic infections?

A. Liver cirrhosis
B. Pulmonary embolism
C. Esophageal sarcoma or fibrosarcoma
D. Diabetes mellitus

Answer: ✅ C. Esophageal sarcoma or fibrosarcoma

Dipetalonema reconditum

1. What is the primary mode of transmission of *Dipetalonema reconditum* in dogs?

A. Mosquito bite
B. Flea bite
C. Ingestion of contaminated water
D. Direct dog-to-dog contact

Answer: ✅ B. Flea bite

2. *Dipetalonema reconditum* microfilariae are usually found in which part of the dog's body?

A. Lungs
B. Heart
C. Bloodstream
D. Intestine

Answer: ✅ C. Bloodstream

3. How can *Dipetalonema reconditum* microfilariae be differentiated from *Dirofilaria immitis* microfilariae?

A. D. reconditum is longer and wider
B. D. reconditum has a straight body and tail
C. D. reconditum has a curved or "button-hook" tail
D. D. reconditum is found only in puppies

Answer: ✅ C. D. reconditum has a curved or "button-hook" tail

4. What is the clinical significance of *Dipetalonema reconditum* in dogs?

A. Causes severe respiratory distress
B. Typically non-pathogenic
C. Major cause of heart failure
D. Leads to kidney dysfunction

Answer: ✅ B. Typically non-pathogenic

5. Which diagnostic test is commonly used to detect microfilariae of *Dipetalonema reconditum*?

A. ELISA
B. SNAP test

C. Modified Knott's test
D. PCR only

Answer: ✅ C. Modified Knott's test

Dirofilaria immitis

1. What is the definitive host of Dirofilaria immitis?

A) Mosquito
B) Dog
C) Cat
D) Human

Correct Answer: B) Dog
Explanation: The dog is the definitive host where the adult heartworms live and reproduce. Mosquitoes are intermediate hosts.

2. How is Dirofilaria immitis transmitted to dogs?

A) Ingestion of contaminated water
B) Inhalation of larvae
C) Bite of an infected mosquito
D) Direct contact with infected dogs

Correct Answer: C) Bite of an infected mosquito
Explanation: Heartworms are transmitted when an infected mosquito bites a dog and deposits L3 larvae into the skin.

3. Where do adult Dirofilaria immitis worms reside in infected dogs?

A) Liver and spleen
B) Brain and spinal cord

C) Pulmonary arteries and right heart
D) Small intestine

Correct Answer: C) Pulmonary arteries and right heart
Explanation: Adult worms typically reside in the pulmonary arteries and sometimes extend into the right ventricle.

4. Which diagnostic test is commonly used to detect heartworm infection in dogs?

A) Fecal flotation
B) Blood smear for microfilariae
C) Antigen test
D) Urinalysis

Correct Answer: C) Antigen test
Explanation: Antigen tests detect proteins from adult female heartworms and are a common method for diagnosis.

5. What is a common clinical sign of heartworm disease in dogs?

A) Diarrhea
B) Coughing and exercise intolerance
C) Seizures
D) Skin lesions

Correct Answer: B) Coughing and exercise intolerance
Explanation: Heartworm affects the lungs and heart, leading to coughing, fatigue, and sometimes heart failure.

Trichuris vulpis

1. What type of parasite is *Trichuris vulpis*?
A) Cestode
B) Nematode
C) Trematode
D) Protozoa

Answer: B) Nematode

2. What is the primary site of infection of *Trichuris vulpis* in dogs?
A) Small intestine
B) Large intestine (cecum and colon)
C) Stomach
D) Liver

Answer: B) Large intestine (cecum and colon)

3. What is the typical clinical sign of *Trichuris vulpis* infection in dogs?
A) Severe coughing
B) Vomiting and diarrhea with blood
C) Excessive scratching
D) Hair loss

Answer: B) Vomiting and diarrhea with blood

4. How is *Trichuris vulpis* primarily transmitted to dogs?
A) Ingestion of infected fleas
B) Ingestion of embryonated eggs from the environment
C) Transplacental transmission
D) Bite from infected mosquito

Answer: B) Ingestion of embryonated eggs from the environment

5. Which diagnostic method is most commonly used to detect *Trichuris vulpis* infection in dogs?
A) Blood smear
B) Fecal flotation

C) Urinalysis
D) Skin scraping

Answer: B) Fecal flotation

PROTOZOA OF DOGSA_D CATS
PROTOZOA

Phylum Sarcomastigophora
Class Mastigophora (flagellates)
Hemoflagellates

***Leishmania* spp.**

1. What is the primary species of Leishmania that infects dogs?

A. Leishmania major
B. Leishmania mexicana
C. Leishmania infantum
D. Leishmania donovani

Answer: ✅ C. Leishmania infantum

2. How is Leishmania typically transmitted to dogs?

A. Direct contact with infected animals
B. Ingestion of contaminated food
C. Bite of infected sandflies
D. Through ticks and fleas

Answer: ✅ C. Bite of infected sandflies

3. Which of the following is a common clinical sign of canine leishmaniasis?

A. Seizures
B. Hair loss and skin lesions

C. Aggression
D. Vomiting blood

Answer: ✅ B. Hair loss and skin lesions

4. What type of organism is Leishmania?

A. Bacterium
B. Virus
C. Protozoan
D. Fungus

Answer: ✅ C. Protozoan

5. What is a common diagnostic method used to confirm leishmaniasis in dogs?

A. Blood culture
B. ELISA serology or PCR
C. Radiography
D. Fecal flotation

Answer: ✅ B. ELISA serology or PCR

Trypanosoma cruzi

MCQ 1: What disease does *Trypanosoma cruzi* cause in dogs?

A. Leishmaniasis
B. Chagas disease
C. Babesiosis
D. Ehrlichiosis

✅ **Answer: B. Chagas disease**

Explanation: *Trypanosoma cruzi* is the protozoan parasite responsible for Chagas disease, which affects both humans and dogs.

MCQ 2: What is the primary mode of transmission of *T. cruzi* in dogs?

A. Tick bite
B. Mosquito bite
C. Feces of triatomine bugs
D. Inhalation of spores

✅ **Answer: C. Feces of triatomine bugs**

Explanation: Dogs are infected primarily through contamination of mucous membranes or wounds with the feces of infected triatomine insects (also called "kissing bugs").

MCQ 3: Which clinical sign is most commonly associated with chronic *T. cruzi* infection in dogs?

A. Vomiting
B. Seizures
C. Dilated cardiomyopathy
D. Skin ulcers

✅ **Answer: C. Dilated cardiomyopathy**

Explanation: Chronic *T. cruzi* infection often leads to cardiac damage, especially **dilated cardiomyopathy**, which is a major cause of heart failure in infected dogs.

MCQ 4: Which diagnostic test is most reliable for detecting chronic *T. cruzi* infection in dogs?

A. Blood smear
B. ELISA or IFA serology
C. Fecal flotation
D. Skin biopsy

✅ **Answer: B. ELISA or IFA serology**

Explanation: Serological tests such as ELISA or Indirect Fluorescent Antibody (IFA) are most reliable for detecting chronic infections when the parasite is no longer present in peripheral blood.

MCQ 5: What is the primary concern with *T. cruzi* infection in dogs from a public health perspective?

A. Dogs can act as reservoirs and contribute to human infections
B. Dogs are vectors of the parasite
C. Infected dogs shed the parasite in saliva
D. There is direct dog-to-human transmission through bites

✅ **Answer: A. Dogs can act as reservoirs and contribute to human infections**

Explanation: Although dogs don't directly transmit *T. cruzi* to humans, they can serve as important **reservoirs**, maintaining the parasite in domestic environments and increasing the risk of human exposure.

Enteric flagellates

Giardia canis

1. What type of organism is *Giardia canis*?

A. Bacterium
B. Virus
C. Protozoan parasite
D. Fungi

✅ **Correct Answer:** C. **Protozoan parasite**

Giardia canis is a flagellated protozoan that infects the intestines of dogs and other animals.

2. What is the most common clinical sign of *Giardia* infection in dogs?

A. Vomiting
B. Seizures
C. Chronic diarrhea
D. Hair loss

✅ **Correct Answer:** C. **Chronic diarrhea**

Diarrhea, often soft or watery and foul-smelling, is the primary symptom of giardiasis.

3. How is *Giardia canis* most commonly transmitted between dogs?

A. Airborne droplets
B. Bite wounds
C. Ingestion of contaminated water or feces
D. Blood transfusion

✅ **Correct Answer:** C. **Ingestion of contaminated water or feces**

Transmission is fecal-oral, typically through contaminated water, food, or surfaces.

4. Which diagnostic test is commonly used to detect *Giardia* infection in dogs?

A. ELISA antigen test
B. Skin scrape test

C. Complete blood count (CBC)
D. Heartworm test

✅ **Correct Answer:** A. **ELISA antigen test**

An ELISA test or a fecal float with zinc sulfate is commonly used to detect Giardia cysts or antigens in feces.

5. Which of the following medications is commonly used to treat *Giardia canis* in dogs?

A. Amoxicillin
B. Metronidazole
C. Ivermectin
D. Prednisone

✅ **Correct Answer:** B. **Metronidazole**

Metronidazole and fenbendazole are commonly used antiprotozoal medications for treating Giardia infections.

Pentatrichomonas hominis

MCQ 1:

What type of organism is *Pentatrichomonas hominis*?
A. Bacterium
B. Virus
C. Protozoan
D. Fungus

Answer: ✅ C. Protozoan

MCQ 2:

Where in the dog's body is *Pentatrichomonas hominis* typically found?
A. Lungs
B. Small intestine
C. Colon
D. Bloodstream

Answer: ✅ C. Colon

MCQ 3:

Which diagnostic method is commonly used to detect *Pentatrichomonas hominis* in dogs?
A. ELISA
B. Fecal flotation
C. Direct fecal smear with microscopy
D. Hematology panel

Answer: ✅ C. Direct fecal smear with microscopy

MCQ 4:

What is the typical clinical significance of *Pentatrichomonas hominis* in dogs?
A. It is always pathogenic and causes severe diarrhea
B. It is a commensal organism and usually non-pathogenic
C. It causes neurological symptoms
D. It leads to liver failure

Answer: ✅ B. It is a commensal organism and usually non-pathogenic

MCQ 5:

Which of the following is a potential differential diagnosis when *Pentatrichomonas hominis* is found in a dog with diarrhea?

A. Giardia spp.
B. Parvovirus
C. Clostridium perfringens
D. All of the above

Answer: ✅ D. All of the above

Phylum Apicomplexa
Class Coccidia

Cryptosporidium canis

1. What is Cryptosporidium canis?

A. A virus that infects the respiratory system of dogs
B. A bacterial pathogen causing skin infections
C. A protozoan parasite that infects the gastrointestinal tract of dogs
D. A fungal infection affecting dog paws

Answer: ✅ C. A protozoan parasite that infects the gastrointestinal tract of dogs

2. What is the most common clinical sign of Cryptosporidium canis infection in dogs?

A. Coughing and sneezing
B. Hair loss and itching
C. Diarrhea, often watery
D. Vomiting only

Answer: ✅ C. Diarrhea, often watery

3. How is Cryptosporidium canis primarily transmitted between dogs?

A. Airborne transmission
B. Blood-to-blood contact
C. Fecal-oral route (ingestion of oocysts in contaminated food/water)
D. Through ticks and fleas

Answer: ✅ C. Fecal-oral route (ingestion of oocysts in contaminated food/water)

4. Which group is at higher risk of severe illness from Cryptosporidium canis?

A. Healthy adult dogs
B. Elderly humans
C. Immunocompromised dogs and puppies
D. Cats

Answer: ✅ C. Immunocompromised dogs and puppies

5. What is a common method for diagnosing Cryptosporidium canis infection?

A. X-ray of the abdomen
B. Blood culture
C. Fecal examination using acid-fast staining or PCR
D. Urine test

Answer: ✅ C. Fecal examination using acid-fast staining or PCR

Hammondia heydorni

1. What type of organism is *Hammondia heydorni*?

A. Bacterium
B. Fungus
C. Protozoan parasite
D. Virus

Answer: ✅ C. Protozoan parasite

2. How do dogs typically become infected with *Hammondia heydorni*?

A. Inhalation of spores
B. Direct skin contact
C. Ingestion of raw or undercooked meat containing tissue cysts
D. Bite from an infected tick

Answer: ✅ C. Ingestion of raw or undercooked meat containing tissue cysts

3. What is the primary clinical significance of *Hammondia heydorni* infection in dogs?

A. Causes severe neurological disease
B. Usually asymptomatic or mild gastrointestinal signs
C. Leads to fatal cardiac failure
D. Causes respiratory distress

Answer: ✅ B. Usually asymptomatic or mild gastrointestinal signs

4. Which diagnostic method is commonly used to identify *Hammondia heydorni* in dogs?

A. Blood smear
B. Fecal flotation to detect oocysts
C. Skin scraping
D. ELISA test for antibodies

Answer: ✅ B. Fecal flotation to detect oocysts

5. *Hammondia heydorni* is closely related to which of the following parasites?

A. *Giardia lamblia*
B. *Toxoplasma gondii*
C. *Neospora caninum*
D. *Cryptosporidium parvum*

Answer: ✅ C. *Neospora caninum*

Hepatozoon canis

1. What is the primary mode of transmission of Hepatozoon canis in dogs?

A. Tick bite
B. Mosquito bite
C. Ingestion of infected tick
D. Inhalation of oocysts

Answer: ✅ C. Ingestion of infected tick

2. Which tick species is commonly associated with the transmission of Hepatozoon canis?

A. *Rhipicephalus sanguineus*
B. *Ixodes scapularis*
C. *Dermacentor variabilis*
D. *Amblyomma americanum*

Answer: ✅ A. Rhipicephalus sanguineus

3. What is a common clinical sign of Hepatozoon canis infection in dogs?

A. Hyperactivity
B. Severe coughing
C. Lethargy and muscle wasting
D. Skin rash

Answer: ✅ C. Lethargy and muscle wasting

4. Which diagnostic method is commonly used to detect Hepatozoon canis?

A. ELISA test for antibodies
B. PCR testing of blood
C. Skin scraping
D. Radiography

Answer: ✅ B. PCR testing of blood

5. What type of organism is Hepatozoon canis?

A. Bacterium
B. Fungus
C. Protozoan parasite
D. Virus

Answer: ✅ C. Protozoan parasite

Isospora canis

1. What type of organism is *Isospora canis*?

A. Bacteria
B. Virus
C. Protozoa
D. Fungus

✅ **Answer:** C. **Protozoa**
Explanation: Isospora canis is a protozoan parasite that causes coccidiosis in dogs.

2. What is the most common clinical sign of *Isospora canis* infection in puppies?

A. Coughing
B. Seizures
C. Diarrhea
D. Vomiting

✅ **Answer:** C. **Diarrhea**
Explanation: The most common symptom of *Isospora canis* in puppies is watery or bloody diarrhea due to intestinal damage.

3. How is *Isospora canis* transmitted among dogs?

A. Through insect bites
B. Direct contact with infected blood

C. Ingestion of sporulated oocysts from contaminated environment
D. Airborne droplets

✅ **Answer:** C. **Ingestion of sporulated oocysts from contaminated environment**
Explanation: Dogs become infected by ingesting oocysts from contaminated feces, water, or food.

4. Which group of dogs is most susceptible to *Isospora canis* infection?

A. Adult dogs with strong immunity
B. Senior dogs
C. Puppies and immunocompromised dogs
D. Pregnant females

✅ **Answer:** C. **Puppies and immunocompromised dogs**
Explanation: Young and immunocompromised animals are more likely to show clinical signs.

5. What is the common treatment for *Isospora canis* infection?

A. Antibiotics like amoxicillin
B. Antiprotozoal drugs like sulfadimethoxine
C. Antifungals like ketoconazole
D. Corticosteroids

✅ **Answer:** B. **Antiprotozoal drugs like sulfadimethoxine**
Explanation: Sulfadimethoxine (Albon) is commonly used to treat coccidiosis caused by *Isospora canis*.

Neospora caninum

1. What is the most common clinical sign of Neospora caninum infection in young dogs?

A. Seizures
B. Progressive hindlimb paralysis
C. Vomiting
D. Coughing

Answer: ✅ B. Progressive hindlimb paralysis

2. How is Neospora caninum most commonly transmitted to puppies?

A. Direct contact with infected urine
B. Ingestion of contaminated water
C. Transplacental transmission from an infected dam
D. Tick bites

Answer: ✅ C. Transplacental transmission from an infected dam

3. Which tissue is primarily affected in dogs with Neospora caninum infection?

A. Liver
B. Lungs
C. Muscle and central nervous system
D. Skin

Answer: ✅ C. Muscle and central nervous system

4. Which diagnostic test is commonly used to confirm Neospora caninum infection in dogs?

A. ELISA for antibodies
B. Fecal flotation

C. Skin scraping
D. Coombs test

Answer: ✅ A. ELISA for antibodies

5. What is the treatment of choice for Neospora caninum infection in dogs?

A. Penicillin and corticosteroids
B. Clindamycin or Trimethoprim-sulfonamide
C. Ivermectin
D. Ketoconazole

Answer: ✅ B. Clindamycin or Trimethoprim-sulfonamide

Class Piroplasmidia

Babesia canis

1. What is the primary mode of transmission of *Babesia canis* in dogs?

A. Fecal-oral route
B. Inhalation of spores
C. Tick bite (Rhipicephalus sanguineus)
D. Direct contact with infected urine

✅ Answer: C. Tick bite (Rhipicephalus sanguineus)
Explanation: Babesia canis is transmitted mainly through the bite of infected ticks, especially the brown dog tick.

2. What type of organism is *Babesia canis*?

A. Bacteria
B. Virus

C. Protozoa
D. Fungus

✅ **Answer: C. Protozoa**
Explanation: Babesia canis is a protozoan parasite that infects red blood cells.

3. Which clinical sign is commonly associated with *Babesia canis* infection in dogs?

A. Diarrhea
B. Jaundice (icterus)
C. Lameness
D. Seizures

✅ **Answer: B. Jaundice (icterus)**
Explanation: Jaundice occurs due to hemolysis of red blood cells, a hallmark of Babesia infections.

4. Which diagnostic test is most commonly used to confirm *Babesia canis* infection?

A. Urinalysis
B. Blood smear microscopy
C. Skin scraping
D. ELISA for heartworm

✅ **Answer: B. Blood smear microscopy**
Explanation: Microscopic examination of a stained blood smear can reveal Babesia organisms inside red blood cells.

5. What is the most effective drug used to treat *Babesia canis* infection in dogs?

A. Enrofloxacin
B. Ivermectin

C. Imidocarb dipropionate
D. Prednisolone

✅ **Answer: C. Imidocarb dipropionate**
Explanation: Imidocarb is commonly used to treat Babesia infections in dogs.

Babesia gibsoni

1. What type of organism is *Babesia gibsoni*?

A. Bacteria
B. Virus
C. Protozoa
D. Fungus

Answer: ✅ C. Protozoa

2. How is *Babesia gibsoni* primarily transmitted in dogs?

A. Airborne droplets
B. Fecal-oral route
C. Tick bite (especially *Rhipicephalus sanguineus*)
D. Mosquito bite

Answer: ✅ C. Tick bite (especially *Rhipicephalus sanguineus*)

3. Which clinical sign is commonly associated with *Babesia gibsoni* infection in dogs?

A. Diarrhea
B. Seizures

C. Hemolytic anemia
D. Skin ulcers

Answer: ✅ C. Hemolytic anemia

4. Which diagnostic method is most commonly used to confirm *Babesia gibsoni* infection?

A. Urinalysis
B. Blood smear microscopy
C. Fecal floatation
D. X-ray

Answer: ✅ B. Blood smear microscopy
(*PCR is also used for more sensitive detection*)

5. What is the commonly recommended treatment for *Babesia gibsoni* in dogs?

A. Amoxicillin
B. Doxycycline only
C. Atovaquone + Azithromycin
D. Ivermectin

Answer: ✅ C. Atovaquone + Azithromycin

PART THREE :ECTOPARASITES

Linguatula serrate

1. What is the common name of the parasite ***Linguatula serrata***?

A. Dog tapeworm
B. Tongue worm
C. Nasal fluke
D. Canine whipworm

Answer: ✅ B. Tongue worm

2. What is the primary site of infection of ***Linguatula serrata*** in dogs?

A. Small intestine
B. Nasal cavity and nasopharynx
C. Liver
D. Lungs

Answer: ✅ B. Nasal cavity and nasopharynx

3. How do dogs most commonly become infected with ***Linguatula serrata***?

A. Inhalation of infective larvae from the environment
B. Biting insects
C. Ingestion of raw viscera from intermediate hosts (e.g., sheep or goats)
D. Drinking contaminated water

Answer: ✅ C. Ingestion of raw viscera from intermediate hosts (e.g., sheep or goats)

4. Which clinical sign is most associated with ***Linguatula serrata*** infection in dogs?

A. Diarrhea
B. Seizures

C. Sneezing and nasal discharge
D. Hindlimb paralysis

Answer: ✅ C. Sneezing and nasal discharge

5. ***Linguatula serrata*** belongs to which group of parasites?

A. Nematodes
B. Trematodes
C. Pentastomids
D. Cestodes

Answer: ✅ C. Pentastomids

Demodex canis

1. What type of organism is ***Demodex canis***?

A. Bacterium
B. Fungus
C. Mite
D. Virus

Answer: ✅ C. Mite

2. ***Demodex canis*** primarily inhabits which part of the dog's body?

A. Bloodstream
B. Intestinal tract
C. Hair follicles and sebaceous glands
D. Lungs

Answer: ✅ C. Hair follicles and sebaceous glands

3. Which condition is caused by an overgrowth of ***Demodex canis*** in dogs?

A. Ringworm
B. Demodectic mange (demodicosis)
C. Sarcoptic mange
D. Otitis externa

Answer: ✅ B. Demodectic mange (demodicosis)

4. Which of the following is a common clinical sign of demodicosis in dogs?

A. Vomiting
B. Hair loss (alopecia)
C. Seizures
D. Coughing

Answer: ✅ B. Hair loss (alopecia)

5. How is ***Demodex canis*** most commonly transmitted?

A. Through contaminated water
B. Through tick bites
C. From mother to pup during nursing
D. Airborne droplets

Answer: ✅ C. From mother to pup during nursing

Sarcoptes scabiei* var. *canis

1. What is the primary host of ***Sarcoptes scabiei*** var. ***canis***?

A) Cats
B) Dogs

C) Humans
D) Horses

Answer: ✅ B) Dogs

2. What is a common clinical sign of ***Sarcoptes scabiei*** var. ***canis*** infestation in dogs?

A) Vomiting
B) Diarrhea
C) Intense pruritus (itching)
D) Lameness

Answer: ✅ C) Intense pruritus (itching)

3. How is ***Sarcoptes scabiei*** var. ***canis*** most commonly transmitted?

A) Airborne droplets
B) Contaminated food
C) Direct contact with infested animals
D) Insect bites

Answer: ✅ C) Direct contact with infested animals

4. Which of the following diagnostic tests is commonly used to detect *Sarcoptes scabiei* **mites?**

A) Blood culture
B) Skin scraping
C) Urinalysis
D) Fecal flotation

Answer: ✅ B) Skin scraping

5. Can ***Sarcoptes scabiei*** var. ***canis*** infect humans?

A) No, it is species-specific
B) Yes, it can cause a temporary zoonotic skin condition
C) Yes, it causes long-term scabies in humans
D) No, it only infects rodents

Answer: ✅ B) Yes, it can cause a temporary zoonotic skin condition

Notoedric *sp.*

1. What is the causative agent of Notoedric mange?

A. *Sarcoptes scabiei*
B. *Demodex canis*
C. *Notoedres cati*
D. *Otodectes cynotis*

✅ **Correct Answer: C.** *Notoedres cati*
(*Notoedres cati* primarily affects cats but can also infect dogs and humans in rare cases.)

2. Which of the following is the primary mode of transmission of Notoedric mange?

A. Ingestion of contaminated food
B. Airborne droplets
C. Direct contact with infected animals
D. Mosquito bites

✅ **Correct Answer: C. Direct contact with infected animals**
(The mites are spread by close contact, especially in multi-pet households or shelters.)

3. Which clinical sign is MOST commonly associated with Notoedric mange?

A. Limping
B. Intense itching and crusting around the ears and face
C. Vomiting and diarrhea
D. Hind limb paralysis

✅ **Correct Answer: B. Intense itching and crusting around the ears and face**
(This mange starts on the face and ears, spreading with intense pruritus.)

4. Which diagnostic method is typically used to confirm Notoedric mange?

A. Blood culture
B. Urinalysis
C. Skin scraping and microscopic examination
D. Chest X-ray

✅ **Correct Answer: C. Skin scraping and microscopic examination**
(Mites are usually found in deep skin scrapings and are easy to identify.)

5. Which treatment is commonly effective against Notoedric mange in dogs?

A. Antibiotics only
B. Antifungal creams
C. Ivermectin or other acaricidal medications
D. Corticosteroids alone

✅ **Correct Answer: C. Ivermectin or other acaricidal medications**
(Acaricidal treatments like ivermectin, selamectin, or lime sulfur dips are effective.)

Ctenocephalides canis.

1. What is the primary host of ***Ctenocephalides canis***?

A. Humans
B. Cats
C. Dogs
D. Rodents

Answer: ✅ C. Dogs

2. How can ***Ctenocephalides canis*** be differentiated from ***Ctenocephalides felis*** (cat flea)?

A. Presence of a longer head
B. Presence of longer legs
C. More rounded head and shorter first genal comb spine
D. It is larger in size than the cat flea

Answer: ✅ C. More rounded head and shorter first genal comb spine

3. What type of parasite is *Ctenocephalides canis***?**

A. Endoparasite
B. Ectoparasite
C. Protozoan parasite
D. Hemoparasite

Answer: ✅ B. Ectoparasite

4. What disease can *Ctenocephalides canis* **potentially transmit?**

A. Malaria
B. Bubonic plague
C. Dipylidiasis (*Dipylidium caninum*)
D. Leptospirosis

Answer: ✅ C. Dipylidiasis (*Dipylidium caninum*)

5. What is the typical life cycle stage of *Ctenocephalides canis* that infests the host?

A. Egg
B. Larva
C. Pupa
D. Adult

Answer: ✅ D. Adult

TICKS: *Ixodes sp.,Rhipicephalus sp. . Dermacentor sp. . Amblyomma americanum . Haemaphysalis longicornis* **.**

1. Which tick species is commonly known as the "brown dog tick"?

A. *Ixodes scapularis*
B. *Dermacentor variabilis*
C. *Rhipicephalus sanguineus*
D. *Amblyomma americanum*

Answer: ✅ C. *Rhipicephalus sanguineus*

2. Which tick species is also called the "lone star tick"?

A. *Haemaphysalis longicornis*
B. *Ixodes scapularis*
C. *Dermacentor andersoni*
D. *Amblyomma americanum*

Answer: ✅ D. *Amblyomma americanum*

3. Which tick is an invasive species originally from Asia, now found on dogs in the U.S.?

A. *Ixodes pacificus*
B. *Haemaphysalis longicornis*
C. *Dermacentor variabilis*
D. *Amblyomma maculatum*

Answer: ✅ B. *Haemaphysalis longicornis*

4. Which tick is the primary vector of Lyme disease and may parasitize dogs?

A. *Ixodes scapularis*
B. *Rhipicephalus sanguineus*
C. *Dermacentor variabilis*
D. *Amblyomma americanum*

Answer: ✅ A. *Ixodes scapularis*

5. Which tick species is known for causing tick paralysis in dogs in North America?

A. *Ixodes pacificus*
B. *Haemaphysalis longicornis*

C. *Dermacentor variabilis*
D. *Rhipicephalus sanguineus*

Answer: ✅ C. *Dermacentor variabilis*

Trichodectes canis

1. What type of parasite is *Trichodectes canis*?

A) Nematode
B) Cestode
C) Louse (Insect)
D) Mite

Answer: C) **Louse (Insect)**
Explanation: *Trichodectes canis* is a chewing louse that infests dogs.

2. What is the primary host of *Trichodectes canis*?

A) Cats
B) Humans
C) Cattle
D) Dogs

Answer: D) **Dogs**
Explanation: *Trichodectes canis* specifically infests dogs and is a host-specific ectoparasite.

3. What kind of mouthparts does *Trichodectes canis* have?

A) Piercing-sucking
B) Sponging
C) Chewing
D) Lapping

Answer: C) **Chewing**
Explanation: It belongs to the Mallophaga group (chewing lice), which have chewing mouthparts.

4. What is a possible medical importance of *Trichodectes canis* beyond causing irritation?

A) Causes rabies
B) Intermediate host for *Dipylidium caninum*
C) Vector for Lyme disease
D) Causes mange

Answer: B) **Intermediate host for *Dipylidium caninum***
Explanation: Dogs can become infected with *Dipylidium caninum* (a tapeworm) by ingesting lice carrying its larval stage.

5. How is *Trichodectes canis* primarily transmitted?

A) Through contaminated food
B) Through water
C) Direct contact between animals
D) Mosquito bite

Answer: C) **Direct contact between animals**
Explanation: The louse is transmitted via close physical contact, especially in kennels or shared bedding.

ZOONOTIC PARASITES FROM DOGS AND CATS

1. Which of the following parasites is a common cause of cutaneous larva migrans in humans?

A. *Toxocara canis*
B. *Ancylostoma braziliense*
C. *Dipylidium caninum*
D. *Giardia duodenalis*

✅ **Answer: B. *Ancylostoma braziliense***

2. Which parasite, transmitted by ingestion of infective eggs from dog feces, can cause visceral and ocular larva migrans in humans?

A. *Toxocara canis*
B. *Taenia pisiformis*
C. *Trichuris vulpis*
D. *Isospora canis*

✅ **Answer: A. *Toxocara canis***

3. What zoonotic parasite from dogs or cats is commonly transmitted by ingesting infected fleas?

A. *Toxoplasma gondii*
B. *Dipylidium caninum*
C. *Giardia lamblia*
D. *Ancylostoma duodenale*

✅ **Answer: B. *Dipylidium caninum***

4. Which protozoan parasite, shed in cat feces, can cause congenital infections in humans?

A. *Cryptosporidium parvum*
B. *Giardia lamblia*
C. *Toxoplasma gondii*
D. *Balantidium coli*

✅ **Answer: C. *Toxoplasma gondii***

5. How can humans become infected with *Echinococcus granulosus* from dogs?

A. By eating undercooked pork
B. By ingesting contaminated water
C. By ingesting eggs from dog feces
D. Through mosquito bites

✅ **Answer: C. By ingesting eggs from dog feces**

6. Which parasite is associated with hydatid cyst disease in humans?

A. *Toxocara cati*
B. *Ancylostoma caninum*
C. *Echinococcus granulosus*
D. *Giardia duodenalis*

✅ **Answer: C. *Echinococcus granulosus***

7. Which zoonotic parasite is most likely to be acquired by contact with contaminated soil in areas with stray dogs and cats?

A. *Isospora felis*
B. *Toxoplasma gondii*
C. *Ancylostoma spp.*
D. *Cryptosporidium parvum*

✅ **Answer: C. *Ancylostoma spp.***

8. What is the main mode of transmission of *Toxoplasma gondii* from cats to humans?

A. Tick bites
B. Drinking cat urine
C. Ingestion of oocysts from cat feces
D. Aerosol inhalation

✅ **Answer: C. Ingestion of oocysts from cat feces**

9. *Giardia duodenalis* can be transmitted to humans from dogs and cats mainly through:

A. Flea bites
B. Contaminated food and water
C. Tick infestation
D. Scratches and bites

✅ **Answer: B. Contaminated food and water**

10. Which of the following is NOT a zoonotic parasite from dogs or cats?

A. *Toxocara canis*
B. *Ancylostoma caninum*
C. *Tritrichomonas foetus*
D. *Echinococcus multilocularis*

✅ **Answer: C. *Tritrichomonas foetus***

CHAPTER FOUR :POULTRY PARASITES QUESTIONS

HELMINTH PARASITES OF POULTRY

NEMATODES OF THE DIGESTIVE TRACT

Ascaridia galli

1. What type of parasite is Ascaridia galli?

A. Ectoparasite
B. Endoparasite
C. Facultative parasite
D. Free-living organism

Answer: B. Endoparasite
Explanation: Ascaridia galli lives inside the host's intestine, making it an endoparasite.

2. What is the primary host of Ascaridia galli?

A. Cattle
B. Dog
C. Chicken
D. Human

Answer: C. Chicken
Explanation: Ascaridia galli primarily infects domestic chickens and other birds.

3. Where in the host does Ascaridia galli reside?

A. Liver
B. Crop
C. Intestine
D. Lungs

Answer: C. Intestine
Explanation: The adult worms live in the small intestine of birds.

4. What is the mode of transmission of Ascaridia galli?

A. Skin penetration
B. Inhalation
C. Ingestion of infective eggs
D. Sexual contact

Answer: C. Ingestion of infective eggs
Explanation: Birds get infected by eating food or water contaminated with embryonated eggs.

5. What type of lifecycle does Ascaridia galli have?

A. Indirect lifecycle
B. Direct lifecycle
C. Complex lifecycle
D. Zoonotic lifecycle

Answer: B. Direct lifecycle
Explanation: The parasite does not require intermediate hosts to complete its lifecycle.

6. What is the infective stage of Ascaridia galli?

A. L1 larva
B. L2 larva
C. Embryonated egg containing L3 larva
D. Adult worm

Answer: C. Embryonated egg containing L3 larva
Explanation: The infective stage is the embryonated egg containing the third-stage larva (L3).

7. Which of the following clinical signs is commonly associated with Ascaridia galli infection?

A. Coughing
B. Diarrhea
C. Feather loss
D. Lameness

Answer: B. Diarrhea
Explanation: Infected birds may show diarrhea, stunted growth, weight loss, and reduced egg production.

8. How can Ascaridia galli be diagnosed?

A. Skin scraping
B. ELISA
C. Fecal flotation
D. X-ray

Answer: C. Fecal flotation
Explanation: Eggs of A. galli can be detected in feces using fecal flotation techniques.

9. Which drug is commonly used to treat Ascaridia galli infections in poultry?

A. Metronidazole
B. Albendazole
C. Praziquantel
D. Ivermectin

Answer: B. Albendazole
Explanation: Albendazole or fenbendazole are commonly used anthelmintics against A. galli.

10. What is the shape of Ascaridia galli eggs?

A. Lemon-shaped
B. Oval and thick-shelled
C. Barrel-shaped
D. Crescent-shaped

Answer: B. Oval and thick-shelled
Explanation: Eggs of A. galli are oval, smooth, and thick-shelled, and appear yellow-brown under the microscope.

Porrocaecum crissum

MCQs on *Porrocaecum* (Nematoda / Ascaridoidea)

1. **In *Porrocaecum*, the anterior end typically has how many lips?**
   A. Two
   B. Three
   C. Four
   D. Five
   Answer: B. Three
2. Which structure is ***absent*** in ***Porrocaecum*** among these?
   A. Cervical alae
   B. Intestinal caecum
   C. Muscular esophagus
   D. Dorsal lip with papillae
   Answer: A. Cervical alae

3. **In the life cycle of *Porrocaecum ensicaudatum*, the second-stage larvae infect which host?**

A. Definitive vertebrate host
B. Terrestrial oligochaetes (earthworms)
C. Aquatic crustacean
D. Mollusc
Answer: B. Terrestrial oligochaetes

4. **Which of the following is true about the development inside the egg of *Porrocaecum ensicaudatum*?**
A. Development stops above 30 °C
B. First-stage larvae moult within the egg
C. Larvae are released externally immediately after egg laying
D. There is direct development without larval stages
Answer: B. First-stage larvae moult within the egg

5. **Which is a known definitive host for *Porrocaecum decipiens*?**
A. Fish
B. Birds
C. Seals
D. Earthworms
Answer: C. Seals Canadian Science Publishing

6. **Which taxonomic rank is just above genus *Porrocaecum*?**
A. Order
B. Family
C. Subfamily
D. Class
Answer: C. Subfamily

7. **In *Porrocaecum*, the ventriculus (stomach) is typically described as:**
A. Wider than long
B. Rectangular with length > width
C. Spherical
D. Absent
Answer: B. Rectangular with length > width

8. **Which best describes the tail in *Porrocaecum* adults?**
   A. Blunt and short
   B. Filiform
   C. Conical with a mucron
   D. Spirally coiled
   Answer: C. Conical with a mucron

9. **Which is *not* typically a host or stage in the *Porrocaecum* life cycle?**
   A. Earthworms
   B. Fish
   C. Birds
   D. Insects like beetles
   Answer: D. Insects like beetles

10. **Molecular phylogenetic analyses of *Porrocaecum* species suggest**
    A. *Porrocaecum* belongs to Cestoda
    B. That subfamily **Porrocaecinae** should be recognized
    C. *Porrocaecum* is more closely related to trematodes
    D. All species have identical mitochondrial genomes
    Answer: B. That subfamily Porrocaecinae should be recognized

MCQs on *Histomonas meleagridis* and *Heterakis gallinarum*:

1. What disease is caused by *Histomonas meleagridis* in turkeys?
A. Coccidiosis
B. Newcastle disease
C. Histomoniasis (Blackhead disease)
D. Marek's disease
C. Histomoniasis (Blackhead disease)

2. What is the primary vector for *Histomonas meleagridis*?
A. Ascaridia galli
B. Heterakis gallinarum
C. Eimeria tenella
D. Trichomonas gallinae
B. Heterakis gallinarum

3. What is the typical lesion seen in the liver of birds infected with *Histomonas meleagridis*?
A. Granulomas
B. Hemorrhagic spots
C. Circular necrotic lesions
D. Fibrotic nodules
→ **C. Circular necrotic lesions**

4. Which of the following birds is most susceptible to blackhead disease?
A. Chickens
B. Ducks
C. Turkeys
D. Geese
→ **C. Turkeys**

5. How does *Histomonas meleagridis* reach the bird's body?
A. Direct ingestion from contaminated water
B. Transovarian transmission
C. Ingestion of *Heterakis gallinarum* eggs containing the protozoa
D. Inhalation of spores
→ **C. Ingestion of *Heterakis gallinarum* eggs containing the protozoa**

6. What type of organism is *Histomonas meleagridis*?
A. Bacterium
B. Nematode
C. Protozoan
D. Fungus
→ **C. Protozoan**

7. Which organ systems are primarily affected by *Histomonas meleagridis*?
A. Respiratory and nervous
B. Digestive and liver
C. Circulatory and skin
D. Musculoskeletal and renal
→ **B. Digestive and liver**

8. What is the role of *Heterakis gallinarum* in the life cycle of *Histomonas meleagridis*?
A. Final host
B. Vector and intermediate host
C. Irrelevant to transmission
D. Only mechanical carrier
→ **B. Vector and intermediate host**

9. What control measure helps reduce transmission of histomoniasis?
A. Vaccination
B. Reducing water supply
C. Deworming to eliminate *Heterakis gallinarum*
D. Use of antibiotics
→ **C. Deworming to eliminate *Heterakis gallinarum***

10. Which of the following is a common symptom of histomoniasis in turkeys?
A. Blue comb and lethargy
B. Sneezing and nasal discharge
C. Leg paralysis
D. Crop impaction
→ **A. Blue comb and lethargy**

Subulura brumpti

1. Subulura brumpti primarily infects which type of host?

A. Ruminants
B. Poultry
C. Dogs
D. Humans
Answer: B. Poultry

2. The adult Subulura brumpti is typically found in which part of the host?

A. Lungs
B. Intestine (cecum)
C. Liver
D. Crop
Answer: B. Intestine (cecum)

3. What is the intermediate host for Subulura brumpti?

A. Mosquito
B. Earthworm
C. Beetle
D. Ant
Answer: C. Beetle

4. The eggs of Subulura brumpti resemble those of which parasite?

A. Ascaridia galli
B. Capillaria spp.
C. Heterakis gallinarum
D. Trichuris spp.
Answer: C. Heterakis gallinarum

5. What is the shape of the Subulura brumpti egg?

A. Oval with polar plugs
B. Barrel-shaped
C. Spherical
D. Elliptical with smooth shell
Answer: D. Elliptical with smooth shell

6. How is Subulura brumpti transmitted to the definitive host?

A. Inhalation of larvae
B. Direct skin penetration
C. Ingestion of infected beetles
D. Transplacental transmission
Answer: C. Ingestion of infected beetles

7. Which of the following is a common clinical sign of subuluriasis in poultry?

A. Diarrhea and poor growth
B. Convulsions
C. Coughing
D. Feather loss
Answer: A. Diarrhea and poor growth

8. Subulura brumpti is more commonly seen in which species?

A. Ducks
B. Pigeons
C. Turkeys
D. Quail
Answer: C. Turkeys

9. What is the main control strategy for Subulura brumpti infection?

A. Vaccination
B. Vector control
C. Deworming and controlling beetle population
D. Isolation of infected birds
Answer: C. Deworming and controlling beetle population

10. Which class of anthelmintics is commonly used against Subulura brumpti?

A. Tetracyclines
B. Benzimidazoles
C. Fluoroquinolones
D. Macrolides
Answer: B. Benzimidazoles

Strongyloides avium

1. What is Strongyloides avium?

A. A protozoan parasite
B. A fungal infection
C. A nematode parasite
D. A bacterial disease
Answer: C. A nematode parasite

2. What is the typical host for Strongyloides avium?

A. Humans
B. Dogs
C. Birds (especially ducks and geese)
D. Rodents
Answer: C. Birds (especially ducks and geese)

3. Where in the host does Strongyloides avium primarily reside?

A. Liver
B. Small intestine
C. Lungs
D. Bloodstream
Answer: B. Small intestine

4. What is the typical mode of transmission for Strongyloides avium?

A. Inhalation
B. Ingestion of contaminated food or water
C. Skin penetration by infective larvae
D. Vector-borne via mosquitoes
Answer: C. Skin penetration by infective larvae

5. Which stage of Strongyloides avium is infective to the host?

A. Egg
B. Rhabditiform larva
C. Filariform larva
D. Adult worm
Answer: C. Filariform larva

6. What is a common clinical sign of Strongyloides avium infection in birds?

A. Feather loss
B. Respiratory distress
C. Diarrhea and weight loss
D. Paralysis
Answer: C. Diarrhea and weight loss

7. How can Strongyloides avium be diagnosed in birds?

A. Blood smear
B. Fecal flotation or larval culture
C. X-ray
D. Skin scraping
Answer: B. Fecal flotation or larval culture

8. Which of the following best describes the life cycle of Strongyloides avium?

A. Direct life cycle without free-living stage
B. Indirect life cycle involving an intermediate host
C. Both parasitic and free-living life cycle phases
D. Only a free-living life cycle
Answer: C. Both parasitic and free-living life cycle phases

9. Which drug is commonly used to treat Strongyloides infections in birds?

A. Ivermectin
B. Amoxicillin
C. Ketoconazole
D. Praziquantel
Answer: A. Ivermectin

10. Which environmental condition favors the development of Strongyloides larvae?

A. Cold and dry environments
B. High-altitude regions
C. Warm and moist environments
D. Saline water
Answer: C. Warm and moist environments

C. annulata

1. What is the primary host for *Capillaria annulata*?

A) Humans
B) Dogs
C) Poultry (chickens, turkeys, etc.)
D) Cattle
Answer: ✅ C) Poultry (chickens, turkeys, etc.)

2. Which part of the body does *Capillaria annulata* primarily infect?

A) Intestine
B) Trachea
C) Crop and esophagus
D) Lungs
Answer: ✅ C) Crop and esophagus

3. What is the typical mode of transmission for *Capillaria annulata*?

A) Direct skin penetration
B) Inhalation
C) Ingestion of embryonated eggs or infected earthworms
D) Blood-sucking insects
Answer: ✅ C) Ingestion of embryonated eggs or infected earthworms

4. Which of the following is a clinical sign of *Capillaria annulata* infection in birds?

A) Feather loss
B) Sneezing
C) Emaciation and difficulty swallowing
D) Excessive salivation
Answer: ✅ C) Emaciation and difficulty swallowing

5. What type of life cycle does *Capillaria annulata* have?

A) Direct
B) Indirect (requires intermediate host)
C) Parthenogenetic
D) No life cycle
Answer: ✅ B) Indirect (requires intermediate host – usually earthworms)

6. What is the shape of *Capillaria annulata* eggs?

A) Oval with a thick shell
B) Barrel-shaped with bipolar plugs
C) Round with a single operculum
D) Oval with pointed ends
Answer: ✅ B) Barrel-shaped with bipolar plugs

7. Which diagnostic method is commonly used to detect *Capillaria annulata*?

A) Blood smear
B) Radiography
C) Fecal flotation and crop scraping
D) PCR test only
Answer: ✅ C) Fecal flotation and crop scraping

8. What is the best preventive strategy for *Capillaria annulata* infection?

A) Regular deworming only
B) Isolating infected birds
C) Preventing access to earthworms and maintaining hygiene
D) Using antibiotics regularly
Answer: ✅ C) Preventing access to earthworms and maintaining hygiene

9. What is a potential consequence of heavy *Capillaria annulata* infestation in poultry?

A) Egg binding
B) Crop impaction and death
C) Feather pecking
D) Foot rot
Answer: ✅ B) Crop impaction and death

10. Which of the following anthelmintics is commonly used to treat *Capillaria annulata*?

A) Amoxicillin
B) Levamisole
C) Tylosin
D) Ivermectin
Answer: ✅ B) Levamisole

Capillaria caudinflata

1. What is the primary host of *Capillaria caudinflata*?

A. Humans
B. Cattle
C. Birds (especially poultry)
D. Dogs
Answer: C. Birds (especially poultry)

2. Where in the host does *Capillaria caudinflata* typically localize?

A. Trachea
B. Intestine and caecum
C. Liver
D. Lungs
Answer: B. Intestine and caecum

3. What is the life cycle type of *Capillaria caudinflata*?

A. Direct only
B. Indirect only
C. Both direct and indirect
D. Requires three hosts
Answer: C. Both direct and indirect

4. What intermediate host can be involved in the indirect life cycle of *Capillaria caudinflata*?

A. Earthworm
B. Mosquito
C. Snail
D. Tick
Answer: A. Earthworm

5. What is the shape of *Capillaria caudinflata* eggs?

A. Oval and smooth
B. Barrel-shaped with bipolar plugs
C. Round and rough
D. Elongated and striated
Answer: B. Barrel-shaped with bipolar plugs

6. What is a common clinical sign in birds infected with *Capillaria caudinflata*?

A. Sneezing
B. Bloody diarrhea
C. Weight loss and reduced egg production
D. Skin lesions
Answer: C. Weight loss and reduced egg production

7. How can *Capillaria caudinflata* infection be diagnosed?

A. PCR only
B. Radiography
C. Fecal flotation to detect eggs
D. Blood smear
Answer: C. Fecal flotation to detect eggs

8. Which drug is commonly used to treat *Capillaria caudinflata* infection in poultry?

A. Ivermectin
B. Levamisole
C. Albendazole
D. All of the above
Answer: D. All of the above

9. Which of the following best describes the appearance of adult *Capillaria caudinflata* worms?

A. Flat and segmented
B. Thread-like, slender nematodes
C. Leaf-shaped flukes
D. Hook-shaped roundworms
Answer: B. Thread-like, slender nematodes

10. How can *Capillaria caudinflata* infections be controlled in poultry farms?

A. Regular deworming
B. Proper disposal of litter
C. Avoiding access to intermediate hosts like earthworms
D. All of the above
Answer: D. All of the above

Capillaria bursata

1. What type of organism is *Capillaria bursata*?

A. Protozoan
B. Trematode
C. Cestode
D. Nematode
Answer: D. Nematode

2. What is the primary host of *Capillaria bursata*?

A. Humans
B. Birds
C. Rodents
D. Cats
Answer: C. Rodents

3. Where in the host is *Capillaria bursata* primarily found?

A. Liver
B. Intestines
C. Lungs
D. Urinary bladder
Answer: B. Intestines

4. *Capillaria bursata* belongs to which family?

A. Ascarididae
B. Trichuridae
C. Capillariidae
D. Strongylidae
Answer: C. Capillariidae

5. What is the characteristic shape of *Capillaria bursata* eggs?

A. Oval with thick shell
B. Barrel-shaped with bipolar plugs
C. Spherical with operculum
D. Crescent-shaped
Answer: B. Barrel-shaped with bipolar plugs

6. What is the mode of transmission of *Capillaria bursata*?

A. Skin penetration
B. Ingestion of infective eggs
C. Biting insects
D. Vertical transmission
Answer: B. Ingestion of infective eggs

7. What kind of lifecycle does *Capillaria bursata* have?

A. Direct
B. Indirect with intermediate host
C. Both direct and indirect
D. Parthenogenetic
Answer: A. Direct

8. What is a common symptom in rodents infected with *Capillaria bursata*?

A. Anemia
B. Diarrhea
C. Cough
D. Seizures
Answer: B. Diarrhea

9. Which diagnostic method is commonly used to detect *Capillaria bursata* infection?

A. Blood smear
B. Skin scraping
C. Fecal flotation
D. ELISA
Answer: C. Fecal flotation

10. What is the most effective way to control *Capillaria bursata* infection in lab animals?

A. Vaccination
B. Deworming and sanitation
C. Isolation of infected humans
D. Antibiotic therapy
Answer: B. Deworming and sanitation

Tetrameres Americana

1. What type of organism is *Tetrameres americana*?

A. Bacterium
B. Virus
C. Parasitic nematode
D. Fungus
Answer: C. Parasitic nematode

2. Which host is primarily infected by *Tetrameres americana*?

A. Humans
B. Chickens and other birds
C. Dogs
D. Fish
Answer: B. Chickens and other birds

3. Where in the host's body is *Tetrameres americana* usually found?

A. Intestine
B. Lungs
C. Proventriculus
D. Liver
Answer: C. Proventriculus

4. What is the role of intermediate hosts in the life cycle of *Tetrameres americana*?

A. They are not involved
B. They transmit the parasite through the air
C. They carry the larval stages of the parasite
D. They provide immunity to the parasite
Answer: C. They carry the larval stages of the parasite

5. What is a common intermediate host for *Tetrameres americana*?

A. Earthworms
B. Mosquitoes
C. Grasshoppers
D. Ants
Answer: C. Grasshoppers

6. How do birds typically become infected with *Tetrameres americana*?

A. Inhalation of spores
B. Eating infected intermediate hosts
C. Contact with infected birds
D. Drinking contaminated water
Answer: B. Eating infected intermediate hosts

7. What is a common clinical sign of heavy *Tetrameres americana* infection in birds?

A. Feathers falling off
B. Blood in stool
C. Emaciation and poor growth
D. Aggression
Answer: C. Emaciation and poor growth

8. What does the female *Tetrameres americana* look like?

A. Small and thread-like
B. Red, globular, and embedded in tissue
C. Flat and leaf-shaped
D. Segmented like a tapeworm
Answer: B. Red, globular, and embedded in tissue

9. What diagnostic method is most effective for detecting *Tetrameres americana* infection?

A. Blood smear
B. X-ray
C. Necropsy and examination of the proventriculus
D. Fecal flotation only
Answer: C. Necropsy and examination of the proventriculus

10. What is the most effective way to control *Tetrameres americana* infections in poultry?

A. Vaccination
B. Antiviral treatment
C. Breaking the life cycle by controlling intermediate hosts
D. Increasing water supply
Answer: C. Breaking the life cycle by controlling intermediate hosts

Dispharynx nasuta *(Acuaria spiralis)*

1. What type of organism is *Dispharynx nasuta*?

A) Bacteria
B) Nematode parasite
C) Protozoan
D) Fungus

Answer: B) Nematode parasite

2. *Dispharynx nasuta* primarily infects which host?

A) Humans
B) Fish
C) Birds
D) Mammals

Answer: C) Birds

3. What is the primary site of infection of *Dispharynx nasuta* in its host?

A) Liver
B) Intestine
C) Stomach
D) Esophagus

Answer: D) Esophagus

4. The infection caused by *Dispharynx nasuta* is commonly known as:

A) Ascariasis
B) Esophageal worm infection
C) Tapeworm infection
D) Malaria

Answer: B) Esophageal worm infection

5. Which of the following best describes the life cycle of *Dispharynx nasuta*?

A) Direct life cycle without intermediate host
B) Indirect life cycle involving an intermediate host
C) Sexual reproduction outside the host
D) None of the above

Answer: B) Indirect life cycle involving an intermediate host

6. What is the intermediate host commonly involved in the life cycle of *Dispharynx nasuta*?

A) Earthworms
B) Snails
C) Mosquitoes
D) Fleas

Answer: A) Earthworms

7. How is *Dispharynx nasuta* transmitted to the definitive host?

A) Ingestion of contaminated water
B) Bite of an infected insect
C) Eating infected intermediate host
D) Airborne spores

Answer: C) Eating infected intermediate host

8. Which of the following symptoms is commonly observed in birds infected with *Dispharynx nasuta*?

A) Diarrhea
B) Respiratory distress
C) Difficulty swallowing and weight loss
D) Skin lesions

Answer: C) Difficulty swallowing and weight loss

9. Which diagnostic method is most commonly used to identify *Dispharynx nasuta* infection?

A) Blood smear
B) Fecal examination for eggs
C) Skin biopsy
D) Urine analysis

Answer: B) Fecal examination for eggs

10. The treatment for *Dispharynx nasuta* infection usually involves:

A) Antibiotics
B) Anthelmintic drugs
C) Antiviral drugs
D) Vaccination

Answer: B) Anthelmintic drugs

Acuaria uncinata

1. What is Acuaria uncinata?

a) A species of plant
b) A parasitic nematode
c) A type of bacteria
d) A virus

Answer: b) A parasitic nematode

2. Acuaria uncinata primarily infects which type of host?

a) Humans
b) Fish
c) Birds
d) Mammals

Answer: c) Birds

3. The scientific classification of Acuaria uncinata belongs to which phylum?

a) Arthropoda
b) Nematoda
c) Platyhelminthes
d) Annelida

Answer: b) Nematoda

4. What is the common mode of transmission for Acuaria uncinata?

a) Airborne spores
b) Ingestion of infected intermediate hosts
c) Direct skin contact
d) Blood transfusion

Answer: b) Ingestion of infected intermediate hosts

5. Which intermediate host is commonly involved in the life cycle of Acuaria uncinata?

a) Snails
b) Insects such as beetles or grasshoppers
c) Fish
d) Rodents

Answer: b) Insects such as beetles or grasshoppers

6. What is the main pathological effect of Acuaria uncinata in its bird hosts?

a) Respiratory distress
b) Intestinal blockage and damage
c) Skin lesions
d) Neurological symptoms

Answer: b) Intestinal blockage and damage

7. Which part of the bird is mainly affected by Acuaria uncinata?

a) Lungs
b) Intestines
c) Liver
d) Brain

Answer: b) Intestines

8. How can infection by Acuaria uncinata be diagnosed in birds?

a) Blood test for antibodies
b) Identification of eggs or adult worms in feces
c) Skin biopsy
d) X-ray imaging

Answer: b) Identification of eggs or adult worms in feces

9. Which of the following is a control measure for Acuaria uncinata infection?

a) Vaccination
b) Use of anthelmintics (dewormers)
c) Quarantine of infected birds only
d) Increasing bird exposure to intermediate hosts

Answer: b) Use of anthelmintics (dewormers)

10. The genus Acuaria is primarily studied in relation to which field?

a) Veterinary parasitology
b) Botany
c) Microbiology
d) Virology

Answer: a) Veterinary parasitology

Eustrongyloides papillosus

1. What type of organism is *Eustrongyloides papillosus*?

A) Protozoan
B) Nematode
C) Trematode
D) Cestode

Answer: B) Nematode

2. What is the primary host of *Eustrongyloides papillosus*?

A) Humans
B) Cattle and sheep
C) Birds
D) Fish

Answer: B) Cattle and sheep

3. *Eustrongyloides papillosus* primarily infects which part of the host?

A) Lungs
B) Intestine
C) Liver
D) Muscle

Answer: B) Intestine

4. What is the common mode of transmission of *Eustrongyloides papillosus*?

A) Ingestion of contaminated water
B) Skin penetration by larvae
C) Direct contact with infected animals
D) Inhalation of airborne eggs

Answer: B) Skin penetration by larvae

5. Which stage of *Eustrongyloides papillosus* is

infective to the host?

A) Egg
B) First-stage larva (L1)
C) Third-stage larva (L3)
D) Adult worm

Answer: C) Third-stage larva (L3)

6. What is the typical diagnostic method for detecting *Eustrongyloides papillosus* infection?

A) Blood smear
B) Fecal examination for eggs
C) Urine analysis
D) Skin biopsy

Answer: B) Fecal examination for eggs

7. What kind of lifecycle does *Eustrongyloides papillosus* have?

A) Direct lifecycle
B) Indirect lifecycle with intermediate host
C) Complex lifecycle involving multiple hosts
D) Free-living only

Answer: A) Direct lifecycle

8. What is a common clinical sign of *Eustrongyloides papillosus* infection in livestock?

A) Diarrhea and weight loss
B) Coughing and nasal discharge
C) Skin lesions
D) Paralysis

Answer: A) Diarrhea and weight loss

9. Which of the following drugs is commonly used to treat *Eustrongyloides papillosus* infection?

A) Praziquantel
B) Albendazole
C) Chloroquine
D) Penicillin

Answer: B) Albendazole

10. *Eustrongyloides papillosus* larvae can survive in which environmental condition?

A) Dry and hot soil
B) Moist and shaded soil
C) Saltwater
D) Frozen soil

Answer: B) Moist and shaded soil

Acuaria hamulosa

1. What type of organism is *Acuaria hamulosa*?

A) Bacteria
B) Fungus
C) Parasitic nematode
D) Algae

Answer: C) Parasitic nematode

2. *Acuaria hamulosa* primarily infects which host?

A) Humans
B) Fish
C) Birds
D) Mammals

Answer: C) Birds

3. What is the common site of infection for *Acuaria hamulosa* in birds?

A) Intestine
B) Liver
C) Lungs
D) Stomach

Answer: D) Stomach

4. What is the typical morphology of *Acuaria hamulosa*?

A) Flatworm with segmented body
B) Roundworm with hooks on the head
C) Ciliated protozoan
D) Filamentous fungus

Answer: B) Roundworm with hooks on the head

5. How is *Acuaria hamulosa* transmitted to its avian host?

A) Through contaminated water
B) By ingestion of intermediate hosts like insects
C) Direct contact with infected birds
D) Airborne spores

Answer: B) By ingestion of intermediate hosts like insects

6. Which stage of *Acuaria hamulosa* life cycle is infective to birds?

A) Egg
B) Larva inside intermediate host
C) Adult worm
D) Free-living larva

Answer: B) Larva inside intermediate host

7. What kind of pathology does *Acuaria hamulosa* cause in infected birds?

A) Respiratory distress
B) Gastric ulcers and inflammation
C) Neurological damage
D) Skin lesions

Answer: B) Gastric ulcers and inflammation

8. Which group of birds is most commonly affected by *Acuaria hamulosa*?

A) Waterfowl
B) Passerines (songbirds)
C) Raptors
D) Domestic poultry

Answer: B) Passerines (songbirds)

9. How can infection with *Acuaria hamulosa* be diagnosed?

A) Blood test
B) Stool examination for eggs
C) Radiography
D) Skin biopsy

Answer: B) Stool examination for eggs

10. What is the recommended control measure for *Acuaria hamulosa* in birds?

A) Antibiotic treatment
B) Anthelmintic drugs and controlling insect intermediate hosts
C) Vaccination
D) Isolation of infected birds only

Answer: B) Anthelmintic drugs and controlling insect intermediate hosts

Amidostomum nodulosum

1. What type of organism is *Amidostomum nodulosum*?

a) Bacterium
b) Virus
c) Nematode
d) Protozoa

Answer: c) Nematode

2. *Amidostomum nodulosum* primarily infects which part of the host?

a) Intestines
b) Lungs
c) Crop and gizzard
d) Liver

Answer: c) Crop and gizzard

3. What is the common host for *Amidostomum nodulosum*?

a) Humans
b) Birds, especially waterfowl
c) Cattle
d) Fish

Answer: b) Birds, especially waterfowl

4. How is *Amidostomum nodulosum* transmitted?

a) Direct contact with infected birds
b) Ingestion of infective eggs
c) Through blood transfusion
d) Airborne droplets

Answer: b) Ingestion of infective eggs

5. What is the main pathology caused by *Amidostomum nodulosum*?

a) Liver cirrhosis
b) Crop and gizzard inflammation and nodules
c) Intestinal blockage
d) Respiratory distress

Answer: b) Crop and gizzard inflammation and nodules

6. What is the shape of *Amidostomum nodulosum* eggs?

a) Oval and thick-shelled
b) Round and thin-shelled
c) Elongated and segmented
d) Spiral and motile

Answer: a) Oval and thick-shelled

7. Which diagnostic method is commonly used to detect *Amidostomum nodulosum* infection?

a) Blood smear
b) Fecal flotation and egg identification
c) Skin scraping
d) Urine analysis

Answer: b) Fecal flotation and egg identification

8. What kind of life cycle does *Amidostomum nodulosum* have?

a) Direct life cycle
b) Indirect life cycle with intermediate host
c) Complex life cycle involving multiple hosts
d) Parasitic only in larvae form

Answer: a) Direct life cycle

9. What is the typical clinical sign of *Amidostomum nodulosum* infection in birds?

a) Coughing and sneezing
b) Weight loss and poor growth
c) Diarrhea and dehydration
d) Neurological symptoms

Answer: b) Weight loss and poor growth

10. Which of the following is a common treatment for *Amidostomum nodulosum* infection?

a) Antibiotics
b) Anthelmintics (e.g., fenbendazole)
c) Vaccination
d) Antiviral drugs

Answer: b) Anthelmintics (e.g., fenbendazole)

Strongylus anseris* or *Strongylus orispinum

1. What type of organism is *Strongylus anseris*?

A) Bacterium
B) Parasite
C) Virus
D) Fungus

Answer: B) Parasite

2. *Strongylus anseris* primarily infects which host?

A) Cattle
B) Horses
C) Geese
D) Dogs

Answer: C) Geese

3. What is the common site of infection of *Strongylus orispinum* in its host?

A) Liver
B) Intestines
C) Lungs
D) Brain

Answer: B) Intestines

4. What is the main clinical sign of *Strongylus* infection in birds?

A) Neurological symptoms
B) Diarrhea and weight loss
C) Skin lesions
D) Respiratory distress

Answer: B) Diarrhea and weight loss

5. How are *Strongylus* species typically transmitted?

A) Through contaminated water
B) Skin penetration by larvae
C) Ingestion of infective larvae
D) Vector-borne via ticks

Answer: C) Ingestion of infective larvae

6. Which stage of *Strongylus* life cycle is infective?

A) Egg
B) L1 Larvae
C) L3 Larvae
D) Adult

Answer: C) L3 Larvae

7. What is the diagnostic method commonly used for detecting *Strongylus* infections?

A) Blood smear
B) Fecal egg count
C) Skin biopsy
D) Urine analysis

Answer: B) Fecal egg count

8. What is the common treatment for *Strongylus* infection?

A) Antibiotics
B) Anthelmintics (dewormers)
C) Antivirals
D) Steroids

Answer: B) Anthelmintics (dewormers)

9. Which genus do *Strongylus anseris* and *Strongylus orispinum* belong to?

A) Ascaris
B) Strongylus
C) Trichuris
D) Fasciola

Answer: B) Strongylus

10. What is a preventive measure against *Strongylus* infections?

A) Vaccination
B) Proper sanitation and pasture management
C) Isolating infected animals in cold storage
D) High-dose vitamin supplements

Answer: B) Proper sanitation and pasture management

Amidostomum Anatinum

1. Amidostomum anatinum primarily infects which type of animal?

A) Cattle
B) Waterfowl (ducks and geese)
C) Cats
D) Pigs

Answer: B) Waterfowl (ducks and geese)

2. Amidostomum anatinum is classified as which type of parasite?

A) Cestode
B) Trematode
C) Nematode
D) Protozoan

Answer: C) Nematode

3. What is the primary site of infection for Amidostomum anatinum in its host?

A) Liver
B) Small intestine
C) Large intestine (ceca)
D) Lungs

Answer: C) Large intestine (ceca)

4. The primary mode of transmission for Amidostomum anatinum is through:

A) Skin penetration by larvae
B) Ingestion of embryonated eggs
C) Direct contact with infected birds
D) Bites from infected insects

Answer: B) Ingestion of embryonated eggs

5. What is the main clinical sign in birds infected with Amidostomum anatinum?

A) Respiratory distress
B) Anemia and weight loss
C) Neurological symptoms
D) Diarrhea with blood

Answer: B) Anemia and weight loss

6. Which of the following is a characteristic feature of Amidostomum anatinum eggs?

A) Operculated eggs
B) Thick-shelled, oval eggs
C) Thin-shelled, larvated eggs at laying
D) Eggs with polar plugs

Answer: B) Thick-shelled, oval eggs

7. Amidostomum anatinum belongs to which family?

A) Ascarididae
B) Strongylidae
C) Amidostomatidae
D) Trichuridae

Answer: C) Amidostomatidae

8. Which of the following control measures is most effective against Amidostomum anatinum?

A) Vaccination
B) Regular anthelmintic treatment and sanitation
C) Isolation of infected birds
D) Vector control

Answer: B) Regular anthelmintic treatment and sanitation

9. Amidostomum anatinum is commonly found in which geographic regions?

A) Tropical regions only
B) Worldwide, especially in temperate regions
C) Only in the Americas
D) Only in Africa

Answer: B) Worldwide, especially in temperate regions

10. What is the typical lifespan of Amidostomum anatinum in its host?

A) A few days
B) Several months
C) Several years
D) Lifelong

Answer: B) Several months

Trichostrongylus tenuis

1. What type of organism is *Trichostrongylus tenuis*?

A) Bacterium
B) Virus
C) Nematode (roundworm)
D) Protozoan

Answer: C) Nematode (roundworm)

2. *Trichostrongylus tenuis* primarily infects which host?

A) Humans
B) Sheep
C) Red grouse (bird)
D) Cattle

Answer: C) Red grouse (bird)

3. The main site of infection of *Trichostrongylus tenuis* in its host is the:

A) Intestine
B) Lungs
C) Caeca (part of the gut)
D) Liver

Answer: C) Caeca (part of the gut)

4. What is the mode of transmission of *Trichostrongylus tenuis*?

A) Ingestion of contaminated water
B) Skin penetration by larvae
C) Ingestion of infective larvae from vegetation
D) Bite from an insect vector

Answer: C) Ingestion of infective larvae from vegetation

5. The larvae of *Trichostrongylus tenuis* develop to the infective stage in:

A) Water
B) Soil and vegetation
C) Intermediate host
D) Host bloodstream

Answer: B) Soil and vegetation

6. What is the main effect of *Trichostrongylus tenuis* infection on the red grouse population?

A) Respiratory distress
B) Damage to caecal mucosa causing reduced nutrient absorption and mortality
C) Skin lesions
D) Neurological disorders

Answer: B) Damage to caecal mucosa causing reduced nutrient absorption and mortality

7. The eggs of *Trichostrongylus tenuis* are passed out of the host through:

A) Saliva
B) Urine
C) Feces
D) Blood

Answer: C) Feces

8. Which of the following is NOT true about *Trichostrongylus tenuis*?

A) It is a nematode parasite
B) It can infect humans frequently
C) It causes damage in the caeca of birds
D) It transmits via ingestion of larvae on plants

Answer: B) It can infect humans frequently

9. What control measure is commonly recommended for managing *Trichostrongylus tenuis* infection in wild bird populations?

A) Antibiotics
B) Anthelmintic treatment (deworming)
C) Vaccination
D) Vector control

Answer: B) Anthelmintic treatment (deworming)

10. The lifecycle of *Trichostrongylus tenuis* involves:

A) Direct lifecycle (no intermediate host)
B) Indirect lifecycle (with intermediate host)
C) Vector-borne transmission
D) Multiple hosts including mammals and birds

Answer: A) Direct lifecycle (no intermediate host)

NEMATODES IN OTHER ORGANS AND TISSUES

Oxyspirura mansoni

Oxyspirura mansoni MCQs

1. **What type of organism is Oxyspirura mansoni?**
   A) Bacteria
   B) Virus
   C) Nematode (roundworm)
   D) Protozoa

   Answer: C) Nematode (roundworm)

2. **Oxyspirura mansoni primarily infects which part of its host?**
   A) Intestine
   B) Eye and surrounding tissues
   C) Blood
   D) Liver

   Answer: B) Eye and surrounding tissues

3. **The common host of Oxyspirura mansoni is:**
   A) Dogs
   B) Poultry (chickens and other birds)
   C) Cattle
   D) Humans

   Answer: B) Poultry (chickens and other birds)

4. **What is the intermediate host of Oxyspirura mansoni?**
   A) Snails
   B) Cockroaches or other insects
   C) Fish
   D) Rodents

   Answer: B) Cockroaches or other insects

5. **What is the main clinical sign of Oxyspirura mansoni infection in birds?**
   A) Diarrhea
   B) Respiratory distress
   C) Eye irritation and conjunctivitis
   D) Weight loss

   Answer: C) Eye irritation and conjunctivitis

6. **Which stage of Oxyspirura mansoni is infectious to the definitive host?**
   A) Egg
   B) Larva inside intermediate host
   C) Adult worm
   D) Free-living larva in environment

   Answer: B) Larva inside intermediate host

7. **How is Oxyspirura mansoni transmitted to the definitive host?**
   A) Ingestion of contaminated water
   B) Skin penetration by larvae
   C) Ingestion of infected intermediate host (cockroach)
   D) Inhalation of eggs

   Answer: C) Ingestion of infected intermediate host (cockroach)

8. **Which diagnostic method is commonly used for detecting Oxyspirura mansoni infection?**
   A) Blood smear
   B) Fecal flotation for eggs
   C) Examination of eye secretions or conjunctival scrapings
   D) X-ray imaging

   Answer: C) Examination of eye secretions or conjunctival scrapings

9. **Which drug is commonly used to treat Oxyspirura mansoni infections?**
   A) Antibiotics
   B) Antifungals
   C) Anthelmintics like albendazole or ivermectin
   D) Antivirals

   Answer: C) Anthelmintics like albendazole or ivermectin

10. **What is the significance of controlling cockroach populations in managing Oxyspirura mansoni infections?**
A) Cockroaches are the definitive hosts
B) Cockroaches carry the infective larval stages and act as intermediate hosts
C) Cockroaches increase fecal contamination
D) Cockroaches spread viral infections

Answer: B) Cockroaches carry the infective larval stages and act as intermediate hosts

Syngamus trachea

Syngamus MCQs

1. **What is the common name of Syngamus trachea?**
a) Lungworm
b) Gapeworm
c) Intestinal worm
d) Liver fluke
Answer: b) Gapeworm

2. **Syngamus trachea primarily infects which organ in birds?**
a) Liver
b) Intestine
c) Trachea
d) Kidney
Answer: c) Trachea

3. **What type of organism is Syngamus trachea?**
a) Bacterium
b) Virus
c) Nematode (roundworm)
d) Trematode (fluke)
Answer: c) Nematode (roundworm)

4. **How is Syngamus trachea transmitted to birds?**
   a) Through contaminated water
   b) Through ingestion of infective larvae from the environment or intermediate hosts like earthworms
   c) By direct contact with infected birds
   d) Via airborne spores
   Answer: b) Through ingestion of infective larvae from the environment or intermediate hosts like earthworms

5. **What clinical sign is most characteristic of syngamiasis in birds?**
   a) Diarrhea
   b) Coughing and gasping for air (gaping)
   c) Feather loss
   d) Lameness
   Answer: b) Coughing and gasping for air (gaping)

6. **What is the typical appearance of Syngamus trachea worms when found in the trachea?**
   a) Small white threads
   b) Bright red Y-shaped worms
   c) Flat, leaf-like structures
   d) Round, segmented worms
   Answer: b) Bright red Y-shaped worms

7. **Which birds are most commonly affected by Syngamus trachea?**
   a) Only wild birds
   b) Only domestic birds like chickens and turkeys
   c) Both domestic and wild birds
   d) Only aquatic birds
   Answer: c) Both domestic and wild birds

8. **Which of the following is NOT an effective control measure for syngamiasis?**
   a) Proper sanitation and removal of intermediate hosts
   b) Regular deworming of birds
   c) Vaccination against Syngamus trachea
   d) Avoiding overcrowding
   Answer: c) Vaccination against Syngamus trachea

9. **How are Syngamus trachea eggs typically diagnosed?**
   a) Blood test
   b) Fecal flotation to detect eggs
   c) Skin scraping
   d) Urine analysis
   Answer: b) Fecal flotation to detect eggs

10. **What is the lifecycle of Syngamus trachea?**
   a) Direct lifecycle with no intermediate host
   b) Indirect lifecycle involving an intermediate host like earthworms or snails
   c) Lifecycle completed inside water only
   d) Requires a mammalian host for development
   Answer: b) Indirect lifecycle involving an intermediate host like earthworms or snails

CESTODES OF POULTRY

Raillietina

Echinobothrida

1. What type of parasite is *Raillietina echinobothrida*?

A) Nematode
B) Trematode
C) Cestode
D) Protozoa

Answer: C) Cestode

2. The primary host of *Raillietina echinobothrida* is:

A) Humans
B) Cattle
C) Poultry (chickens)
D) Fish

Answer: C) Poultry (chickens)

3. The intermediate host of *Raillietina echinobothrida* is usually:

A) Snail
B) Earthworm
C) Insect (beetle or ant)
D) Fish

Answer: C) Insect (beetle or ant)

4. Which part of the chicken does *Raillietina echinobothrida* primarily infect?

A) Liver
B) Intestine
C) Lungs
D) Muscle

Answer: B) Intestine

5. The body of *Raillietina echinobothrida* is:

A) Segmented with proglottids
B) Non-segmented and round
C) Flat and leaf-shaped without segments
D) Round and unsegmented

Answer: A) Segmented with proglottids

6. Which feature is characteristic of *Raillietina echinobothrida*'s scolex?

A) No hooks or suckers
B) Four suckers and hooks arranged in a rostellum
C) Only suckers, no hooks
D) Only hooks, no suckers

Answer: B) Four suckers and hooks arranged in a rostellum

7. The mode of transmission of *Raillietina echinobothrida* is:

A) Direct ingestion of eggs
B) Ingestion of infected intermediate host (insect)
C) Skin penetration by larvae
D) Blood transfusion

Answer: B) Ingestion of infected intermediate host (insect)

8. The diagnosis of *Raillietina echinobothrida* infection is mainly by:

A) Blood smear
B) Fecal examination for proglottids or eggs
C) Skin biopsy
D) Radiography

Answer: B) Fecal examination for proglottids or eggs

9. What is a common pathological effect of *Raillietina echinobothrida* in chickens?

A) Liver cirrhosis
B) Intestinal irritation and enteritis
C) Kidney failure
D) Brain damage

Answer: B) Intestinal irritation and enteritis

10. The treatment for *Raillietina echinobothrida* infection in poultry typically involves:

A) Antibiotics
B) Anthelmintics like praziquantel or niclosamide
C) Vaccination
D) Surgical removal

Answer: B) Anthelmintics like praziquantel or niclosamide

Raillientina cesticillus

1. What type of organism is *Raillietina cesticillus*?

A) Bacteria
B) Protozoan
C) Tapeworm (Cestode)
D) Nematode

Answer: C) Tapeworm (Cestode)

2. What is the primary host of *Raillietina cesticillus*?

A) Humans
B) Cattle
C) Poultry (chickens)
D) Fish

Answer: C) Poultry (chickens)

3. What is the common site of infection by *Raillietina cesticillus* in its host?

A) Small intestine
B) Liver
C) Lungs
D) Bloodstream

Answer: A) Small intestine

4. How is *Raillietina cesticillus* transmitted?

A) Ingestion of contaminated water
B) Ingestion of intermediate hosts like beetles or ants
C) Direct contact with infected poultry
D) Airborne spores

Answer: B) Ingestion of intermediate hosts like beetles or ants

5. What is the intermediate host for *Raillietina cesticillus*?

A) Mosquito
B) Earthworm
C) Beetle or ant
D) Snail

Answer: C) Beetle or ant

6. Which part of *Raillietina cesticillus* helps it attach to the host's intestine?

A) Scolex with suckers and hooks
B) Proglottids
C) Neck
D) Segments

Answer: A) Scolex with suckers and hooks

7. What type of lifecycle does *Raillietina cesticillus* have?

A) Direct lifecycle
B) Indirect lifecycle with intermediate host
C) Asexual reproduction only
D) Parthenogenetic lifecycle

Answer: B) Indirect lifecycle with intermediate host

8. What is a common symptom in poultry infected with *Raillietina cesticillus*?

A) Diarrhea and weight loss
B) Paralysis
C) Skin rash
D) Coughing

Answer: A) Diarrhea and weight loss

9. Which method is commonly used to diagnose *Raillietina cesticillus* infection?

A) Blood smear
B) Fecal examination for eggs or proglottids
C) Skin biopsy
D) X-ray

Answer: B) Fecal examination for eggs or proglottids

10. What is an effective treatment for *Raillietina cesticillus* infection in poultry?

A) Antibiotics
B) Anthelmintics like Praziquantel or Niclosamide
C) Vaccination
D) Anti-inflammatory drugs

Answer: B) Anthelmintics like Praziquantel or Niclosamide

Raillietina echinobothrida

1. What type of organism is *Raillietina echinobothrida*?

A) Bacterium
B) Protozoan
C) Cestode (tapeworm)
D) Nematode

Answer: C) Cestode (tapeworm)

2. The primary host for *Raillietina echinobothrida* is:

A) Humans
B) Poultry (chickens and turkeys)
C) Cattle
D) Fish

Answer: B) Poultry (chickens and turkeys)

3. What is the intermediate host of *Raillietina echinobothrida*?

A) Snail
B) Earthworm
C) Ant or beetle
D) Mosquito

Answer: C) Ant or beetle

4. *Raillietina echinobothrida* primarily infects which part of the host?

A) Liver
B) Intestine
C) Lungs
D) Blood

Answer: B) Intestine

5. The adult *Raillietina echinobothrida* attaches to the host using:

A) Suckers
B) Hooks on the scolex
C) Teeth
D) Claws

Answer: B) Hooks on the scolex

6. What is the main symptom in poultry infected with *Raillietina echinobothrida*?

A) Coughing
B) Diarrhea and weight loss
C) Skin lesions
D) Neurological signs

Answer: B) Diarrhea and weight loss

7. How is *Raillietina echinobothrida* transmitted to the definitive host?

A) Ingestion of contaminated water
B) Ingestion of intermediate host (ant or beetle) containing cysticercoid
C) Skin penetration by larvae
D) Inhalation of eggs

Answer: B) Ingestion of intermediate host (ant or beetle) containing cysticercoid

8. What stage of *Raillietina echinobothrida* is infective to the definitive host?

A) Egg
B) Miracidium
C) Cysticercoid
D) Adult worm

Answer: C) Cysticercoid

9. Which drug is commonly used to treat *Raillietina echinobothrida* infection in poultry?

A) Albendazole
B) Praziquantel
C) Metronidazole
D) Ivermectin

Answer: B) Praziquantel

10. Diagnosis of *Raillietina echinobothrida* infection is usually done by:

A) Blood smear
B) Fecal examination for eggs
C) Skin biopsy
D) Urine test

Answer: B) Fecal examination for eggs

Raillietina tetragona

1. What type of organism is *Raillietina tetragona*?

A) Bacterium
B) Protozoan
C) Cestode (tapeworm)
D) Nematode

Answer: C) Cestode (tapeworm)

2. *Raillietina tetragona* primarily infects which host?

A) Humans
B) Poultry (chickens)
C) Fish
D) Cattle

Answer: B) Poultry (chickens)

3. What is the intermediate host of *Raillietina tetragona*?

A) Snail
B) Earthworm
C) Beetle
D) Mosquito

Answer: C) Beetle

4. Which part of the host does *Raillietina tetragona* inhabit?

A) Liver
B) Intestine
C) Lungs
D) Stomach

Answer: B) Intestine

5. What is the main mode of transmission of *Raillietina tetragona* to poultry?

A) Ingestion of contaminated water
B) Skin penetration by larvae
C) Ingestion of infected beetles
D) Direct contact with infected birds

Answer: C) Ingestion of infected beetles

6. The body of *Raillietina tetragona* is segmented and called:

A) Proglottids
B) Scolex
C) Cysticercoid
D) Trophozoite

Answer: A) Proglottids

7. What is the function of the scolex in *Raillietina tetragona*?

A) Reproduction
B) Attachment to the host intestine
C) Digestion
D) Movement

Answer: B) Attachment to the host intestine

8. Which structure does *Raillietina tetragona* use to attach to the host's intestinal wall?

A) Hooks and suckers on the scolex
B) Flagella
C) Cilia
D) Pseudopodia

Answer: A) Hooks and suckers on the scolex

9. What is a common symptom in poultry infected with *Raillietina tetragona*?

A) Diarrhea and weight loss
B) Coughing
C) Skin rash
D) Paralysis

Answer: A) Diarrhea and weight loss

10. How can *Raillietina tetragona* infection in poultry be controlled?

A) Regular deworming and controlling beetle population
B) Vaccination
C) Isolation of infected birds only
D) Feeding antibiotics

Answer: A) Regular deworming and controlling beetle population

Cotugnia digonopora

Cotugnia digonopora: MCQs

1. **Cotugnia digonopora is classified as a type of:**
   - A) Bacteria
   - B) Protozoa
   - C) Cestode (tapeworm)
   - D) Nematode

   Answer: C) Cestode (tapeworm)
2. **What is the primary host of Cotugnia digonopora?**
   - A) Humans
   - B) Birds
   - C) Fish
   - D) Mammals

   Answer: B) Birds
3. **The infection caused by Cotugnia digonopora is primarily found in the:**
   - A) Intestines
   - B) Liver
   - C) Lungs
   - D) Bloodstream

   Answer: A) Intestines
4. **How is Cotugnia digonopora usually transmitted?**
   - A) Through contaminated water
   - B) By ingesting intermediate hosts such as insects
   - C) Through airborne spores
   - D) Direct skin penetration

   Answer: B) By ingesting intermediate hosts such as insects
5. **Cotugnia digonopora is part of which family?**
   - A) Taeniidae
   - B) Davaineidae
   - C) Dipylidiidae
   - D) Hymenolepididae

   Answer: B) Davaineidae
6. **The intermediate host of Cotugnia digonopora is usually:**
   - A) Snail
   - B) Cockroach
   - C) Beetle
   - D) Earthworm

   Answer: C) Beetle

7. **Which part of Cotugnia digonopora helps it attach to the host's intestinal wall?**
   - A) Scolex
   - B) Proglottids
   - C) Hooks
   - D) Suckers

   Answer: A) Scolex
8. **The gravid proglottids of Cotugnia digonopora contain:**
   - A) Larvae
   - B) Eggs
   - C) Cysts
   - D) Spores

   Answer: B) Eggs
9. **The disease caused by Cotugnia digonopora is typically called:**
   - A) Cysticercosis
   - B) Cotugniasis
   - C) Hydatidosis
   - D) Taeniasis

   Answer: B) Cotugniasis
10. **Which diagnostic method is commonly used to detect Cotugnia digonopora infection?**
    - A) Blood smear
    - B) Stool examination for eggs or proglottids
    - C) Urine analysis
    - D) X-ray imaging

    Answer: B) Stool examination for eggs or proglottids

Amoebotaenia cuneate

1. What type of organism is Amoebotaenia cuneata?

A) Bacterium
B) Protozoan
C) Cestode (tapeworm)
D) Nematode

Answer: C) Cestode (tapeworm)

2. What is the primary host of Amoebotaenia cuneata?

A) Humans
B) Fish
C) Birds (especially chickens)
D) Cattle

Answer: C) Birds (especially chickens)

3. Which class does Amoebotaenia cuneata belong to?

A) Trematoda
B) Cestoda
C) Nematoda
D) Annelida

Answer: B) Cestoda

4. The larvae of Amoebotaenia cuneata typically develop in which type of intermediate host?

A) Fish
B) Arthropods
C) Earthworms
D) Snails

Answer: C) Earthworms

5. The scolex of Amoebotaenia cuneata is characterized by:

A) Presence of hooks and suckers
B) Absence of hooks and suckers
C) Only hooks, no suckers
D) Only suckers, no hooks

Answer: B) Absence of hooks and suckers

6. Which part of the host does Amoebotaenia cuneata mainly infect?

A) Intestine
B) Liver
C) Blood vessels
D) Muscle tissue

Answer: A) Intestine

7. How is Amoebotaenia cuneata transmitted to its definitive host?

A) By ingestion of infected water
B) By ingestion of infected intermediate hosts (earthworms)
C) Through skin penetration
D) Via insect bites

Answer: B) By ingestion of infected intermediate hosts (earthworms)

8. Which of the following best describes the body shape of Amoebotaenia cuneata?

A) Segmented and ribbon-like
B) Round and unsegmented
C) Flat and unsegmented
D) Cylindrical and segmented

Answer: A) Segmented and ribbon-like

9. What is the primary symptom in chickens infected with Amoebotaenia cuneata?

A) Diarrhea
B) Weight loss and decreased egg production
C) Coughing
D) Skin lesions

Answer: B) Weight loss and decreased egg production

10. Which of the following is a common diagnostic method for Amoebotaenia cuneata infection?

A) Blood smear
B) Fecal examination for eggs
C) Skin scraping
D) Serological test

Answer: B) Fecal examination for eggs

Davainea proglottina

1. What type of organism is *Davainea proglottina*?
A) Bacterium
B) Protozoan
C) Tapeworm (cestode)
D) Nematode

Answer: C) Tapeworm (cestode)

2. *Davainea proglottina* primarily infects which host?
A) Humans
B) Fish
C) Birds
D) Mammals

Answer: C) Birds

3. What is the intermediate host for *Davainea proglottina*?
A) Earthworm
B) Snail
C) Beetle
D) Ant

Answer: B) Snail

4. Which part of the bird does *Davainea proglottina* typically infect?
A) Intestine
B) Liver
C) Lungs
D) Brain

Answer: A) Intestine

5. How does *Davainea proglottina* attach to the host's intestine?
A) Using hooks on its scolex
B) Using suction cups
C) By burrowing into the tissue
D) It does not attach, it floats freely

Answer: A) Using hooks on its scolex

6. What is the common disease caused by *Davainea proglottina* infection in birds?
A) Coccidiosis
B) Davaineiasis
C) Histomoniasis
D) Aspergillosis

Answer: B) Davaineiasis

7. What is the main symptom in birds infected with *Davainea proglottina*?
A) Respiratory distress
B) Diarrhea and weight loss
C) Feather loss
D) Neurological symptoms

Answer: B) Diarrhea and weight loss

8. How is *Davainea proglottina* transmitted to birds?
A) Ingestion of infected snails
B) Direct contact with infected birds
C) Inhalation of eggs
D) Through mosquito bite

Answer: A) Ingestion of infected snails

9. Which class does *Davainea proglottina* belong to?
A) Trematoda
B) Cestoda
C) Nematoda
D) Protozoa

Answer: B) Cestoda

10. What is the diagnostic method for *Davainea proglottina* infection?
A) Blood smear examination
B) Fecal examination for eggs or proglottids
C) Skin biopsy
D) X-ray imaging

Choanotaenia infundibulum

1. What type of organism is *Choanotaenia infundibulum*?

A) Bacteria
B) Protozoa
C) Cestode (tapeworm)
D) Nematode

Answer: C) Cestode (tapeworm)

2. *Choanotaenia infundibulum* is primarily found in which host?

A) Humans
B) Birds
C) Fish
D) Mammals

Answer: B) Birds

3. What is the common intermediate host of *Choanotaenia infundibulum*?

A) Earthworm
B) Mosquito
C) Ant
D) Beetle larva

Answer: D) Beetle larva

4. What is the primary site of infection of *Choanotaenia infundibulum* in the definitive host?

A) Intestine
B) Liver
C) Blood
D) Muscle

Answer: A) Intestine

5. *Choanotaenia infundibulum* belongs to which family?

A) Taeniidae
B) Davaineidae
C) Hymenolepididae
D) Dipylidiidae

Answer: B) Davaineidae

6. The body of *Choanotaenia infundibulum* is:

A) Segmented
B) Unsegmented
C) Cylindrical and smooth
D) Flattened but unsegmented

Answer: A) Segmented

7. What is the mode of transmission for *Choanotaenia infundibulum*?

A) Direct contact
B) Ingestion of infected intermediate host
C) Vector bite
D) Inhalation

Answer: B) Ingestion of infected intermediate host

8. The larval stage of *Choanotaenia infundibulum* found in the intermediate host is called:

A) Miracidium
B) Cysticercus
C) Oncosphere
D) Procercoid

Answer: C) Oncosphere

9. Which of the following symptoms is commonly seen in birds infected with *Choanotaenia infundibulum*?

A) Diarrhea and weight loss
B) Neurological symptoms
C) Respiratory distress
D) Skin lesions

Answer: A) Diarrhea and weight loss

10. How can infection with *Choanotaenia infundibulum* be prevented in poultry farms?

A) Regular vaccination
B) Avoiding intermediate host exposure
C) Using antibiotics
D) Quarantine of infected birds

Answer: B) Avoiding intermediate host exposure

Hymenolepis cantaniana

1. What type of organism is *Hymenolepis cantaniana*?

A) Bacterium
B) Protozoan
C) Cestode (tapeworm)
D) Nematode

Answer: C) Cestode (tapeworm)

2. *Hymenolepis cantaniana* primarily infects which type of host?

A) Humans
B) Rodents
C) Birds
D) Fish

Answer: B) Rodents

3. The intermediate host for *Hymenolepis cantaniana* is typically:

A) Snails
B) Insects
C) Fish
D) Amphibians

Answer: B) Insects

4. Which part of the host does *Hymenolepis cantaniana* inhabit?

A) Liver
B) Intestine
C) Bloodstream
D) Muscle tissue

Answer: B) Intestine

5. The life cycle of *Hymenolepis cantaniana* involves:

A) Direct transmission without an intermediate host
B) One intermediate host
C) Multiple intermediate hosts
D) No intermediate host, only paratenic hosts

Answer: B) One intermediate host

6. What is the infective stage of *Hymenolepis cantaniana* for the definitive host?

A) Egg
B) Oncosphere
C) Cysticercoid larva
D) Adult worm

Answer: C) Cysticercoid larva

7. Which diagnostic method is commonly used to detect *Hymenolepis cantaniana* infection?

A) Blood smear
B) Stool examination for eggs
C) Skin biopsy
D) Urine test

Answer: B) Stool examination for eggs

8. What kind of symptoms would a heavy infection of *Hymenolepis cantaniana* likely cause in the host?

A) Respiratory distress
B) Gastrointestinal disturbances
C) Neurological symptoms
D) Skin rashes

Answer: B) Gastrointestinal disturbances

9. Which of the following best describes the body structure of *Hymenolepis cantaniana*?

A) Segmented flatworm with a scolex
B) Roundworm with a simple digestive system
C) Unsegmented worm with a coelom
D) Ciliated protozoan

Answer: A) Segmented flatworm with a scolex

10. Control and prevention of *Hymenolepis cantaniana* infection primarily involve:

A) Avoiding contact with contaminated water
B) Proper cooking of fish
C) Controlling rodent and insect populations
D) Vaccination

Answer: C) Controlling rodent and insect populations

TREMATODES
Echinostoma revolutum

1. What type of organism is *Echinostoma revolutum*?

A) Bacterium
B) Virus
C) Trematode (fluke)
D) Nematode (roundworm)

Answer: C) Trematode (fluke)

2. What is the primary habitat of adult *Echinostoma revolutum*?

A) Liver
B) Intestine
C) Lungs
D) Blood vessels

Answer: B) Intestine

3. What is the intermediate host commonly involved in the life cycle of *Echinostoma revolutum*?

A) Fish
B) Snails
C) Mosquitoes
D) Humans

Answer: B) Snails

4. How do humans usually acquire *Echinostoma revolutum* infection?

A) Inhaling contaminated air
B) Eating raw or undercooked freshwater snails or fish
C) Direct skin penetration by larvae
D) Contact with contaminated soil

Answer: B) Eating raw or undercooked freshwater snails or fish

5. Which stage of *Echinostoma revolutum* is infective to humans?

A) Miracidium
B) Sporocyst
C) Cercaria
D) Metacercaria

Answer: D) Metacercaria

6. What is the characteristic feature of *Echinostoma revolutum* under a microscope?

A) Presence of a rosette of spines around the oral sucker
B) Segmented body
C) Long tail in adults
D) Hooks on the posterior end

Answer: A) Presence of a rosette of spines around the oral sucker

7. Which of the following symptoms is commonly associated with *Echinostoma revolutum* infection?

A) Intestinal discomfort and diarrhea
B) Severe cough and hemoptysis
C) Liver enlargement
D) Skin rash

Answer: A) Intestinal discomfort and diarrhea

8. Which diagnostic method is commonly used for *Echinostoma revolutum* infection?

A) Blood serology
B) Stool examination for eggs
C) Urine microscopy
D) Skin biopsy

Answer: B) Stool examination for eggs

9. What is the preferred treatment for *Echinostoma revolutum* infection?

A) Metronidazole
B) Praziquantel
C) Albendazole
D) Ivermectin

Answer: B) Praziquantel

10. Which of the following preventive measures can reduce the risk of *Echinostoma revolutum* infection?

A) Avoiding swimming in freshwater lakes
B) Boiling or cooking snails and fish thoroughly before consumption
C) Wearing gloves while gardening
D) Vaccination

Answer: B) Boiling or cooking snails and fish thoroughly before consumption

Prosthogonimus spp.:

1. What type of organism is *Prosthogonimus* spp.?

a) Bacteria
b) Protozoa
c) Trematode (fluke)
d) Nematode (roundworm)

Answer: c) Trematode (fluke)

2. What is the primary host of *Prosthogonimus* spp.?

a) Humans
b) Birds
c) Fish
d) Mammals

Answer: b) Birds

3. Which part of the bird is mainly infected by *Prosthogonimus* spp.?

a) Intestine
b) Liver
c) Oviduct and bursa of Fabricius
d) Lungs

Answer: c) Oviduct and bursa of Fabricius

4. What is the intermediate host of *Prosthogonimus* spp.?

a) Snails
b) Fish
c) Earthworms
d) Mosquitoes

Answer: a) Snails

5. How do birds typically get infected by *Prosthogonimus* spp.?

a) Ingesting infected snails
b) Drinking contaminated water
c) Eating infected insects
d) Ingesting cercariae on vegetation

Answer: d) Ingesting cercariae on vegetation

6. The life cycle of *Prosthogonimus* spp. involves which of the following stages?

a) Egg → Miracidium → Sporocyst → Redia → Cercaria → Metacercaria → Adult
b) Egg → Larva → Pupa → Adult
c) Egg → Nymph → Adult
d) Egg → Cyst → Adult

Answer: a) Egg → Miracidium → Sporocyst → Redia → Cercaria → Metacercaria → Adult

7. What disease condition is caused by *Prosthogonimus* spp. in birds?

a) Coccidiosis
b) Prosthogonimiasis
c) Newcastle disease
d) Avian influenza

Answer: b) Prosthogonimiasis

8. Which of the following symptoms is commonly seen in birds infected with *Prosthogonimus* spp.?

a) Diarrhea and dehydration
b) Egg-laying reduction and oviduct inflammation
c) Respiratory distress
d) Neurological signs

Answer: b) Egg-laying reduction and oviduct inflammation

9. How can *Prosthogonimus* infection be diagnosed in birds?

a) Blood smear
b) Fecal egg examination
c) Skin biopsy
d) Urine test

Answer: b) Fecal egg examination

10. What is the best method to control *Prosthogonimus* spp. infections in poultry?

a) Antibiotic treatment
b) Avoiding ingestion of snails and controlling snail populations
c) Vaccination
d) Quarantine of infected birds

Intestinal coccidiosis

. Which organism is primarily responsible for intestinal coccidiosis in poultry?

A. *Eimeria* species
B. *Ascaridia* species
C. *Histomonas* species
D. *Capillaria* species

Answer: A. *Eimeria* species
Explanation: Intestinal coccidiosis is caused by protozoan parasites of the genus Eimeria.

2. Which species of *Eimeria* is considered the most pathogenic in chickens?

A. *E. acervulina*
B. *E. maxima*
C. *E. tenella*
D. *E. mitis*

Answer: C. *E. tenella*
Explanation: E. tenella causes severe hemorrhagic cecal coccidiosis, often with high mortality.

3. How is intestinal coccidiosis in poultry primarily transmitted?

A. Through contaminated feed
B. By blood-sucking insects
C. Through ingestion of sporulated oocysts in feces
D. Through respiratory secretions

Answer: C. Through ingestion of sporulated oocysts in feces
Explanation: Transmission occurs via the fecal-oral route, mainly by ingesting infective oocysts.

4. Which clinical sign is most commonly associated with coccidiosis in poultry?

A. Sneezing
B. Diarrhea, often bloody
C. Leg paralysis
D. Feather loss

Answer: B. Diarrhea, often bloody
Explanation: Bloody diarrhea is a hallmark of severe Eimeria tenella infection.

5. What is the prepatent period of most *Eimeria* species in chickens?

A. 1–2 hours
B. 1–2 days
C. 4–7 days
D. 10–14 days

Answer: C. 4–7 days
Explanation: The prepatent period is typically around 4–7 days, depending on the species.

6. Which of the following is a common method of diagnosing coccidiosis in poultry?

A. ELISA test
B. PCR from blood samples
C. Fecal flotation and lesion scoring
D. X-ray imaging

Answer: C. Fecal flotation and lesion scoring
Explanation: Diagnosis is usually based on clinical signs, fecal examination, and postmortem lesion scoring.

7. What type of drug is commonly used to control coccidiosis in poultry?

A. Antibiotic
B. Anthelmintic
C. Coccidiostat
D. Antifungal

Answer: C. Coccidiostat
Explanation: Coccidiostats are added to feed to prevent coccidiosis (e.g., amprolium, salinomycin).

8. Why is rotation of coccidiostats recommended in poultry production?

A. To reduce feed cost
B. To improve egg quality
C. To prevent drug resistance
D. To enhance growth rate

Answer: C. To prevent drug resistance
Explanation: Continuous use of the same coccidiostat can lead to resistance in Eimeria populations.

9. Which management practice helps reduce the incidence of coccidiosis?

A. Overcrowding birds
B. Wet litter conditions
C. Frequent cleaning and dry litter
D. Mixed-age housing

Answer: C. Frequent cleaning and dry litter
Explanation: Dry, clean environments reduce oocyst sporulation and transmission.

10. What is the role of vaccination in coccidiosis control?

A. It is not effective
B. Used only in emergency outbreaks
C. Provides immunity through exposure to live oocysts
D. Replaces all biosecurity measures

Answer: C. Provides immunity through exposure to live oocysts
Explanation: Live vaccines expose birds to attenuated or low-dose pathogenic Eimeria to build immunity.

***Eimeria necatrix* – MCQs**

1. What type of organism is *Eimeria necatrix*?
A. Bacterium
B. Fungus
C. Protozoan
D. Virus
Answer: ✅ C. Protozoan

2. *Eimeria necatrix* primarily affects which species?
A. Cattle
B. Chickens
C. Pigs
D. Sheep
Answer: ✅ B. Chickens

3. In which part of the chicken's intestine does *Eimeria necatrix* mainly cause lesions?
A. Duodenum
B. Cecum
C. Mid-intestine (jejunum/ileum)
D. Rectum
Answer: ✅ C. Mid-intestine (jejunum/ileum)

4. What is a characteristic clinical sign of *Eimeria necatrix* infection?
A. Green droppings
B. Blood in feces
C. Nasal discharge
D. Lameness
Answer: ✅ B. Blood in feces

5. ***Eimeria necatrix*** **causes which form of coccidiosis?**
A. Mild coccidiosis
B. Cecal coccidiosis
C. Hemorrhagic intestinal coccidiosis
D. Nervous coccidiosis
Answer: ✅ C. Hemorrhagic intestinal coccidiosis

6. At which stage does *Eimeria necatrix* release oocysts?
A. Inside the liver
B. In the intestinal lumen
C. In the blood
D. In the muscle tissue
Answer: ✅ B. In the intestinal lumen

7. How are chickens infected by *Eimeria necatrix*?
A. Inhalation of spores
B. Contaminated feed and water
C. Skin penetration
D. Tick bite
Answer: ✅ B. Contaminated feed and water

8. What type of life cycle does *Eimeria necatrix* follow?
A. Direct life cycle
B. Indirect life cycle with intermediate host
C. Both direct and indirect
D. No life cycle
Answer: ✅ A. Direct life cycle

9. Which of the following control measures is effective against *Eimeria necatrix*?
A. Antibiotics
B. Vaccination and anticoccidial drugs
C. Antiviral therapy
D. Deworming
Answer: ✅ B. Vaccination and anticoccidial drugs

10. What is a common histological finding in the intestine infected with *Eimeria necatrix*?
A. Villous hypertrophy
B. Schizonts in epithelial cells
C. Neutrophil infiltration in liver
D. Fibrosis of the cecum
Answer: ✅ B. Schizonts in epithelial cells

Eimeria maxima – MCQs

1. What is the primary host for *Eimeria maxima*?
A) Cattle
B) Chickens
C) Sheep
D) Humans

✅ **Answer:** B) Chickens

2. *Eimeria maxima* primarily infects which part of the chicken's gastrointestinal tract?
A) Crop
B) Duodenum
C) Mid-intestine (jejunum)
D) Cecum

✅ **Answer:** C) Mid-intestine (jejunum)

3. What type of parasite is *Eimeria maxima*?
A) Nematode
B) Trematode
C) Protozoan
D) Bacterium

✅ **Answer:** C) Protozoan

4. How is *Eimeria maxima* transmitted?
A) Airborne spores
B) Skin contact
C) Ingestion of sporulated oocysts
D) Blood transfusion

✅ **Answer:** C) Ingestion of sporulated oocysts

5. What is the typical prepatent period (time from infection to shedding of oocysts) for *Eimeria maxima*?
A) 1–2 days
B) 4–5 days
C) 10–12 days
D) 20–25 days

✅ **Answer:** B) 4–5 days

6. What clinical sign is most associated with *Eimeria maxima* infection?
A) Neurological symptoms
B) Yellow-orange diarrhea
C) Respiratory distress
D) Lameness

✅ **Answer:** B) Yellow-orange diarrhea

7. What stage of the *Eimeria maxima* life cycle is infective to chickens?
A) Unsporulated oocyst
B) Sporulated oocyst
C) Trophozoite
D) Merozoite

✅ **Answer:** B) Sporulated oocyst

8. What is a common method for controlling *Eimeria maxima* in poultry farms?
A) Antibiotic treatment
B) Vaccination and anticoccidial drugs
C) Antiviral drugs
D) Genetic selection of parasites

✅ **Answer:** B) Vaccination and anticoccidial drugs

9. Which diagnostic method is most commonly used to detect *Eimeria maxima* infection?
A) Blood test
B) Skin biopsy
C) Fecal flotation and microscopic examination
D) X-ray

✅ **Answer:** C) Fecal flotation and microscopic examination

10. What is the impact of *Eimeria maxima* on poultry production?
A) Improves growth rate
B) No significant impact
C) Causes reduced weight gain and poor feed conversion
D) Enhances immunity to all diseases

✅ **Answer:** C) Causes reduced weight gain and poor feed conversion

1. What type of organism is *Eimeria tenella*?

A. Bacteria
B. Virus
C. Protozoa
D. Fungus

Answer: C. Protozoa
Explanation: E. tenella is a protozoan parasite belonging to the phylum Apicomplexa.

2. Which part of the chicken does *Eimeria tenella* primarily infect?

A. Liver
B. Small intestine
C. Cecum
D. Lungs

Answer: C. Cecum
Explanation: E. tenella targets the epithelial cells of the ceca in chickens, causing severe damage.

3. What disease is caused by *Eimeria tenella* in poultry?

A. Newcastle disease
B. Coccidiosis
C. Salmonellosis
D. Avian influenza

Answer: B. Coccidiosis
Explanation: Eimeria species cause coccidiosis, a parasitic disease of the intestinal tract.

4. How is *Eimeria tenella* transmitted among chickens?

A. Through air
B. Through contaminated water
C. Through oocysts in feces
D. Through direct blood contact

Answer: C. Through oocysts in feces
Explanation: Chickens ingest sporulated oocysts from contaminated litter, feed, or water.

5. Which stage of *E. tenella* is infective to chickens?

A. Trophozoite
B. Merozoite
C. Sporulated oocyst
D. Unsporulated oocyst

Answer: C. Sporulated oocyst
Explanation: Only sporulated oocysts are infective and capable of initiating infection in chickens.

6. What is the best method for diagnosing *Eimeria tenella* infection in chickens?

A. Blood test
B. Fecal flotation and microscopy
C. Radiography
D. Urinalysis

Answer: B. Fecal flotation and microscopy
Explanation: Oocysts can be identified in feces using fecal flotation techniques.

7. What is the primary control measure for *E. tenella* in poultry farms?

A. Antibiotics
B. Vaccination and coccidiostats
C. Isolation of infected birds only
D. Spraying insecticides

Answer: B. Vaccination and coccidiostats
Explanation: Control is mainly through anticoccidial drugs (coccidiostats) and live vaccines.

8. What type of life cycle does *E. tenella* follow?

A. Direct life cycle
B. Indirect life cycle with intermediate host
C. Asexual only
D. None of the above

Answer: A. Direct life cycle
Explanation: The entire life cycle occurs in a single host (chicken), without intermediate hosts.

9. What is the prepatent period of *Eimeria tenella* in chickens?

A. 1–2 hours
B. 3–5 days
C. 10–14 days
D. 21 days

Answer: B. 3–5 days
Explanation: The time from ingestion of oocysts to the shedding of new oocysts is about 3–5 days.

10. What is a common clinical sign of *Eimeria tenella* infection in chickens?

A. Sneezing
B. Bloody diarrhea
C. Feather loss
D. Lameness

Answer: B. Bloody diarrhea
Explanation: E. tenella causes hemorrhagic lesions in the ceca, leading to bloody droppings.

1. What is the causative agent of coccidiosis in turkeys?

A. Bacteria
B. Virus
C. Protozoa
D. Fungus

✅ **Answer: C. Protozoa**
Explanation: Coccidiosis is caused by protozoan parasites of the genus *Eimeria.*

2. Which of the following species of *Eimeria* commonly affects turkeys?

A. *Eimeria tenella*
B. *Eimeria meleagrimitis*
C. *Eimeria maxima*
D. *Eimeria acervulina*

✅ **Answer: B. *Eimeria meleagrimitis***
Explanation: *Eimeria meleagrimitis* is one of the primary species causing coccidiosis in turkeys.

3. What is the primary site of infection for *Eimeria meleagrimitis* in turkeys?

A. Cecum
B. Small intestine
C. Crop
D. Proventriculus

✅ **Answer: B. Small intestine**
Explanation: *E. meleagrimitis* mainly affects the small intestine, leading to enteritis and diarrhea.

4. What is the most common clinical sign of coccidiosis in turkeys?

A. Sneezing
B. Lameness
C. Bloody droppings
D. Diarrhea

✅ **Answer: D. Diarrhea**
Explanation: Diarrhea (sometimes bloody or watery) is a hallmark of intestinal coccidiosis.

5. How is coccidiosis primarily transmitted among turkeys?

A. Through the air
B. Contaminated feed and water
C. Direct contact with infected blood
D. Through insect vectors

✅ **Answer: B. Contaminated feed and water**
Explanation: Turkeys ingest sporulated oocysts from contaminated environments, including feed, water, or litter.

6. What diagnostic method is commonly used to detect coccidiosis in turkeys?

A. PCR
B. X-ray
C. Fecal flotation
D. Skin scraping

✅ **Answer: C. Fecal flotation**
Explanation: Fecal flotation is commonly used to detect *Eimeria* oocysts in the feces of infected birds.

7. Which of the following is a common control measure for coccidiosis in turkeys?

A. Antibiotics
B. Vaccination
C. Anticoccidial drugs in feed
D. Probiotics only

✅ **Answer: C. Anticoccidial drugs in feed**
Explanation: Prophylactic use of anticoccidial drugs in feed is a common and effective control strategy.

8. Which of the following anticoccidial drugs is commonly used in turkeys?

A. Amprolium
B. Penicillin
C. Tylosin
D. Enrofloxacin

✅ **Answer: A. Amprolium**
Explanation: Amprolium is an anticoccidial drug often used to prevent or treat coccidiosis in poultry, including turkeys.

9. Which management practice helps reduce the risk of coccidiosis outbreaks?

A. Increasing flock density
B. Keeping litter wet
C. Frequent litter removal and sanitation
D. Feeding raw meat

✅ **Answer: C. Frequent litter removal and sanitation**
Explanation: Good hygiene and dry, clean litter help reduce oocyst buildup and prevent outbreaks.

10. Which age group of turkeys is most susceptible to coccidiosis?

A. 1-3 days old
B. 1-6 weeks old
C. 12-16 weeks old
D. Adult breeders

✅ **Answer: B. 1–6 weeks old**
Explanation: Young turkeys are more vulnerable due to their immature immune systems.

Eimeria meleagrimitis

1. What type of organism is *Eimeria meleagrimitis*?

A) Bacterium
B) Virus
C) Protozoan
D) Fungus

Answer: C) Protozoan

2. What disease is caused by *Eimeria meleagrimitis* in turkeys?

A) Newcastle disease
B) Coccidiosis
C) Salmonellosis
D) Aspergillosis

Answer: B) Coccidiosis

3. *Eimeria meleagrimitis* primarily infects which part of the turkey's intestine?

A) Duodenum
B) Cecum
C) Jejunum and ileum
D) Colon

Answer: C) Jejunum and ileum

4. What is the primary mode of transmission for *Eimeria meleagrimitis*?

A) Aerosol
B) Fecal-oral
C) Vertical (through egg)
D) Vector-borne

Answer: B) Fecal-oral

5. Which life cycle stage of *Eimeria meleagrimitis* is infective to turkeys?

A) Trophozoite
B) Merozoite
C) Unsporulated oocyst
D) Sporulated oocyst

Answer: D) Sporulated oocyst

6. How can coccidiosis caused by *Eimeria meleagrimitis* be prevented in poultry farms?

A) Use of antibiotics
B) Vaccination and coccidiostats
C) Antifungal treatment
D) Isolation of adult birds

Answer: B) Vaccination and coccidiostats

7. What is a common clinical sign of *Eimeria meleagrimitis* infection in turkeys?

A) Neurological signs
B) Coughing
C) Diarrhea (sometimes bloody)
D) Lameness

Answer: C) Diarrhea (sometimes bloody)

8. Which of the following best describes the reproductive strategy of *Eimeria meleagrimitis*?

A) Binary fission
B) Sexual and asexual reproduction
C) Budding
D) Fragmentation

Answer: B) Sexual and asexual reproduction

9. What laboratory method is commonly used to diagnose *Eimeria meleagrimitis* infection?

A) Blood smear
B) PCR of blood samples
C) Fecal flotation and microscopic examination
D) Urine culture

Answer: C) Fecal flotation and microscopic examination

10. In the life cycle of *Eimeria meleagrimitis*, what occurs after ingestion of sporulated oocysts?

A) Merozoites are released directly
B) Sporozoites invade the intestinal lining
C) Gametocytes are excreted
D) Trophozoites multiply in the blood

Answer: B) Sporozoites invade the intestinal lining

Cryptosporidium* spp. (c. *baileyi* and C. *meleagridis)

1. Which of the following Cryptosporidium species primarily infects birds?

A. *C. parvum*
B. *C. hominis*
C. *C. meleagridis*
D. *C. muris*

Answer: C. *C. meleagridis*

2. *Cryptosporidium baileyi* primarily infects which system in birds?

A. Digestive system
B. Respiratory system
C. Nervous system
D. Reproductive system

Answer: B. Respiratory system

3. What is the primary mode of transmission of *Cryptosporidium spp.* in birds and humans?

A. Vector-borne
B. Sexual contact
C. Fecal-oral route
D. Airborne droplets

Answer: C. Fecal-oral route

4. Which Cryptosporidium species is most commonly associated with zoonotic infections in humans from birds?

A. *C. parvum*
B. *C. meleagridis*
C. *C. baileyi*
D. *C. canis*

Answer: B. *C. meleagridis*

5. Which avian species is most commonly infected by *C. baileyi*?

A. Turkey
B. Parrot
C. Falcon
D. Duck

Answer: A. Turkey

6. What is a common clinical sign of *C. baileyi* infection in birds?

A. Diarrhea
B. Coughing and dyspnea
C. Seizures
D. Feather loss

Answer: B. Coughing and dyspnea

7. *C. meleagridis* has been reported to infect which human population most commonly?

A. Healthy adults
B. Immunocompromised individuals
C. Infants only
D. Pregnant women only

Answer: B. Immunocompromised individuals

8. What is the main diagnostic method for detecting *Cryptosporidium* oocysts?

A. ELISA
B. PCR
C. Modified Ziehl-Neelsen staining
D. Hemagglutination assay

Answer: C. Modified Ziehl-Neelsen staining

9. Which of the following is a characteristic of *Cryptosporidium* oocysts?

A. Large and easily visible under low magnification
B. Acid-fast and resistant to chlorine disinfection
C. Motile with flagella
D. Encapsulated spores

Answer: B. Acid-fast and resistant to chlorine disinfection

10. Which species is most likely to serve as a reservoir for *C. meleagridis*?

A. Cattle
B. Poultry (especially turkeys and chickens)
C. Rodents
D. Dogs

Answer: B. Poultry (especially turkeys and chickens)

Histomonas meleagridis

1. What disease is caused by Histomonas meleagridis?

A) Coccidiosis
B) Blackhead disease
C) Marek's disease
D) Newcastle disease

Answer: B) Blackhead disease

2. Which poultry species is most susceptible to Histomonas meleagridis?

A) Chickens
B) Ducks
C) Turkeys
D) Quails

Answer: C) Turkeys

3. What is the primary mode of transmission of Histomonas meleagridis?

A) Aerosol
B) Through contaminated water
C) Ingestion of Heterakis gallinarum eggs
D) Direct contact with infected birds

Answer: C) Ingestion of *Heterakis gallinarum* eggs

4. What type of organism is Histomonas meleagridis?

A) Bacterium
B) Nematode
C) Protozoan
D) Fungus

Answer: C) Protozoan

5. What is a common clinical sign of blackhead disease in turkeys?

A) Bright red comb
B) Yellow, sulfur-colored droppings
C) Excessive egg production
D) Limping

Answer: B) Yellow, sulfur-colored droppings

6. What is the role of Heterakis gallinarum in the life cycle of Histomonas meleagridis?

A) It acts as a virus carrier
B) It serves as a vector and host
C) It destroys the protozoa
D) It has no role

Answer: B) It serves as a vector and host

7. What organ is primarily affected by Histomonas meleagridis in turkeys?

A) Heart
B) Lungs
C) Liver and cecum
D) Kidneys

Answer: C) Liver and cecum

8. What pathological lesion is commonly found in the liver due to blackhead disease?

A) Hemorrhages
B) Caseous nodules
C) Ulcers
D) Fibrosi

Answer: B) Caseous nodules

9. Can chickens carry Histomonas meleagridis without severe symptoms?

A) Yes
B) No
C) Only in summer
D) Only if vaccinated

Answer: A) Yes

10. Which of the following is a method to control the spread of Histomonas meleagridis?

A) Antibiotic treatment
B) Use of anticoccidials
C) Control of Heterakis gallinarum
D) Vaccination

Trichomonas gallinae

1. What type of organism is *Trichomonas gallinae*?

A. Bacteria
B. Virus
C. Fungi
D. Protozoan

✅ **Answer: D. Protozoan**

2. Which type of animals are most commonly affected by *Trichomonas gallinae*?

A. Mammals
B. Amphibians
C. Birds
D. Reptiles

✅ **Answer: C. Birds**

3. What is the primary mode of transmission of *Trichomonas gallinae* in birds?

A. Airborne droplets
B. Ingestion of contaminated food or water
C. Skin contact
D. Blood-feeding insects

✅ **Answer: B. Ingestion of contaminated food or water**
Especially during feeding of young birds (squabs) by adults or shared water sources.

4. What disease does *Trichomonas gallinae* cause in birds?

A. Avian pox
B. Trichomoniasis
C. Aspergillosis
D. Psittacosis

✅ **Answer: B. Trichomoniasis**

5. What is a common clinical sign of trichomoniasis in pigeons?

A. Feather loss
B. Lesions in the mouth and throat
C. Lameness
D. Sneezing

✅ **Answer: B. Lesions in the mouth and throat**
These are often yellowish caseous plaques, leading to difficulty in eating or breathing.

6. Which of the following is a diagnostic method for *Trichomonas gallinae*?

A. Blood smear
B. PCR from feces
C. Wet mount microscopy of oral swabs
D. Chest X-ray

✅ **Answer: C. Wet mount microscopy of oral swabs**
Motile trophozoites can be seen under the microscope.

7. What is the morphological stage found in *Trichomonas gallinae* infections?

A. Trophozoite
B. Cyst
C. Spore
D. Merozoite

✅ **Answer: A. Trophozoite**
*It does **not** form cysts, which makes it vulnerable to desiccation.*

8. Which treatment is commonly used against *Trichomonas gallinae* infections in birds?

A. Amoxicillin
B. Ivermectin
C. Metronidazole
D. Enrofloxacin

✅ **Answer: C. Metronidazole**

9. Which bird species are considered important reservoirs of *Trichomonas gallinae*?

A. Sparrows and finches
B. Pigeons and doves
C. Parrots and cockatoos
D. Hawks and falcons

✅ **Answer: B. Pigeons and doves**

10. Why is *Trichomonas gallinae* considered a threat to raptors (e.g., hawks, falcons)?

A. They are directly infected from the air
B. They get infected from eating infected prey
C. They get infected from standing water
D. They are born with the parasite

✅ **Answer: B. They get infected from eating infected prey**
Predatory birds often acquire the parasite by consuming infected pigeons or doves.

ECTOPARASITES OF POULTRY

Argas persicus **Syn.** The fowl tick

1. What is the common name of Argas persicus?

A. Cattle tick
B. Fowl tick
C. Dog tick
D. Lone star tick

✅ **Answer:** B. Fowl tick

2. Argas persicus belongs to which family of ticks?

A. Ixodidae
B. Argasidae
C. Dermacentoridae
D. Rhipicephalidae

✅ **Answer:** B. Argasidae

3. Which type of tick is Argas persicus?

A. Hard tick
B. Soft tick
C. Seed tick
D. Nymphal tick

✅ **Answer:** B. Soft tick

4. The main host of Argas persicus is:

A. Cattle
B. Humans
C. Poultry (e.g., chickens)
D. Dogs

✅ **Answer:** C. Poultry (e.g., chickens)

5. What is a major disease transmitted by Argas persicus?

A. Lyme disease
B. Avian spirochetosis
C. Babesiosis
D. Ehrlichiosis

✅ **Answer:** B. Avian spirochetosis

6. Which of the following is a characteristic feature of Argas persicus?

A. Has a scutum
B. Body is leathery and lacks a hard shield
C. Lives only on the host
D. Active only in the daytime

✅ **Answer:** B. Body is leathery and lacks a hard shield

7. Where does Argas persicus typically hide when not feeding?

A. On the host's body
B. Underground
C. In cracks and crevices of poultry houses
D. On vegetation

✅ **Answer:** C. In cracks and crevices of poultry houses

8. Argas persicus feeds primarily during:

A. The day
B. Winter
C. The night
D. Rainy season

✅ **Answer:** C. The night

9. Which life stage of Argas persicus feeds on blood?

A. Larva only
B. Nymph only
C. All stages except egg
D. Adults only

✅ **Answer:** C. All stages except egg

10. Which control method is most effective against Argas persicus in poultry farms?

A. Spraying animals with insecticides
B. Applying systemic antibiotics
C. Treating housing and hiding places with acaricides
D. Vaccination

✅ **Answer:** C. Treating housing and hiding places with acaricides

Dermanyssus gallinae Syn. The red mite, Omithonyssus Sylviarum

1. What is the common name of *Dermanyssus gallinae*?

A) Bed bug
B) Red mite
C) Tick
D) Flea

Answer: B) Red mite

2. *Dermanyssus gallinae* primarily parasitizes which type of host?

A) Humans
B) Birds
C) Mammals
D) Reptiles

Answer: B) Birds

3. Which of the following diseases is *Dermanyssus gallinae* known to potentially transmit?

A) Lyme disease
B) Avian spirochetosis
C) Malaria
D) Plague

Answer: B) Avian spirochetosis

4. What is the primary habitat of *Dermanyssus gallinae* during the day?

A) On the host
B) In the soil
C) In cracks and crevices away from the host
D) On plants

Answer: C) In cracks and crevices away from the host

5. Which order do *Dermanyssus gallinae* belong to?

A) Coleoptera
B) Hymenoptera
C) Acari
D) Diptera

Answer: C) Acari

6. What is the main method for controlling *Dermanyssus gallinae* infestations in poultry?

A) Antibiotics
B) Pesticides/insecticides
C) Vaccination
D) Quarantine

Answer: B) Pesticides/insecticides

7. What is the synonym for *Dermanyssus gallinae*?

A) *Ornithonyssus sylviarum*
B) *Ixodes scapularis*
C) *Cimex lectularius*
D) *Rhipicephalus sanguineus*

Answer: A) *Ornithonyssus sylviarum*

8. How does *Dermanyssus gallinae* primarily feed?

A) By biting and sucking blood
B) By ingesting skin flakes
C) By feeding on feathers
D) By eating dead tissue

Answer: A) By biting and sucking blood

9. What time of day is *Dermanyssus gallinae* most active in feeding on hosts?

A) Morning
B) Afternoon
C) Night
D) Always active

Answer: C) Night

10. Why is *Dermanyssus gallinae* infestation a concern in poultry farming?

A) It causes decreased egg production
B) It spreads bacterial infections
C) It causes anemia and stress in birds
D) All of the above

Answer: D) All of the above

Cnemidocoptes mutans

1. What type of organism is *Cnemidocoptes mutans*?

A) Bacteria
B) Virus
C) Mite
D) Fungus

Answer: C) Mite

2. *Cnemidocoptes mutans* primarily causes which condition in birds?

A) Feather mites
B) Scaly leg disease
C) Respiratory infection
D) Beak deformities

Answer: B) Scaly leg disease

3. Which part of the bird's body is mostly affected by *Cnemidocoptes mutans*?

A) Beak
B) Legs and feet
C) Wings
D) Eyes

Answer: B) Legs and feet

4. How is *Cnemidocoptes mutans* transmitted among birds?

A) Through contaminated water
B) Direct contact with infected birds
C) Airborne droplets
D) Through insect vectors

Answer: B) Direct contact with infected birds

5. What is the typical symptom of an infestation by *Cnemidocoptes mutans*?

A) Feather loss
B) Swelling and crusty scales on legs
C) Coughing
D) Blindness

Answer: B) Swelling and crusty scales on legs

6. *Cnemidocoptes mutans* belongs to which family of mites?

A) Sarcoptidae
B) Trombiculidae
C) Demodicidae
D) Psoroptidae

Answer: A) Sarcoptidae

7. What is the primary method for diagnosing *Cnemidocoptes mutans* infestation?

A) Blood test
B) Skin scraping and microscopic examination
C) X-ray
D) Fecal examination

Answer: B) Skin scraping and microscopic examination

8. Which treatment is commonly used against *Cnemidocoptes mutans* in birds?

A) Antibiotics
B) Antifungals
C) Topical or systemic acaricides
D) Antivirals

Answer: C) Topical or systemic acaricides

9. In which types of birds is *Cnemidocoptes mutans* infestation most commonly seen?

A) Waterfowl
B) Raptors
C) Poultry and pet birds like canaries and pigeons
D) Parrots only

Answer: C) Poultry and pet birds like canaries and pigeons

10. What is the nature of the damage caused by *Cnemidocoptes mutans* to the bird's legs?

A) Tissue necrosis
B) Formation of thickened, crusty, and scaly skin
C) Hemorrhaging
D) Ulcerative lesions

Answer: B) Formation of thickened, crusty, and scaly skin

Northern fowl mites (*Ornithonyssus sylviarum*)

1. What is the primary host of Northern fowl mites (Ornithonyssus sylviarum)?

A) Cattle
B) Chickens
C) Dogs
D) Horses

Answer: B) Chickens

2. Northern fowl mites primarily feed on:

A) Feathers
B) Blood
C) Skin cells
D) Eggs

Answer: B) Blood

3. Where do Northern fowl mites typically live on the host?

A) Around the vent area
B) Inside the beak
C) On the feet
D) On the comb and wattles

Answer: A) Around the vent area

4. How quickly can Northern fowl mites complete their life cycle under favorable conditions?

A) 2 days
B) 7 days
C) 14 days
D) 30 days

Answer: B) 7 days

5. Which of the following is a common symptom of Northern fowl mite infestation?

A) Feather loss and irritation
B) Excessive egg production
C) Swelling of the legs
D) Increased appetite

Answer: A) Feather loss and irritation

6. How are Northern fowl mites usually transmitted?

A) Through contaminated feed
B) Direct contact between birds
C) Airborne spores
D) Infected water

Answer: B) Direct contact between birds

7. What type of parasite is the Northern fowl mite?

A) External ectoparasite
B) Internal parasite
C) Protozoan parasite
D) Nematode parasite

Answer: A) External ectoparasite

8. Which of these control methods is commonly used against Northern fowl mites?

A) Antibiotics
B) Insecticides or acaricides
C) Antifungals
D) Vaccination

Answer: B) Insecticides or acaricides

9. What effect do Northern fowl mites have on poultry production?

A) No significant effect
B) Increased egg size
C) Reduced egg production and weight loss
D) Enhanced growth rate

Answer: C) Reduced egg production and weight loss

10. Northern fowl mites are best identified by:

A) Their large size and slow movement
B) Their reddish color after feeding
C) Their presence inside the respiratory tract
D) Their ability to jump long distances

Answer: B) Their reddish color after feeding

Echidnophaga gallinacea

Syn. Sticktight flea

1. What is the common name for *Echidnophaga gallinacea*?

A) Dog flea
B) Cat flea
C) Sticktight flea
D) Human flea

Answer: C) Sticktight flea

2. Which animals are primarily affected by *Echidnophaga gallinacea*?

A) Cattle and horses
B) Chickens and other poultry
C) Dogs and cats
D) Humans

Answer: B) Chickens and other poultry

3. Where do *Echidnophaga gallinacea* fleas typically attach on their host?

A) Ears
B) Skin around the eyes and face
C) Legs and under wings
D) Tail and back

Answer: C) Legs and under wings

4. What type of parasite is *Echidnophaga gallinacea*?

A) Endoparasite
B) Ectoparasite
C) Free-living organism
D) Commensal organism

Answer: B) Ectoparasite

5. What is a common symptom caused by *Echidnophaga gallinacea* infestation in poultry?

A) Diarrhea
B) Severe itching and skin lesions
C) Respiratory distress
D) Weight gain

Answer: B) Severe itching and skin lesions

6. How does *Echidnophaga gallinacea* reproduce?

A) Laying eggs on the host
B) Laying eggs in the environment
C) Giving live birth
D) Budding

Answer: B) Laying eggs in the environment

7. What is a typical treatment approach for *Echidnophaga gallinacea* infestation?

A) Antibiotics
B) Antiparasitic insecticides
C) Antifungal medications
D) Vitamin supplements

Answer: B) Antiparasitic insecticides

8. Which life stage of *Echidnophaga gallinacea* is responsible for blood-feeding?

A) Larva
B) Pupa
C) Adult flea
D) Egg

Answer: C) Adult flea

9. ***Echidnophaga gallinacea*** **is capable of causing:**

A) Myiasis
B) Anemia in heavy infestations
C) Skin cancer
D) Neurological disease

Answer: B) Anemia in heavy infestations

10. What distinguishes ***Echidnophaga gallinacea*** **from other fleas?**

A) It jumps long distances
B) It embeds its head into the skin (sticktight behavior)
C) It is aquatic
D) It lives only on mammals

Answer: B) It embeds its head into the skin (sticktight behavior)

POULTRY LICE

chicken body louse (*Menacanthus stramineus*)

1. What is the common name of ***Menacanthus stramineus*****?**

A) Chicken head louse
B) Chicken mite
C) Chicken body louse
D) Poultry tick

Answer: C) Chicken body louse

2. Where on the chicken's body is ***Menacanthus stramineus*** **most commonly found?**

A) Comb and wattles
B) Under wings and around the vent
C) Beak and eyes
D) Legs and feet

Answer: B) Under wings and around the vent

3. What is the primary diet of the chicken body louse?

A) Blood
B) Feather material and skin debris
C) Muscle tissue
D) Chicken feed

Answer: B) Feather material and skin debris
(*Note:* It may occasionally feed on blood through broken skin.)

4. How does *Menacanthus stramineus* reproduce?

A) Live birth
B) Spore formation
C) Lays eggs (nits) on feathers
D) Budding

Answer: C) Lays eggs (nits) on feathers

5. Which stage of the louse life cycle is infectious to the host?

A) Egg
B) Nymph
C) Adult
D) Both B and C

Answer: D) Both B and C

6. What is the typical life cycle duration of *Menacanthus stramineus* under optimal conditions?

A) 1–2 days
B) 4–5 days
C) 10–15 days
D) 30–40 days

Answer: C) 10–15 days

7. What are common signs of a *Menacanthus stramineus* infestation in chickens?

A) Coughing and sneezing
B) Feather loss, restlessness, reduced egg production
C) Limping and leg swelling
D) Sudden death without symptoms

Answer: B) Feather loss, restlessness, reduced egg production

8. How is *Menacanthus stramineus* primarily transmitted among chickens?

A) Through feed
B) Through air
C) Direct contact between birds
D) Mosquito bites

Answer: C) Direct contact between birds

9. What is a common method of controlling chicken body lice?

A) Antibiotics
B) Vaccination
C) Insecticidal dust or spray (e.g., permethrin)
D) Antifungal medication

Answer: C) Insecticidal dust or spray (e.g., permethrin)

10. Which type of housing management helps prevent louse infestations in poultry?

A) Overcrowding
B) Dirt flooring
C) Regular cleaning and dust bathing areas
D) High humidity housing

Answer: C) Regular cleaning and dust bathing areas

Shaft louse (*Menopon gallinae*)

1. What is the scientific name of the shaft louse?

A. Menacanthus stramineus
B. Goniocotes gallinae
C. Menopon gallinae
D. Lipeurus caponis

Answer: C. *Menopon gallinae*

2. What is the primary host of the shaft louse?

A. Cattle
B. Sheep
C. Poultry (especially chickens)
D. Dogs

Answer: C. Poultry (especially chickens)

3. Where is the shaft louse commonly found on the host?

A. Inside the ears
B. On the vent area
C. Along the feather shafts and breast/thigh regions
D. Between the toes

Answer: C. Along the feather shafts and breast/thigh regions

4. What is the feeding habit of *Menopon gallinae*?

A. Sucks blood
B. Feeds on skin scales and feathers
C. Eats muscle tissue
D. Feeds on feces

Answer: B. Feeds on skin scales and feathers

5. Which of the following is a symptom of heavy *Menopon gallinae* infestation?

A. Coughing and nasal discharge
B. Lameness
C. Feather damage and restlessness
D. Vomiting

Answer: C. Feather damage and restlessness

6. What is the life cycle type of *Menopon gallinae*?

A. Complete metamorphosis
B. Incomplete metamorphosis
C. Parthenogenesis
D. Holometabolous

Answer: B. Incomplete metamorphosis

7. How long does it typically take for *Menopon gallinae* to complete its life cycle?

A. 2-3 days
B. 1-2 weeks
C. 3-4 weeks
D. 6-8 weeks

Answer: C. 3–4 weeks

8. Which of the following is a control measure for shaft lice in poultry?

A. Deworming with albendazole
B. Spraying with insecticides like permethrin
C. Administering antibiotics
D. Vaccination

Answer: B. Spraying with insecticides like permethrin

9. How are *Menopon gallinae* transmitted among birds?

A. Through water
B. Through the air
C. By direct contact or shared nesting areas
D. Via contaminated feed

Answer: C. By direct contact or shared nesting areas

10. Which stage of *Menopon gallinae* is parasitic?

A. Only adult
B. Only nymph
C. Egg
D. Both nymph and adult

Answer: D. Both nymph and adult

BLOOD PARASITES OF POULTRY

MCQs on *Leucocytozoon caulleryi*

1. What type of organism is *Leucocytozoon caulleryi*?

A) Bacteria
B) Virus
C) Protozoa
D) Fungus

Answer: ✅ C) Protozoa

2. What is the primary host for *Leucocytozoon caulleryi*?

A) Ducks
B) Turkeys
C) Chickens
D) Pigeons

Answer: ✅ C) Chickens

3. How is *Leucocytozoon caulleryi* transmitted to chickens?

A) Through contaminated water
B) Via fecal-oral route
C) By insect vectors (biting midges)
D) Direct contact with infected birds

Answer: ✅ C) By insect vectors (biting midges)

Explanation: Mainly transmitted by biting midges (e.g., Culicoides spp.) and blackflies.

4. Which of the following is a clinical sign of *Leucocytozoon caulleryi* infection in chickens?

A) Increased egg production
B) Nervous signs only
C) Hemorrhages and anemia
D) Diarrhea with blood

Answer: ✅ C) Hemorrhages and anemia

5. In which organ are schizonts of *Leucocytozoon caulleryi* commonly found?

A) Intestine
B) Liver
C) Lungs
D) Pancreas

Answer: ✅ B) Liver

Leucocytozoon macleani

1. What type of organism is *Leucocytozoon macleani*?

A. Bacterium
B. Nematode
C. Protozoan parasite
D. Fungus

Answer: ✅ C. Protozoan parasite

2. *Leucocytozoon macleani* is known to primarily infect which of the following animals?

A. Domestic chickens
B. Falcons and other raptors
C. Amphibians
D. Reptiles

Answer: ✅ B. Falcons and other raptors

3. What is the main site of infection for *Leucocytozoon macleani* in its avian host?

A. Intestines
B. Lungs
C. Blood cells (erythrocytes and leukocytes)
D. Nervous system

Answer: ✅ C. Blood cells (erythrocytes and leukocytes)

4. What is the primary mode of transmission for *Leucocytozoon macleani*?

A. Ingestion of contaminated food
B. Direct contact with infected birds
C. Bite of infected blackflies (Simuliidae)
D. Airborne spores

Answer: ✅ C. Bite of infected blackflies (Simuliidae)

5. Which of the following is a key diagnostic feature used to identify *Leucocytozoon macleani* in blood smears?

A. Flagellated trophozoites
B. Cysts in liver tissue
C. Gametocytes distorting host blood cells
D. Large round eggs in fecal samples

Answer: ✅ C. Gametocytes distorting host blood cells

Leucocytozoon simondi

1. What type of organism is *Leucocytozoon simondi*?

A) Bacterium
B) Virus
C) Protozoan parasite
D) Fungi

Answer: ✅ C) Protozoan parasite

2. What is the primary host of *Leucocytozoon simondi*?

A) Chickens
B) Turkeys
C) Ducks and geese
D) Pigeons

Answer: ✅ C) Ducks and geese

3. Which insect acts as the vector for *Leucocytozoon simondi*?

A) Mosquito
B) Blackfly (*Simulium* spp.)
C) Tick
D) Flea

Answer: ✅ B) Blackfly (*Simulium* spp.)

4. Which cells are primarily infected by *Leucocytozoon simondi* in the host?

A) Red blood cells and hepatocytes
B) White blood cells and liver cells
C) Platelets and neurons
D) Muscle cells and epithelial cells

Answer: ✅ B) White blood cells and liver cells

5. What is a common clinical sign of *Leucocytozoon simondi* infection in birds?

A) Diarrhea
B) Respiratory distress
C) Anemia and sudden death
D) Feather loss

Answer: ✅ C) Anemia and sudden death

Leucocytozoon smithi

1. What type of organism is *Leucocytozoon smithi*?

A. Bacterium
B. Virus
C. Protozoan parasite
D. Fungus

Answer: ✅ C. Protozoan parasite

2. Which host is primarily affected by *Leucocytozoon smithi*?

A. Cattle
B. Chicken
C. Turkey
D. Pigeon

Answer: ✅ C. Turkey

3. What is the vector for transmission of *Leucocytozoon smithi*?

A. Tick
B. Mosquito (*Culex*)
C. Blackfly (*Simulium*)
D. Louse

Answer: ✅ C. Blackfly (*Simulium*)

4. Where does *Leucocytozoon smithi* undergo asexual reproduction (schizogony)?

A. Intestinal epithelium
B. Liver cells
C. Red blood cells
D. Endothelial cells of liver and spleen

Answer: ✅ D. Endothelial cells of liver and spleen

5. What is a common clinical sign of *Leucocytozoon smithi* infection in turkeys?

A. Diarrhea
B. Nervous signs
C. Sudden death with anemia
D. Feather loss

Answer: ✅ C. Sudden death with anemia

Haemoproteus* spp. *(H. columbae* and H. *danilewskii)

1. Which of the following is the primary host for *Haemoproteus columbae*?

A) Chickens
B) Pigeons and doves
C) Crows
D) Ducks

Correct Answer: B) *Pigeons and doves*
Explanation: *Haemoproteus columbae* is commonly found in pigeons and doves and is transmitted by pigeon flies (hippoboscid flies).

2. How is *Haemoproteus spp.* primarily transmitted to its avian hosts?

A) Mosquitoes
B) Fleas
C) Hippoboscid flies and biting midges
D) Ticks

Correct Answer: C) *Hippoboscid flies and biting midges*
Explanation: *Haemoproteus spp.* are transmitted by blood-sucking insects such as hippoboscid flies (*H. columbae*) and biting midges (*H. danilewskii*).

3. In which type of host cells do *Haemoproteus* gametocytes typically develop?

A) Liver cells
B) White blood cells
C) Red blood cells
D) Intestinal epithelial cells

Correct Answer: C) *Red blood cells*
Explanation: Gametocytes of *Haemoproteus* are found in the erythrocytes (RBCs) of infected birds and can be seen during blood smear examination.

4. What is the clinical significance of *Haemoproteus* infection in birds such as pigeons?

A) Always fatal
B) Usually asymptomatic or mild
C) Causes rapid death
D) Leads to permanent sterility

Correct Answer: B) *Usually asymptomatic or mild*
Explanation: Most *Haemoproteus* infections are mild or subclinical, although stress or co-infection may exacerbate disease signs.

5. Which of the following statements is TRUE about *Haemoproteus danilewskii*?

A) It infects mammals
B) It is transmitted by ticks
C) It infects passerine birds
D) It only occurs in tropical regions

Correct Answer: C) *It infects passerine birds*
Explanation: *Haemoproteus danilewskii* primarily infects passerine birds (songbirds) and is transmitted by biting midges.

Plasmodium gallinaceum

1. What is the primary host of *Plasmodium gallinaceum*?

A. Humans
B. Chickens
C. Dogs
D. Frogs

Answer: B. Chickens

2. Which mosquito genus is the vector for *Plasmodium gallinaceum* transmission?

A. Anopheles
B. Culex
C. Aedes
D. Mansonia

Answer: C. Aedes

3. What is a characteristic symptom of *Plasmodium gallinaceum* infection in birds?

A. Hair loss
B. Diarrhea
C. Anemia and enlarged spleen
D. Skin ulcers

Answer: C. Anemia and enlarged spleen

4. *Plasmodium gallinaceum* belongs to which group of protozoa?

A. Flagellates
B. Amoeboids
C. Sporozoans (Apicomplexa)
D. Ciliates

Answer: C. Sporozoans (Apicomplexa)

5. Why is *Plasmodium gallinaceum* often used in research?

A. It infects humans directly
B. It has a short life cycle in humans
C. It serves as a model for studying human malaria
D. It causes cancer in birds

Answer: C. It serves as a model for studying human malaria

Aegyptinella pullorum.:

1. What is *Aegyptinella pullorum* primarily known to infect?

A. Humans
B. Reptiles
C. Birds
D. Amphibians

Answer: ✅ C. Birds

2. Which group of protozoa does *Aegyptinella pullorum* belong to?

A. Amoebozoa
B. Apicomplexa
C. Euglenozoa
D. Ciliophora

Answer: ✅ B. Apicomplexa

3. In which host cells is *Aegyptinella pullorum* found?

A. Red blood cells
B. Liver cells
C. Intestinal epithelial cells
D. Skin cells

Answer: ✅ A. Red blood cells

4. How is *Aegyptinella pullorum* typically transmitted?

A. Ingestion of cysts in contaminated food
B. Airborne spores
C. Vector-borne via blood-sucking arthropods
D. Direct contact between birds

Answer: ✅ C. Vector-borne via blood-sucking arthropods

5. Which staining technique is commonly used to identify *Aegyptinella pullorum* in blood smears?

A. Gram stain
B. Giemsa stain
C. Ziehl-Neelsen stain
D. Acid-fast stain

Answer: ✅ B. Giemsa stain

CHAPTER FIVE :RABBIT PARASITES QUESTIONS

Trematodes of Rabbits MCQ

1. Which of the following is a trematode commonly found in rabbits?

A. *Fasciola hepatica*
B. *Taenia pisiformis*
C. *Trichostrongylus retortaeformis*
D. *Eimeria stiedae*

Answer: A. *Fasciola hepatica*
(Note: Although rare, rabbits can be accidental hosts of Fasciola hepatica, a liver fluke.)

2. What is the primary site of infection for *Fasciola hepatica* **in rabbits?**

A. Lungs
B. Small intestine
C. Liver and bile ducts
D. Kidneys

Answer: C. Liver and bile ducts

3. How do rabbits typically acquire trematode infections like *Fasciola hepatica*?

A. Direct contact with infected animals
B. Inhalation of spores
C. Ingestion of contaminated water or vegetation
D. Transplacental transmission

Answer: C. Ingestion of contaminated water or vegetation
(Through ingestion of metacercariae on aquatic plants.)

4. Which diagnostic method is commonly used to detect trematode eggs in rabbits?

A. Skin scraping
B. Fecal sedimentation
C. ELISA test
D. Blood smear

Answer: B. Fecal sedimentation
(Trematode eggs are heavy and often missed by flotation methods.)

5. Which of the following is a potential clinical sign of trematode infection in rabbits?

A. Seizures
B. Jaundice
C. Alopecia
D. Head tilt

Answer: B. Jaundice
(Due to liver damage caused by migrating flukes.)

Trematodes of Rabbits MCQ

1. Which of the following is a trematode commonly found in rabbits?

A. *Fasciola hepatica*
B. *Taenia pisiformis*
C. *Trichostrongylus retortaeformis*
D. *Eimeria stiedae*

Answer: A. *Fasciola hepatica*
(Note: Although rare, rabbits can be accidental hosts of Fasciola hepatica, a liver fluke.)

2. What is the primary site of infection for *Fasciola hepatica* **in rabbits?**

A. Lungs
B. Small intestine
C. Liver and bile ducts
D. Kidneys

Answer: C. Liver and bile ducts

3. How do rabbits typically acquire trematode infections like *Fasciola hepatica*?

A. Direct contact with infected animals
B. Inhalation of spores
C. Ingestion of contaminated water or vegetation
D. Transplacental transmission

Answer: C. Ingestion of contaminated water or vegetation
(Through ingestion of metacercariae on aquatic plants.)

4. Which diagnostic method is commonly used to detect trematode eggs in rabbits?

A. Skin scraping
B. Fecal sedimentation
C. ELISA test
D. Blood smear

Answer: B. Fecal sedimentation
(Trematode eggs are heavy and often missed by flotation methods.)

5. Which of the following is a potential clinical sign of trematode infection in rabbits?

A. Seizures
B. Jaundice
C. Alopecia
D. Head tilt

Answer: B. Jaundice
(Due to liver damage caused by migrating flukes.)

Trematodes of Rabbits MCQ

1. Which of the following is a trematode commonly found in rabbits?

A. *Fasciola hepatica*
B. *Taenia pisiformis*
C. *Trichostrongylus retortaeformis*
D. *Eimeria stiedae*

Answer: A. *Fasciola hepatica*
(Note: Although rare, rabbits can be accidental hosts of Fasciola hepatica, a liver fluke.)

2. What is the primary site of infection for *Fasciola hepatica* in rabbits?

A. Lungs
B. Small intestine
C. Liver and bile ducts
D. Kidneys

Answer: C. Liver and bile ducts

3. How do rabbits typically acquire trematode infections like *Fasciola hepatica*?

A. Direct contact with infected animals
B. Inhalation of spores
C. Ingestion of contaminated water or vegetation
D. Transplacental transmission

Answer: C. Ingestion of contaminated water or vegetation
(Through ingestion of metacercariae on aquatic plants.)

4. Which diagnostic method is commonly used to detect trematode eggs in rabbits?

A. Skin scraping
B. Fecal sedimentation
C. ELISA test
D. Blood smear

Answer: B. Fecal sedimentation
(Trematode eggs are heavy and often missed by flotation methods.)

5. Which of the following is a potential clinical sign of trematode infection in rabbits?

A. Seizures
B. Jaundice
C. Alopecia
D. Head tilt

Answer: B. Jaundice
(Due to liver damage caused by migrating flukes.)

Hydatid echinococcosis in Rabbits MCQ

1. What is the causative agent of hydatid echinococcosis in rabbits?
A. *Taenia pisiformis*
B. *Echinococcus granulosus*
C. *Eimeria stiedae*
D. *Toxoplasma gondii*
Answer: B. *Echinococcus granulosus*

2. How do rabbits typically become intermediate hosts for *Echinococcus granulosus*?
A. Ingestion of oocysts in contaminated water
B. Bite from an infected tick
C. Inhalation of parasitic spores
D. Ingestion of eggs from contaminated environment or feces
Answer: D. Ingestion of eggs from contaminated environment or feces

3. Which of the following organs in rabbits is most commonly affected by hydatid cysts?
A. Brain
B. Heart
C. Liver
D. Kidney
Answer: C. Liver

4. Which diagnostic method is commonly used to detect hydatid cysts in live rabbits?
A. Skin scraping
B. Fecal flotation
C. Ultrasonography
D. ELISA for antibodies
Answer: C. Ultrasonography

5. What is the primary way to control and prevent hydatid echinococcosis in rabbit populations?
A. Vaccination of rabbits
B. Treating rabbits with anthelmintics

C. Breaking the cycle by deworming dogs and controlling their access to rabbit carcasses
D. Isolating infected rabbits
Answer: C. Breaking the cycle by deworming dogs and controlling their access to rabbit carcasses

Rabbit ear mites Questions

1. What are ear mites in rabbits and what causes them?

Ear mites in rabbits are **tiny parasitic insects**, most commonly *Psoroptes cuniculi*, that **live in the ear canal**. They cause intense irritation and inflammation. Mites spread through **direct contact with infected rabbits** or contaminated objects (e.g., bedding, grooming tools).

2. What are the symptoms of ear mite infestation in rabbits?

Symptoms may include:

- Frequent **scratching** at the ears or head shaking
- **Crusty, scaly buildup** inside the ears
- **Hair loss** around the ears
- Redness, swelling, and sometimes a **foul odor**
- In severe cases, rabbits may lose balance or show neurological signs

3. How are rabbit ear mites diagnosed?

A veterinarian usually diagnoses ear mites by:

- **Visual examination** of the ears for scabs and crusts
- **Microscopic analysis** of ear discharge to identify the mites

4. What treatments are available for ear mites in rabbits?

Common treatments include:

- **Topical or injectable antiparasitic medications** (like ivermectin or selamectin)
- **Cleaning of the ears** (done carefully to avoid damage)

- Treating the rabbit's **environment and other pets** to prevent reinfestation Always follow a **vet's guidance**, as improper cleaning or medication can worsen symptoms.

5. Can humans or other pets get ear mites from rabbits?

Psoroptes cuniculi is **species-specific**, so humans are **unlikely** to be infected. However, **other rabbits and possibly other small pets** can catch mites through contact or shared items. It's essential to isolate affected animals and **disinfect their living spaces**.

Rabbit ear mites MCQ

1. What is the most common species of ear mite affecting rabbits?
A) Sarcoptes scabiei
B) Otodectes cynotis
C) Psoroptes cuniculi
D) Demodex canis

Correct Answer: C) Psoroptes cuniculi

2. Which of the following is a common clinical sign of ear mite infestation in rabbits?
A) Sudden weight gain
B) Thick, crusty discharge in the ears
C) Persistent sneezing
D) Excessive water drinking

Correct Answer: B) Thick, crusty discharge in the ear

3. How are ear mites in rabbits typically diagnosed?
A) Blood test
B) Radiography
C) Microscopic examination of ear debris
D) Urinalysis

Correct Answer: C) Microscopic examination of ear debris

4. What is the best initial treatment for Psoroptes cuniculi in rabbits?
A) Oral antibiotics
B) Cleaning the ears aggressively with water
C) Topical or systemic anti-parasitic medication (e.g., ivermectin or selamectin)
D) Corticosteroids only

Correct Answer: C) Topical or systemic anti-parasitic medication (e.g., ivermectin or selamectin)

5. Which of the following statements is TRUE regarding rabbit ear mites?
A) They are typically asymptomatic.
B) They are not contagious to other rabbits.
C) They can cause secondary bacterial infections if left untreated.
D) They are self-limiting and resolve without treatment.

Correct Answer: C) They can cause secondary bacterial infections if left untreated.

Sarcoptes ***scabiei in Rabbits Questions***

1. What is *Sarcoptes scabiei* and how does it affect rabbits?

Sarcoptes scabiei is a microscopic mite that burrows into the skin of rabbits, causing **sarcoptic mange**. This leads to intense itching, crusting, hair loss, and skin thickening. If left untreated, it can result in secondary bacterial infections and severe discomfort.

2. What are the clinical signs of *Sarcoptes scabiei* infestation in rabbits?

- Intense **pruritus (itching)**
- **Alopecia (hair loss)**, especially around the nose, ears, and legs
- **Crusting and thickening** of the skin (hyperkeratosis)
- **Lethargy** and reduced appetite in severe cases
- Possible **secondary infections**

3. How is *Sarcoptes scabiei* diagnosed in rabbits?

Diagnosis is typically made by:

- **Skin scrapings** examined under a microscope to detect the mites
- **Clinical signs** and history
- In some cases, **PCR testing** or **biopsy** may be used if mites are not found but suspicion remains high

4. What treatment options are available for *Sarcoptes scabiei* in rabbits?

- **Topical or injectable ivermectin** or **selamectin**
- **Anti-inflammatory medications** (if needed)
- **Antibiotics** for secondary infections
- Thorough **environmental cleaning** to prevent reinfestation
- **Isolation** of affected animals

5. Can *Sarcoptes scabiei* be transmitted to humans or other animals?

Yes. *Sarcoptes scabiei* is **zoonotic**, meaning it can be transmitted to humans, causing a temporary dermatitis. It can also infect other mammals, so **cross-infection prevention** is important through proper hygiene and quarantine.

Sarcoptes ***scabiei in Rabbits MCQ***

1. What is the primary clinical sign of *Sarcoptes scabiei* infestation in rabbits?
A. Diarrhea
B. Alopecia and intense pruritus
C. Sneezing and nasal discharge
D. Hind limb paralysis

Answer: B. Alopecia and intense pruritus

2. Which diagnostic method is most commonly used to confirm *Sarcoptes scabiei* infestation in rabbits?
A. Blood culture
B. Skin scraping
C. Urinalysis
D. Radiography

Answer: B. Skin scraping

3. *Sarcoptes scabiei* is classified as which type of parasite?
A. Protozoan
B. Trematode
C. Burrowing mite
D. Flea

Answer: C. Burrowing mite

4. Which of the following is a recommended treatment for sarcoptic mange in rabbits?
A. Ivermectin
B. Amoxicillin
C. Ketoconazole
D. Furosemide

Answer: A. Ivermectin

5. How is *Sarcoptes scabiei* transmitted among rabbits?
A. Contaminated food
B. Aerosol droplets
C. Direct contact with infested animals
D. Vertical transmission only

Answer: C. Direct contact with infested animals

Sarcoptes ***scabiei in Rabbits Questions***

1. What is *Sarcoptes scabiei* and how does it affect rabbits?

Sarcoptes scabiei is a microscopic mite that burrows into the skin of rabbits, causing **sarcoptic mange**. This leads to intense itching, crusting, hair loss, and skin thickening. If left untreated, it can result in secondary bacterial infections and severe discomfort.

2. What are the clinical signs of *Sarcoptes scabiei* infestation in rabbits?

- Intense **pruritus (itching)**
- **Alopecia (hair loss)**, especially around the nose, ears, and legs
- **Crusting and thickening** of the skin (hyperkeratosis)
- **Lethargy** and reduced appetite in severe cases
- Possible **secondary infections**

3. How is *Sarcoptes scabiei* diagnosed in rabbits?

Diagnosis is typically made by:

- **Skin scrapings** examined under a microscope to detect the mites
- **Clinical signs** and history
- In some cases, **PCR testing** or **biopsy** may be used if mites are not found but suspicion remains high

4. What treatment options are available for *Sarcoptes scabiei* in rabbits?

- **Topical or injectable ivermectin** or **selamectin**
- **Anti-inflammatory medications** (if needed)
- **Antibiotics** for secondary infections
- Thorough **environmental cleaning** to prevent reinfestation
- **Isolation** of affected animals

5. Can *Sarcoptes scabiei* be transmitted to humans or other animals?

Yes. *Sarcoptes scabiei* is **zoonotic**, meaning it can be transmitted to humans, causing a temporary dermatitis. It can also infect other mammals, so **cross-infection prevention** is important through proper hygiene and quarantine.

*Sarcoptes **scabiei in Rabbits MCQ***

1. What is the primary clinical sign of *Sarcoptes scabiei* infestation in rabbits?
A. Diarrhea
B. Alopecia and intense pruritus
C. Sneezing and nasal discharge
D. Hind limb paralysis

Answer: B. Alopecia and intense pruritus

2. Which diagnostic method is most commonly used to confirm *Sarcoptes scabiei* infestation in rabbits?
A. Blood culture
B. Skin scraping
C. Urinalysis
D. Radiography

Answer: B. Skin scraping

3. *Sarcoptes scabiei* is classified as which type of parasite?
A. Protozoan
B. Trematode
C. Burrowing mite
D. Flea

Answer: C. Burrowing mite

4. Which of the following is a recommended treatment for sarcoptic mange in rabbits?
A. Ivermectin
B. Amoxicillin
C. Ketoconazole
D. Furosemide

Answer: A. Ivermectin

5. How is *Sarcoptes scabiei* transmitted among rabbits?
A. Contaminated food
B. Aerosol droplets
C. Direct contact with infested animals
D. Vertical transmission only

Answer: C. Direct contact with infested animals

Sarcoptes scabiei in Rabbits Questions

1. What is *Sarcoptes scabiei* and how does it affect rabbits?

Sarcoptes scabiei is a microscopic mite that burrows into the skin of rabbits, causing **sarcoptic mange**. This leads to intense itching, crusting, hair loss, and skin thickening. If left untreated, it can result in secondary bacterial infections and severe discomfort.

2. What are the clinical signs of *Sarcoptes scabiei* infestation in rabbits?

- Intense **pruritus (itching)**
- **Alopecia (hair loss)**, especially around the nose, ears, and legs
- **Crusting and thickening** of the skin (hyperkeratosis)
- **Lethargy** and reduced appetite in severe cases
- Possible **secondary infections**

3. How is *Sarcoptes scabiei* diagnosed in rabbits?

Diagnosis is typically made by:

- **Skin scrapings** examined under a microscope to detect the mites
- **Clinical signs** and history
- In some cases, **PCR testing** or **biopsy** may be used if mites are not found but suspicion remains high

4. What treatment options are available for *Sarcoptes scabiei* in rabbits?

- **Topical or injectable ivermectin** or **selamectin**
- **Anti-inflammatory medications** (if needed)
- **Antibiotics** for secondary infections
- Thorough **environmental cleaning** to prevent reinfestation
- **Isolation** of affected animals

5. Can *Sarcoptes scabiei* be transmitted to humans or other animals?

Yes. *Sarcoptes scabiei* is **zoonotic**, meaning it can be transmitted to humans, causing a temporary dermatitis. It can also infect other mammals, so **cross-infection prevention** is important through proper hygiene and quarantine.

Sarcoptes scabiei in Rabbits MCQ

1. What is the primary clinical sign of *Sarcoptes scabiei* infestation in rabbits?
A. Diarrhea
B. Alopecia and intense pruritus
C. Sneezing and nasal discharge
D. Hind limb paralysis

Answer: B. Alopecia and intense pruritus

2. Which diagnostic method is most commonly used to confirm *Sarcoptes scabiei* infestation in rabbits?
A. Blood culture
B. Skin scraping
C. Urinalysis
D. Radiography

Answer: B. Skin scraping

3. *Sarcoptes scabiei* is classified as which type of parasite?
A. Protozoan
B. Trematode
C. Burrowing mite
D. Flea

Answer: C. Burrowing mite

4. Which of the following is a recommended treatment for sarcoptic mange in rabbits?
A. Ivermectin
B. Amoxicillin
C. Ketoconazole
D. Furosemide

Answer: A. Ivermectin

5. How is *Sarcoptes scabiei* transmitted among rabbits?
A. Contaminated food
B. Aerosol droplets
C. Direct contact with infested animals
D. Vertical transmission only

Answer: C. Direct contact with infested animals

Myiasis (fly-strike) in Rabbits Questions

1. What is myiasis (fly-strike) in rabbits?

Answer: Myiasis is a condition where flies, usually *Lucilia sericata* (green bottle fly), lay eggs on a rabbit's skin, typically around the rear. The eggs hatch into maggots that burrow into the flesh, causing severe tissue damage, infection, and often death if untreated.

2. What are the common signs and symptoms of fly-strike in rabbits?

Answer:

- Sudden lethargy or collapse
- Loss of appetite
- Strong odor from the rear
- Visible maggots in or around the skin
- Red, inflamed, or wet fur near the back end

3. What causes fly-strike in rabbits?

Answer:

- Poor hygiene (dirty bottoms or soiled bedding)
- Warm, humid weather (summer months)
- Overweight or arthritic rabbits that can't groom properly
- Diarrhea or urinary problems causing a moist rear

4. How is fly-strike treated in rabbits?

Answer:

- Immediate veterinary care is critical
- Removal of maggots (under sedation if necessary)
- Cleaning and treating wounds
- Antibiotics and pain relief
- In severe cases, euthanasia may be considered due to extensive damage

5. **How can fly-strike be prevented in rabbits?**

Answer:

- Daily checking of your rabbit, especially in summer
- Keeping the rear area clean and dry
- Using fly repellents or protective sprays (vet-approved)
- Keeping hutches clean and fly-proof
- Ensuring a healthy diet to prevent diarrhea and obesity

Myiasis (fly-strike) in Rabbits MCQ

1. What is the primary cause of fly-strike (myiasis) in rabbits?

A) Viral infection
B) Infestation by parasitic worms
C) Infestation by fly larvae (maggots)
D) Bacterial infection

Correct Answer: C) Infestation by fly larvae (maggots)

2. Which of the following is a major risk factor for a rabbit developing fly-strike?

A) Eating too much hay
B) Living indoors
C) Having soiled fur or wounds
D) Being under 1 year old

Correct Answer: C) Having soiled fur or wounds

3. What species of fly is most commonly associated with fly-strike in rabbits in the UK and Europe?

A) Tabanus bromius (Horse fly)
B) Lucilia sericata (Green bottle fly)
C) Musca domestica (House fly)
D) Calliphora vomitoria (Bluebottle fly)

Correct Answer: B) Lucilia sericata (Green bottle fly)

4. What is a common sign of fly-strike in rabbits?

A) Excessive grooming
B) Dry nose
C) Presence of maggots in the fur
D) Increased appetite

Correct Answer: C) Presence of maggots in the fur

5. What is the most effective way to prevent fly-strike in rabbits?

A) Feeding only pellets
B) Daily cleaning and regular health checks
C) Keeping the rabbit in direct sunlight
D) Using antibiotics regularly

Correct Answer: B) Daily cleaning and regular health checks

Myiasis (fly-strike) in Rabbits Questions

1. What is myiasis (fly-strike) in rabbits?

Answer: Myiasis is a condition where flies, usually *Lucilia sericata* (green bottle fly), lay eggs on a rabbit's skin, typically around the rear. The eggs hatch into maggots that burrow into the flesh, causing severe tissue damage, infection, and often death if untreated.

2. What are the common signs and symptoms of fly-strike in rabbits?

Answer:

- Sudden lethargy or collapse
- Loss of appetite
- Strong odor from the rear
- Visible maggots in or around the skin
- Red, inflamed, or wet fur near the back end

3. What causes fly-strike in rabbits?

Answer:

- Poor hygiene (dirty bottoms or soiled bedding)
- Warm, humid weather (summer months)
- Overweight or arthritic rabbits that can't groom properly
- Diarrhea or urinary problems causing a moist rear

4. How is fly-strike treated in rabbits?

Answer:

- Immediate veterinary care is critical
- Removal of maggots (under sedation if necessary)
- Cleaning and treating wounds
- Antibiotics and pain relief
- In severe cases, euthanasia may be considered due to extensive damage

5. How can fly-strike be prevented in rabbits?

Answer:

- Daily checking of your rabbit, especially in summer
- Keeping the rear area clean and dry
- Using fly repellents or protective sprays (vet-approved)
- Keeping hutches clean and fly-proof
- Ensuring a healthy diet to prevent diarrhea and obesity

Myiasis (fly-strike) in Rabbits MCQ

1. What is the primary cause of fly-strike (myiasis) in rabbits?

A) Viral infection
B) Infestation by parasitic worms
C) Infestation by fly larvae (maggots)
D) Bacterial infection

Correct Answer: C) Infestation by fly larvae (maggots)

2. Which of the following is a major risk factor for a rabbit developing fly-strike?

A) Eating too much hay
B) Living indoors
C) Having soiled fur or wounds
D) Being under 1 year old

Correct Answer: C) Having soiled fur or wounds

3. What species of fly is most commonly associated with fly-strike in rabbits in the UK and Europe?

A) Tabanus bromius (Horse fly)
B) Lucilia sericata (Green bottle fly)
C) Musca domestica (House fly)
D) Calliphora vomitoria (Bluebottle fly)

Correct Answer: B) Lucilia sericata (Green bottle fly)

4. What is a common sign of fly-strike in rabbits?

A) Excessive grooming
B) Dry nose
C) Presence of maggots in the fur
D) Increased appetite

Correct Answer: C) Presence of maggots in the fur

5. What is the most effective way to prevent fly-strike in rabbits?

A) Feeding only pellets
B) Daily cleaning and regular health checks
C) Keeping the rabbit in direct sunlight
D) Using antibiotics regularly

Correct Answer: B) Daily cleaning and regular health checks

Rabbit ear mites Questions

1. What are ear mites in rabbits and what causes them?

Ear mites in rabbits are **tiny parasitic insects**, most commonly *Psoroptes cuniculi*, that **live in the ear canal**. They cause intense irritation and inflammation. Mites spread through **direct contact with infected rabbits** or contaminated objects (e.g., bedding, grooming tools).

2. What are the symptoms of ear mite infestation in rabbits?

Symptoms may include:

- Frequent **scratching** at the ears or head shaking
- **Crusty, scaly buildup** inside the ears
- **Hair loss** around the ears
- Redness, swelling, and sometimes a **foul odor**
- In severe cases, rabbits may lose balance or show neurological signs

3. How are rabbit ear mites diagnosed?

A veterinarian usually diagnoses ear mites by:

- **Visual examination** of the ears for scabs and crusts
- **Microscopic analysis** of ear discharge to identify the mites

4. What treatments are available for ear mites in rabbits?

Common treatments include:

- **Topical or injectable antiparasitic medications** (like ivermectin or selamectin)
- **Cleaning of the ears** (done carefully to avoid damage)

- Treating the rabbit's **environment and other pets** to prevent reinfestation Always follow a **vet's guidance**, as improper cleaning or medication can worsen symptoms.

5. Can humans or other pets get ear mites from rabbits?

Psoroptes cuniculi is **species-specific**, so humans are **unlikely** to be infected. However, **other rabbits and possibly other small pets** can catch mites through contact or shared items. It's essential to isolate affected animals and **disinfect their living spaces**.

Rabbit ear mites MCQ

1. What is the most common species of ear mite affecting rabbits?
A) Sarcoptes scabiei
B) Otodectes cynotis
C) Psoroptes cuniculi
D) Demodex canis

Correct Answer: C) Psoroptes cuniculi

2. Which of the following is a common clinical sign of ear mite infestation in rabbits?
A) Sudden weight gain
B) Thick, crusty discharge in the ears
C) Persistent sneezing
D) Excessive water drinking

Correct Answer: B) Thick, crusty discharge in the ear

3. How are ear mites in rabbits typically diagnosed?
A) Blood test
B) Radiography
C) Microscopic examination of ear debris
D) Urinalysis

Correct Answer: C) Microscopic examination of ear debris

4. What is the best initial treatment for Psoroptes cuniculi in rabbits?
A) Oral antibiotics
B) Cleaning the ears aggressively with water
C) Topical or systemic anti-parasitic medication (e.g., ivermectin or selamectin)
D) Corticosteroids only

Correct Answer: C) Topical or systemic anti-parasitic medication (e.g., ivermectin or selamectin)

5. Which of the following statements is TRUE regarding rabbit ear mites?
A) They are typically asymptomatic.
B) They are not contagious to other rabbits.
C) They can cause secondary bacterial infections if left untreated.
D) They are self-limiting and resolve without treatment.

Correct Answer: C) They can cause secondary bacterial infections if left untreated.

Haemaphysalis leporispalustris (the rabbit tick) Questions

1. What is *Haemaphysalis leporispalustris*?

It is a species of **hard tick** (family *Ixodidae*) that primarily feeds on **lagomorphs** (rabbits and hares), although it may also feed on birds and other small mammals.

2. Where is the rabbit tick commonly found?

It is widely distributed across **North and Central America**, including the United States, Canada, Mexico, and parts of Central America. It prefers **cooler, wooded environments**.

3. What hosts does it prefer?

The rabbit tick has a strong preference for **cottontail rabbits** and **snowshoe hares**, but it may also infest **ground-feeding birds** and small mammals during its larval and nymph stages.

4. Is *H. leporispalustris* a vector for any diseases?

Yes. While not a major human pest, it can transmit **Rickettsia rickettsii** (the agent of Rocky Mountain spotted fever) and **Francisella tularensis** (which causes tularemia) to wildlife and potentially humans.

5. What is the lifecycle of *Haemaphysalis leporispalustris*?

It has a **three-host lifecycle** (larva, nymph, adult), each stage feeding on a different host. The cycle can take **several months to a year**, depending on environmental conditions.

Haemaphysalis leporispalustris (the rabbit tick) MCQ

1. What is the primary host of *Haemaphysalis leporispalustris*?

A. Deer
B. Rabbits and hares
C. Cattle
D. Dogs

Answer: B. Rabbits and hares

2. Which of the following best describes the geographic distribution of *Haemaphysalis leporispalustris*?

A. Exclusive to Africa
B. Found mainly in tropical Asia
C. Widespread across North and Central America
D. Endemic to Australia

Answer: C. Widespread across North and Central America

3. What disease is *Haemaphysalis leporispalustris* known to potentially transmit?

A. Malaria
B. Rocky Mountain spotted fever
C. Lyme disease
D. Anaplasmosis

Answer: B. Rocky Mountain spotted fever
(It is a potential vector of Rickettsia rickettsii, the agent of RMSF.)

4. Which of the following best describes the life cycle of *Haemaphysalis leporispalustris*?

A. Two-host tick
B. One-host tick
C. Three-host tick
D. Does not require a host

Answer: C. Three-host tick

5. In which habitat is *Haemaphysalis leporispalustris* most commonly found?

A. Desert scrubland
B. Arctic tundra
C. Wooded and brushy areas
D. Open ocean shores

Answer: C. Wooded and brushy areas

Fleas of Rabbits Questions

1. Can rabbits get fleas, and if so, how?

Yes, rabbits can get fleas, especially if they come into contact with other infested animals like cats or dogs, or if they spend time outdoors. Fleas can jump from one host to another or be picked up from environments with flea eggs or larvae.

2. What are the symptoms of fleas on a rabbit?

Common signs include:

- Excessive scratching or biting at fur
- Bald patches or hair loss
- Red, irritated skin
- Flea dirt (small black specks) in fur

- Lethargy or anemia in severe infestations

3. Are fleas dangerous to rabbits?

Yes. Besides discomfort and skin irritation, fleas can cause **anemia** due to blood loss, especially in small or young rabbits.

Fleas can also transmit diseases like **myxomatosis** and **Rabbit Hemorrhagic Disease Virus (RHDV)** in some areas.

4. How can you safely treat a rabbit for fleas?

Use only **rabbit-safe flea treatments**, often prescribed by a vet.

Some topical treatments for cats may be fatal to rabbits.

Avoid over-the-counter products unless approved by a veterinarian.

Clean bedding, living areas, and any other pets at the same time to prevent reinfestation.

5. Can you prevent flea infestations in rabbits?

Yes. Keep indoor rabbits away from flea-prone pets. Regularly clean their habitat and vacuum floors. If your rabbit goes outside, limit time in high-risk areas. Vets may recommend preventative treatments in flea-heavy regions.

Fleas of Rabbits MCQ

1. What is the most common flea species found on rabbits?

A) *Ctenocephalides felis* (cat flea)
B) *Spilopsyllus cuniculi* (rabbit flea)
C) *Pulex irritans* (human flea)
D) *Xenopsylla cheopis* (rat flea)

Answer: B) *Spilopsyllus cuniculi*

2. What role does *Spilopsyllus cuniculi* play in rabbit populations in the wild?

A) Helps with grooming
B) Transmits myxomatosis virus
C) Pollinates plants
D) Acts as a predator of lice

Answer: B) Transmits myxomatosis virus

3. Which of the following signs may indicate a rabbit is infested with fleas?

A) Lethargy and watery eyes
B) Hair loss and excessive scratching
C) Limping and ear drooping
D) Weight gain and increased appetite

Answer: B) Hair loss and excessive scratching

4. What is the safest way to treat a pet rabbit for fleas?

A) Use dog flea shampoo
B) Use a permethrin-based flea spray
C) Use a rabbit-safe flea treatment prescribed by a vet
D) Use garlic in their food

Answer: C) Use a rabbit-safe flea treatment prescribed by a vet

5. How can you prevent flea infestations in indoor rabbits?

A) Bathing them weekly
B) Allowing them outside to build resistance
C) Regularly cleaning bedding and using flea control on other pets
D) Keeping them in dark, humid environments

Answer: C) Regularly cleaning bedding and using flea control on other pets

BLOOD PARASITES OF RABBITS MCQ

Trypanosoma cuniculi MCQ

1. **Which of the following statements about Trypanosoma cuniculicida infection in rabbits is correct?**
   A. Rabbits are highly susceptible and show rapid, severe disease.
   B. Rabbits are relatively resistant to infection and rarely develop disease. ERA+1
   C. The main route of infection is ingestion of contaminated feed.
   D. The parasite is mainly transmitted by ticks.

   Answer: B. In the study of T. cuniculicida, rabbits were described as "relatively insusceptible to experimental infection". ERA+1

2. **Which vector is implicated in the transmission of a rabbit trypanosome species in Australia?**
   A. Mosquito
   B. Tick
   C. Rabbit flea, Spilopsyllus cuniculi PubMed
   D. Sandfly

   Answer: C. In Australia the rabbit flea *Spilopsyllus cuniculi* was implicated as the vector for Trypanosoma nabiasi (a rabbit trypanosome). PubMed

3. **Which of the following laboratory / haematological changes might you expect in rabbits experimentally infected with a trypanosome (e.g., T. brucei or T. congolense)?**
   A. Increased red-blood-cell count
   B. Elevated hemoglobin
   C. Reduced RBC count and hemoglobin level njap.org.ng
   D. No changes in WBC count

   Answer: C. In one comparative study in rabbits infected with T. brucei or T. congolense, there was a **significant reduction** in RBC count and haemoglobin levels. njap.org.ng

4. **Which of the following best describes the epidemiological significance of trypanosomiasis in rabbits (according to older literature)?**
A. Corroborated as a major spontaneous disease in commercial rabbitries worldwide
B. Rabbits frequently serve as major reservoirs for human trypanosomiasis
C. Few data; infection in rabbits appears experimental or under special circumstances FAOHome+1
D. It is mainly transmitted vertically (from doe to kits) in rabbits

Answer: C. Older sources indicate there are "few data on this disease" in rabbits; most information is about experimental infections rather than major natural outbreaks. FAOHome+1

5. **Which of the following is TRUE about the host-parasite relationship of T. cuniculicida in rabbits?**
A. Rats, mice and guinea-pigs can be infected equally as rabbits.
B. Passage of the parasite in rabbits was accomplished via infestation with fleas. ERA+1
C. Rabbit serum shows strong trypanocidal activity against the parasite.
D. Experimental infection is easily achieved via oral ingestion of parasites.

Answer: B. The original study noted successful passage in rabbits by (1) infestation with *Spilopsyllus cuniculi* fleas from an infected rabbit, and (2) intravenous inoculation of infected blood

Plasmodium berghei MCQ

1. Plasmodium berghei is primarily a parasite of:

A. Humans
B. Monkeys
C. Rodents
D. Rabbits

✅ **Answer:** C. Rodents
Explanation: *Plasmodium berghei* is a rodent malaria parasite, commonly infecting *mice* and *rats*, not rabbits or humans.

2. Why is Plasmodium berghei used in laboratory research involving rabbits?

A. It causes natural malaria infection in rabbits
B. It is used to study host immune responses using rabbit-derived antibodies
C. Rabbits are the definitive host
D. Rabbits serve as vectors for transmission

✅ **Answer:** B. It is used to study host immune responses using rabbit-derived antibodies
Explanation: Although rabbits do **not** develop malaria from *P. berghei*, rabbit antisera (antibodies) are often used to study the parasite in immunological assays or vaccine testing.

3. What is the natural route of infection for Plasmodium berghei in its primary host?

A. Ingestion of contaminated food
B. Bite of infected Anopheles mosquito
C. Direct contact with infected blood
D. Airborne transmission

✅ **Answer:** B. Bite of infected *Anopheles* mosquito
Explanation: Like human malaria parasites, *P. berghei* is transmitted through the bite of an infected *Anopheles* mosquito in its natural rodent hosts.

4. What happens when Plasmodium berghei is inoculated into a rabbit?

A. Rabbit develops clinical malaria
B. Parasite multiplies in rabbit erythrocytes
C. No infection occurs
D. Rabbit becomes a carrier

✅ **Answer:** C. No infection occurs
Explanation: Rabbits are **non-permissive hosts** for *P. berghei* — the parasite cannot invade or multiply in rabbit red blood cells.

5. In malaria research, rabbits are often used with Plasmodium berghei to:

A. Model cerebral malaria directly
B. Produce anti-sera for immunological detection
C. Serve as reservoir hosts
D. Maintain the parasite lifecycle

✅ **Answer:** B. Produce anti-sera for immunological detection
Explanation: Rabbit immune systems are used to produce antibodies against *P. berghei* antigens for diagnostic and research purposes.

6. What type of malaria does Plasmodium berghei typically cause in its natural host?

A. Relapsing malaria
B. Cerebral malaria
C. Vivax-type malaria
D. Chronic low-grade malaria

✅ **Answer:** B. Cerebral malaria
Explanation: In mice, certain strains of *P. berghei* (like ANKA) can cause cerebral malaria, a model used to study severe human malaria.

7. Which of the following is *not* a characteristic of Plasmodium berghei?

A. Rodent malaria parasite
B. Used in malaria vaccine research
C. Infects rabbits naturally
D. Transmitted by Anopheles mosquito

✅ **Answer:** C. Infects rabbits naturally
Explanation: Rabbits do **not** get natural infections from *P. berghei*.

Hepatozoon spp. in RabbitsMCQ

1. Which of the following best describes *Hepatozoon* spp.?

A. Coccidian parasite transmitted by ingestion of oocysts from feces
B. Haemoprotozoan parasite transmitted by ingestion of infected arthropods
C. Nematode parasite transmitted by mosquito bites
D. Trematode parasite transmitted via snails

✅ **Answer:** B. Haemoprotozoan parasite transmitted by ingestion of infected arthropods

Explanation:
Hepatozoon species are apicomplexan parasites (haemogregarines) transmitted when a host ingests an infected arthropod vector, such as a tick.

2. What is the primary site of *Hepatozoon* spp. infection in rabbits?

A. Liver and spleen
B. Intestinal mucosa
C. Skin and subcutaneous tissue
D. Respiratory epithelium

✅ **Answer:** A. Liver and spleen

Explanation:
In rabbits, *Hepatozoon* parasites often localize in the liver, spleen, and sometimes in circulating leukocytes.

3. Which stage of *Hepatozoon* spp. is typically observed in peripheral blood smears?

A. Oocyst
B. Schizont
C. Gamont
D. Sporozoite

✅ **Answer:** C. Gamont

Explanation:
Gamonts of *Hepatozoon* spp. are seen within leukocytes (especially neutrophils and monocytes) in stained blood smears.

4. How do rabbits most likely become infected with *Hepatozoon* spp.?

A. Tick bite during blood feeding
B. Ingestion of an infected tick or arthropod
C. Vertical transmission from doe to kits
D. Contaminated water ingestion

✅ **Answer:** B. Ingestion of an infected tick or arthropod

Explanation:
Unlike many blood parasites, *Hepatozoon* is not transmitted by bites but by ingestion of infected arthropods.

5. Which diagnostic technique is most reliable for identifying *Hepatozoon* infection in rabbits?

A. Fecal flotation test
B. Blood smear examination under microscopy
C. Skin scraping
D. Urinalysis

✅ **Answer:** B. Blood smear examination under microscopy

Explanation:
Microscopic identification of gamonts within leukocytes on Giemsa-stained blood smears is the most common diagnostic method.

Trypanosoma nabiasi MCQ

1. The primary vector (intermediate host) responsible for transmission of Trypanosoma nabiasi to rabbits is:
A) Tsetse fly (Glossina)
B) Rabbit flea (Spilopsyllus cuniculi)

C) Sand fly (Phlebotomus)
D) Tick (Ixodes)
Answer: B) Rabbit flea (Spilopsyllus cuniculi)
Explanation: The life-cycle of T. nabiasi involves the rabbit flea S. cuniculi as the arthropod vector. Cambridge University Press & Assessment+2MDPI+2

2. In rabbits experimentally infected with T. nabiasi, what is the approximate pre-patent period (time until parasites appear in blood) under experimental conditions?
A) 1-2 days
B) 3-4 days
C) 5-12 days
D) 20-30 days
Answer: C) 5-12 days
Explanation: In experimentally infected rabbits, incubation (or pre-patent) period varied from 5 to 12 days. Cambridge University Press & Assessment+1

3. Which of the following best describes the pathogenicity of T. nabiasi in its normal rabbit host?
A) Highly pathogenic, causing severe anemia and death
B) Moderately pathogenic, causing chronic wasting
C) Mildly pathogenic, causing occasional signs
D) Essentially non-pathogenic, with minimal effect
Answer: D) Essentially non-pathogenic, with minimal effect
Explanation: The parasite is described as non-pathogenic (or minimally pathogenic) in its normal rabbit host. Cambridge University Press & Assessment+1

4. Which of the following is *not* a recognized route by which rabbits may become infected by T. nabiasi?
A) Bite of infected rabbit flea
B) Ingestion of infected flea
C) Contamination of skin/mucosa with flea faeces
D) Direct rabbit-to-rabbit blood contact
Answer: D) Direct rabbit-to-rabbit blood contact
Explanation: The known routes include ingestion of the flea or contamination via flea faeces on skin/mucosa. Direct rabbit-to-rabbit blood contact is not documented. PMC+1

5. After infection and subsequent recovery from T. nabiasi, what is the status of immunity in the rabbit host?

A) No immunity, rabbits can be re-infected immediately
B) Partial immunity, rabbits show milder re-infection
C) Rabbits become immune to reinfection for some time
D) Immunity only occurs if fleas are absent
Answer: C) Rabbits become immune to reinfection for some time
Explanation: Following recovery, rabbits were shown to become immune to reinfection with T. nabiasi. Cambridge University Press & Assessment+1

Besnoitia oryctofelisi MCQ

1. *Besnoitia oryctofelisi* primarily infects which host species?

A. Cattle
B. Domestic rabbit (*Oryctolagus cuniculus*)
C. Cat (*Felis catus*)
D. Dog (*Canis lupus familiaris*)

Answer: ✅ B. Domestic rabbit (*Oryctolagus cuniculus*)
Explanation: *Besnoitia oryctofelisi* is a protozoan parasite found in rabbits, with the cat acting as the definitive host.

2. What type of organism is *Besnoitia oryctofelisi*?

A. Trematode
B. Cestode
C. Protozoan (Apicomplexan)
D. Nematode

Answer: ✅ C. Protozoan (Apicomplexan)
Explanation: *Besnoitia oryctofelisi* is a coccidian protozoan belonging to the phylum **Apicomplexa**, related to *Toxoplasma* and *Neospora*.

3. Which animal acts as the definitive host for *Besnoitia oryctofelisi*?

A. Rabbit
B. Fox
C. Cat
D. Cow

Answer: ✅ C. Cat
Explanation: The cat serves as the **definitive host**, where sexual reproduction of the parasite occurs in the intestinal epithelium.

4. What is the main site of tissue cyst formation in the intermediate host (rabbit)?

A. Liver
B. Brain
C. Subcutaneous tissues and connective tissue
D. Lungs

Answer: ✅ C. Subcutaneous tissues and connective tissue
Explanation: Infected rabbits develop cysts in **subcutaneous and connective tissues**, typical of *Besnoitia* infections.

5. How is *Besnoitia oryctofelisi* transmitted to the definitive host (cat)?

A. Ingestion of sporulated oocysts in feces
B. Ingestion of infected rabbit tissues containing cysts
C. Bite from infected insects
D. Transplacental transmission

Answer: ✅ B. Ingestion of infected rabbit tissues containing cysts
Explanation: Cats acquire infection by **eating infected rabbit tissues** containing bradyzoite cysts.

Hepatozoon cuniculi MCQ

1. What type of organism is *Hepatozoon cuniculi*?

A. Bacterium
B. Virus
C. Protozoan parasite
D. Fungus

✅ **Answer:** C. Protozoan parasite
Explanation: *Hepatozoon cuniculi* is a protozoan parasite belonging to the phylum **Apicomplexa**, similar to *Hepatozoon canis* and *Hepatozoon americanum* in dogs.

2. What is the primary site of *Hepatozoon cuniculi* infection in rabbits?

A. Intestinal mucosa
B. Liver and spleen
C. Kidneys
D. Respiratory tract

✅ **Answer:** B. Liver and spleen
Explanation: The parasite mainly infects the **hepatic (liver) and splenic tissues**, where schizonts can be observed in histological sections.

3. Which of the following is the most common route of transmission for *Hepatozoon cuniculi* in rabbits?

A. Ingestion of infected arthropods
B. Direct contact with infected rabbits
C. Transplacental transmission
D. Bite from infected mosquitoes

✅ **Answer:** A. Ingestion of infected arthropods
Explanation: Similar to other *Hepatozoon* species, infection typically occurs when rabbits **ingest infected arthropods** containing mature oocysts.

4. What histopathological feature is characteristic of *Hepatozoon cuniculi* infection?

A. Granulomatous inflammation in lungs
B. Intracellular schizonts within hepatocytes and Kupffer cells
C. Necrosis of intestinal villi
D. Cyst formation in kidney tubules

✅ **Answer:** B. Intracellular schizonts within hepatocytes and Kupffer cells
Explanation: Histopathology reveals **intracellular schizonts** in **liver and spleen macrophages (Kupffer cells)**, confirming infection.

5. Which diagnostic method is most reliable for confirming *Hepatozoon cuniculi* infection?

A. Fecal flotation
B. PCR or histopathology of tissue samples
C. Serology (ELISA)
D. Blood culture

✅ **Answer:** B. PCR or histopathology of tissue samples
Explanation: Diagnosis is usually confirmed by **PCR** detection of *Hepatozoon* DNA or **microscopic examination** of tissue sections showing characteristic schizonts.

Toxoplasma gondii in Rabbits MCQ

1. Which of the following is the definitive host of *Toxoplasma gondii*?

A. Rabbit
B. Dog
C. Cat
D. Rat

Answer: ✅ C. Cat
Explanation: Cats (domestic and wild felids) are the only definitive hosts that can shed *T. gondii* oocysts in feces.

2. How do rabbits most commonly acquire *Toxoplasma gondii* infection?

A. Inhalation of oocysts
B. Bite from infected cat
C. Ingestion of oocysts from contaminated feed or water
D. Transplacental infection from the doe

Answer: ✅ C. Ingestion of oocysts from contaminated feed or water
Explanation: Rabbits become infected by ingesting sporulated oocysts from contaminated environments.

3. What is the usual clinical presentation of *Toxoplasma gondii* infection in rabbits?

A. Severe diarrhea
B. Often subclinical, but may cause neurological signs or abortion
C. Jaundice and hepatic necrosis
D. Chronic cough and dyspnea

Answer: ✅ B. Often subclinical, but may cause neurological signs or abortion
Explanation: Infection in rabbits is mostly subclinical; in severe cases, it can cause encephalitis, paralysis, or reproductive issues.

4. Which diagnostic method is most reliable for confirming *Toxoplasma gondii* infection in rabbits?

A. Blood glucose test
B. Microscopic examination of feces
C. Serological tests (e.g., ELISA, IFAT) or PCR
D. Skin scraping

Answer: ✅ C. Serological tests (e.g., ELISA, IFAT) or PCR
Explanation: Diagnosis is based on detection of antibodies or parasite DNA, since rabbits do not shed oocysts.

5. How can *Toxoplasma gondii* infection be prevented in rabbit farms?

A. Regular vaccination of rabbits
B. Keeping cats away from feed and water, and proper hygiene

C. Routine deworming with ivermectin
D. Feeding raw meat to rabbits

Answer: ✅ B. Keeping cats away from feed and water, and proper hygiene
Explanation: Preventing contamination of feed and water with cat feces is the main control strategy

Brugia lepori in Rabbits MCQ

1. Brugia lepori belongs to which group of parasites?

A. Trematodes
B. Cestodes
C. Nematodes
D. Protozoa

✅ **Answer:** C. Nematodes

Explanation: *Brugia lepori* is a filarial nematode (roundworm) that infects rabbits.

2. What is the primary site of infection of *Brugia lepori* in rabbits?

A. Intestinal tract
B. Subcutaneous tissues and lymphatic vessels
C. Liver parenchyma
D. Lungs and bronchi

✅ **Answer:** B. Subcutaneous tissues and lymphatic vessels

Explanation: *Brugia lepori* is a filarial worm found mainly in the lymphatic system and subcutaneous tissue of rabbits.

3. Which arthropod acts as the vector for transmission of *Brugia lepori*?

A. Fleas
B. Ticks
C. Mosquitoes
D. Lice

✅ **Answer:** C. Mosquitoes

Explanation: *Brugia lepori* is transmitted by mosquitoes, similar to other *Brugia* species that cause lymphatic filariasis.

4. Which of the following is the diagnostic stage of *Brugia lepori* in the host?

A. Adult worms in lymph nodes
B. Eggs in feces
C. Microfilariae in peripheral blood
D. Larvae in the lungs

✅ **Answer:** C. Microfilariae in peripheral blood

Explanation: Diagnosis is usually made by detecting microfilariae in the blood of infected rabbits.

5. *Brugia lepori* infection in rabbits is mainly used as a model for which human disease?

A. Ascariasis
B. Filariasis (Lymphatic filariasis)
C. Schistosomiasis
D. Leishmaniasis

✅ **Answer:** B. Filariasis (Lymphatic filariasis)

Explanation: *Brugia lepori* infection in rabbits is an experimental model for studying lymphatic filariasis caused by *Brugia malayi* in humans.

Brugia lepori in Rabbits MCQ

1. Brugia lepori belongs to which group of parasites?

A. Trematodes
B. Cestodes
C. Nematodes
D. Protozoa

✅ **Answer:** C. Nematodes

Explanation: *Brugia lepori* is a filarial nematode (roundworm) that infects rabbits.

2. What is the primary site of infection of *Brugia lepori* in rabbits?

A. Intestinal tract
B. Subcutaneous tissues and lymphatic vessels
C. Liver parenchyma
D. Lungs and bronchi

✅ **Answer:** B. Subcutaneous tissues and lymphatic vessels

Explanation: *Brugia lepori* is a filarial worm found mainly in the lymphatic system and subcutaneous tissue of rabbits.

3. Which arthropod acts as the vector for transmission of *Brugia lepori*?

A. Fleas
B. Ticks
C. Mosquitoes
D. Lice

✅ **Answer:** C. Mosquitoes

Explanation: *Brugia lepori* is transmitted by mosquitoes, similar to other *Brugia* species that cause lymphatic filariasis.

4. Which of the following is the diagnostic stage of *Brugia lepori* in the host?

A. Adult worms in lymph nodes
B. Eggs in feces
C. Microfilariae in peripheral blood
D. Larvae in the lungs

✅ **Answer:** C. Microfilariae in peripheral blood

Explanation: Diagnosis is usually made by detecting microfilariae in the blood of infected rabbits.

5. *Brugia lepori* infection in rabbits is mainly used as a model for which human disease?

A. Ascariasis
B. Filariasis (Lymphatic filariasis)
C. Schistosomiasis
D. Leishmaniasis

✅ **Answer:** B. Filariasis (Lymphatic filariasis)

Explanation: *Brugia lepori* infection in rabbits is an experimental model for studying lymphatic filariasis caused by *Brugia malayi* in humans.

BLOOD PARASITES OF RABBITS MCQ

Trypanosoma cuniculi MCQ

2. **Which of the following statements about Trypanosoma cuniculicida infection in rabbits is correct?**
   A. Rabbits are highly susceptible and show rapid, severe disease.
   B. Rabbits are relatively resistant to infection and rarely develop disease. ERA+1
   C. The main route of infection is ingestion of contaminated feed.
   D. The parasite is mainly transmitted by ticks.

   Answer: B. In the study of T. cuniculicida, rabbits were described as "relatively insusceptible to experimental infection". ERA+1

3. **Which vector is implicated in the transmission of a rabbit trypanosome species in Australia?**
   A. Mosquito
   B. Tick
   C. Rabbit flea, Spilopsyllus cuniculi PubMed
   D. Sandfly

   Answer: C. In Australia the rabbit flea *Spilopsyllus cuniculi* was implicated as the vector for Trypanosoma nabiasi (a rabbit trypanosome). PubMed

4. **Which of the following laboratory / haematological changes might you expect in rabbits experimentally infected with a trypanosome (e.g., T. brucei or T. congolense)?**
   A. Increased red-blood-cell count
   B. Elevated hemoglobin
   C. Reduced RBC count and hemoglobin level njap.org.ng
   D. No changes in WBC count

   Answer: C. In one comparative study in rabbits infected with T. brucei or T. congolense, there was a **significant reduction** in RBC count and haemoglobin levels. njap.org.ng

5. **Which of the following best describes the epidemiological significance of trypanosomiasis in rabbits (according to older literature)?**
A. Corroborated as a major spontaneous disease in commercial rabbitries worldwide
B. Rabbits frequently serve as major reservoirs for human trypanosomiasis
C. Few data; infection in rabbits appears experimental or under special circumstances FAOHome+1
D. It is mainly transmitted vertically (from doe to kits) in rabbits

Answer: C. Older sources indicate there are "few data on this disease" in rabbits; most information is about experimental infections rather than major natural outbreaks. FAOHome+1

6. **Which of the following is TRUE about the host-parasite relationship of T. cuniculicida in rabbits?**
A. Rats, mice and guinea-pigs can be infected equally as rabbits.
B. Passage of the parasite in rabbits was accomplished via infestation with fleas. ERA+1
C. Rabbit serum shows strong trypanocidal activity against the parasite.
D. Experimental infection is easily achieved via oral ingestion of parasites.

Answer: B. The original study noted successful passage in rabbits by (1) infestation with *Spilopsyllus cuniculi* fleas from an infected rabbit, and (2) intravenous inoculation of infected blood

Plasmodium berghei MCQ

1. Plasmodium berghei is primarily a parasite of:

A. Humans
B. Monkeys
C. Rodents
D. Rabbits

✅ **Answer:** C. Rodents
Explanation: *Plasmodium berghei* is a rodent malaria parasite, commonly infecting *mice* and *rats*, not rabbits or humans.

2. Why is Plasmodium berghei used in laboratory research involving rabbits?

A. It causes natural malaria infection in rabbits
B. It is used to study host immune responses using rabbit-derived antibodies
C. Rabbits are the definitive host
D. Rabbits serve as vectors for transmission

✅ **Answer:** B. It is used to study host immune responses using rabbit-derived antibodies
Explanation: Although rabbits do **not** develop malaria from *P. berghei*, rabbit antisera (antibodies) are often used to study the parasite in immunological assays or vaccine testing.

3. What is the natural route of infection for Plasmodium berghei in its primary host?

A. Ingestion of contaminated food
B. Bite of infected Anopheles mosquito
C. Direct contact with infected blood
D. Airborne transmission

✅ **Answer:** B. Bite of infected *Anopheles* mosquito
Explanation: Like human malaria parasites, *P. berghei* is transmitted through the bite of an infected *Anopheles* mosquito in its natural rodent hosts.

4. What happens when Plasmodium berghei is inoculated into a rabbit?

A. Rabbit develops clinical malaria
B. Parasite multiplies in rabbit erythrocytes
C. No infection occurs
D. Rabbit becomes a carrier

✅ **Answer:** C. No infection occurs
Explanation: Rabbits are **non-permissive hosts** for *P. berghei* — the parasite cannot invade or multiply in rabbit red blood cells.

5. In malaria research, rabbits are often used with Plasmodium berghei to:

A. Model cerebral malaria directly
B. Produce anti-sera for immunological detection
C. Serve as reservoir hosts
D. Maintain the parasite lifecycle

✅ **Answer:** B. Produce anti-sera for immunological detection
Explanation: Rabbit immune systems are used to produce antibodies against *P. berghei* antigens for diagnostic and research purposes.

6. What type of malaria does Plasmodium berghei typically cause in its natural host?

A. Relapsing malaria
B. Cerebral malaria
C. Vivax-type malaria
D. Chronic low-grade malaria

✅ **Answer:** B. Cerebral malaria
Explanation: In mice, certain strains of *P. berghei* (like ANKA) can cause cerebral malaria, a model used to study severe human malaria.

7. Which of the following is *not* a characteristic of Plasmodium berghei?

A. Rodent malaria parasite
B. Used in malaria vaccine research
C. Infects rabbits naturally
D. Transmitted by Anopheles mosquito

✅ **Answer:** C. Infects rabbits naturally
Explanation: Rabbits do **not** get natural infections from *P. berghei*.

Hepatozoon spp. in RabbitsMCQ

1. Which of the following best describes *Hepatozoon* spp.?

A. Coccidian parasite transmitted by ingestion of oocysts from feces
B. Haemoprotozoan parasite transmitted by ingestion of infected arthropods
C. Nematode parasite transmitted by mosquito bites
D. Trematode parasite transmitted via snails

✅ **Answer:** B. Haemoprotozoan parasite transmitted by ingestion of infected arthropods

Explanation:
Hepatozoon species are apicomplexan parasites (haemogregarines) transmitted when a host ingests an infected arthropod vector, such as a tick.

2. What is the primary site of *Hepatozoon* spp. infection in rabbits?

A. Liver and spleen
B. Intestinal mucosa
C. Skin and subcutaneous tissue
D. Respiratory epithelium

✅ **Answer:** A. Liver and spleen

Explanation:
In rabbits, *Hepatozoon* parasites often localize in the liver, spleen, and sometimes in circulating leukocytes.

3. Which stage of *Hepatozoon* spp. is typically observed in peripheral blood smears?

A. Oocyst
B. Schizont
C. Gamont
D. Sporozoite

✅ **Answer:** C. Gamont

Explanation:
Gamonts of *Hepatozoon* spp. are seen within leukocytes (especially neutrophils and monocytes) in stained blood smears.

4. How do rabbits most likely become infected with *Hepatozoon* spp.?

A. Tick bite during blood feeding
B. Ingestion of an infected tick or arthropod
C. Vertical transmission from doe to kits
D. Contaminated water ingestion

✅ **Answer:** B. Ingestion of an infected tick or arthropod

Explanation:
Unlike many blood parasites, *Hepatozoon* is not transmitted by bites but by ingestion of infected arthropods.

5. Which diagnostic technique is most reliable for identifying *Hepatozoon* infection in rabbits?

A. Fecal flotation test
B. Blood smear examination under microscopy
C. Skin scraping
D. Urinalysis

✅ **Answer:** B. Blood smear examination under microscopy

Explanation:
Microscopic identification of gamonts within leukocytes on Giemsa-stained blood smears is the most common diagnostic method.

Trypanosoma nabiasi MCQ

1. The primary vector (intermediate host) responsible for transmission of Trypanosoma nabiasi to rabbits is:
A) Tsetse fly (Glossina)
B) Rabbit flea (Spilopsyllus cuniculi)

C) Sand fly (Phlebotomus)
D) Tick (Ixodes)
Answer: B) Rabbit flea (Spilopsyllus cuniculi)
Explanation: The life-cycle of T. nabiasi involves the rabbit flea S. cuniculi as the arthropod vector. Cambridge University Press & Assessment+2MDPI+2

2. In rabbits experimentally infected with T. nabiasi, what is the approximate pre-patent period (time until parasites appear in blood) under experimental conditions?
A) 1-2 days
B) 3-4 days
C) 5-12 days
D) 20-30 days
Answer: C) 5-12 days
Explanation: In experimentally infected rabbits, incubation (or pre-patent) period varied from 5 to 12 days. Cambridge University Press & Assessment+1

3. Which of the following best describes the pathogenicity of T. nabiasi in its normal rabbit host?
A) Highly pathogenic, causing severe anemia and death
B) Moderately pathogenic, causing chronic wasting
C) Mildly pathogenic, causing occasional signs
D) Essentially non-pathogenic, with minimal effect
Answer: D) Essentially non-pathogenic, with minimal effect
Explanation: The parasite is described as non-pathogenic (or minimally pathogenic) in its normal rabbit host. Cambridge University Press & Assessment+1

4. Which of the following is *not* a recognized route by which rabbits may become infected by T. nabiasi?
A) Bite of infected rabbit flea
B) Ingestion of infected flea
C) Contamination of skin/mucosa with flea faeces
D) Direct rabbit-to-rabbit blood contact
Answer: D) Direct rabbit-to-rabbit blood contact
Explanation: The known routes include ingestion of the flea or contamination via flea faeces on skin/mucosa. Direct rabbit-to-rabbit blood contact is not documented. PMC+1

5. After infection and subsequent recovery from T. nabiasi, what is the status of immunity in the rabbit host?

A) No immunity, rabbits can be re-infected immediately
B) Partial immunity, rabbits show milder re-infection
C) Rabbits become immune to reinfection for some time
D) Immunity only occurs if fleas are absent
Answer: C) Rabbits become immune to reinfection for some time
Explanation: Following recovery, rabbits were shown to become immune to reinfection with T. nabiasi. Cambridge University Press & Assessment+1

Besnoitia oryctofelisi MCQ

1. *Besnoitia oryctofelisi* primarily infects which host species?

A. Cattle
B. Domestic rabbit (*Oryctolagus cuniculus*)
C. Cat (*Felis catus*)
D. Dog (*Canis lupus familiaris*)

Answer: ✅ B. Domestic rabbit (*Oryctolagus cuniculus*)
Explanation: *Besnoitia oryctofelisi* is a protozoan parasite found in rabbits, with the cat acting as the definitive host.

2. What type of organism is *Besnoitia oryctofelisi*?

A. Trematode
B. Cestode
C. Protozoan (Apicomplexan)
D. Nematode

Answer: ✅ C. Protozoan (Apicomplexan)
Explanation: *Besnoitia oryctofelisi* is a coccidian protozoan belonging to the phylum **Apicomplexa**, related to *Toxoplasma* and *Neospora*.

3. Which animal acts as the definitive host for *Besnoitia oryctofelisi*?

A. Rabbit
B. Fox
C. Cat
D. Cow

Answer: ✅ C. Cat
Explanation: The cat serves as the **definitive host**, where sexual reproduction of the parasite occurs in the intestinal epithelium.

4. What is the main site of tissue cyst formation in the intermediate host (rabbit)?

A. Liver
B. Brain
C. Subcutaneous tissues and connective tissue
D. Lungs

Answer: ✅ C. Subcutaneous tissues and connective tissue
Explanation: Infected rabbits develop cysts in **subcutaneous and connective tissues**, typical of *Besnoitia* infections.

5. How is *Besnoitia oryctofelisi* transmitted to the definitive host (cat)?

A. Ingestion of sporulated oocysts in feces
B. Ingestion of infected rabbit tissues containing cysts
C. Bite from infected insects
D. Transplacental transmission

Answer: ✅ B. Ingestion of infected rabbit tissues containing cysts
Explanation: Cats acquire infection by **eating infected rabbit tissues** containing bradyzoite cysts.

Hepatozoon cuniculi MCQ

1. What type of organism is *Hepatozoon cuniculi*?

A. Bacterium
B. Virus
C. Protozoan parasite
D. Fungus

✅ **Answer:** C. Protozoan parasite
Explanation: *Hepatozoon cuniculi* is a protozoan parasite belonging to the phylum **Apicomplexa**, similar to *Hepatozoon canis* and *Hepatozoon americanum* in dogs.

2. What is the primary site of *Hepatozoon cuniculi* infection in rabbits?

A. Intestinal mucosa
B. Liver and spleen
C. Kidneys
D. Respiratory tract

✅ **Answer:** B. Liver and spleen
Explanation: The parasite mainly infects the **hepatic (liver) and splenic tissues**, where schizonts can be observed in histological sections.

3. Which of the following is the most common route of transmission for *Hepatozoon cuniculi* in rabbits?

A. Ingestion of infected arthropods
B. Direct contact with infected rabbits
C. Transplacental transmission
D. Bite from infected mosquitoes

✅ **Answer:** A. Ingestion of infected arthropods
Explanation: Similar to other *Hepatozoon* species, infection typically occurs when rabbits **ingest infected arthropods** containing mature oocysts.

4. What histopathological feature is characteristic of *Hepatozoon cuniculi* infection?

A. Granulomatous inflammation in lungs
B. Intracellular schizonts within hepatocytes and Kupffer cells
C. Necrosis of intestinal villi
D. Cyst formation in kidney tubules

✅ **Answer:** B. Intracellular schizonts within hepatocytes and Kupffer cells
Explanation: Histopathology reveals **intracellular schizonts** in **liver and spleen macrophages (Kupffer cells)**, confirming infection.

5. Which diagnostic method is most reliable for confirming *Hepatozoon cuniculi* infection?

A. Fecal flotation
B. PCR or histopathology of tissue samples
C. Serology (ELISA)
D. Blood culture

✅ **Answer:** B. PCR or histopathology of tissue samples
Explanation: Diagnosis is usually confirmed by **PCR** detection of *Hepatozoon* DNA or **microscopic examination** of tissue sections showing characteristic schizonts.

Toxoplasma gondii in Rabbits MCQ

1. Which of the following is the definitive host of *Toxoplasma gondii*?

A. Rabbit
B. Dog
C. Cat
D. Rat

Answer: ✅ C. Cat
Explanation: Cats (domestic and wild felids) are the only definitive hosts that can shed *T. gondii* oocysts in feces.

2. How do rabbits most commonly acquire *Toxoplasma gondii* infection?

A. Inhalation of oocysts
B. Bite from infected cat
C. Ingestion of oocysts from contaminated feed or water
D. Transplacental infection from the doe

Answer: ✅ C. Ingestion of oocysts from contaminated feed or water
Explanation: Rabbits become infected by ingesting sporulated oocysts from contaminated environments.

3. What is the usual clinical presentation of *Toxoplasma gondii* infection in rabbits?

A. Severe diarrhea
B. Often subclinical, but may cause neurological signs or abortion
C. Jaundice and hepatic necrosis
D. Chronic cough and dyspnea

Answer: ✅ B. Often subclinical, but may cause neurological signs or abortion
Explanation: Infection in rabbits is mostly subclinical; in severe cases, it can cause encephalitis, paralysis, or reproductive issues.

4. Which diagnostic method is most reliable for confirming *Toxoplasma gondii* infection in rabbits?

A. Blood glucose test
B. Microscopic examination of feces
C. Serological tests (e.g., ELISA, IFAT) or PCR
D. Skin scraping

Answer: ✅ C. Serological tests (e.g., ELISA, IFAT) or PCR
Explanation: Diagnosis is based on detection of antibodies or parasite DNA, since rabbits do not shed oocysts.

5. How can *Toxoplasma gondii* infection be prevented in rabbit farms?

A. Regular vaccination of rabbits
B. Keeping cats away from feed and water, and proper hygiene

C. Routine deworming with ivermectin
D. Feeding raw meat to rabbits

Answer: ✅ B. Keeping cats away from feed and water, and proper hygiene
Explanation: Preventing contamination of feed and water with cat feces is the main control strategy.

Brugia lepori in Rabbits MCQ

1. Brugia lepori belongs to which group of parasites?

A. Trematodes
B. Cestodes
C. Nematodes
D. Protozoa

✅ **Answer:** C. Nematodes

Explanation: *Brugia lepori* is a filarial nematode (roundworm) that infects rabbits.

2. What is the primary site of infection of *Brugia lepori* in rabbits?

A. Intestinal tract
B. Subcutaneous tissues and lymphatic vessels
C. Liver parenchyma
D. Lungs and bronchi

✅ **Answer:** B. Subcutaneous tissues and lymphatic vessels

Explanation: *Brugia lepori* is a filarial worm found mainly in the lymphatic system and subcutaneous tissue of rabbits.

3. Which arthropod acts as the vector for transmission of *Brugia lepori*?

A. Fleas
B. Ticks
C. Mosquitoes
D. Lice

✅ **Answer:** C. Mosquitoes

Explanation: *Brugia lepori* is transmitted by mosquitoes, similar to other *Brugia* species that cause lymphatic filariasis.

4. Which of the following is the diagnostic stage of *Brugia lepori* in the host?

A. Adult worms in lymph nodes
B. Eggs in feces
C. Microfilariae in peripheral blood
D. Larvae in the lungs

✅ **Answer:** C. Microfilariae in peripheral blood

Explanation: Diagnosis is usually made by detecting microfilariae in the blood of infected rabbits.

5. *Brugia lepori* infection in rabbits is mainly used as a model for which human disease?

A. Ascariasis
B. Filariasis (Lymphatic filariasis)
C. Schistosomiasis
D. Leishmaniasis

✅ **Answer:** B. Filariasis (Lymphatic filariasis)

Explanation: *Brugia lepori* infection in rabbits is an experimental model for studying lymphatic filariasis caused by *Brugia malayi* in humans.

Brugia lepori in Rabbits MCQ

1. Brugia lepori belongs to which group of parasites?

A. Trematodes
B. Cestodes
C. Nematodes
D. Protozoa

✅ **Answer:** C. Nematodes

Explanation: *Brugia lepori* is a filarial nematode (roundworm) that infects rabbits.

2. What is the primary site of infection of *Brugia lepori* in rabbits?

A. Intestinal tract
B. Subcutaneous tissues and lymphatic vessels
C. Liver parenchyma
D. Lungs and bronchi

✅ **Answer:** B. Subcutaneous tissues and lymphatic vessels

Explanation: *Brugia lepori* is a filarial worm found mainly in the lymphatic system and subcutaneous tissue of rabbits.

3. Which arthropod acts as the vector for transmission of *Brugia lepori*?

A. Fleas
B. Ticks
C. Mosquitoes
D. Lice

✅ **Answer:** C. Mosquitoes

Explanation: *Brugia lepori* is transmitted by mosquitoes, similar to other *Brugia* species that cause lymphatic filariasis.

4. Which of the following is the diagnostic stage of *Brugia lepori* in the host?

A. Adult worms in lymph nodes
B. Eggs in feces
C. Microfilariae in peripheral blood
D. Larvae in the lungs

✅ **Answer:** C. Microfilariae in peripheral blood

Explanation: Diagnosis is usually made by detecting microfilariae in the blood of infected rabbits.

5. *Brugia lepori* infection in rabbits is mainly used as a model for which human disease?

A. Ascariasis
B. Filariasis (Lymphatic filariasis)
C. Schistosomiasis
D. Leishmaniasis

✅ **Answer:** B. Filariasis (Lymphatic filariasis)

Explanation: *Brugia lepori* infection in rabbits is an experimental model for studying lymphatic filariasis caused by *Brugia malayi* in humans.

CHAPTER SIX :FISH PARASITES QUESTIONS

Dactylogyrus vastator

1. What type of parasite is ***Dactylogyrus vastator***?

A) Nematode
B) Cestode
C) Monogenean
D) Trematode

Answer: ✅ C) Monogenean

2. Which part of the fish is primarily affected by ***Dactylogyrus vastator***?

A) Intestines
B) Skin
C) Gills
D) Liver

Answer: ✅ C) Gills

3. ***Dactylogyrus vastator*** mainly affects which of the following fish species?

A) Tilapia
B) Salmon
C) Carp
D) Catfish

Answer: ✅ C) Carp

4. How is ***Dactylogyrus vastator*** typically transmitted between fish?

A) Through contaminated feed
B) Direct contact with infected water or fish
C) By bird carriers
D) Through mosquito bites

Answer: ✅ B) Direct contact with infected water or fish

5. Which of the following is a common symptom in fish heavily infected with ***Dactylogyrus vastator***?

A) Excessive appetite
B) Rapid gill movement and gasping
C) Scale discoloration
D) Tail rot

Answer: ✅ B) Rapid gill movement and gasping

Gill fluke

1. What type of organism is a gill fluke?

A. Bacterium
B. Nematode
C. Trematode
D. Protozoan

Answer: ✅ **C. Trematode**
Explanation: Gill flukes are parasitic flatworms belonging to the class Trematoda, specifically Monogenea (like *Dactylogyrus*).

2. What is a common sign of gill fluke infestation in fish?

A. Fin rot
B. Flashing (rubbing against surfaces)
C. Bloating
D. Cloudy eyes

Answer: ✅ B. Flashing (rubbing against surfaces)
Explanation: Infected fish often show irritation and may rub their bodies against objects.

3. Which species of monogenean is commonly referred to as a gill fluke?

A. *Ichthyophthirius multifiliis*
B. *Dactylogyrus spp.*
C. *Gyrodactylus salaris*
D. *Trichodina spp.*

Answer: ✅ B. *Dactylogyrus spp.*
Explanation: *Dactylogyrus* is a common gill fluke affecting freshwater fish, especially carp and goldfish.

4. How are gill flukes commonly diagnosed?

A. Blood test
B. X-ray
C. Gill biopsy or skin scraping under microscope
D. Behavior observation only

Answer: ✅ C. Gill biopsy or skin scraping under microscope
Explanation: Definitive diagnosis requires microscopic examination of gill or skin samples.

5. What is a commonly used treatment for gill flukes in aquaculture?

A. Antibiotics
B. Formalin or Praziquantel
C. Saltwater immersion only
D. Increased oxygen supply

Answer: ✅ **B. Formalin or Praziquantel**
Explanation: Praziquantel and formalin baths are effective treatments against gill flukes.

Macrogyrodactylus congolensis

1. What type of parasite is *Macrogyrodactylus congolensis*?

A. Protozoan
B. Nematode
C. Monogenean
D. Cestode

Answer: ✅ C. Monogenean

2. *Macrogyrodactylus congolensis* primarily infects which part of the fish?

A. Intestine
B. Liver
C. Gills and skin
D. Swim bladder

Answer: ✅ C. Gills and skin

3. Which fish species is commonly associated as a host for *Macrogyrodactylus congolensis*?

A. Tilapia (*Oreochromis niloticus*)
B. African catfish (*Clarias gariepinus*)
C. Common carp (*Cyprinus carpio*)
D. Salmon (*Salmo salar*)

Answer: ✅ B. African catfish (*Clarias gariepinus*)

4. How is *Macrogyrodactylus congolensis* typically transmitted between fish?

A. Ingestion of infected prey
B. Through water as free-living larvae
C. Direct contact or close proximity
D. Via intermediate host

Answer: ✅ C. Direct contact or close proximity

5. What is a common method used to control *Macrogyrodactylus congolensis* in aquaculture?

A. Antibiotics
B. Vaccination
C. Chemical baths (e.g., formalin or potassium permanganate)
D. UV sterilization of eggs

Answer: ✅ C. Chemical baths (e.g., formalin or potassium permanganate)

Skin fluke

1. What is the most common genus of skin flukes affecting freshwater fish?

A. Gyrodactylus
B. Dactylogyrus
C. Ichthyophthirius
D. Argulus

Answer: A. Gyrodactylus

2. Skin flukes are classified under which type of parasite?

A. Protozoa
B. Cestodes
C. Monogeneans
D. Nematodes

Answer: C. Monogeneans

3. How do skin flukes primarily reproduce?

A. Sexual reproduction with two hosts
B. Asexual binary fission
C. Hermaphroditic reproduction on a single host
D. Spore formation

Answer: C. Hermaphroditic reproduction on a single host

4. Which of the following is a common symptom of a skin fluke infestation in fish?

A. Bulging eyes
B. Rapid gill movement and flashing
C. Swim bladder dysfunction
D. Fin rot

Answer: B. Rapid gill movement and flashing

5. What is a commonly used treatment for skin flukes in aquaculture?

A. Salt bath
B. Antibiotics
C. Copper sulfate
D. Formalin

Answer: D. Formalin
(*Note: Salt baths may also be effective, but formalin is widely used in controlled aquaculture settings.*)

Ligula intestinalis

1. What type of parasite is *Ligula intestinalis*?

A) Nematode
B) Trematode
C) Cestode
D) Protozoa

Answer: C) Cestode
Explanation: *Ligula intestinalis* is a cestode (tapeworm) belonging to the class Cestoda.

2. What is the primary intermediate host of *Ligula intestinalis*?

A) Fish
B) Birds
C) Snail
D) Amphibians

Answer: A) Fish
Explanation: The plerocercoid larval stage of *Ligula intestinalis* develops in freshwater fish, which act as intermediate hosts.

3. Which of the following acts as the definitive host for *Ligula intestinalis*?

A) Humans
B) Fish
C) Piscivorous birds (e.g., herons)
D) Amphibians

Answer: C) Piscivorous birds (e.g., herons)
Explanation: Birds that eat fish serve as the definitive host, where the adult worm matures in the intestine.

4. What pathological effect does ***Ligula intestinalis*** have on its fish intermediate host?

A) Enhances reproductive capacity
B) Causes liver cirrhosis
C) Leads to reproductive inhibition and abdominal swelling
D) No noticeable effects

Answer: C) Leads to reproductive inhibition and abdominal swelling
Explanation: The plerocercoid larvae can grow very large inside the fish, inhibiting reproduction and causing abdominal distension.

5. How is ***Ligula intestinalis*** transmitted to the definitive host?

A) Ingestion of contaminated water
B) Direct skin penetration
C) Ingestion of infected fish
D) Inhalation of spores

Answer: C) Ingestion of infected fish
Explanation: Birds become infected by eating fish that contain the plerocercoid larvae.

Camallanus sp.

1. What type of parasite is ***Camallanus*** sp.?

A) Ectoparasite
B) Endoparasite
C) Epiphyte
D) Commensal

Answer: B) Endoparasite
Explanation: *Camallanus* sp. is a parasitic nematode that lives inside the gastrointestinal tract of fish.

2. Which part of the fish's body is primarily affected by *Camallanus* worms?

A) Gills
B) Skin
C) Intestine
D) Liver

Answer: C) Intestine
Explanation: These worms reside in the intestines and are often seen protruding from the anus of infected fish.

3. What is a common visible sign of *Camallanus* infection in aquarium fish?

A) White patches on the body
B) Red, thread-like worms protruding from the anus
C) Loss of scales
D) Bulging eyes

Answer: B) Red, thread-like worms protruding from the anus
Explanation: Adult *Camallanus* worms are often visible as red worms extending from the fish's anus.

4. What is the mode of transmission of *Camallanus* sp. in fish?

A) Airborne spores
B) Direct skin contact
C) Ingestion of infected intermediate hosts
D) Through egg deposition on substrate

Answer: C) Ingestion of infected intermediate hosts
Explanation: *Camallanus* has an indirect life cycle involving crustacean intermediate hosts (e.g., copepods), which fish consume.

5. Which class of drugs is commonly used to treat *Camallanus* infections in fish?

A) Antibiotics
B) Antifungals
C) Anthelmintics
D) Vaccines

Answer: C) Anthelmintics
Explanation: Anthelmintic medications like levamisole, fenbendazole, or praziquantel are used to treat nematode infections.

Clinostomum complanatum

1. Clinostomum complanatum *is commonly known as:*

A. Liver fluke
B. Fish fluke
C. Lung fluke
D. Intestinal fluke

✅ **Answer: B. Fish fluke**

2. The definitive host of Clinostomum complanatum is:

A. Fish
B. Snail
C. Bird
D. Human

✅ **Answer: C. Bird**
(*Primarily piscivorous birds like herons and egrets*)

3. Humans are infected by Clinostomum complanatum by:

A. Drinking contaminated water
B. Eating undercooked fish
C. Insect bites
D. Skin penetration in water

✅ **Answer: B. Eating undercooked fish**

4. In humans, Clinostomum complanatum most commonly causes:

A. Hepatitis
B. Intestinal obstruction
C. Laryngopharyngitis
D. Pneumonia

✅ **Answer: C. Laryngopharyngitis**
(*Due to migration of the parasite to the throat region*)

5. The larval form of Clinostomum complanatum found in fish is called:

A. Cercaria
B. Sporocyst
C. Redia
D. Metacercaria

✅ **Answer: D. Metacercaria**

Ichthyobodo necator

1. What type of organism is ***Ichthyobodo necator***?

A) Bacterium
B) Protozoan
C) Fungus
D) Nematode

Answer: B) Protozoan

2. Which part of the fish does ***Ichthyobodo necator*** primarily infect?

A) Digestive tract
B) Swim bladder
C) Skin and gills
D) Heart

Answer: C) Skin and gills

3. What is a common clinical sign of ***Ichthyobodo necator*** infection in fish?

A) Fin rot
B) Flashing (rubbing against objects)
C) Bulging eyes
D) Enlarged abdomen

Answer: B) Flashing (rubbing against objects)

4. Which of the following environmental conditions most favors the spread of ***Ichthyobodo necator***?

A) High salinity
B) High temperature
C) Poor water quality and overcrowding
D) Strong water current

Answer: C) Poor water quality and overcrowding

5. Which treatment is commonly used to control ***Ichthyobodo necator*** infections?

A) Antibiotics
B) Formalin bath
C) Copper sulfate injection
D) Saltwater diet

Answer: B) Formalin bath

Ichthyophthirius multifiliis

1. What type of organism is ***Ichthyophthirius multifiliis***?

A. Bacterium
B. Virus
C. Protozoan parasite
D. Fungi

Answer: ✅ C. Protozoan parasite

2. What disease is caused by ***Ichthyophthirius multifiliis*** in freshwater fish?

A. Fin rot
B. Columnaris
C. White spot disease
D. Dropsy

Answer: ✅ C. White spot disease

3. Which stage of ***Ichthyophthirius multifiliis*** is infective to fish?

A. Trophont
B. Tomont
C. Theront
D. Cyst

Answer: ✅ C. Theront

4. What is the typical sign of infection by ***Ichthyophthirius multifiliis*** in fish?

A. Cloudy eyes
B. Ulcers on the body
C. White cyst-like spots on skin and gills
D. Bloated abdomen

Answer: ✅ C. White cyst-like spots on skin and gills

5. Which of the following is a common method to control or treat ***Ichthyophthirius multifiliis*** infection in aquaculture?

A. Use of antibiotics
B. Increasing salinity drastically
C. Formalin or salt bath treatments
D. Vaccination

Answer: ✅ C. Formalin or salt bath treatment

Chilodonella hexasticha

1. What type of organism is ***Chilodonella hexasticha***?

A. Bacterium
B. Virus
C. Parasitic protozoan
D. Fungi

Answer: C. Parasitic protozoan

2. What part of the fish does ***Chilodonella hexasticha*** primarily infect?

A. Liver
B. Gills and skin
C. Intestines
D. Swim bladder

Answer: B. Gills and skin

3. Which of the following is a common symptom in fish infected with ***Chilodonella hexasticha***?

A. Red lesions on the fins
B. Flashing and rubbing against surfaces
C. Swollen eyes
D. Loss of scales only on the tail

Answer: B. Flashing and rubbing against surfaces

4. What is the most favorable condition for ***Chilodonella hexasticha*** outbreaks?

A. High salinity
B. Cold, crowded freshwater environments
C. Clean and warm water
D. Saltwater with high oxygen levels

Answer: B. Cold, crowded freshwater environments

5. Which method is commonly used to diagnose ***Chilodonella hexasticha*** infection in fish?

A. Blood test
B. X-ray
C. Wet mount microscopic examination of gill or skin scrapings
D. DNA fingerprinting

Answer: C. Wet mount microscopic examination of gill or skin scrapings

Whirling disease (black tail) in fish

1. What organism causes Whirling Disease in fish?

A) Bacteria
B) Virus
C) Parasite
D) Fungus

Answer: C) Parasite

2. Whirling Disease primarily affects which part of the fish's body?

A) Gills
B) Nervous system and cartilage
C) Scales
D) Liver

Answer: B) Nervous system and cartilage

3. Which fish species is most commonly affected by Whirling Disease?

A) Catfish
B) Trout
C) Salmon
D) Carp

Answer: B) Trout

4. What is a common symptom of Whirling Disease in infected fish?

A) Black tail and whirling swimming behavior
B) Excessive mucus production
C) Loss of scales
D) Red spots on fins

Answer: A) Black tail and whirling swimming behavior

5. How is Whirling Disease primarily transmitted among fish?

A) Through water contaminated with spores
B) Direct fish-to-fish contact only
C) Through eating infected plants
D) By airborne particles

Answer: A) Through water contaminated with spores

***Trichodina** sp*

1. What type of organism is Trichodina sp.?

A) Bacteria
B) Protozoan
C) Virus
D) Fungus

Answer: B) Protozoan

2. Which class does Trichodina sp. belong to?

A) Ciliophora
B) Amoebozoa
C) Apicomplexa
D) Euglenozoa

Answer: A) Ciliophora

3. What is the primary habitat of Trichodina sp.?

A) Soil
B) Freshwater and marine environments
C) Airborne
D) Inside mammals

Answer: B) Freshwater and marine environments

4. What is the common role of Trichodina sp. in aquatic ecosystems?

A) Photosynthetic producer
B) Parasite or ectocommensal on fish and invertebrates
C) Decomposer of organic matter
D) Predator of small fish

Answer: B) Parasite or ectocommensal on fish and invertebrates

5. How does Trichodina sp. attach to its host?

A) Using cilia to swim only
B) Using specialized adhesive disc on the underside
C) By penetrating host tissues with a proboscis
D) Through spore formation

Answer: B) Using specialized adhesive disc on the underside

Henneguya sp.

1. Henneguya sp. is a type of:

A. Bacteria
B. Virus
C. Myxosporean parasite
D. Fungal pathogen

Answer: ✅ C. Myxosporean parasite

2. The common site of infection of Henneguya sp. in fish is:

A. Intestine
B. Liver
C. Gills
D. Skin

Answer: ✅ C. Gills

3. Which of the following is a characteristic feature of Henneguya spores?

A. Absence of polar capsules
B. Oval shape with flagella
C. Two polar capsules and long caudal appendages
D. Circular spores without appendages

Answer: ✅ C. Two polar capsules and long caudal appendages

4. Henneguya infections are mainly transmitted through:

A. Direct fish-to-fish contact
B. Contaminated feed
C. Intermediate hosts (annelid worms)
D. Airborne spores

Answer: ✅ C. Intermediate hosts (annelid worms)

5. Henneguya infections in fish primarily lead to:

A. Liver necrosis
B. Swim bladder malfunction
C. Gill damage and respiratory distress
D. Skin ulcers

Answer: ✅ C. Gill damage and respiratory distress

Myxobolus cerebralis

1. What type of organism is ***Myxobolus cerebralis***?

A. Bacterium
B. Virus
C. Myxozoan parasite
D. Fungi

✅ **Answer: C. Myxozoan parasite**

2. Which fish species is most commonly affected by ***Myxobolus cerebralis***?

A. Tuna
B. Salmon
C. Trout
D. Catfish

✅ **Answer: C. Trout**
(*Especially rainbow trout*)

3. What is the primary symptom of whirling disease in fish?

A. Lesions on the skin
B. Hemorrhaging of fins
C. Erratic tail-chasing swimming behavior
D. Loss of scales

✅ **Answer: C. Erratic tail-chasing swimming behavior**
(*This behavior resembles "whirling", hence the name of the disease*)

4. What is the intermediate host of *Myxobolus cerebralis* **in its life cycle?**

A. Mosquito larvae
B. Tubifex worm
C. Water flea
D. Snail

✅ **Answer: B. Tubifex worm**

5. How is ***Myxobolus cerebralis*** primarily transmitted to fish?

A. Through bites of insects
B. Via ingestion of infected worms or spores in water
C. Through direct fish-to-fish contact
D. By contaminated fishing gear only

✅ **Answer: B. Via ingestion of infected worms or spores in water**

Sanguinicola sp

1. What type of parasite is ***Sanguinicola*** sp.?

A) Intestinal nematode
B) Blood fluke
C) Gill copepod
D) Cestode

Answer: B) Blood fluke

2. Which organ system is primarily affected by ***Sanguinicola*** sp. in fish?

A) Digestive system
B) Nervous system
C) Circulatory system
D) Muscular system

Answer: C) Circulatory system

3. How are *Sanguinicola* sp. typically transmitted to fish?

A) Through ingestion of infected prey
B) Through skin contact with contaminated sediment
C) Via penetration by cercariae released from intermediate hosts (snails)
D) Inhalation of spores

Answer: C) Via penetration by cercariae released from intermediate hosts (snails)

4. What is a common pathological effect of *Sanguinicola* infection in fish?

A) Liver failure
B) Anemia and gill hemorrhage
C) Skin ulceration
D) Swim bladder dysfunction

Answer: B) Anemia and gill hemorrhage

5. Which diagnostic method is most commonly used to detect *Sanguinicola* infections in fish?

A) Blood smear microscopy
B) Skin scraping
C) X-ray imaging
D) PCR and histopathology

Answer: D) PCR and histopathology

Contracaecum sp

1. What type of parasite is *Contracaecum*?

A) Protozoan
B) Nematode
C) Cestode
D) Trematode

Answer: ✅ B) Nematode

2. What is the definitive host of *Contracaecum* spp.?

A) Fish
B) Snails
C) Birds (e.g., piscivorous birds)
D) Amphibians

Answer: ✅ C) Birds (e.g., piscivorous birds)

3. In which organ are *Contracaecum* larvae usually found in fish?

A) Gills
B) Intestine
C) Liver and body cavity
D) Skin

Answer: ✅ C) Liver and body cavity

4. How do fish become infected with *Contracaecum*?

A) Ingesting eggs from the water
B) Contact with infected birds
C) Eating infected crustaceans or intermediate hosts
D) Through gill penetration

Answer: ✅ C) Eating infected crustaceans or intermediate hosts

5. Why is *Contracaecum* significant to human and animal health?

A) It improves fish nutrition
B) It can be used in vaccines
C) It is zoonotic and can infect humans
D) It prevents other parasites from infecting fish

Answer: ✅ C) It is zoonotic and can infect humans

Argulus sp (Fish lice)

1. What type of organism is *Argulus* sp.?

A. Nematode
B. Cestode
C. Crustacean
D. Fungi

Answer: ✅ C. Crustacean

2. Which part of the fish does *Argulus* commonly attach to?

A. Gills and fins
B. Eyes
C. Digestive tract
D. Swim bladder

Answer: ✅ A. Gills and fins

3. How does *Argulus* sp. feed on its host?

A. By engulfing whole cells
B. By scraping algae from the host
C. By sucking blood and body fluids
D. By absorbing nutrients through the skin

Answer: ✅ C. By sucking blood and body fluids

4. What is a common symptom of *Argulus* infestation in fish?

A. Fin regrowth
B. Lethargy and flashing behavior

C. Increased feeding
D. Darkened skin only

Answer: ✅ B. Lethargy and flashing behavior
(*Flashing* refers to rubbing or scratching against surfaces due to irritation.)

5. Which method is commonly used to treat *Argulus* infestations in aquaculture?

A. Antibiotics
B. Formalin or organophosphate baths
C. Increased feeding
D. Oxygen depletion

Answer: ✅ B. Formalin or organophosphate baths

Ergasilus sp.

1. What type of organism is ***Ergasilus*** sp.?

A. Bacterium
B. Fungal parasite
C. Copepod parasite
D. Trematode

Answer: ✅ C. Copepod parasite

2. ***Ergasilus*** sp. most commonly parasitizes which part of a fish's body?

A. Liver
B. Intestines
C. Skin
D. Gills

Answer: ✅ D. Gills

3. Which life stage of ***Ergasilus*** is parasitic in fish?

A. Nauplius
B. Copepodid
C. Adult female
D. Adult male

Answer: ✅ C. Adult female
(Only adult females are parasitic; males are free-living.)

4. How does ***Ergasilus*** sp. affect the host fish?

A. Causes neurological damage
B. Interferes with respiration by damaging gill tissue
C. Enhances nutrient absorption
D. Improves immunity

Answer: ✅ B. Interferes with respiration by damaging gill tissue

5. What is a common method for controlling ***Ergasilus*** infestations in aquaculture?

A. Antibiotics
B. Copper sulfate treatment
C. UV sterilization
D. Vaccination

Answer: ✅ B. Copper sulfate treatment

Lernaea sp.(Anchor worm)

1. What type of organism is ***Lernaea*** (Anchor worm)?

A. Virus
B. Bacteria
C. Parasitic crustacean
D. Protozoa

✅ **Answer: C. Parasitic crustacean**

2. What is the primary host for ***Lernaea*** species?

A. Amphibians
B. Mammals
C. Freshwater fish
D. Reptiles

✅ **Answer: C. Freshwater fish**

3. Where is the adult female ***Lernaea*** typically found on its host?

A. Inside the gills
B. Attached deep into the skin and muscle
C. Floating in blood
D. In the intestines

✅ **Answer: B. Attached deep into the skin and muscle**

4. What is a visible symptom of ***Lernaea*** infestation in fish?

A. Bulging eyes
B. Cotton-like growth
C. Worm-like structures protruding from the body
D. Rapid breathing

✅ **Answer: C. Worm-like structures protruding from the body**

5. What is the best method to control ***Lernaea*** infestation in aquaculture?

A. Use of antibiotics
B. Manual removal and chemical treatment (e.g., potassium permanganate)
C. Increasing water temperature
D. Reducing oxygen levels

✅ Answer: B. Manual removal and chemical treatment (e.g., potassium permanganate)

Anisakis simplex larva

Hexamita intestinalis

1. What type of organism is Hexamita intestinalis?

A. Bacterium
B. Nematode
C. Flagellated protozoan
D. Ciliate protozoan

Answer: ✅ C. Flagellated protozoan

2. Which organ system is primarily affected by Hexamita intestinalis?

A. Respiratory system
B. Nervous system
C. Digestive system
D. Circulatory system

Answer: ✅ C. Digestive system

3. What is a common clinical sign of Hexamita intestinalis infection in fish?

A. Fin rot
B. White stringy feces
C. Cloudy eyes
D. Open sores

Answer: ✅ B. White stringy feces

4. How is Hexamita intestinalis primarily transmitted?

A. Airborne spores
B. Skin contact
C. Fecal-oral route
D. Vector-borne transmission

Answer: ✅ C. Fecal-oral route

5. What is a common treatment for Hexamita intestinalis in infected aquarium fish?

A. Penicillin
B. Formalin
C. Metronidazole
D. Tetracycline

Answer: ✅ C. Metronidazole

Anguillicola sp.(Swim bladder)

1. What is *Anguillicola* sp.?

A) A bacterial pathogen of gills
B) A nematode parasite of the swim bladder
C) A fungal parasite of fish skin
D) A protozoan infecting blood

Answer: ✅ B) A nematode parasite of the swim bladder

2. Which fish is primarily affected by *Anguillicola crassus*?

A) Salmon
B) Tilapia
C) European eel (*Anguilla anguilla*)
D) Carp

Answer: ✅ C) European eel (*Anguilla anguilla*)

3. How does *Anguillicola crassus* affect fish health?

A) Causes external skin ulcers
B) Disrupts respiration by infecting gills
C) Damages the swim bladder, impairing buoyancy
D) Blocks intestinal absorption

Answer: ✅ C) Damages the swim bladder, impairing buoyancy

4. What is the mode of transmission of *Anguillicola* in fish?

A) Direct contact with infected water
B) Ingestion of intermediate/paratenic hosts
C) Airborne transmission
D) Vertical transmission from mother to offspring

Answer: ✅ B) Ingestion of intermediate/paratenic hosts

5. Which stage of *Anguillicola* typically inhabits the swim bladder of fish?

A) Egg
B) Larval stage (L2)
C) Adult nematode
D) Cyst stage

Answer: ✅ C) Adult nematode

1-Shows the correct answer:

1-Popular fish tapeworm in Common carp caused by:

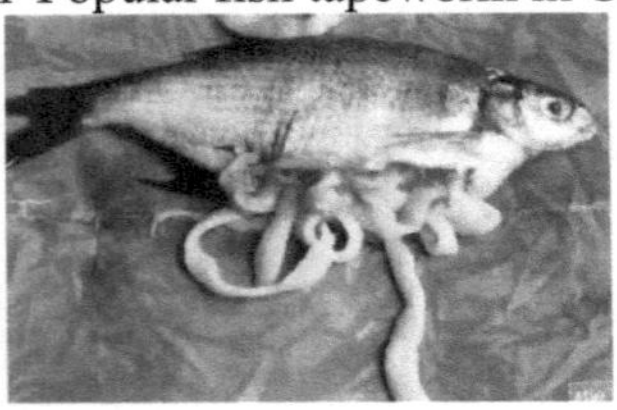

Zafran et al., 2000

A. *Taenia solium*

B. *Ligula intestinalis*

C. *Clonorchis sinensis*

D. Camallanus sp.

Correct Answer :B

2-The causative agent of this disease is :

Koesharyani et al., 2001

A. *Ichthyobodo necator*

B. *Ichthyophthirius multifiliis*

C.Chilodonella hexasticha

D.Trichodina sp.

Correct Answer :B

3-Whirling disease (black tail) in fish caused by :

Koesharyani et al., 2001

A. *Henneguya sp.*

B. Doctylogyrus *vastator*

C. *Myxobolus cerebralis*

D. *Macrogyrodactylus congolensis*

Correct Answer :C

4-Blood fluke disease in *Clarias lazera* caused by :

A. *Clinostomum complanatum*

B. *Contracaecum sp*

C. *Argulus sp*

D. *Sanguinicola sp.*

Correct Answer :D

5-This parasite found on the skin of ornamental fish:

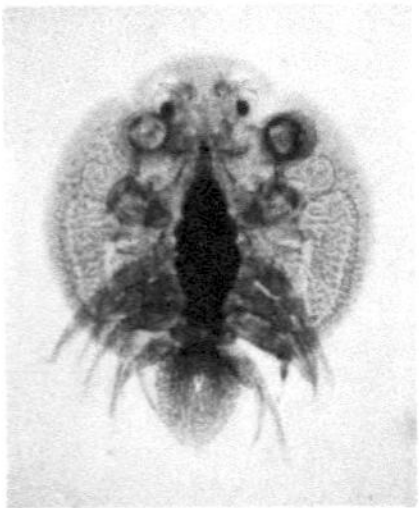

Raef et al, 2002

A. *Macrogyrodactylus sp.*

B. *Ergasilus sp.*

C. *Lernaea sp.*

D. *Argulus sp*

Correct Answer :D

6- This parasite found on the muscles of Tilapia sp

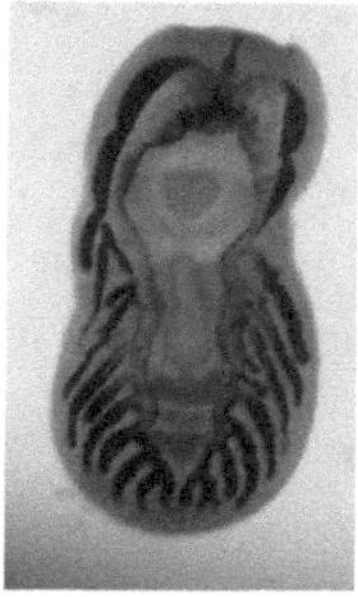

Raef et al, 2004

A. Ichthyophthirius multifiliis

B. Clinostomum adult

C. Clinostomum metacercaria

D. Euoclinostomum metacercaria

Correct Answer :D

7- Which of the following is the most likely organism infect Mugil sp.?

Helal and Yousef (2018)

A. Bacteria

B. Fish lice

C. Isopoda

D. Anchor worm

Correct Answer :C

Fish farm suffering from Fish swim in circles, then rest on the bottom and again begin to whirl in circles. Malformations of vertebral column, which lead to bind the vertebral column in various directions.

Elizabeth and Bartholomew (2000)

What is your diagnosis? Based on what criteria?

A. *Henneguy. alexandrinus*

B. *Dactylogyrus vastator*

C. *Myxosoma cerebralis*

D. *Macrogyrodactylus congolensis*

Correct Answer :C

9- Hamburger Gill Diseases in cat fish caused by:

Abdel-Hadi (2004)

A. *Henneguy. alexandrinus*

B. *Dactylogyrus vastator*

C. *Myxosoma cerebralis*

D. *Sanguinicola Clarias*

Correct Answer :A

10- What parasite does it found in Muscle near the skin of Tilapia sp.?

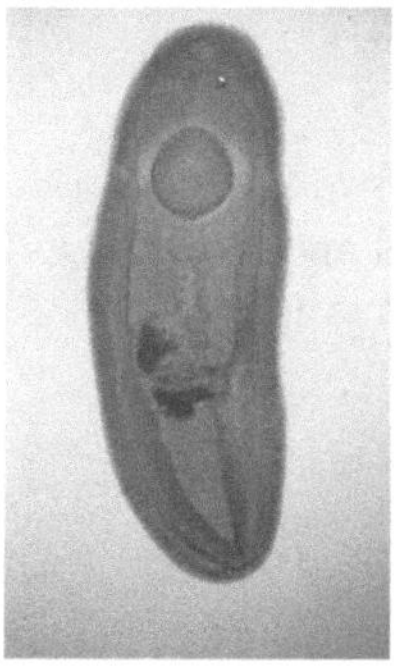

Raef et al, 2004

A. Euoclinostomum metacercaria

B. Clinostomum maginatum adult

C. Clinostomum maginatum metacercaria

D. *Contracaecum*

Correct Answer :C

. *Henneguy. alexandrinus*

11-This parasite found in the preitionial cavity of Tilapia

Ahmed (2011):

A. Contracaecum multipapillatum larva

B. Contracaecum multipapillatuma dult

C.Anisakis simplex larva

D. *Renocila thresherorum*

Correct Answer : A

12-This parasite cause Focal hemorrhage at point of attachment and Skin shows signs of inflammation . What is your diagnosis? Based on what criteria?

Selim (2002)

A. Hook worm

B. Pin worm

C. Anchor worm

D. None of the above

Correct Answer : C

13- These parasites were found on *Mugil cephalus* in Lake Qarun, Egypt.

What species does it represent?

Helal and Yousef (2018

A. Livoneca redmanii

B. Ergasilus sieboldi

C. Argulus foliaceus

D. Argulus japonicus

Correct Answer : A

14- The worm was found attached to the wall of the Skin. The *Claris . gariepinus* suffering from destruction of skin .

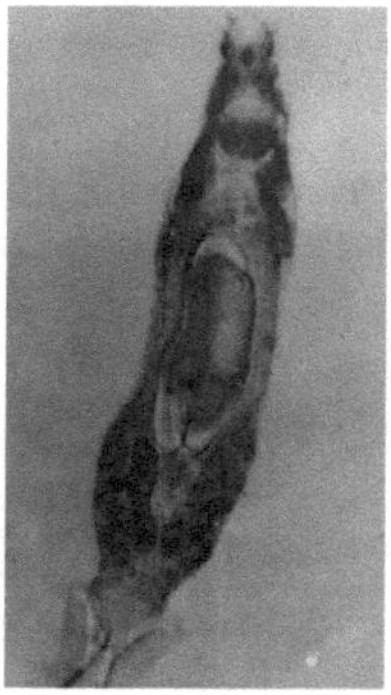

Abd –El Gawad (2004):-

A. Macrogyrodactylus clarii

B. *Dactylogyrus mrigali*

C. *Aphyosemion cameronense*

D. *Polycentropsis abbreviate*

Correct Answer : A

15- The parasite is a common on Tilapia zillii fish in Egypt which feeds by sucking blood. After feeding on the fish, they drop off the host and stay in the substratum while digesting their meal. After the digestive process is finished, they will again attack the fish. Under aquarium conditions, 15-20 of these parasite can kill a 2-3 inch tilapia within 5-6 hr. Peak infection by this parasite is in the rainy season.

This case diagnosed as :-

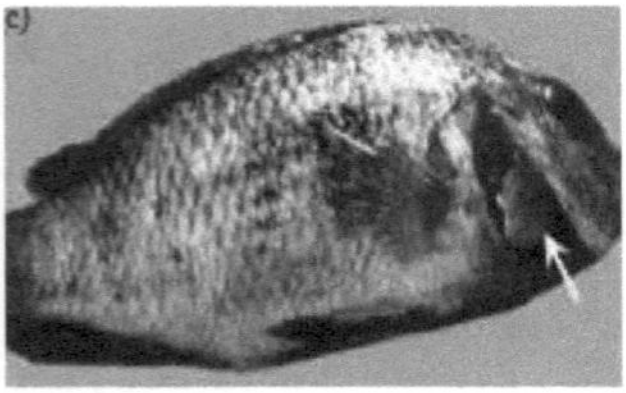

Abd –El Gawad (2004):-

A. Nerocila bivitata

B. Amplicaecum larva

C. Dactylogyrus mrigali

D. Aphyosemion cameronense

Correct Answer : C

16- A 32-year old Egyptian housewife was admitted to the hospital complaining of abdominal pain, fever, and diarrhea for 4 days. She had suffered from abdominal pain for two years . She often ate raw herring and salted salmon and had sampled pieces of raw fish during salting 3 months prior to admission as a patient. Four days prior, she had experienced cramping, increasing abdominal pain, and fever and diarrhea. This case diagnosed as :-

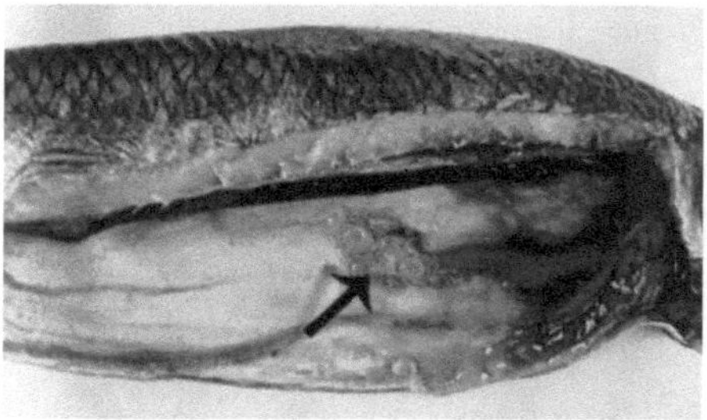

Ahmed (2011)

A. Amplicaecum larva

B.Contracaecum adult

C. Anisakis simplex larva

D. Contracaecum larva

Correct Answer : C

17- Parasite detection in the ornamental fish

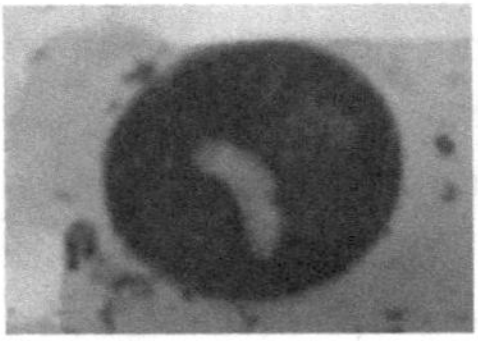

Selim (2002)

A. Ichthyobodo necator

B. Chilodonella hexasticha

C. Hexamita intestinalis

D. Ichthyophthirius multifilliis

Correct Answer : D

18- Which parasite cause this symptoms :

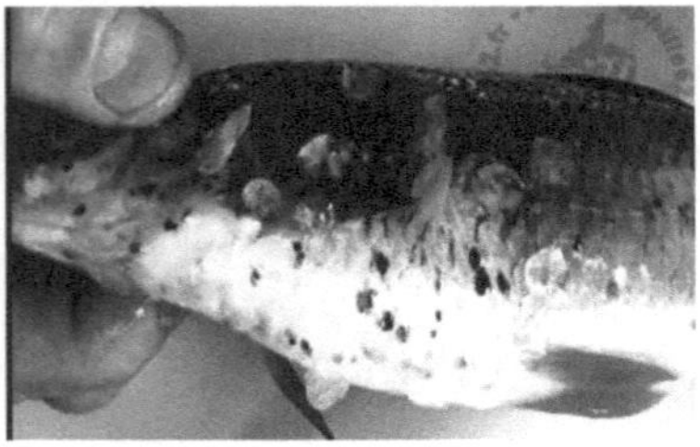

Raef et al, 2004

A. Contracaecum larva

B. Clinostomum maginatum

C. Posthodiplostomum metacercaria

D. Euoclinostomum metacercaria

Correct Answer : C

19- This object was found in swim bladder of Eel

El Dosoky (2007)

A. Capillaria sp.
B. Sanguinicola *sp.*
C. Contracaecum sp.
D. Anguillicola sp.

Correct Answer : D

20-White lesions in the abdominal viscera of fish

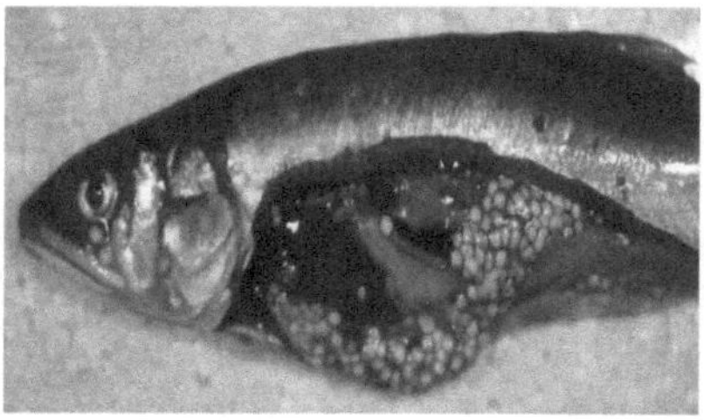

Zafran et al., 2000

A. Microspora
B. Myxosora
C. Henneguya
D. Ichthyobodo

Correct Answer : B

21- Parasitic diseases in fish by swim bladder worm can be diagnosed using

A.radiography

B. gill biopsy.

C.Wood's lamp.

D. ultrasonography.

Correct Answer : D

22-Parasitic infections in fish can cause all of the following except

A. poor growth.

B. poor reproduction.

C. gill hyperplasia.

D. none of the above

Correct Answer : D

23- Which clinical sign is indicative of parasite feeding relative to a parasitic infection?

A. flashing

B. All of the above

C. reddish gills

D. rubbing against the tank wall

Correct Answer : B

24-The most helpful method(s) for external parasite detection in fish is/are

A. lice comb.

B. skin scrapings and gill biopsies.

C. running tape over the skin.

D. microscopic examination of 1 mL of aquarium water.

Correct Answer : D

25-The most common parasites detected in fish are

A. Nematodes.

B. Trematodes.

C. Protozoans.

D. Cestodes.

Correct Answer : C

26- ________ can be seen with the naked eye and removed manually.

A. Lernaea spp

B.Digenean trematodes

C. Cryptocaryon spp

D. Ichthyophthirius multifiliis

Correct Answer : A

27-The most common route for treatment of parasitic diseases in fish is

A. oral.

B.injectable.

C. water bath.

D. direct topical.

Correct Answer : C

28- ________ is one of the most valuable tools for diagnosing infectious disease in fish.

A. Radiology

B. Endoscopy

C. Necropsy

D. Hematology

Correct Answer : C

29-Which components are necessary for a complete fish necropsy?

A. skin scrapings and gill biopsies to check for parasites

B.an overall gross external examination

C. squash preparations of organs

D. all of the above

Correct Answer : D

30-If bacteremia is suspected, the ________ is the best organ for obtaining direct cultures in fish necropsy.

A. liver

B. kidney

C. gill

D. swim bladder

Correct Answer : A

31-This organism was isolated from gills of catfish

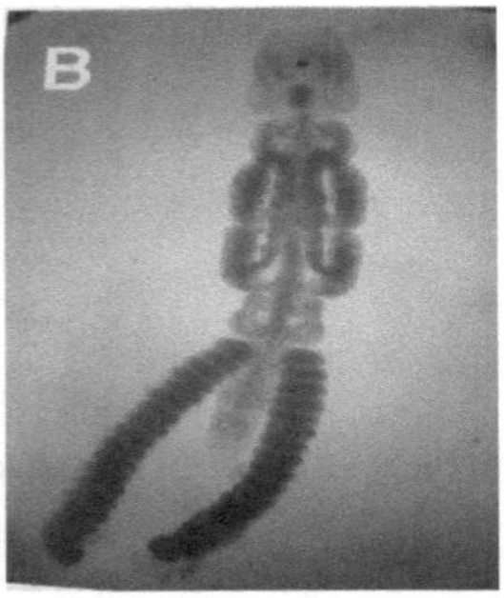

Raef et al., 2000

A. What is it ?
B. Is it male or female
C. What is its clinical significance ?
D. How would you treat infested fish .

Correct Answer :

A- *Lamproglina mondi*

B- Female

C- flashing, poor growth., poor reproduction and gill hyperplasia

D- The most effective treatments against parasites were a freshwater bath or a combined freshwater bath and anaesthesia with 2-phenoxyethanol. Monogeneans on the gills were difficult to control and exophthalmia was an unresolved problem.

32-Microscopic examination of a skin scraping from carp fish in Sharkia, Egypt during routine examination reavels this organism

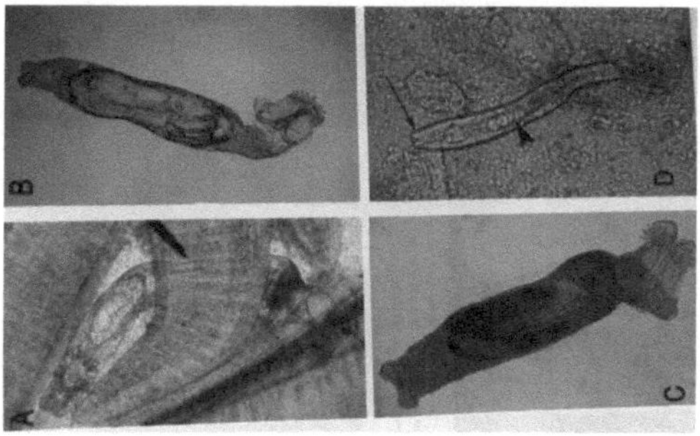

Abd –El Gawad (2004):-

A. What is this organism ?
B. Is it significance ?
C. Describe is it life cycle ?
D. What treatment would you advice ?

Correct Answer :

A. *Gyrodactylus sp.*

B. There are no human health concerns associated with *Gyrodactylus*

C. Direct life cycle

D. Most possible treatments to rid of the infection are not approved by the FDA. For example, praziquantel—a common drug used to cure most parasitic infections—can irritate fish gills and cause death. Monogeneans also have the ability to survive praziquantel treatment because they can be protected by mucus that the fish produces. Hydrogen peroxide (300–560 mg/L) can also cure infection, but is not recommended because a Poeciliids cannot handle a high dosage. Formalin, a solution that is approved by the FDA, can be used to treat freshwater fish; however, it removes a large amount of oxygen from water. As a result, high aeration must be added in conjunction with formalin

33-A gold fish is represented with this organisms

Selim (2002)

A. What is the cause of these structures ?
B. How would you treat the condition ?

Correct Answer :-

A. Lernaea (anchorworm
B. Parasitic females of lernaeids are tolerant to organophosphate and organohalogen insecticides. A dip in potassium permanganate ($KMnO_4$) - 20–25 ppm for 2–3 hours or application of 8 ppm concentration to ponds effectively kills attached female lernaeids

34 - What are those worms that I sometimes see in Tilapia fish in Egypt?

Ahmed (2011):

Fish parasites – trematodes ,roundworms and tapeworms – can be a health concern to humans if ingested in their live state such as : Compete

A- Adult *Heterophes sp.* (Raef, 1994)
B- *Diphyllobothrium*
C- *Capillaria philippinensis*
D- *Anisakis*, *Pseudoterranova*. and *Contracaecum.*

Correct Answer:-D

How can fish parasites be killed ?

Answer :-

Parasites become a concern when consumers eat raw, undercooked or lightly preserved fish such as sashimi, sushi or ceviche. Freezing, as required under the FDA Food Code 2013, kills any parasites that may be present.

How do fish get parasites ?

Answer

The most common way a parasite infestation takes off is when a new fish is added into an established system. The stress from capture, transport, and introduction to a foreign environment causes any parasites on the new fish to quickly spread to the others in the aquarium.

What happens if I eat one of the worms?

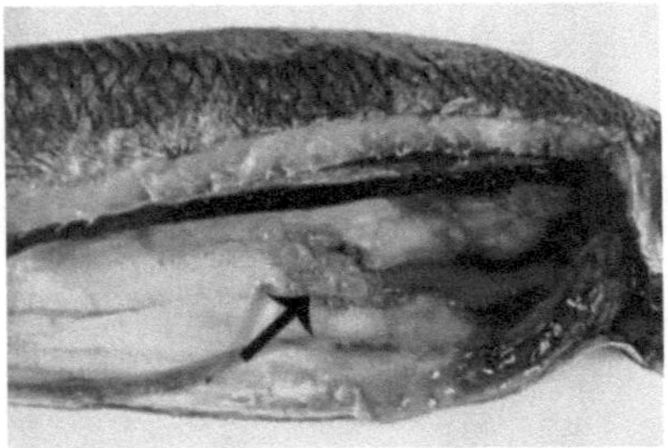

Ahmed (2011)

Answer :-

Anisakis food poisoning frequently occurs within eight hours after eating parasitized seafood raw or near-raw and mainly causes **intense stomach pain**. This may also be accompanied by nausea and vomiting. If you suspect Anisakis food poisoning, consult with a doctor and a Public Health Center.

39-What is a fish tapeworm infection?

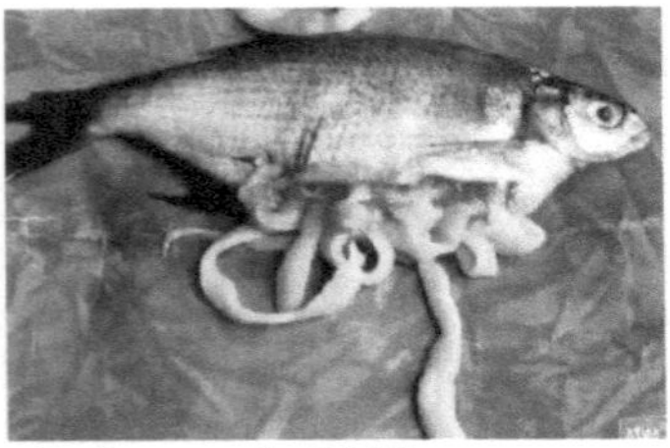

Zafran et al., 2000

Answer :-

Ligula intestinalis

What are the symptoms when a person eats raw or undercooked fish that's contaminated with the parasite *Diphyllobothrium latum*?

Answer :-

Most infections are asymptomatic. However symptoms can include abdominal discomfort, diarrhea, vomiting, and weight loss. Vitamin B12 deficiency leading to pernicious anemia may occur. Complications include intestinal obstruction and gall bladder disease caused by migration of proglottids.

How can you prevent a fish tapeworm infection *Diphyllobothrium latum* ?

Answer :-

Do not eat raw or undercooked fish.

The FDA recommends the following for fish preparation or storage to kill parasites.

- **Cooking**
  - Cook fish adequately (to an internal temperature of at least 145° F [~63° C]).
- **Freezing**
  - At -4°F (-20°C) or below for 7 days (total time), or
  - At -31°F (-35°C) or below until solid, and storing at -31°F (-35°C) or below for 15 hours, or
  - At -31°F (-35°C) or below until solid and storing at -4°F (-20°C) or below for 24 hours.

The monogenean produce young that are fully equipped to immediately attach to the host

A. Gyrodactylids
B. Dactylogyrids
C. Acanothpcephala
D. Isopoda

The correct Answer : A

Tabulate the main differences between the following.

A. Gill flukes and skin flukes

Answer :-

Dactylogyrus predominantly affects the gills, whereas Gyrodactylus is more commonly found on the skin. Monogeneans affecting marine fish include the capsalids; species such as Benedenia and Neobenedenia can infest the skin and gills. Life cycles: Monogeneans may be oviparous (egg laying) or viviparous (live bearers).

C. Ergasillosis and Argulosis .

Answer :-

Ergasillosis

The lice can be found attached to the skin, gill chamber, and mouth. Localized inflammation occurs at the contact site because of mechanical damage from hooks and spines on the stylet and appendages, and irritation from digestive enzymes.

Argulosis

There have been many instances of fish mortality in Indian ponds due to argulosis. The affected fish become very weak and emaciated. Prominent symptoms include stunted growth, peeling off of the scales, and the appearance of red spots at the sites of infection.

D. Clinostomiosis and Sanguinicolinosis .

Answer:-

Clinostomum marginatum is a species of parasitic fluke (class Trematoda) that can grow up to 6.4 millimetres (0.25 in) in the flesh of freshwater fish

Blood fluke :

Fish blood flukes (FBFs) are the most important digenean parasites in marine finfish aquaculture due to their high pathogenicity. Numerous eggs accumulate in gill lamellae and capillary vessels in various organs, interfere the blood flow. This causes fish to suffocate to death or leads to other fatal health problems

Give short notes ON:

A.White spot disease

Answer :-

White spot is a contagious parasitic disease of fish. Caused by **Ichyophthirius multifilis**, the parasite infects the fish after moving from the bottom of the pond. The parasite attaches itself to the fish, moving under the skin where it feeds on cells and body fluids.

C. Anchor worm

Answer :-

Anchor worms are contagious among fish and occur when a new fish is added to an aquarium carrying juvenile anchor worms or a reproductively-active female in their skin. Skipping proper quarantine makes this parasite spread very rapidly

Enumerate Three parasitic diseases and mention the causative agent and the line of treatment of each one

Answer :-

Parasitic diseases of fish such as Ichthyophonus, Nanophyetus salmincola, and whirling diseases pose a significant threat to fish populations. Ichthyophonus is one of the most significant parasites of wild marine fishes, causing recurring population-level impacts during the past century.

46- Monogenetic flukes are so named because they

A- have only one generation in their life cycle.

B- Have a life cycle where only one adult develops from one egg.

C- Are solely external parasites.

D- Both A and B.

The correct Answer : D

47-Anisakiasis, or herring worm disease, is a parasitic disease caused by

A. Nematodes (worms)

B. Monogenea

C. Cestodes (Tapeworms)

D. Digenea

The correct Answer : A

48- Can Anisakiasis be transmitted human to human?
True or False

The correct Answer :T

49-The disease is caused by Myxosporidan protozoa Myxosoma cerebral is only in salmon fish is known as :

A. Costiasis

B. Ichthyophthiriasis

C. Trichodiniasis

D. Whirling disease

The correct Answer :D

50-The disease of fish is caused by ciliate of *Ichthyophthirius multifiliis*

A. Whirling disease

B. White spot disease

C. Black spot disease

D. Yellow grub disease

The correct Answer : B

51-These two parasites are responsible for huge mortality in culture fish is called as:

A. Ergasillus

B. Salmincola

C. Both A and B

D. None of these

The correct Answer : C

52-Pisicola hold on fish and suck fish blood is called :

A. Gyrodactylosis

B. Dactylogyrosis

C. Leeches disease

D. Salmincola

The correct Answer : C

53-The protozoan disease in fish is :

A. Gyrodactylosis
B. Costiasis
C. Dactylogyrosis
D. Diplostomiasis

The correct Answer : B

54-The monogenetic trematode is reported to cause serious infection in carp fish

On the fins and gills is known as :

A. Gyrodactylosis

B. Dactylogyrosis

C. Ergasillus

D. Cymothoid

The correct Answer : A

55-Fish lice is type of :

A. Copepoda

B. Isopoda

C. Branchiura

D. Protozoa

The correct Answer : C

56- Sperm-like structures found inside nodules in the gills of a catfish, what are these?

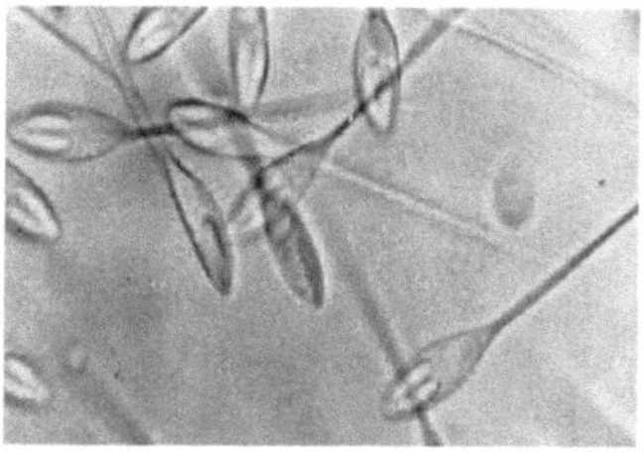

Abd –El Gawad (2004):-

A. Henneguya sp.
B. Myxospora sp.
C. Microspora sp.
D. Myxobolus sp.
E. Kudoa sp.

The correct Answer : A

57- This parasite makes it a bad idea to eat raw or undercooked fish .

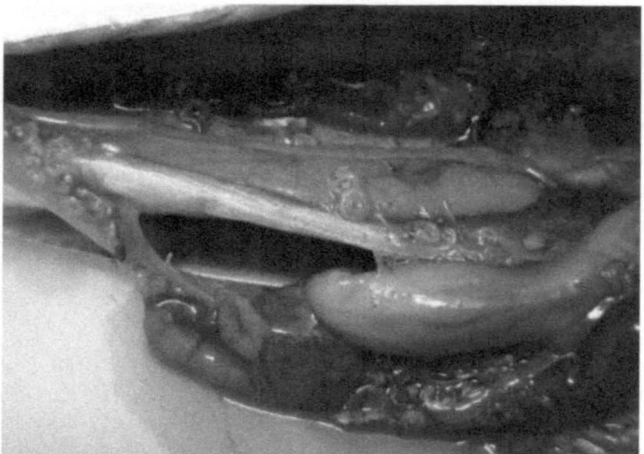

Ahmed (2011)

A.Anisakis.

B.Cryptosporidium

C.Heterakis meleagridis

D. Myxobolus sp.

The correct Answer : A

What's specie name in picture?

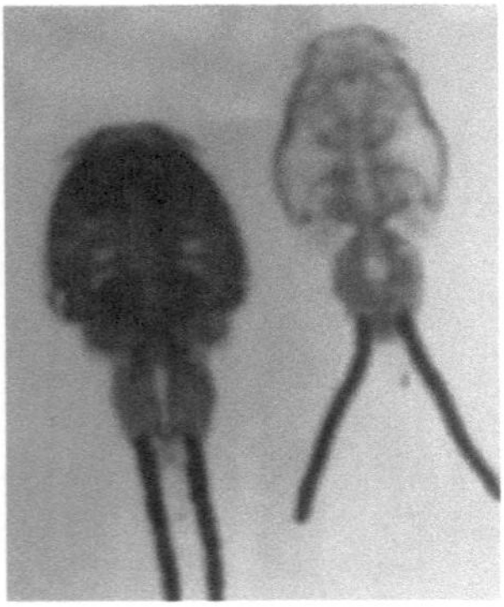

Raef et al., 2000

Answer :Female Ergasilus x100

59- Identify this parasite collected from gills of mugil fish?

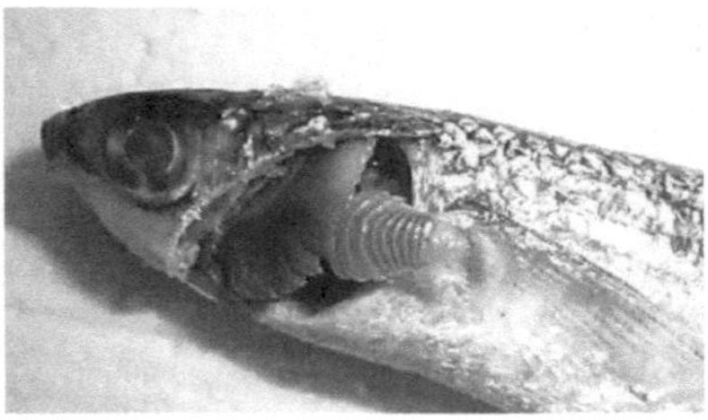

Helal and Yousef (2018

Answer :Isopoda(*Livoneca redmanii)*

60-Anyone have information on this eel parasite?

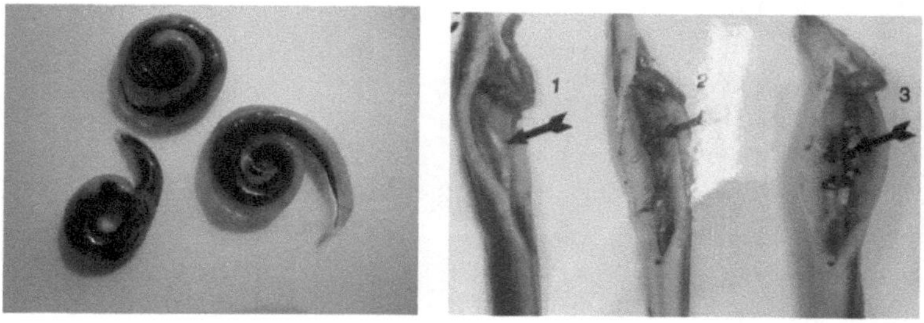

El Dosoky (2007)

Answer:Anguillicoloides crassus a parasitic nematode worm that lives in the swimbladders of eels

61-Does anyone know this worm parasited in the gills of O.niloticus?

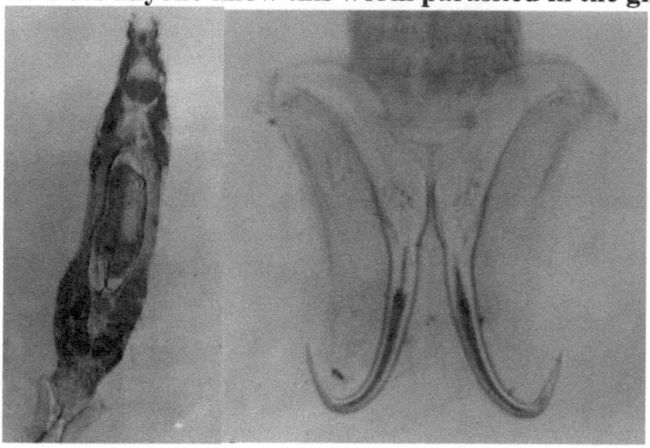

Abd –El Gawad (2004):-

Answer: Macrogyrodactylus congolensis

62-Which parasites form the gut which affect Cat fish?

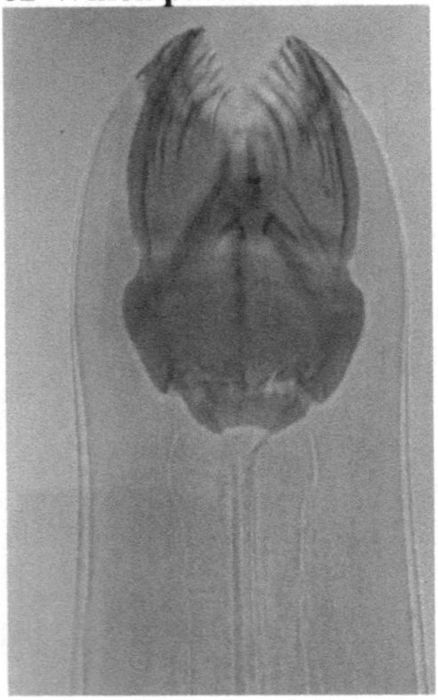

El –Ekiaby (2004).

Answe :Procamallanus laeviconchus

. 63-This parasite is acquired by humans via ingestion of infected fish:

A. Clonorchis sinensis T

B. Taenia saginata F

C. Diphyllobothrium latum T

D. Paragonimus westermani F

E. Schistosoma japonicum F

CHAPTER SENEN:PARASITOLOGY DIAGNOSTIC QUESTIONS

Select the correct answers . One correct answer per question

Identify

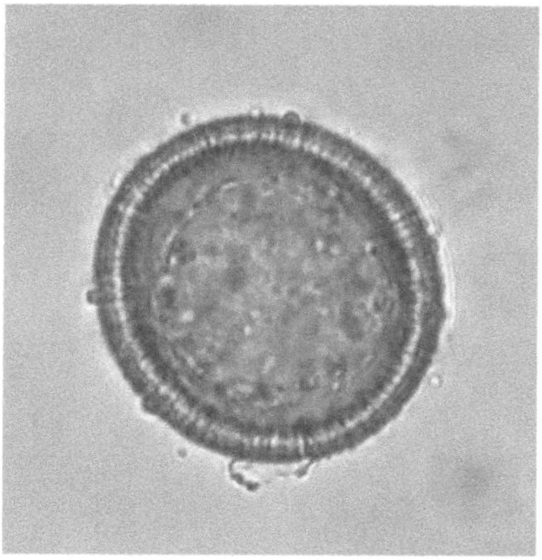

Kaufmann,1996

A. *Taenia taeniaformis*

B. *Dipylidium caninum*

C. *Spirometra* spp.

D. *Paragonimus kellicotti*

The correct Answer :A

2- Feline Fecal Floatation

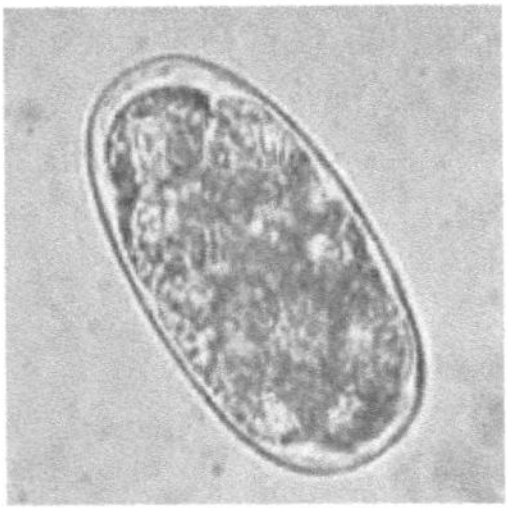

Thienpont et al.,2003

A. *Toxocara cati*

B. *Strongyloides stercoralis*

C. *Hookworm (Ancylostoma*

D. *Toxascaris leonine*

The correct Answer : C

3- Feline Fecal Sedimentation, Sputum direct, or Trans-tracheal wash Identify:

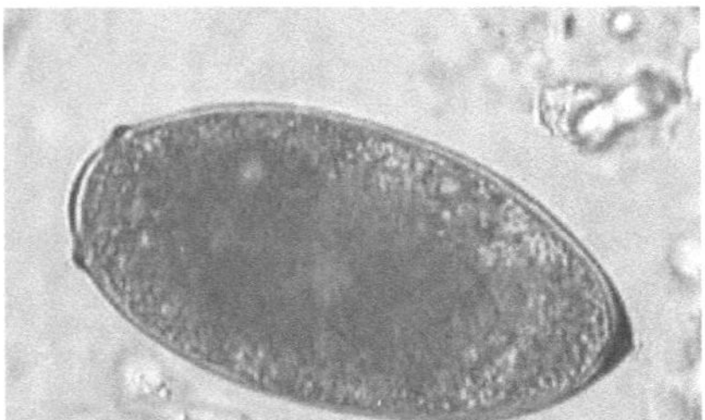

Thienpont et al., 2003

A. *Paragonimus kellicotti*

B .*Spirometra sp.*

C. *Fasciola hepatica*

D. *Ancylostoma tubaeforme*

The correct Answer : A

4-In Feline Feces

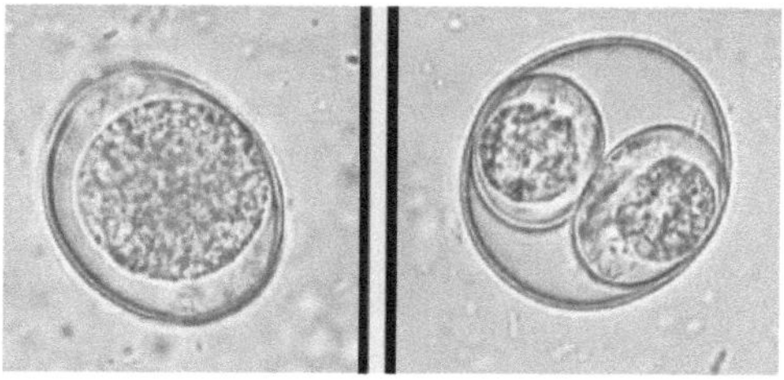

Thienpont et al.,2003

A. *Leishmania donovani*

B. *Giardia sp.*

C .*Sarcocystis sp.*

D. *Isospora sp*

The correct Answer : C

5- From Feline Fecal Sedimentation or Baermann

Identify:

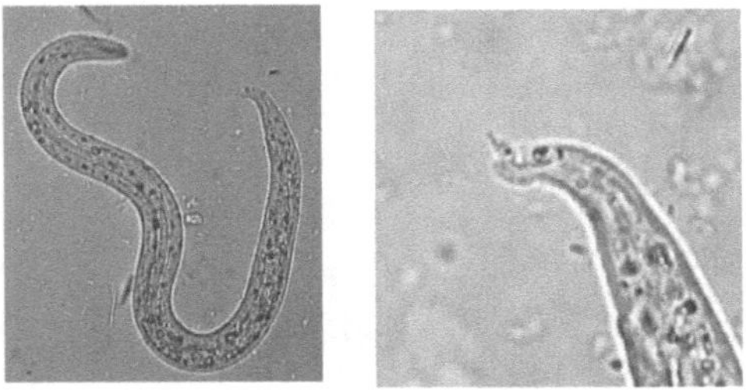

Thienpont et al.,2003

A. *Strongyloides stercoralis*

B.*Toxocara cati*

C.*Toxascaris leonine*

D. *Hookworm (Ancylostoma or Uncinaria)*

The correct Answer : A

6- In Feline Fecal Floatation
Identify

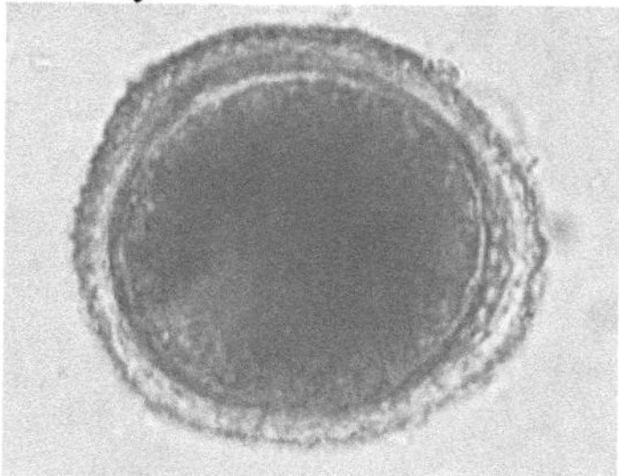

Thienpont et al.,2003

A. *Toxascaris leonine*
B. *Toxocara cati*
C. *Capillaria boehmi*
D. *Giardia sp.cyst*

The correct Answer : A

7-From cat Feces
Identify:-

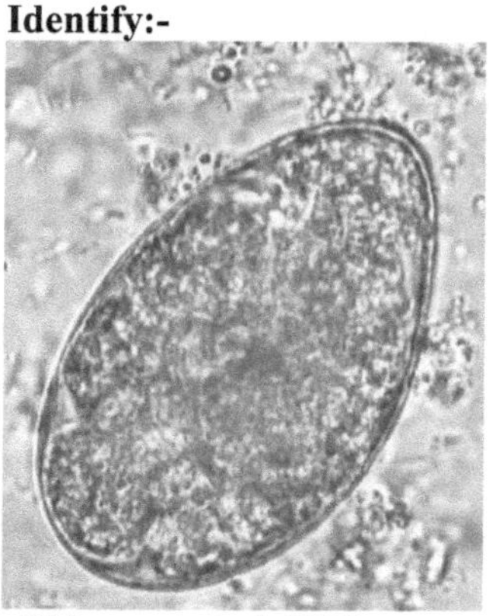

Thienpont et al.,2003

A. *Paragonimus kellicotti*
B. *Taenia taeniaformis*
C. *Dipylidium caninum*
D. *Mesocestoides spp.*

The correct Answer : A

8-From fecal dog
Identify

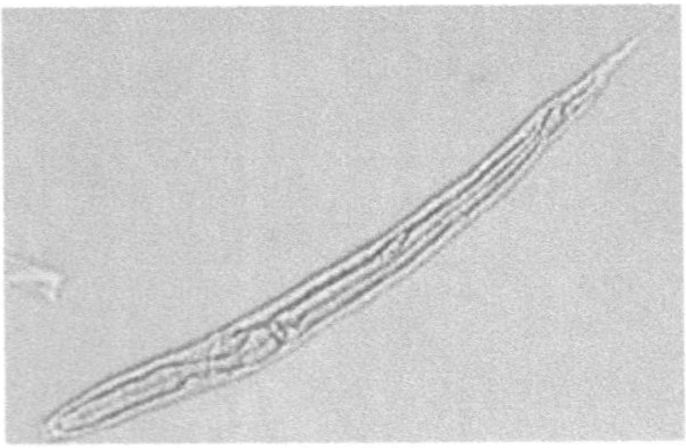

Thienpont et al.,2003

A. *Toxocara cati*
B.*Toxocara canis*
C.*Strongyloides sp.*
D.*Fasciola hepatica*

The correct Answer : C

9-. **Feline Fecal Floatation**
Identify

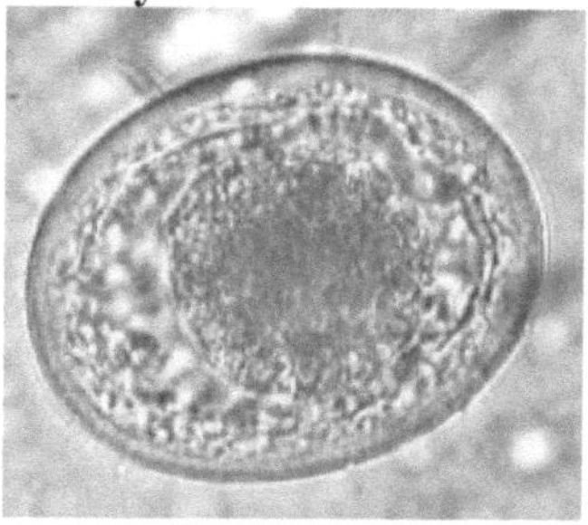

Thienpont et al.,2003

A. *Trichuris vulpis*
B. *Hookworm (Ancylostoma*
C.*Toxascaris leonine*
D.*Toxocara cati*

The correct Answer : C

10-In Cat Feces

Identify

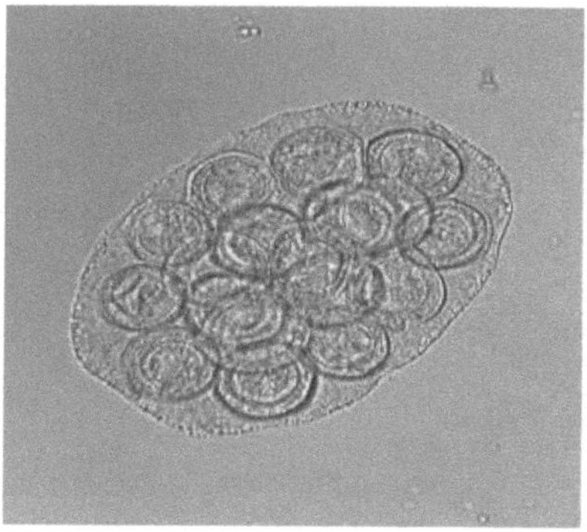

Fig.48 Thienpont et al.,2003

A. *Taenia taeniaformis*

B. *Dipylidium caninum*

C. *Spirometra spp.*

D. *Paragonimus kellicotti*

The correct Answer : B

11- Canine Blood Drop, Knott's, or Filter test

Identify:

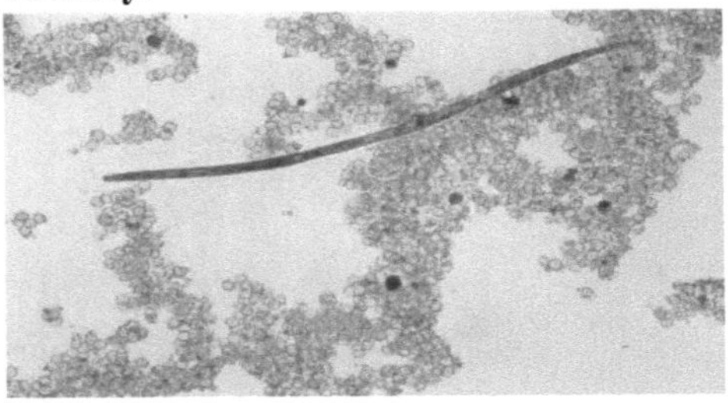

Thienpont et al.,2003

A. *Strongyloides stercoralis*

B. *Dirofilaria immitis*

C. *Toxocara cati*

D. *Aelurostrongylus abstrusus*

The correct Answer : B

12- Canine Fecal Floatation or Nasal discharge

Identify:

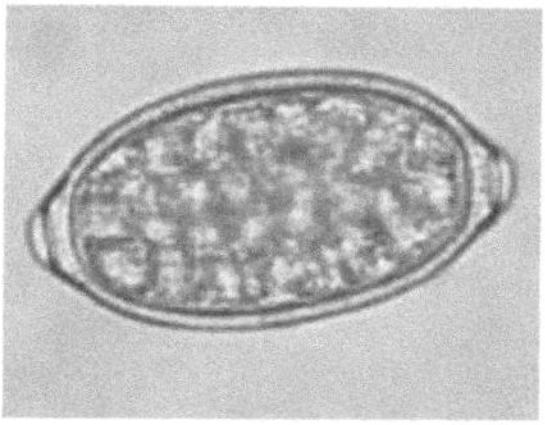

Thienpont et al.,2003

A. *Hookworm*

B.*Trichuris vulpis*

C. *Toxocara canis*

D. *Strongyloides stercoralis*

The correct Answer : B

13- Dog Feces

Identify:

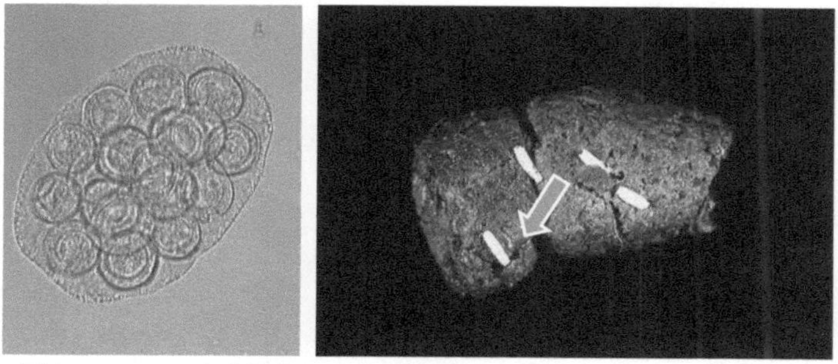

Thienpont et al.,2003 **egg & segment**

A. *Dipylidium caninum*

B. *Spirometra spp.*

C. *Paragonimus kellicotti*

D. *Taenia or Echinococcus*

The correct Answer : A

14- **Canine Fecal Floatation**

Identify:-

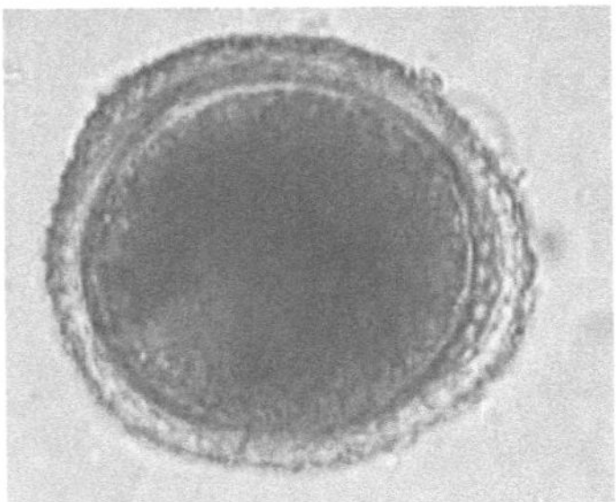

Thienpont et al.,2003

A. Hookworm

B. Toxocara canis

C. Trichuris vulpis

D. Taenia

The correct Answer : B

15- Dog Feces

Identify:-

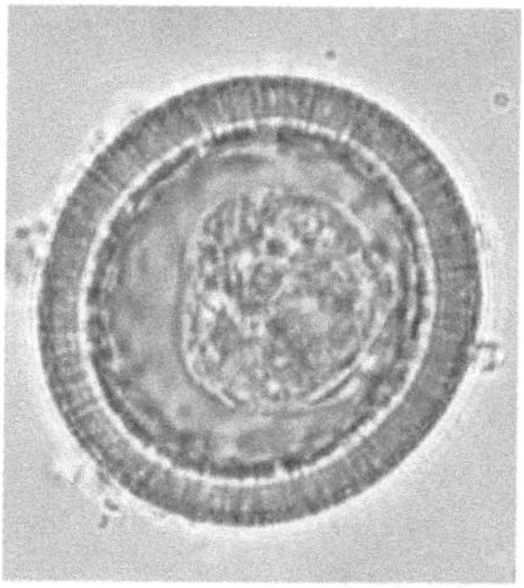

Thienpont et al.,2003

A. Taenia or Echinococcus
B. Dipylidium caninum
C. Paragonimus kellicotti
D. Spirometra spp.

The correct Answer : A

16- Identify this object frommCanine Feces

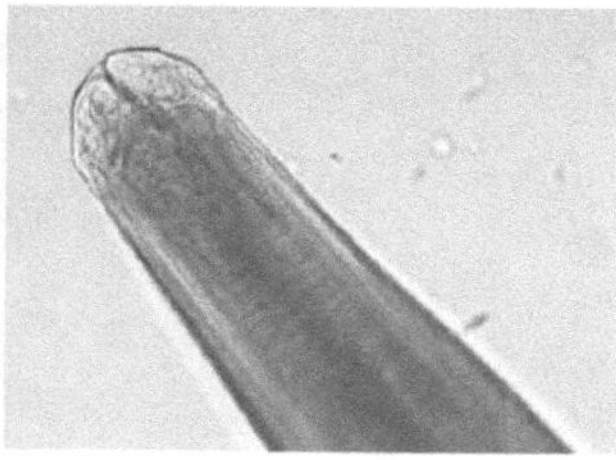

Thienpont et al.,2003

A. Strongyloides stercoralis

B. Toxocara canis

C. Ancylostoma caninum

D. Physaloptera rara

The correct Answer : B

17- Canine Vomitus

Identify :-

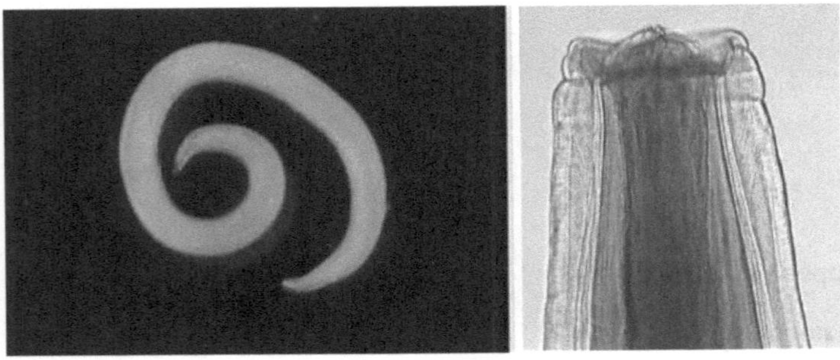

Thienpont et al.,2003

A. Toxocara canis

B. Trichuris vulpis

C. Ancylostoma caninum

D. Physaloptera rara

The correct Answer : D

18- Equine Fecal Float or McMasters

Identify:-

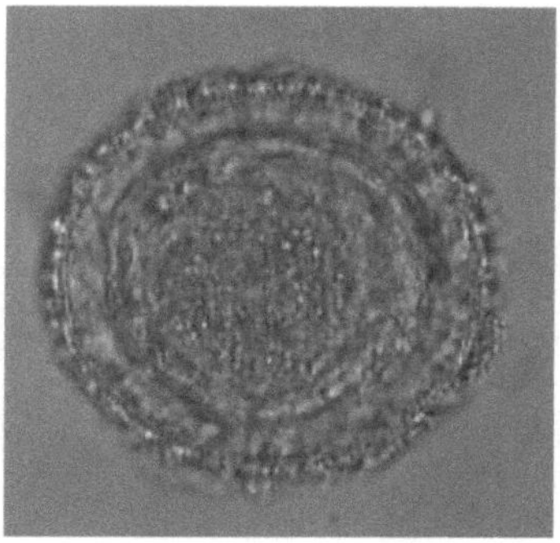

Thienpont et al., 2003

A. Parascaris equorum

B. Oxyuris equi

C. Dictyocaulus arnfeldi

D. Strongyloides westeri

The correct Answer : A

19- Equine Feces

Identify:-

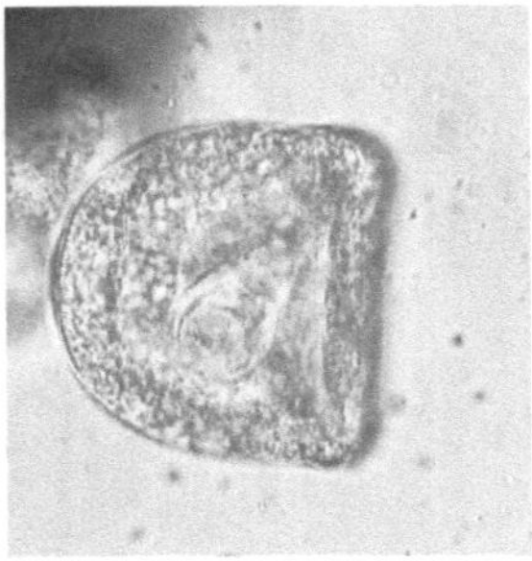

Thienpont et al.,2003

A. Taenia sp.

B. Moniezia spp.

C. Anoplocephala sp.

D. Dipylidium sp.

The correct Answer : B

20- Equine Fecal Float or McMasters

Identify

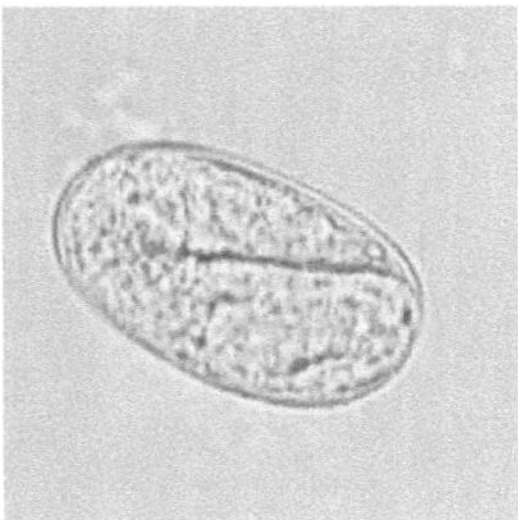

Thienpont et al. ,2003

A. Dictyocaulus arnfeldi

B. Strongyloides westeri

C. Parascaris equorum

D. Oxyuris equi

The correct Answer : A

21- Equine Scotch-tape technique or Fecal Float

Identify

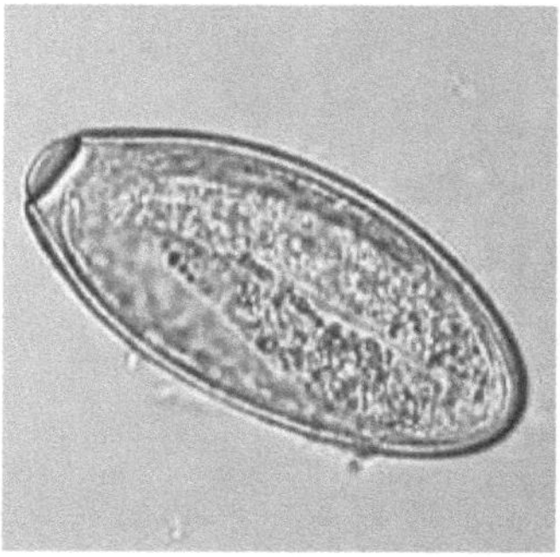

Thienpont et al.,2003

A. Strongyloides westeri

B. Parascaris equorum

C. Oxyuris equi

D. Pseudo-parasite (Pine pollen)

The correct Answer : C

22- Equine Fecal Float or McMasters

Identify

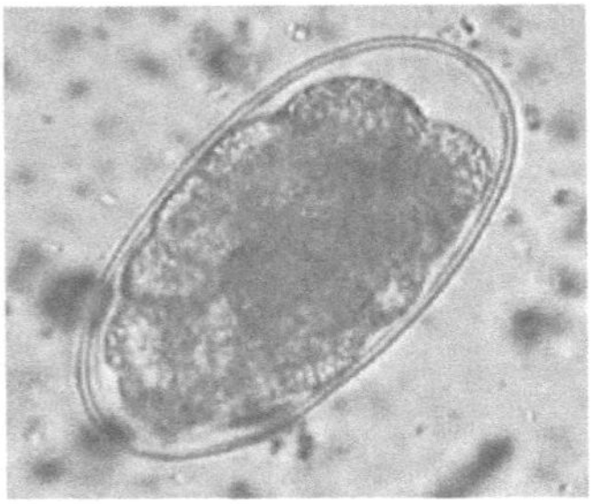

Thienpont et al.,2003

A. Dictyocaulus arnfeldi

B. Oxyuris equi

C. Strongyle-type

D. Parascaris equorum

The correct Answer : C

***23*- Dog Skin or Hair**

Identify:

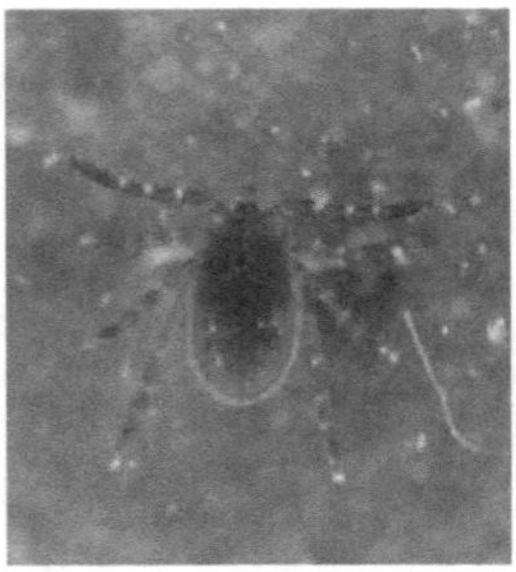

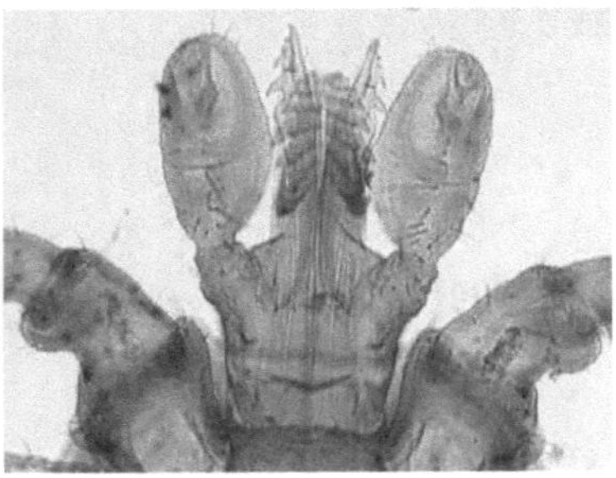

Mathison ,2019

A. Ixodes sp.

B. Argas sp.

C. Boophilus sp.

D. Lice

The correct Answer : A

24- Cow Flaky dermatitis on legs and tail

Identify

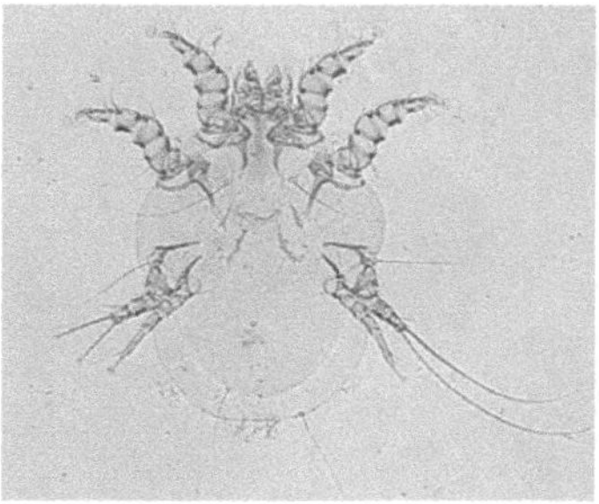

Pérez de León,etal, 2020

A. Psoroptes sp.

B. Chorioptes sp.

C. Sarcoptes sp.

D. Ornithonyssus sp.

The correct Answer : B

25- **Dog Hair Pluck**

Identify:

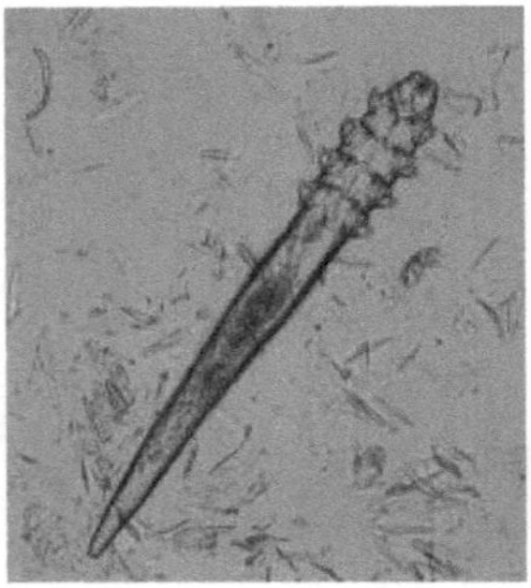 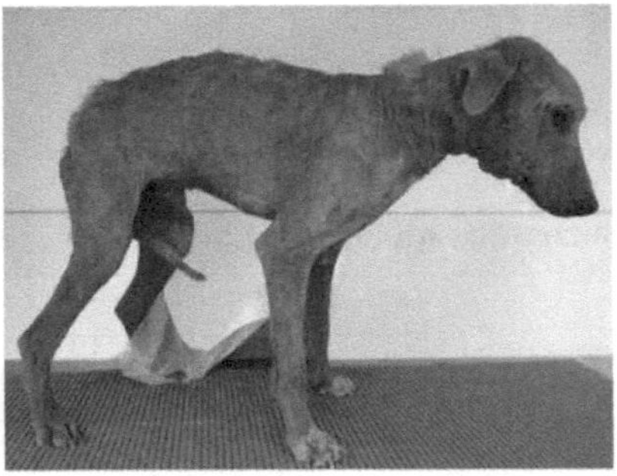

Mehlhorn,2016

A. Chorioptes sp.

B. Demodex sp.

C. Sarcoptes sp.

D. Dermanyssus sp.

The correct Answer : B

26- Feline Skin Scrape of ears and head

Identify

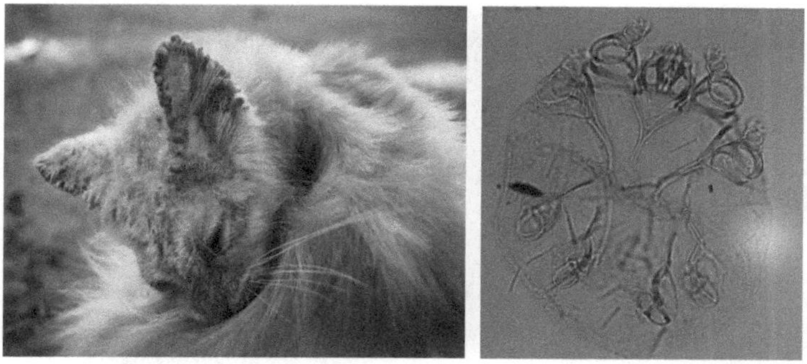

Pérez de León,etal, 2020

A. Sarcoptes sp.

B. Notoedres sp

C. Psoroptes sp.

D. Demodex sp.

The correct Answer : A

27- Feline External Ear Canal

Identify

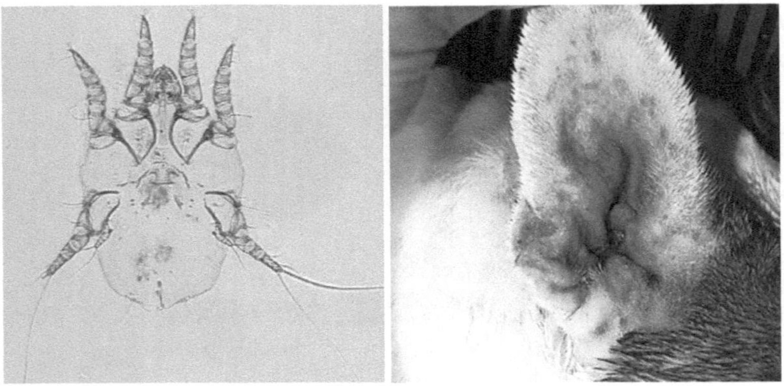

Pérez de León,etal, 2020

A. Demodex sp

B. Sarcoptes sp.

C. Notoedres sp.

D. Otodectes sp.

The correct Answer : D

***28*- Hog Deep Skin Scrape from street dog**

Identify:

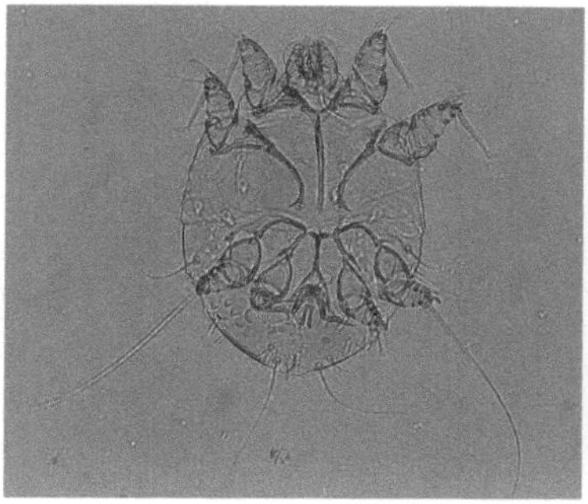

Pérez de León,etal, 2020

A. Sarcoptes sp.

B. Psoroptes sp.

C. Otodectes sp.

D. Demodex sp.

The correct Answer : A

29- Poultry nest or roost

Identify:

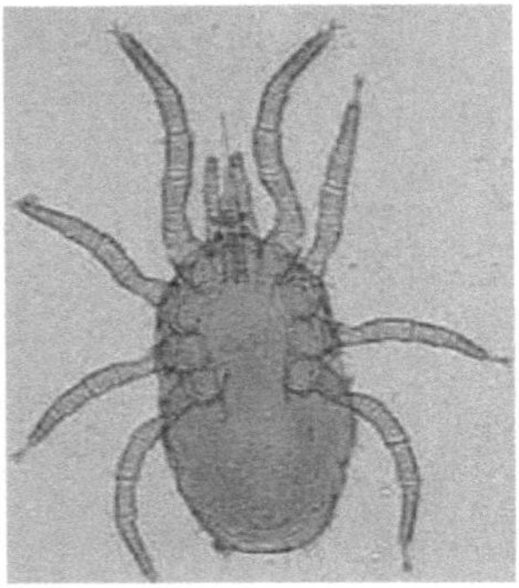

J. F. Butler, UF/IFAS

A. Dermanyssus sp.

B. Demodex sp.

C. Sarcoptes sp.

D. Psoroptes sp.

The correct Answer : A

30- Sheep Under a large skin scab

Identify

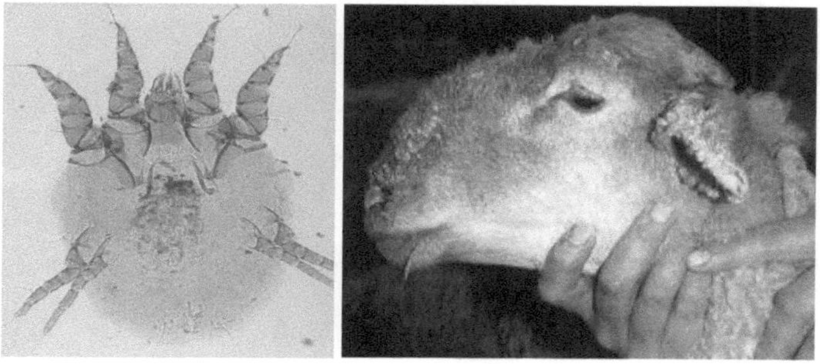

Pérez de León,etal, 2020

A. Psoroptes sp.

B. Sarcoptes sp.

C. Chorioptes sp

D. Domedex sp.

The correct Answer : A

31- Swine Fecal Float

Identify

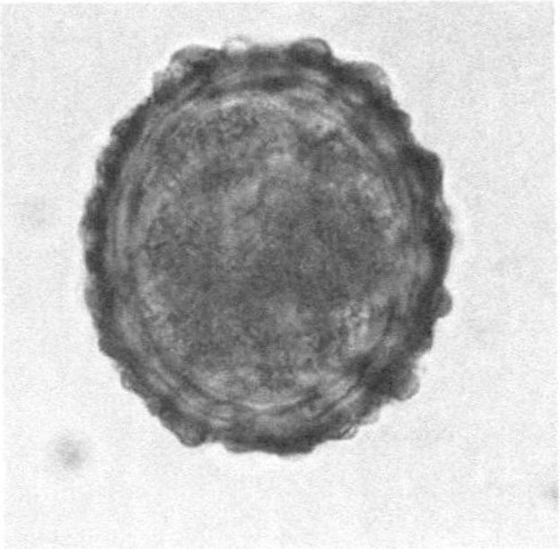

Amer and Ashankyty. 2015

A. Ascaris suum

B. Trichuris suis

C. Strongyloides ransomi

D. Metastrongylus sp.

The correct Answer : A

32- Calf Feces with severe diarrhea

Identify

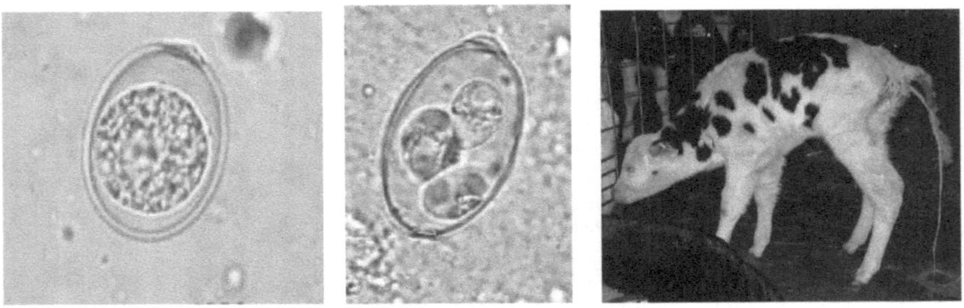

parasite & calf diarrhea Mehlhorn,2016

A. Isospora sp.

B. Sarcocystis sp

C. Eimeria sp.

D. Giardia sp.

The correct Answer : C

33- Swine Fecal Float

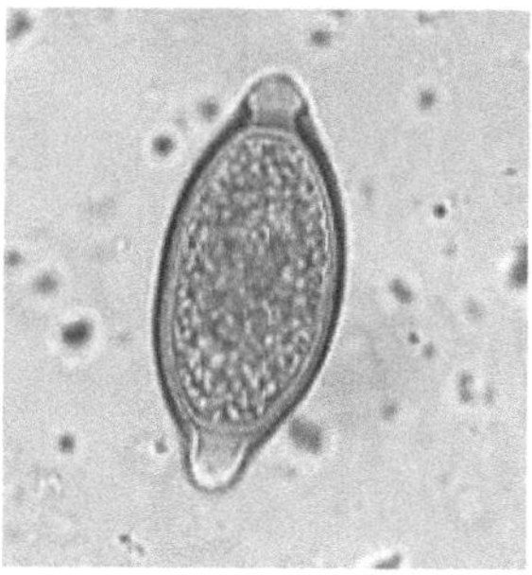

Thienpont et al.,2003

Identify:

A. Ascaris suum

B. Metastrongylus sp

C. Trichuris suis

D. Strongyloides ransomi

The correct Answer : C

34- On Ruminant Skin or Hair

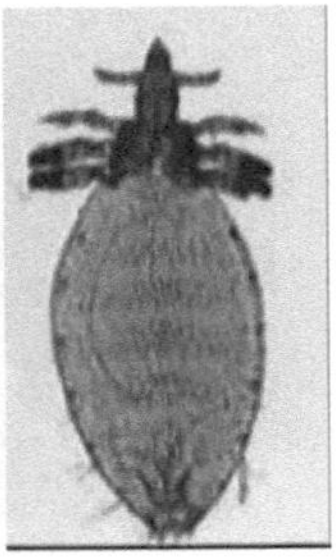

Mehlhorn,2016

Identify:

A. Menopon

B. Haematopinus eurysternus

C. Damalinia sp.

D. Trichodectes sp.

The correct Answer : C

35- Poultry Skin

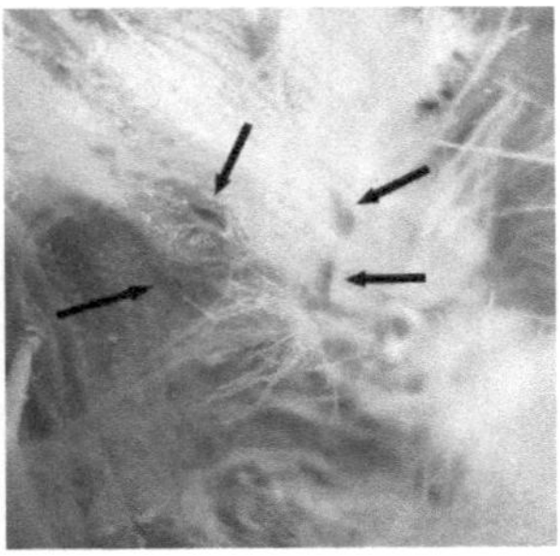

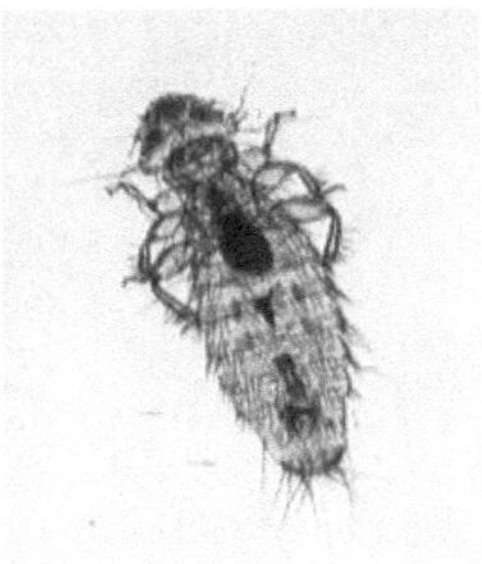

Mehlhorn,2016

Identify:

A. Haematopinus sp

B. Menacanthus or Menopon

C. Linognathus sp

D. Solenoptes sp.

The correct Answer : B

36- On Dog Skin or Hair

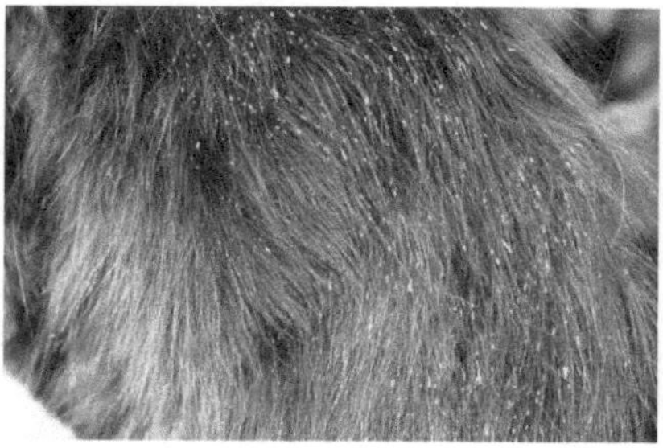

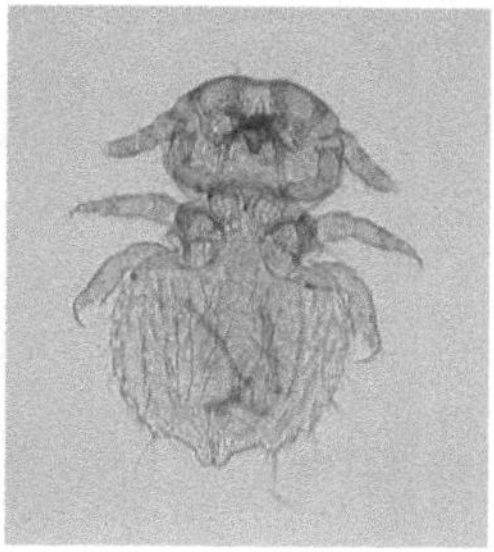

dog hair & parasite Mehlhorn,2016

Identify:

A. Linognathus sp.

B. Phthirus sp.

C. Pediculus sp

D. Felicola sp.

The correct Answer : A

37- Cattle Hair or Skin

Cattle hair & parasites Mehlhorn,2016

Identify:

A. Damalinia (Bovicola) sp.

B. Pediculus sp.

C. Haematopinus eurysternus

D. Solenoptes sp.

The correct Answer : A

38-Horse Skin or Hair

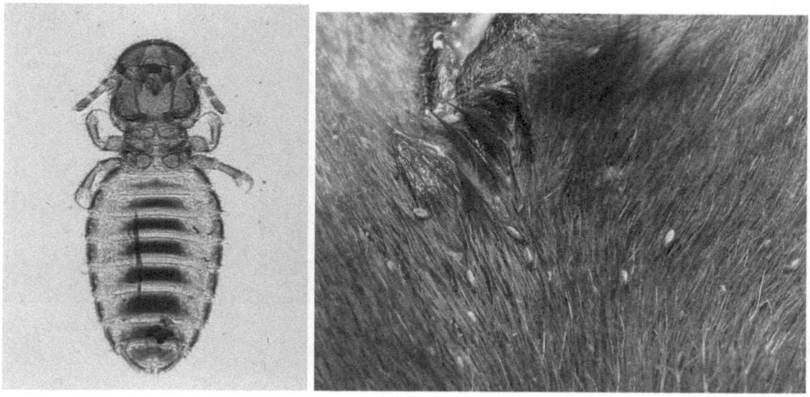

Horse hair & parasite Mehlhorn,2016

Identify:

A. Linognathus sp.

B. Haematopinus sp.

C. Damalinia (Bovicola) sp

D. Menacanthus sp

The correct Answer : B

39- Dog Skin or Hair

Dog hair with parasite Mehlhorn,2016

Identify:

A. Ctenocephalides sp.

B. Echidnophaga gallinacean

C. Pulex irritans

B. Linognathus sp.

The correct Answer : A

40-A number of small (10–20 µm × 5–15 µm), pear-shaped, bilaterally symmetrical trophozoites were observed in the faeces of a cat with a history of diarrhoea. The trophozoites have two nuclei, eight flagella and a large sucking disc on the ventral surface at the broader end. What are these trophozoites?

A. Giardia intestinalis
B. Tritrichomonas foetus
C. Isospora cati
D. Entamoeba histolytica
E. Cryptosporidium feli

The correct Answer : A

41-The following stained blood images are (oil immersion power, 1000x):

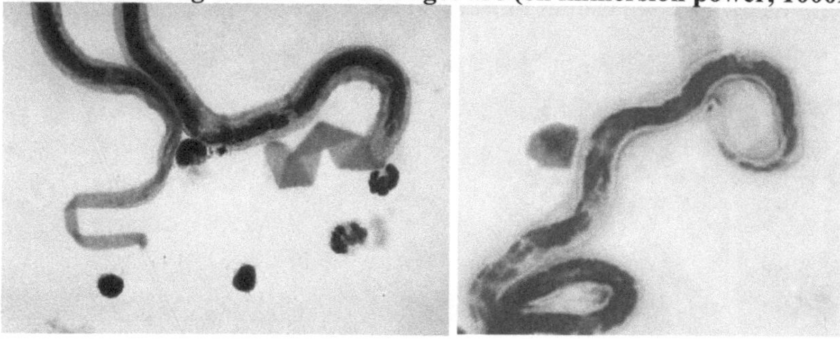

A. Loa loa
B. Brugia malayi
C. Onchocerca volvulus
D. Wuchereria bancrofti

The correct Answer : D

42-You find these worms on the fecal of an 8 week old puppy. Which de-wormer should you use to treat him?

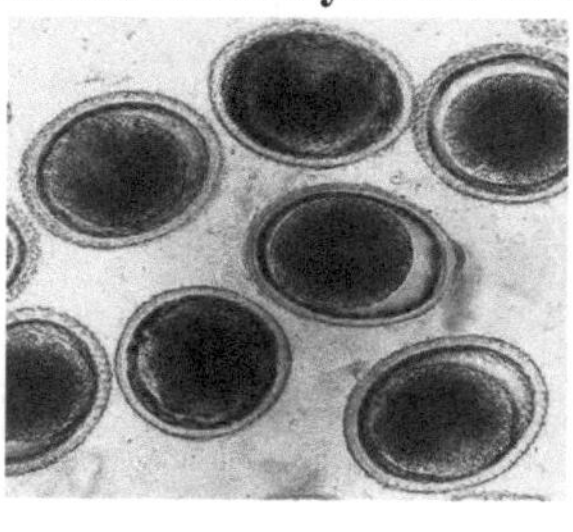

. CDC

A. Pyrantel

B. Fenbendazole

C. Ponazuril

D. Milbemycine oxime

The correct Answer : B

43-On your way to work you notice this in your yard. Besides more conscientious owners, what does this dog need?

D. Thienpont etal ,2003

A.Fipronil

B.Fenbendazole

C.Praziquantel

D.Ivermectin

The correct Answer : C

44- Fenbendazole treats which parasites?

A.Ascarids

B.Strongyles

C.Whipworms

D.Diplyidium caninum

E.Taenia pisiformis

F.Giardia

The correct Answer : A

45- You find this parasite in the fecal of a dog. Which treatment should you use?

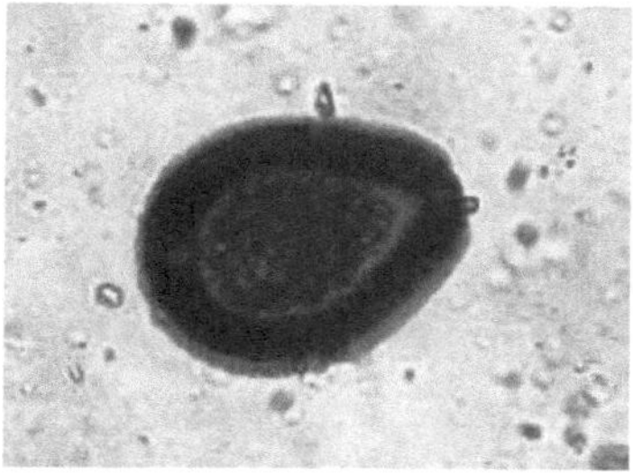

Photo courtesy of Dr. Robert Ridley, College of Veterinary Medicine, Kansas State, University, Manhattan, KS.

A. Ponazuril

B. Febantel

C. Ivermectin

D. Nothing because this is a psuedoparasite.

E. Amprolium

The correct Answer : C

46-This parasite was detected on fecal flotation of a 3-month-old puppy with acute diarrhea. Although many dogs will self-cure this parasite, you decide to prescribe a treatment. What treatment is most appropriate?

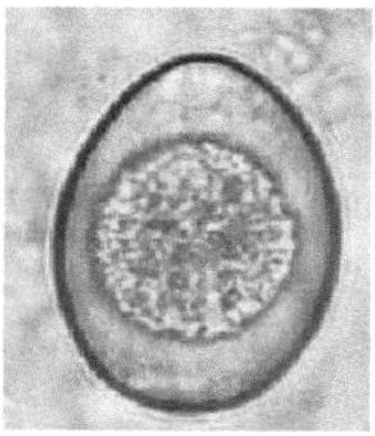

CDC

A. Sulfadimethoxine

B. Fenbendazole

C. Ivermectin

D. Metronidazole

E. Pyrantel

The correct Answer : A

49-This rabbit probably is infested with _________ _________.

Joerg Mayer ,2021

The correct Answer : **Ear mite: *Psoroptes cuniculi***

50-Intestinal Helminths are acquired by .

A. Ingestion of eggs.

B. Direct penetration of larvae through skinC.

C. Both.

D. Neither

The correct Answer : C

CHAPTER EIGHT:CASE STUDIES IN VET.PARASITOLOGY

Case No. 1

A 5-yr-old male Quarter horse is brought to the clinic by his owner. For approximately 1 mo, the patient has had an abscess in his left pectoral region, suggestive of Pigeon fever. In the last week, the patient has had temperatures up to 40° C and has a deep moist cough. He has been treated at home with oral phenylbutazone (unknown dose) for the fevers. A mobile veterinarian examined the patient in the past week and noted increased airway sounds. The horse was referred to the clinic for further examination. Stool examination revealed parasites

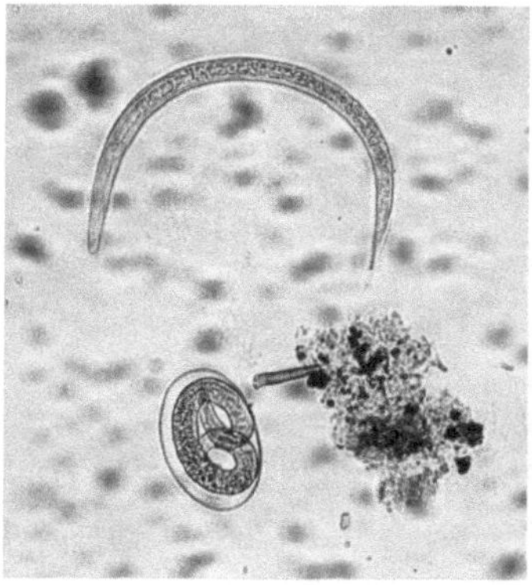

Cough in horses NCVP,2019

1-What is parasite causes the disease?

2-Choose a location where the parasite is most commonly found inside the body.

3-How a horse is takes infection by the parasite?

4-What are the best drugs used for treatment?

Answer the Case No.1

1-Lung worm (*Dictyocaulus arnfieldi*)

2- The lower respiratory tract

3-Ingestion of L3

4-Ivermectin and moxidectin are the most effective treatments for lungworm

Case No.2

A 5-year-old neutered male mixed-breed dog was brought to the clinic by his owner. For approximately 2 wk the patient has had several "lumps" on his body and legs. The owner tells you a few of the lumps burst open recently, and the owners have noticed lameness and less energy. For approximately 1 wk the patient has been coughing and has had a decreased appetite. On blood examination revealed this object (Figure 2)

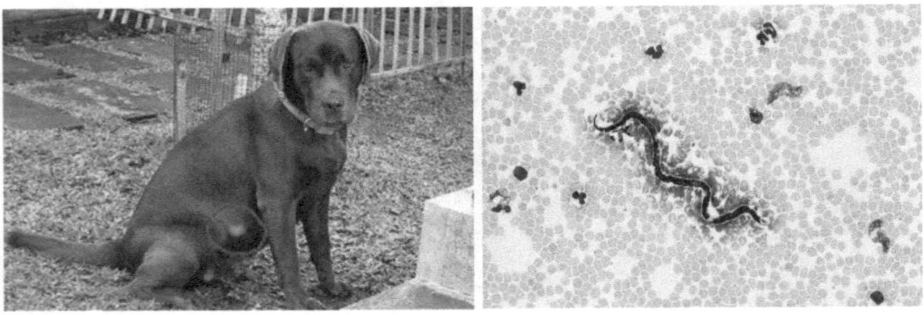

Dog lump & blood object,NCVP,2021

1-What is your identification? Based on what criteria?

2-Choose the habitat of the parasite is most commonly found inside the body?

3-This parasite can be transmitted from dog to human?

Answer the Case No.2

1- Dirofilaria repens
2- subcutaneous nodules
3- Yes

Case No.3

An approximately 8-month-old kitten is brought to the clinic by her owner for evaluation. The kitten was taken in a few weeks ago. The owner says the kitten has been coughing intermittently since being found, but now the coughing has increased in frequency and the cat vomit worm. Stool examination revealed egg

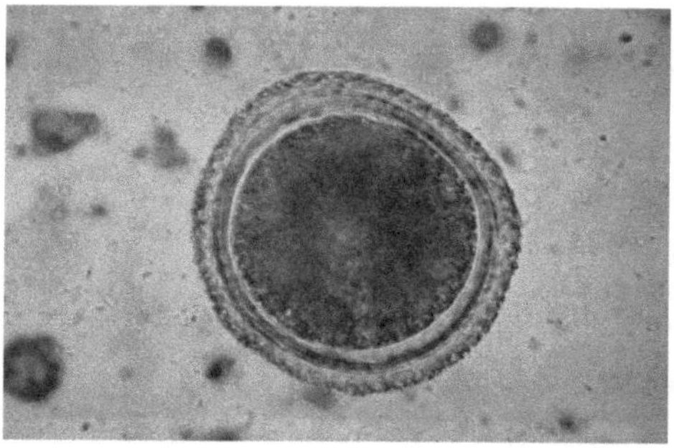

Adult worm & egg, NCVP,2017

1-What is your identification? Based on what criteria?

2-Choose the habitat of the parasite is most commonly found inside the body?

3-This parasite can be transmitted from cat to human ?

Answer the Case No.2

1- Toxocara cati

2-Small intstine

3- Adults and children can become infected by accidentally swallowing dirt that has been contaminated with dog or cat feces that contain infectious Toxocara eggs. Although it is rare, people can also become infected from eating undercooked meat containing Toxocara larvae.

Case No. 4

An 8-month-old mare . Initial clinical signs including anorexia and weight loss, itching the body on hard object and the horse's condition progressively worsened. The horse was humanely euthanatized and submitted for necropsy. Necropsy revealed large numbers of the following organisms:

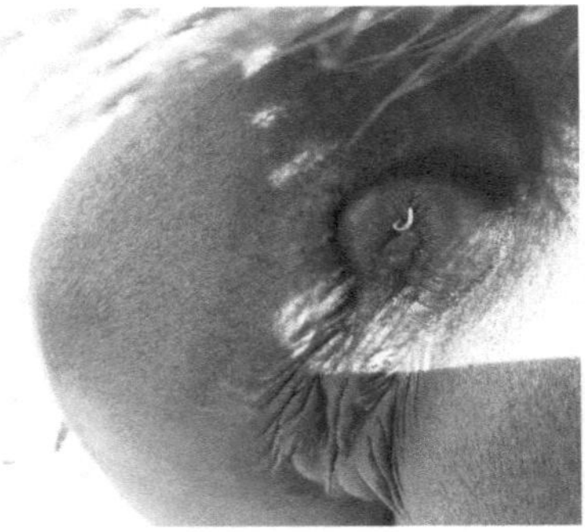

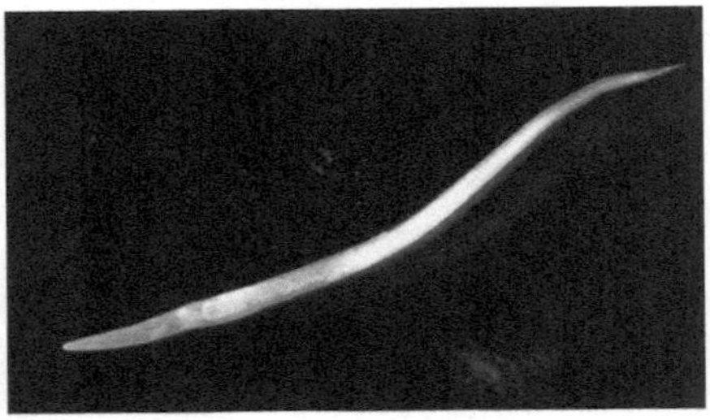

Adult worm Malone etal.,2007

1-Which of the following is the most likely diagnosis?

2- What is the infective stage and diagnostic stage for this parasite ?

3- How this parasite treated?

4-Choose a location where the parasite is most commonly found inside the body?

Answer the Case No.4

1- Oxyuris equi (Pinworm)

2- Eggs containing the infective L3 & The *O. equi* eggs are ovoid, and yellow.

3- Both ivermectin and pyrantel pamoate were greater than 90% effective to remove adult

4- Caecum, large intestine and the rectum.

Case No.5

An 8-month-old male Thoroughbred horse presented to Oklahoma State University's Equine Internal Medicine Service for suspected renal failure. Initial clinical signs including anorexia and weight loss were first observed 3 weeks prior, and the horse's condition progressively worsened. The horse was humanely euthanatized and submitted for necropsy. Necropsy revealed large numbers of the following organisms:

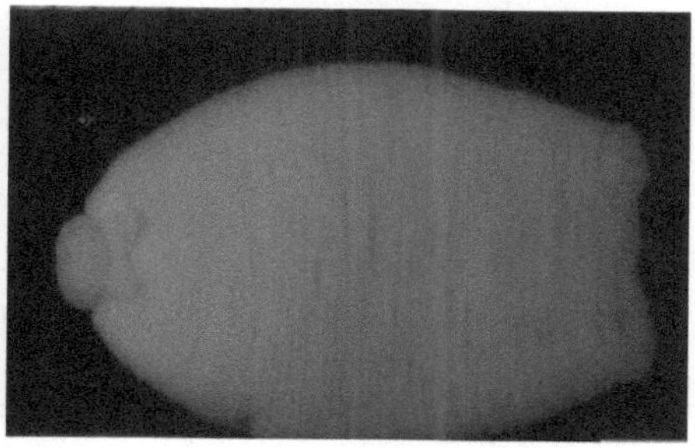

Thienpont et al., 2003

1-What is your diagnosis?

2-What is the mode of infection in 87 & 88 ?

3-Choose a location where the parasite is most commonly found inside the body in 87 & 88?

Answer the Case No.5

1- parascaris equi & Anoplocephala perfoliata
2- Ingestion of egg contain L2 & Cysticercoid
3- Small intestine & common intestinal tapeworm of horses

Case No.6

A litter of three puppies were rescued from a local shelter in Egypt. As part of the clinical exam a fecal analysis was performed. The following eggs and parasites were observed on fecal centrifugation with sugar Sheather's solution .

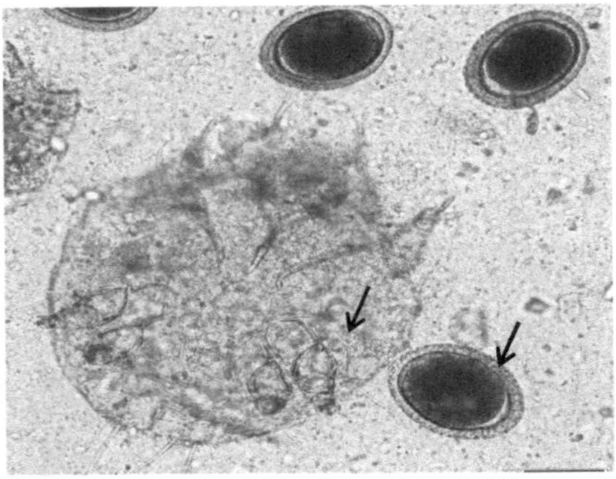

Adult parasite and eggs Jerome,2009

1-Which of the following is the most likely diagnosis?

2- What is the infective stage and diagnostic stage for these parasites?

3- How these parasites treated?

4-Choose a location where the parasites are most commonly found inside the body?

Answer the Case No.6

1-Toxocara canis

2-Egg contain L2 and Diagnostic stage is egg in case of Toxocara but in case of Sarcoptes the eggs hatch in 3-4 days and develop into adult mites in 1–2 weeks. After 4–6 weeks the patient develops an allergic reaction to the presence of mite proteins and faeces in the scabies burrow, causing intense itch and rash. Most individuals are infected with **10–15 mites**.

3- Antiparasitic drugs such as **albendazole or mebendazole** in case of Toxocara canis but in case of Sarcopes **Ivermectin**, injected subcutaneously and delivered multiple times at a dose rate of between 200–400 µg/kg, was found to be the most commonly used acaricide and effective in the treatment of sarcoptic mange

4-Toxocara canis in the small intestine but in Scabies causes severe itching, so dogs that experience prolonged scratching and hair loss are suspect. Symptoms are most often seen on the **ear flaps, elbows, hocks, abdomen, and chest** of infested dogs.

Case No. 7

An emaciated horse with no known previous history was rescued and presented to Large Animal Services at Zagazig University. The horse was humanely euthanized and sent to necropsy the next day. On necropsy, a pathologist found the severe local arteritis, especially in the cranial mesenteric artery, with a worm in the lesion.

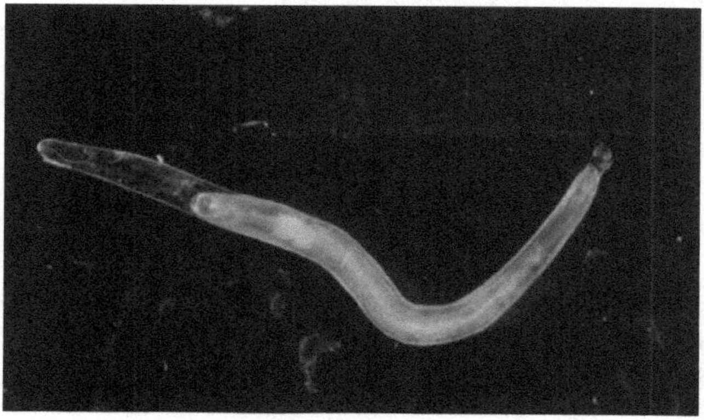

A nematode worm detected in the cranial mesenteric artery. Jerome 2009

1-What's your diagnosis?

2-How was the horse infected?

3- How is the parasite transmitted?

Answer the Case No.7

1- **Strongylus vulgaris** has long been considered as one of the most prevalent and pathogenic parasites of the horse. Adult worms live in the cecum and right ventral colon. Fourth (L4) and fifth (L5) stage larvae are responsible for arteritis, necrosis, and fibrosis of the cranial mesenteric artery and its branches (1).

2- The horse is infected when it consumes grass, feed, or water contaminated with infective larva

3- Infective larvae (L3) of Strongylus vulgaris have limited energy stores for host finding and for infection. For transmission to occur, the larvae must have sufficient energy to (a) migrate onto grass, where they are ingested by their equine host (host finding), and (b) penetrate into the host gut.

Case No.8

A beef cattle herd located in Upper Egypt, started showing weight loss over the past few months. Five cows died during the last week. One of the cows was submitted for necropsy and the following parasites were found on the trachea.

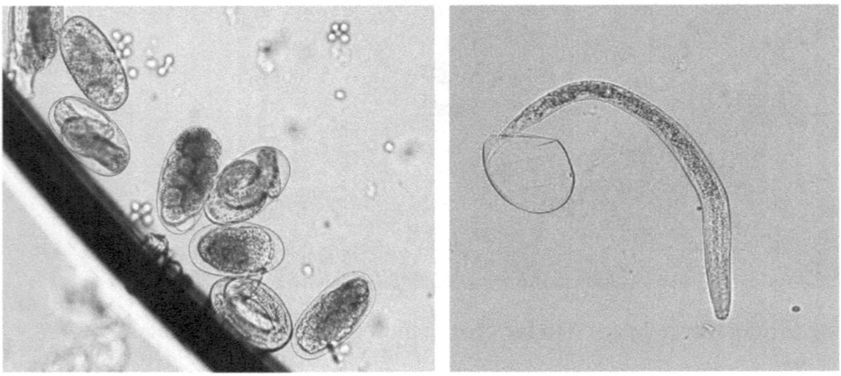

Larvated eggs & Larva hatching from an egg recovered from adult females. Jerome, 2009

1-What's your diagnosis?

2-What is the infective stage and diagnostic stage for this parasite?

3-How these parasites treated?

4-Choose a location where the parasites is most commonly found inside the body?

Answer the Case No.8

1- Lungworm (Dictyocaulus viviparous) is a parasitic infection of the respiratory tract in cattle, which can cause severe disease outbreaks with coughing and respiratory distress. Death can occur in heavy infestations

2- Lungworm infestation is caused by **exposure of grazing animals to nematode (roundworm) larvae on pasture**. The lifecycle of the lungworm is about 4 weeks long i.e. from the ingestion of larvae to the excretion of infective larvae by the affected animal.

3- The larval and adult forms of the lungworms, Dictyocaulus viviparus are highly susceptible to **ivermectin** as 0.2 mg/kg, s.c. of the drug kills 90-100% of these worms in cattle

4- Adult D. viviparus live in the in **trachea and bronchi**. Eggs laid by the females hatch in the airways and first-stage larvae pass in the feces

Case No.9

A fecal sample from a 4 month-old intact male English lop rabbit was submitted for gastrointestinal parasite evaluation. According to the owner, the rabbit has not been doing well lately. A centrifugal fecal flotation with Sheather's sugar solution (specific gravity, 1.26) was performed, and a number of these eggs were observed and sizes ranged from 97.5 x 40 μM to 105 x 47.5 μM .

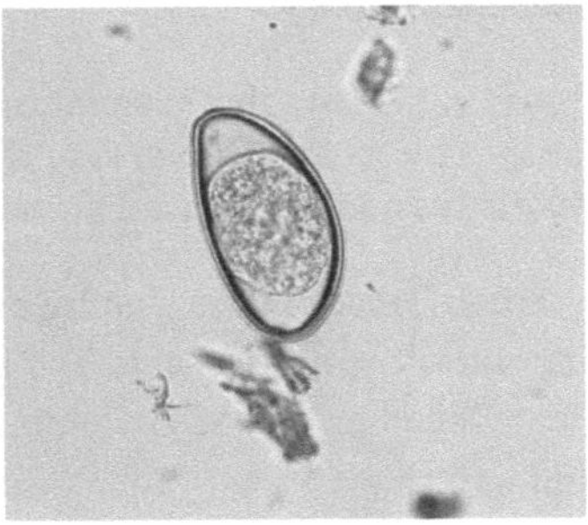

Rabbit & egg Jerome, 2009

1-What's your diagnosis?

2-This parasite can be transmitted from rabbit to human?

Yes Or No Why?

3-Choose a location where the parasite is most commonly found inside the body?

Answer the Case No.9

1- Passalurus ambiguous is **an intestinal parasite**. It does not cause a serious health threat and often live unnoticed in rabbits, but it can cause uncomfortable itching and skin inflammation or redness around their hind ends (anus area).
2- **No.** Rabbit tapeworms cannot be passed to humans
3- Pinworms live in the small intestines, cecum (large intestine), and colon of rabbits.

Case No.10

Three chickens were submitted for necropsy to the Oklahoma Animal Diseases Diagnostic Laboratory. A history of poor feather condition, decreased egg production, and increased mortality was reported. The ceca of the birds were submitted for fecal examination and parasite identification. During gross examination several adult parasites were observed in one of the chicken's cecum .

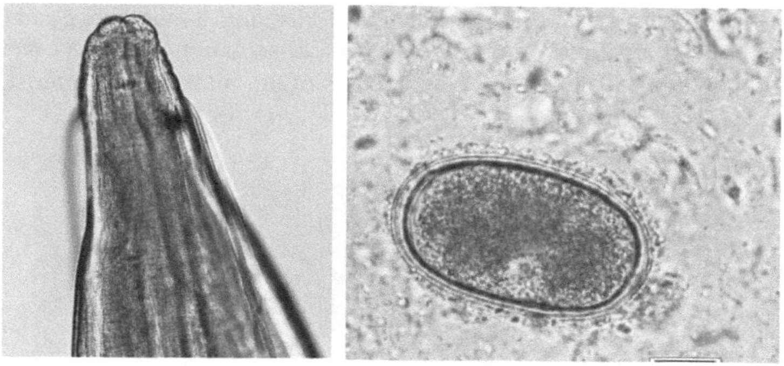

Adult parasites & egg were observed in one of the chicken's cecum Jerome, 2009

1-What's your diagnosis?

2-Name the **habitat** which has been used to demonstrate the parasite on Fig.**95**.

3-Identify the signs of parasites in birds ?

4-What **stage** of the parasite is shown on the field?

5-How this parasite transmitted?

Answer the Case No.10

1- Heterakis gallinarum
2- Caecum
3- Symptoms of a worm infestation in chickens can include: worms in eggs, abnormal droppings, (diarrhea, foamy-looking, etc) weight loss, pale comb/wattles, listlessness, abnormal droppings, dirty vent feathers, worms in droppings or throat, gasping, head-stretching and shaking, reduced egg production and sudden death

4- Adult & egg

Case No.11

An approximately 6-month-old, intact male, recently rescued, domestic short-haired kitten was presented to a small animal clinic in Oklahoma with a 2-week-history of intermittent coughing. A fresh fecal sample was submitted to a parasitology diagnostic lab for a general parasitology examination. Centrifugal fecal flotation with 33% zinc sulfate solution (specific gravity, 1.18) revealed a moderate number of nematode larvae (Figure **aelurostrongylus abstrusus**). Larvae were approximately 400 microns in length, and the terminus of the tail has a characteristic kink and spine .

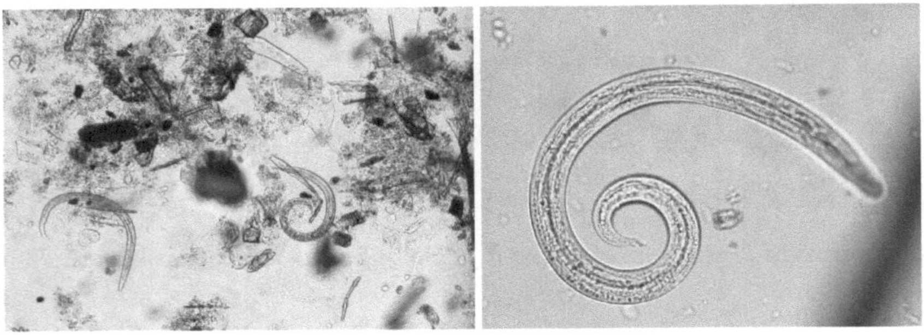

The tail of the larva. Showing the distinctive kink with dorsal spine. 400 x magnifications. Jerome, 2009

1-What's your diagnosis?

2- Choose a location where the parasites is most commonly found inside the body.

3-This parasites can be transmitted from kitten to man ?

Answer the Case No.11

1- *Aelurostrongylus abstrusus*
2- Aelurostrongylus abstrusus, commonly known as feline lungworm, is a globally distributed parasitic nematode that resides in the **terminal bronchioles, alveoli and alveolar ducts** of domestic cats.
3- The feline lungworm Aelurostrongylus abstrusus cannot be transmitted to humans.

Case No.12

A 2-year-old intact male dog was presented to a small animal emergency clinic in Zagazig, , Egypt with a recent onset of lethargy and in appetence and a single episode of vomiting and bloody diarrhea. Physical examination revealed fever of 105.2°F, enlarged lymph nodes, and dehydration.

After providing supportive care, a centrifugal fecal flotation and fecal sedimentation were performed.

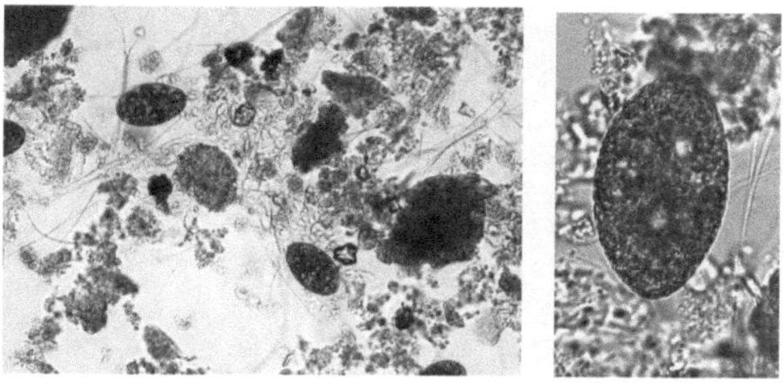

Fecal sedimentation. 100X magnification Jerome, 2009

What's your diagnosis?

Answer the Case No.12

Diphyllobothrium spp

Case No.13

A fecal sample from an approximately 9-month-old, intact female, collie-mixed dog in Cairo was submitted to the parasitology diagnostic laboratory for recheck evaluation post-treatment against persistent *Dipylidium caninum* and *Sarcocystis* spp. infection. Sometimes cause severe catarrh, bleeding and suppuration and may cause much sneezing, difficulty in breathing, irritations and discomfort of upper respiratory tract, when they obstruct the nasal passages and presence of flashy parasite . Also egg shell outer wall were smooth, semi-thickened, and the embryo appeared to have 2-4 short appendages with pairs of chitinous hook-like structures visible using fine focus adjustment of the microscope at 400x magnification .

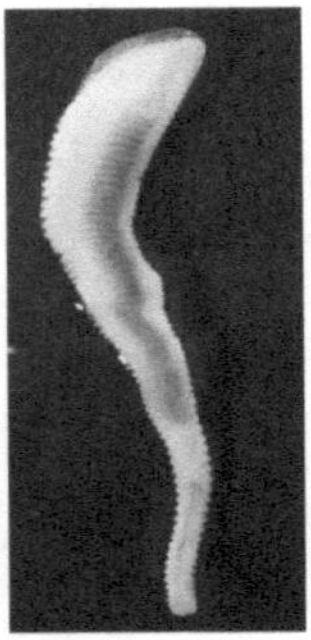
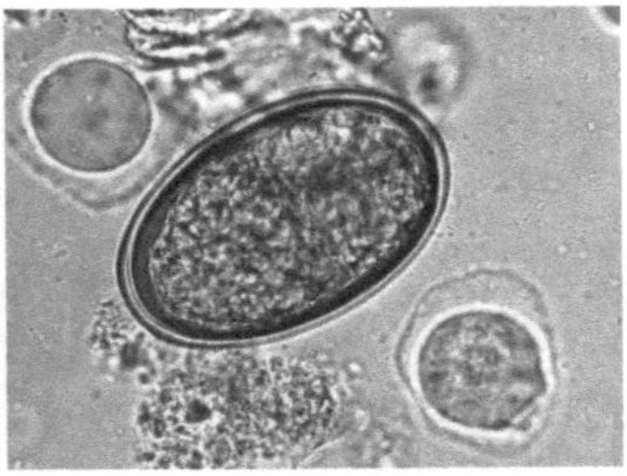

Focused on parasite and egg CDC

1-What's your diagnosis ?

2-This parasites can be transmitted from dog to man ?

Answer the Case No.13

1- Tongue worm disease caused by **the parasite Linguatula serrata** is a blood sucking parasite that belongs to the group Pentastomida. This species generally inhabits the upper respiratory tract of terrestrial, carnivorous vertebrates.

2- In humans, who accidentally serve as intermediate hosts, the infection develops when parasite ova are ingested from respiratory secretions or feces from the final hosts (dogs and other carnivores for Linguatula

CaseNo.14

A 4-month-old intact, male, calf was found dead and submitted to the state diagnostic laboratory for necropsy. Per owner, he was acting weak for a while, but he seemed to gain strength after having hay, protein and sweet feed and with coughing and respiratory distress. A centrifugal fecal flotation revealed the following larva as well as high number of trichostrongyle type of eggs and Eimeria multiple species oocysts. Baermann test was also performed on the fecal sample and recovered the same larvae.

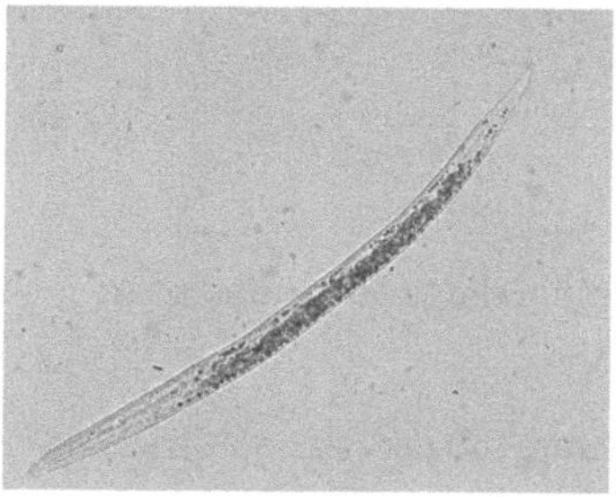

Larva Jerome, 2009

What's your diagnosis?

Answer the Case No.14

Lungworm is a parasitic infection of the respiratory tract in cattle, which can cause severe disease outbreaks with coughing and respiratory distress. Death can occur in heavy infestations.

Case No.15

An 11-year-old, castrated, male, mixed-breed dog is brought to the clinic by his owner for further evaluation suffering from chronic diarrhea. The specimen above is a smear taken from the faeces .

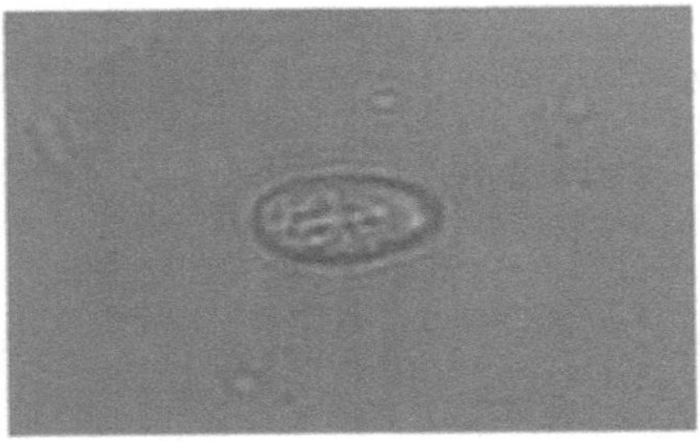

Parasite & dog Omar and Ashankyty. 2015.

1-Which of the following are the most appropriate initial diagnostics studies to obtain?

2-Name the **habitat** which has been used to demonstrate the parasite on this slide.

3- Identify the parasite shown in the field provided (**genus** and **species**)

4- What **stage** of the parasite is shown on the field?

5-How this parasite transmitted?

6-This parasite can be transmitted from dog to man?

Answer the Case No.15

1- Giardia sp.
2- Small intestine
3- Giardia lamblia
4- Giardia lamblia cyst
5- Dogs become infected when they swallow Giardia that may be present in water or other substances that have been soiled with feces.
6- The parasite can be transmitted from dog to man

Case No.16

A 12-year-old spayed female domestic shorthaired cat is brought to the hospital by his owner. The patient has had episodes of vomiting and anorexia for 3 to 4 days with watery, non-bloody diarrhea, Dehydration and extreme weight loss, fever and nausea. The stool reveals the organism seen in the figure below in fresh smear

The patient has not been able to eat solid food and is not drinking. . The cat was started on oral mirtazapine (appetite stimulant) and tramadol (pain medication), but the owner has seen no improvement in the first 24 hr.

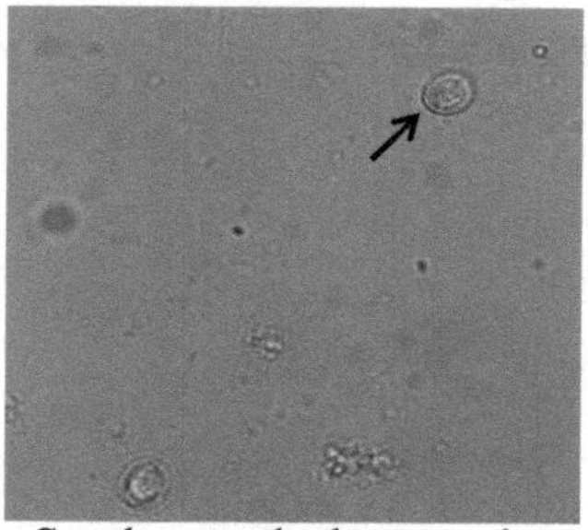

Stools reveals the organism seen in the figure below in fresh smear Omar and Ashankyty. 2015.

1-Which of the following is the most likely diagnosis?

2- What is the special stain used in your diagnosis?

3-How is a person affected by the parasite?

4- What is the infective stage and diagnostic stage for this parasite?

5-How this parasite treated?

6-Choose a location where the parasite is most commonly found inside the body?

Answer the Case No.16

1- Cryptosporidium is an intestinal parasite that is commonly ingested through contaminated water, food or feces. The resulting diseased condition, cryptosporidiosis, can typically be treated effectively with medications. This disease is no more likely to affect one breed than another, and is commonly seen in kittens.
2- Modified Zein nelson stain
3- **Cryptosporidia**, little protozoan parasites, affect **cats**, dogs, rodents, calves, and humans. Symptoms include diarrhea, fever, and lack of appetite.
4- Cyst
5- **A medication called Nitazoxanide** has been effective but causes nausea and diarrhea. Azithromycin and tylosin also have activity against Cryptosporidium and are sometimes used
6- Small itestine

Case No.17

A 2-year-old male neutered American domestic shorthair cat is brought to the clinic by his owner for further evaluation. The cat has been lethargic and anorectic on and off for approximately 6 weeks. The owner tells you that now the cat's appetite has decreased and there is visible weight loss with a distended abdomenwith watery diarrhea,Pale yellow,loose,frothy Diarrhea containing excessive mucus and fat. (Lentilsoup appearance). Stool smear showed no pus cells. However, wet smear showed the following parasite in Figure 24

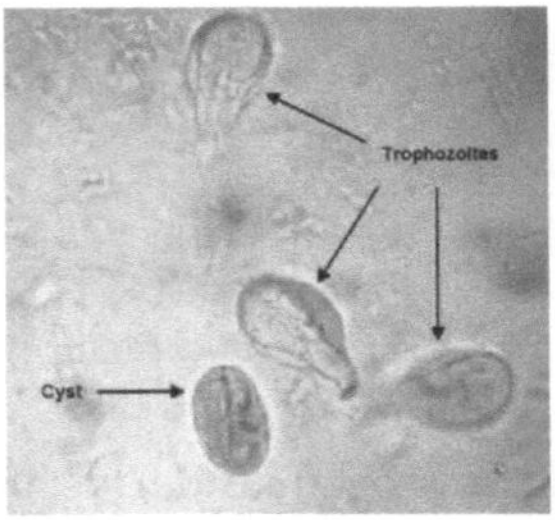

wet smear showed the following parasite Chatterjee, K. D. (2009).

1- What is your diagnosis? Based on what criteria?

2-What are the different methods of diagnosis?

3-Mode of infection and infective stage?

Answer the Case No.17

1- Giardia is a protozoal infectious agent
2- Diagnosis. To diagnose giardiasis, your veterinarian will need to **examine a stool sample**. Because Giardia cysts can be shed intermittently in the stool, they might not be seen on a single stool sample.
3- "Giardiasis can be transmitted by eating or sniffing the cysts from contaminated ground, or by drinking contaminated water." Disease is relatively rare in healthy adult cats. The likelihood of developing disease increases when large numbers of cysts are present in the environment from fecal contamination. The infective stage is cyst

Case No.18

A 4-year-old female, spayed Yorkshire terrier dog is brought to the clinic by his owner for further evaluation. The dog has been anorectic, lethargic, and vomiting for several days . Noticed a wormlike object , cucumber seed shape in the stool. During a visit to the referring veterinarian2 months ago, blood work revealed increased liver enzymes. The dog was started on amoxicillin and a liver support supplement but did not improve. Repeat blood work 1 month later showed a further increase in liver enzymes, and the client was referred for further evaluation.

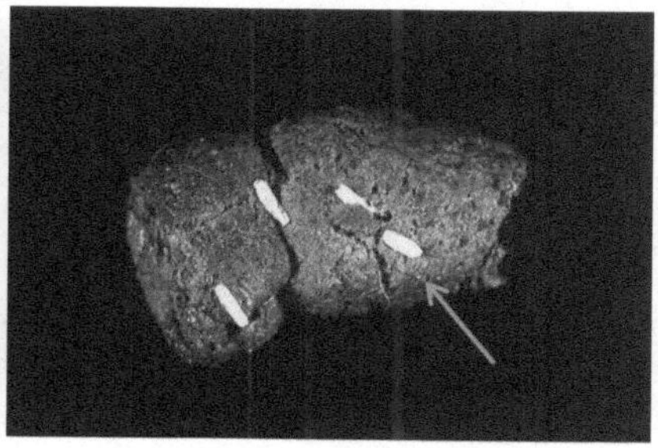

A wormlike object in the stool Chatterjee, K. D. (2009).

1- What is your identification? Based on what criteria?

2-How the species of parasite infect the dog?

3- Can this parasite be transmitted from dog to human? How

Answer the Case No.18

1- Dipylidium caninum, also called the cucumber tapeworm or the double-pore tapeworm, is a cyclophyllid cestode that infects organisms afflicted with fleas, including canids, felids, and pet-owners.

2-D. caninum is the most common tapeworm in of dogs it is acquired by ingesting infected fleas.

3-Dipylidium caninum is a common tapeworm of dogs and cats, but is **occasionally found in humans**. Accidental ingestion of dog fleas.

Case No. 19

A 2-year-old female Holstein cow is brought to the clinic for evaluation. The cow has been coughing and has had nasal discharge for the past several weeks. She recently started to spontaneously bleed from the nose. The owner separated the cow from the herd and attempted to treat the cow for pneumonia with an unknown antibiotic for 3 days ,then the cow died. And on postmortem examination thread like worm was found in lung.

Thread like worm was found in lung. Chatterjee, K. D. (2009).

1- What is your diagnosis? Based on what criteria?

2-What species of parasite infect the cow?

3-What is the infective stage in this parasite?

4-How was the cow acquired the infection?

5-What are the best drugs used for treatment?

Answer the Case No.19

1-Lung worma parasitic infection of the respiratory tract in cattle, which can cause severe disease outbreaks with coughing and respiratory distress. Death can occur in heavy infestations. Other signs can include weight loss, and reduced milk yield in dairy cows.

2-Lungworm (or Husk) is caused by **the parasitic worm Dictyocaulus viviparous**

3-Infective larvae

4-The lifecycle of the lungworm is **about 4 weeks long** i.e. from the **ingestion of larvae** to the excretion of infective larvae by the affected animal. In the worst case, within four weeks of ingesting lungworm larvae, the cow or calf can be shedding literally millions of fresh larvae onto the pasture.

5-Different medications include **ivermectin, fenbendazole (Panacur™), Moxidectin+Imidacloprid (Advantage Multi™), and Milbemycin Oxime+praziquantel (Interceptor Plus™)**. Depending on the severity of the dog's infection, the medication will be prescribed for several weeks to several months.

Case No.20

A 6-year-old female horse is referred to the hospital for additional treatment after being observed eating wilted red maple leaves and passing red urine. The horse has mild signs of colic and appears depressed.

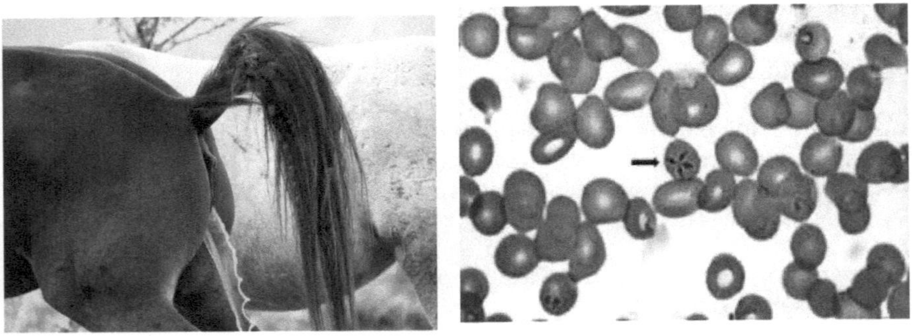

passing red urine & blood parasite Chatterjee, K. D. (2009).

1- What is your diagnosis? Based on what criteria?

2-What species of parasite infect the horse ?

3-What is the infective stage in this parasite?

4-How the horse was acquired the infection?

5-What are the best drugs used for treatment?

Answer the Case No.20

1- Dourine is a contagious disease of equids caused by **the protozoan parasite**
2- *Trypanosoma equiperdum*
3-
4- dourine is transmitted **almost exclusively by coitus**

5- **Quinapyramine sulfate or melarsamine hydrochloride** can be used to treat dourine, but in most countries, confirmed cases are euthanized to prevent further spread of the disease and because recovered horses can still transmit dourine to other horses

Case No.21

A 5-month-old male Quarter horse kept on pasture is brought to the clinic due to an acute colic episode. The colt had been noticed straining to defecate with increased frequency over the past 6 weeks. As recommended, the owner had been soaking the colt's hay after a veterinarian administered mineral oil by nasogastric tube week prior. Also fecal examination revealed an egg as shown in **figure 112**

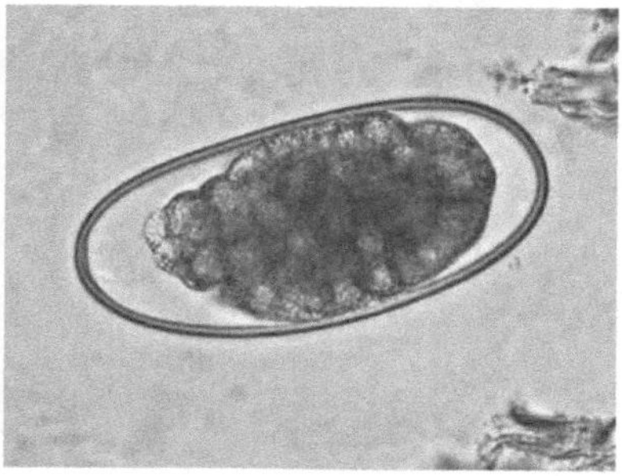

Infected horse & egg Chatterjee, K. D. (2009).

1-What is your diagnosis? Based on what criteria?

2-What species of parasite infect the horse ?

3-What is the infective stage in this parasite?

4-How the horse was acquired the infection?

5-What are the best drugs used for treatment?

Answer the Case No.21

1- **Strongyles** are grouped as either large or small. The three primary species of large **strongyles** that infect the **horse** are Strongylus vulgaris
2- Strongylus vulgaris
3- Third stage larvae
4- The horse is infected when it consumes grass, feed, or water contaminated with infective larvae
5- Treatment options include **ivermectin, tiabendazole and albendazole**. The drug of choice for strongyloidiasis is ivermectin, which kills the worms in the intestine at 200 µg/kg .

Case No.22

A 9-year-old, spayed, female Domestic Shorthair cat is brought to the clinic by her owner for evaluation. She has a worm like object on the nasal planum that has been present for several months. This object has recently increased in size and bleeding occur from nose . The mass was originally noted by the owner after the cat returned home from being missing for several days

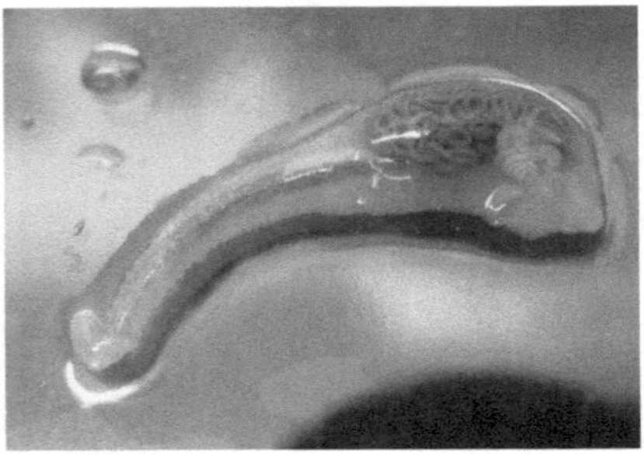

A worm like object on the nasal planum Jerome,2009

1-What is your diagnosis? Based on what criteria?

2-What is the infective stage in this parasite?

3-How the cat was acquired the infection?

Answer the Case No.22

1- Tongue worm disease caused by **the parasite Linguatula serrata** is a blood sucking parasite that belongs to the group Pentastomida
2- Nymph from Intermediate host
3- Ingestion of nymph from lymph node of Cattle , Camels and Sheep

Case No. 23

A young back yard Chickens was noted to have drooping feathers and not roosting in the coop at night. A fecal flotation was performed and revealed the following organisms (400X total magnification)

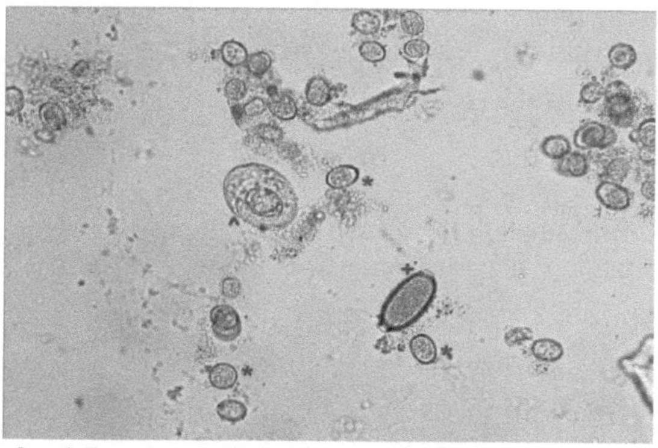

A fecal flotation , Thienpont et.al,2003

What's your diagnosis?

Answer the Case No.23

Capillaria egg, Hymeolepis egg and oocyst of Eimeria

Case No.2 4

A 2-year-old domestic turkey was found dead on a farm and was submitted for necropsy. The following organism was found infesting the feather

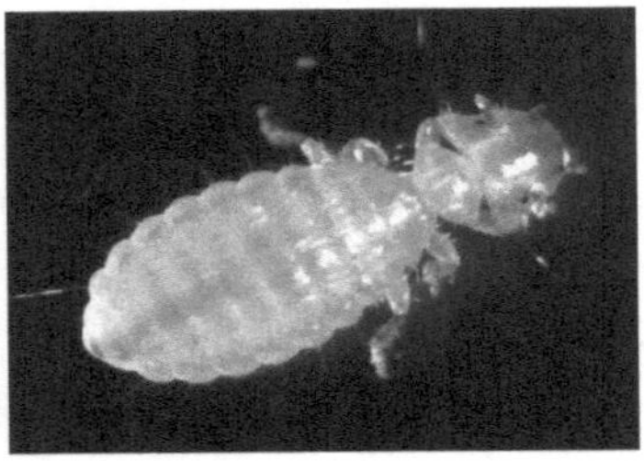

Simon , 2005

What's your diagnosis?

Answer the Case No.24

The most common and economically important louse to both chickens and turkeys is the **chicken body louse, Menacanthus stramineus**

Case No.2 5

A fecal sample was submitted from an adult female cat in Zagazig as part of a routine annual wellness examination. This organism was found on fecal float.

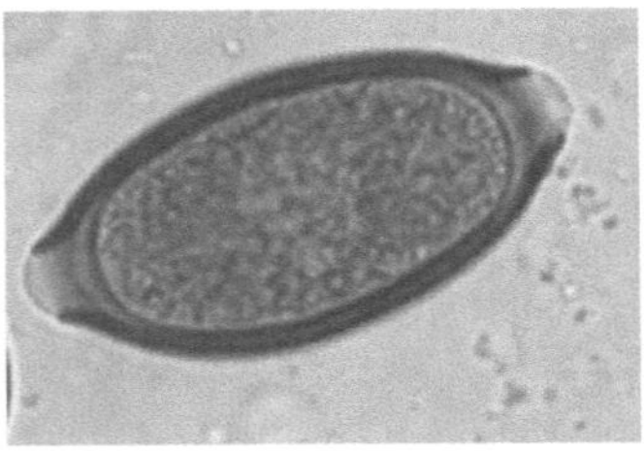

Brian,2019

1-What parasite is this?

2-Choose a location where the parasite is most commonly found inside the body?

Answer the Case No.25

1- *Capillaria* species
2- • *Pearsonema plica* (also known as *Capillaria plica*): This parasite typically invades the wall of the bladder, although it can also lodge in portions of the kidney. This species affects both dogs and cats.
   • *Pearsonema feliscati* (also known as *Capillaria feliscati*): This parasite lives in the bladder, like *Pearsonema plica*, and only affects cats.
   • *Eucoleus aerophilus* (also known as *Capillaria aerophilus*): This parasite affects the respiratory tract, with adult worms attaching both within the lungs and along the trachea. This species affects both dogs and cats.
   • *Eucoleus boehmi* (also known as *Capillaria boehmi*) can live in the membranous tissue of the nasal passages and the sinuses. Dogs are infected more often than cats.

Case No.2 6

A goat kid developed severe, watery diarrhea. These organisms are found on fecal flotation.

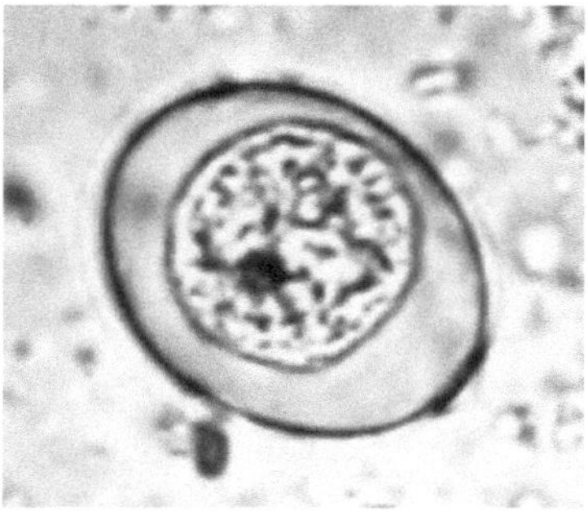

Chatterjee, 2009

1- What are they?

2-Name the **habitat** which has been used to demonstrate the parasite on this slide.

3- Identify the parasite shown in the field provided (**genus** and **species**)

4- What **stage** of the parasite is shown on the field?

Answer the Case No.26

1- Coccidiosis of goats is caused by various Eimeria species of **protozoan parasites**. Transmission of coccidiosis to kids occurs when infected animals shed the organisms in feces, resulting in contaminated feed or water. Contaminated bedding can be a significant source of infection in a herd.
2- Intestine
3- . These species were E. arloingi E. christensini E. alijevi E. pallida , E. hirci E. ninakohliyakimovae E. jolchijevi E. apsheronica and E. punctata Mixed infections were widespread .
4- Unsporulted oocyst

Case No.27

A 5-year-old cat that was housed in a long-term, limited-access shelter developed scaling and hair loss on the head, pinnae, and shoulder. The cat was observed to groom the affected areas frequently.

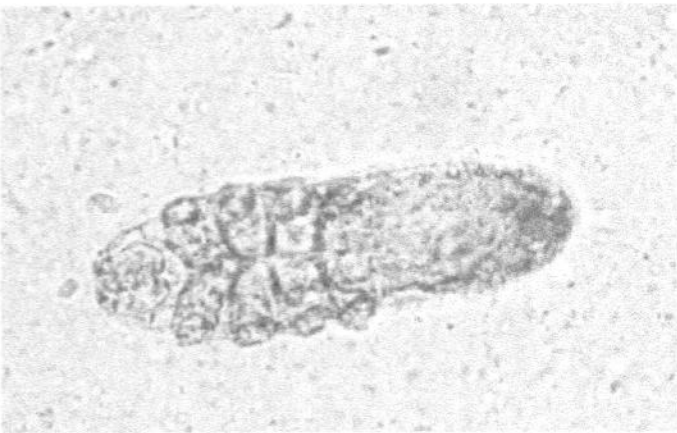

Frédéric et. al,2018

What's your diagnosis ?

Answer the Case No.27

Feline demodicosis is a disease associated with three *Demodex* mites. These are *Demodex* cati and *Demodex* gatoi

Case No.28

A rescue dog from Walpole Island near London, Ontario was euthanitized due to heart failure subsequent to heart worm infection. The dog was posted to collect the heart and *Dirofilaria immitis*. Incidentally, these worms were also collected - three from the right kidney, which was obliterated, and four that were free in the abdomen.

Frédéric et. al,2018

What are these?

Answer the Case No.28

Dioctophyme renale

Case No.29

A veterinarian doing the first pregnancy check of the season on a small beef ranch (20 cows/heifers, 1 bull) finds a high number of open cows. One cow is noted to have a small amount of muco-purulent vaginal discharge. Also, the rancher mentions that he found an aborted calf last week. The rancher recently purchased a new bull, and a breeding soundness exam was performed on the bull prior to purchase, and he has observed the bull mating, but due to the number of open cows, he would like further testing to confirm the bull is fertile.

A preputial wash and culture is performed, and after 48 hours, a sample is spotted onto a slide and fixed/stained. The parasite below is observed under the microscope:

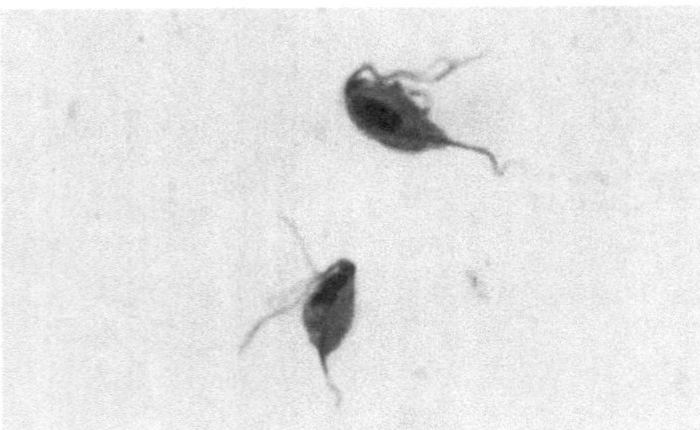

Frédéric et. al,2018

1-What's your diagnosis ?

2-How this parasite transmitted ?

Answer the Case No.29

1- Bovine trichomoniasis is **a venereal disease of cattle**. The parasite Tritrichomonas foetus is transmitted when an infected bull breeds with a susceptible heifer or cow. Infected cows can transmit the disease to uninfected bulls during breeding.
2- Transmitted from cow to cow by infected bullsby coites

Case No.30

Thirteen Dachshund puppies ranging in age from approximately 6 to12 weeks were rescued from an unlicensed breeding facility in Egypt.

The puppies, as well as the dogs used for breeding, had been housed outdoors in metal crates. All of the dogs were emaciated, infested with fleas and ticks, and heavily coated in mud and feces.

The dogs were confiscated and taken to a nearby animal hospital, where they were physically examined to assess overall health. As part of the exam, direct fecal smears and fecal flotations were performed. The following organism (~300 um in length) was found in fecal smears from several of the dogs:

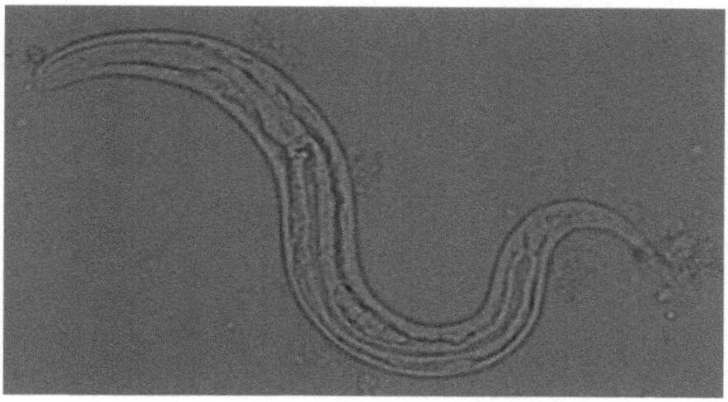

Frédéric et. al,2018

What's your diagnosis ?

How this parasite transmitted?

Answer the Case No.30

1- ***Strongyloides*** stercoralis infections
2- *Penetration to skin*

Case No.31

A 4-yr-old mare was found dead on a farm . Suffering from weight loss, dull hair coat, loose feces, and colic Then death was not apparent and the animal was submitted to the state diagnostic laboratory for necropsy. The following organisms were found in the large intestine (indicated by the black arrow, numerous others also present).

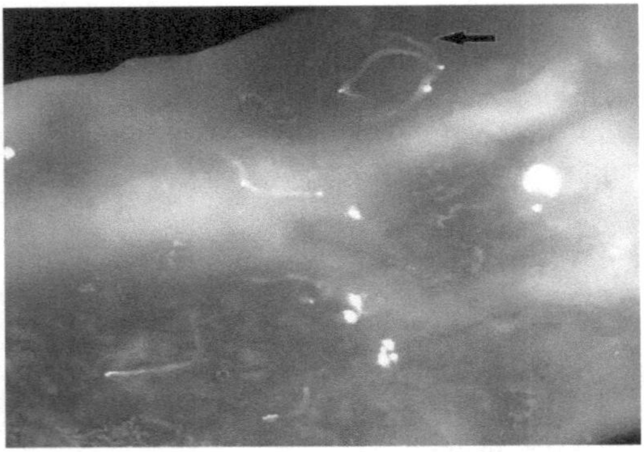

Malone et. al. 2007

1-What's your diagnosis?

2-How was the mare infected?

3-What is the cause of death in mare?

Answer the Case No.31

1- Strongylus vulgaris

2- The mare is infected when it consumes grass, feed, or water contaminated with infective larvae

3- Death often result from bowel infarction secondary to verminous arteritis and thrombosis

Case No. 32

A 7-year-old Thoroughbred horse developed severe colic, abdominal oedema, pyrexia, and diarrhoea. A faecal floatation test was negative, but bright red worms were observed in the faeces.
What is the likely mechanism underpinning this condition?

A. Emergence of dormant cyathostome larvae from the gut wall
B. Extraintestinal migration of *Strongylus edentates*
C. Extraintestinal migration of *Strongylus equinus*
D. Rupture of *Echinococcus granulosus* cyst
E. Rupture of *Cysticercus tenuicollis* (larval stage of *Taenia hydatigena*)

Answer the Case No.32

The correct Answer A

Case Studies in Veterinary Parasitology

Case studies in Fascoiliasis:

- Anaemia and hypoalbuminaemia (more than 0.5 ml blood per fluke can be lost from the bile duct each day).
- Pale mucous membranes.
- Emaciation, decrease the milk yield.
- Intermittent diarrhea and constipation

A dairy farm in a wet, marshy area of northern Egypt reported a sudden drop in milk production, poor body condition, and weight loss among adult cattle over the past 2 months.

Some cows showed signs of diarrhea and reduced appetite.

The farm has access to an irrigation canal that runs through the grazing pasture.

Clinical Examination:

- Pale mucous membranes
- Submandibular edema ("bottle jaw")
- Reduced body condition score (BCS)
- Decreased milk yield
- Mild diarrhea in several cows

Laboratory Tests:

- **Fecal sedimentation** test showed presence of *Fasciola* eggs
- Blood test showed **anemia** and elevated **liver enzymes (AST, GGT)**
- Ultrasonography of the liver revealed thickened bile ducts and liver fibrosis in some animals

Diagnosis:

Chronic **Fascioliasis** due to *Fasciola hepatica*

Treatment:

- Triclabendazole administered orally to affected animals
- Supportive therapy (vitamins, liver tonics)

- Management changes: restrict access to wet grazing areas and drain stagnant water

Outcome:

Clinical signs improved after 3 weeks of treatment. Milk production began to rise. Regular deworming and pasture management were introduced as preventive measures.

■ Case Study Questions:

1. **What is the causative agent of Fascioliasis and its life cycle?**
2. **Which intermediate host is essential for the transmission of Fascioliasis?**
3. **What clinical signs are typically seen in chronic Fascioliasis in cattle?**
4. **How does the location of the farm contribute to the spread of the disease?**
5. **Why was Triclabendazole chosen for treatment, and how does it work?**
6. **What diagnostic methods are used to confirm Fascioliasis?**
7. **What management strategies can prevent future outbreaks of Fascioliasis?**
8. **How does Fascioliasis affect productivity in livestock (e.g., milk yield, weight gain)?**
9. **What are the public health implications, if any, of Fascioliasis in animals?**
10. **Describe the pathology of Fascioliasis in the liver.**

□ Case Study Question:

A 45-year-old farmer visits a veterinary clinic complaining of a sudden decline in the health of his cattle herd, which consists of about 30 animals.

He reports signs of poor appetite, weight loss, lethargy, and persistent watery diarrhea in several cows. He mentions that the animals graze near a stagnant water body where aquatic snails are abundant.

Clinical examination reveals abdominal distension, increased intestinal motility, and loose stools.

Fecal samples are collected and examined microscopically, revealing oval trematode-like eggs.

? Questions:

1. What is the most likely causative parasite? Provide its basic classification.
2. Describe the life cycle of this parasite, emphasizing the intermediate host.
3. What diagnostic methods are used to confirm the infection?
4. How can this parasitic infection be prevented and controlled in herds?
5. Are there any differences between *Paramphistomum cervi* and *P. microbothrium*?

Model Answers:

1. **Most likely parasite & classification:**
    - The most likely parasite is ***Paramphistomum cervi*** or ***P. microbothrium***.
    - **Classification:**
        - **Phylum:** Platyhelminthes
        - **Class:** Trematoda
        - **Order:** Digenea
        - **Family:** Paramphistomidae
        - **Genus:** Paramphistomum
2. **Life cycle:**
    - Paramphistomes have an indirect life cycle involving:
        - **Definitive host:** Ruminants (e.g., cattle, sheep, goats)
        - **Intermediate host:** Aquatic snails (e.g., *Bulinus*, *Planorbis*, *Biomphalaria*)
    - **Stages:**
        1. Eggs are passed in the feces of infected animals.
        2. Miracidia hatch in water and penetrate aquatic snails.

3. Inside snails, they develop through sporocyst → redia → cercaria stages.
4. Cercariae leave the snail and encyst on vegetation as **metacercariae**.
5. Ruminants become infected by ingesting metacercariae while grazing.
6. Juvenile flukes migrate through the duodenum and attach to the rumen wall.

3. **Diagnostic methods:**
    - **Fecal examination**: Detection of large, oval, operculated eggs in feces.
    - **Post-mortem**: Finding adult flukes in the rumen or immature stages in the duodenum.
    - **Sedimentation techniques** are preferred for detecting trematode eggs.
    - **Histopathology** (in severe cases) can show mucosal damage in the small intestine.
4. **Prevention and control:**
    - Avoid grazing near stagnant water sources, especially where snails are present.
    - Use **molluscicides** to control snail populations.
    - Regular **deworming** using anthelmintics effective against trematodes (e.g., oxyclozanide, niclosamide).
    - Improve drainage and pasture management to reduce exposure to infective stages.
5. **Differences between P. cervi and P. microbothrium:**
    - Both are **amphistomes** affecting ruminants and share a similar life cycle.
    - **Morphological differences**:
        - *P. microbothrium* is typically found more in **tropical Africa**, while *P. cervi* is more widespread in **Asia and Europe**.
        - They differ slightly in **size, shape of the acetabulum**, and **genital structures**, which are distinguishable microscopically.
    - **Pathogenicity** may vary slightly, with *P. microbothrium* considered more pathogenic in young animals.

☐ Case Study Question: Gastrodiscus aegyptiacus Infection in a Horse

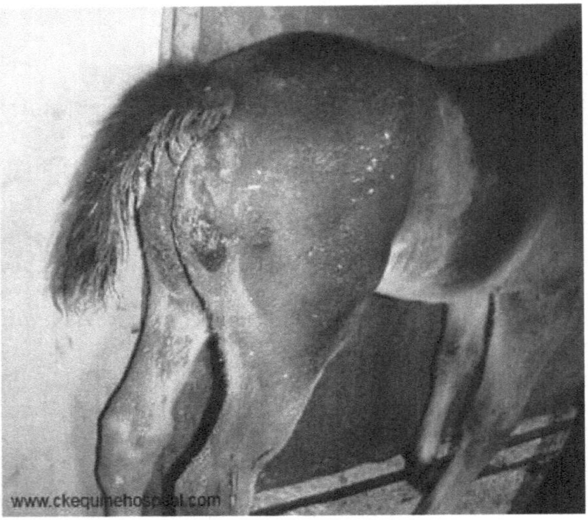

A 4-year-old male Horse from a rural farm in sub-Saharan Africa is presented to the veterinary clinic with a **history of chronic diarrhea**, **weight loss**, and **poor appetite** over the past month.

The owner reports that the donkey grazes freely near a **swampy area** and drinks from an open water source. Clinical examination reveals **moderate dehydration**, **rough hair coat**, and **soft feces with mucus**.

Fecal examination reveals the presence of **large, operculated eggs**, and a sedimentation technique shows trematode-like eggs.

Further investigation suggests the possibility of a paramphistome infection.

A necropsy (conducted after the donkey dies from complications) reveals **numerous red, fleshy, leaf-shaped flukes** attached to the **caecum and colon**.

Question:

1. **Identify the most likely parasite involved and justify your answer.**
2. **Describe the life cycle of *Gastrodiscus aegyptiacus*, highlighting the intermediate host(s).**

3. **Explain the pathogenesis and clinical signs observed in infected animals.**
4. **What diagnostic methods are appropriate for detecting this parasite ante-mortem?**
5. **Discuss control and treatment strategies to prevent future infections on this farm.**

🔬 Case Study 1: Clinical Presentation and Diagnosis

Case:
A 28-year-old man presents with chronic abdominal discomfort, intermittent diarrhea, and fatigue.

He has recently returned from a 3-month work trip to Egypt, where he regularly consumed local dishes containing raw or undercooked fish.

A stool sample is sent for parasitological examination.

Questions:

1. What is the most likely parasitic infection affecting this patient?
2. Describe the life cycle of relevant to human infection.
3. What diagnostic methods can confirm infection?
4. What other parasitic infections should be included in the differential diagnosis?
5. What is the significance of finding embryonated eggs with an operculum in stool?

□ Case Study 2: Epidemiology and Transmission

Case:
A local health authority in a coastal town reports an increase in cases of intestinal fluke infections among residents. Most patients reported eating a popular dish made of lightly fermented mullet fish. Public health officials suspect a fish-borne trematode.

Questions:

1. Explain how *Heterophyes heterophyes* is transmitted to humans.
2. Which intermediate hosts are involved in the parasite's life cycle?

3. How can public health authorities prevent further spread of infection?
4. Why is it important to control snail populations in the environment?
5. Discuss the risk of *Heterophyes heterophyes* establishing itself in non-endemic areas due to changes in food practices.

□ Case Study 3: Complications and Treatment

Case:
A 45-year-old man from the Philippines with a history of chronic gastrointestinal symptoms presents with signs of myocarditis. Further examination suggests systemic spread of a parasitic infection. His diet includes raw freshwater fish.

Questions:

1. How can *Heterophyes heterophyes* lead to extraintestinal complications like myocarditis or brain involvement?
2. What are the key histopathological features seen in *Heterophyes heterophyes* infection?
3. Which antiparasitic medications are used to treat this infection?
4. What are the recommended dosages and treatment regimens?
5. How can reinfection be prevented in endemic areas?

□ Bonus Critical Thinking Questions:

1. Why is *Heterophyes heterophyes* considered a zoonotic parasite?
2. How does the morphology of *Heterophyes heterophyes* help in its identification under the microscope?
3. What are the challenges in diagnosing low-intensity *Heterophyes heterophyes* infections?
4. Why might a traveler returning from Southeast Asia or North Africa be at higher risk?
5. Discuss how molecular techniques could improve the diagnosis and control of this parasite.

1. Canine Heartworm Disease (Dirofilaria immitis)

Species Affected: Dogs (occasionally cats and ferrets)
Case Summary:
A 6-year-old Labrador presents with chronic cough, exercise intolerance, and mild weight loss. Radiographs show right-sided heart enlargement. Blood smear and antigen test confirm **Dirofilaria immitis** infection.
Discussion Points:

- Lifecycle of *D. immitis*
- Role of mosquito vectors
- Preventive protocols
- Adulticidal vs microfilaricidal treatment
- Risk of pulmonary thromboembolism post-treatment

2. Bovine Fascioliasis (Fasciola hepatica)

Species Affected: Cattle
Case Summary:
A dairy farm reports decreased milk yield and chronic weight loss in several cows. Liver fluke infection is suspected. Fecal sedimentation confirms the presence of *Fasciola hepatica* eggs.
Discussion Points:

- Snail as intermediate host
- Liver damage and economic loss
- Seasonal risk (wet grazing areas)
- Control through flukicides (e.g., triclabendazole)
- Pasture management

3. Feline Toxoplasmosis (Toxoplasma gondii)

Species Affected: Cats (definitive host), humans (zoonosis)
Case Summary:
A young, immunocompromised cat shows signs of fever, anorexia, and respiratory distress. Serology reveals high IgM titers for *T. gondii*.
Discussion Points:

- Lifecycle involving felines and intermediate hosts
- Zoonotic importance (especially pregnant women)
- Treatment with clindamycin
- Prevention (feeding cooked meat, litter hygiene)

4. Equine Strongylosis (Strongylus vulgaris)

Species Affected: Horses
Case Summary:
A horse presents with intermittent colic and weight loss. Fecal egg count is high, and larval culture confirms *Strongylus vulgaris*.
Discussion Points:

- Pathogenesis (migration through mesenteric arteries)
- Strategic deworming and fecal monitoring
- Risk of anthelmintic resistance
- Pasture rotation and hygiene

5. Caprine Coccidiosis (Eimeria spp.)

Species Affected: Goats (especially kids)
Case Summary:
A goat farm sees outbreaks of diarrhea, dehydration, and poor growth in kids aged 3–6 weeks. Fecal float reveals oocysts of *Eimeria.*
Discussion Points:

- Stress-related outbreaks (weaning, overcrowding)
- Importance of sanitation
- Use of coccidiostats (e.g., sulfa drugs, toltrazuril)
- Resistance and withdrawal times

6. Poultry Ascaridiasis (Ascaridia galli)

Species Affected: Chickens
Case Summary:
Broilers show signs of weight loss, diarrhea, and poor feed conversion. Necropsy reveals large numbers of adult roundworms in intestines.
Discussion Points:

- Direct lifecycle
- Impact on productivity
- Environmental sanitation
- Anthelmintic use (e.g., piperazine)

7. Trypanosomiasis in Cattle (Trypanosoma spp.)

Species Affected: Cattle (especially in tsetse fly endemic areas)
Case Summary:
Cattle from sub-Saharan Africa show signs of anemia, lethargy, and emaciation. Blood smear reveals motile trypanosomes.
Discussion Points:

- Vector transmission by tsetse fly
- Economic importance
- Drug resistance (e.g., to diminazene)
- Vector control and breeding resistant cattle

CHAPTER NINE: REFERENCES

Abdel-Hadi, Y. M. (2004). *Studies on some diseases affecting the gills of some cultured fishes in Egypt* (Ph.D. thesis).

Abd El-Ghany El-Sayed Ahmed, A. M. (2011). *Parasitological and immunological studies on anisakid parasites* (Ph.D. thesis).

Abdo El-Dosoky, E. S. A. (2007). *Some studies on common ectoparasitic and endoparasitic diseases in eel fishes* (Ph.D. thesis).

Amer, O. H., & Ashankyty, I. M. (2015). *Case Studies in Human Parasitology* (1st ed.). Germany: LAP LAMBERT Academic Publishing.

Arya, R. L., Arya, R., Arya, S., & Kumar, J. (2017). *Indira's Objective Agriculture: MCQ for Competitive Exams*. Scientific Publishers.

Beugnet, F., Halos, L., & Guillot, J. (2018). *Textbook of Clinical Parasitology in Dogs and Cats*.
Copyright © 2018.

Bowman, D. D., & Lynn, R. C. *Atlas of Veterinary Parasitology*. Wiley.

CAB International. (2019). *555 Questions in Veterinary and Tropical Parasitology* (H. M. Elsheikha & X-Q. Zhu).

Chatterjee, K. D. (2009). *Parasitology, Protozoology and Helminthology* (30th ed.). CBS Publishers and Distributors Pvt. Ltd., pp. 298.

Colville, T. *Review Questions for Veterinary Technicians*.

Darwish El-Ekiaby, W. T. (2004). *Studies on endoparasites of some fresh water fishes* (M.Sc. thesis).

Foreyt, W. J. (Ed.). *Veterinary Parasitology Reference Manual* (5th ed.). Wiley-Blackwell.

Garcia, L. S., & Ash, L. (1979). *Diagnostic Parasitology: Clinical Laboratory Manual* (2nd ed.). C.V. Mosby Company, USA, 174 pp.

Goddard, J. (2009). *Infectious Diseases and Arthropods* (2nd ed.).

Helal, A. M., & Yousef, O. E. A. (2018). Infestation study of *Livoneca redmanii* (Isopoda, Cymothoidae) on *Mugil cephalus* in Lake Qarun, Egypt. *Egyptian Academic Journal of Biological Sciences*, 10(1), 1–17.

Herrin, B. (2019). *Diagnosing Intestinal Parasites of Dogs and Cats*.

Koesharyani, I., Roza, D., Mahardika, K., Johnny, F., Zafran, & Yuasa, K. (2001). *Manual for Fish Disease Diagnosis–II: Marine Fish and Crustacean Diseases in Indonesia*. Gondol Research Station for Coastal Fisheries & JICA, Indonesia, 49 p.

Leong, T. S. (1992). Diseases of brackishwater and marine fish cultured in some Asian countries.
In M. Shariff, R. P. Subasinghe & J. R. Arthur (Eds.), *Diseases in Asian Aquaculture I* (pp. 223–236). Asian Fisheries Society, Manila, Philippines.

MacConnell, E., & Bartholomew, J. L. (2000). *Whirling Disease of Salmonids*.

Malone, R. J., Baker, D., Klei, T., & Miller, J. (2007). *Introduction to Parasitology* (VMED 5235 – Fall). Louisiana State University.

Meana, A., & Rojo, F. A. *60 Q&A on Bovine Parasitology*. Edra Publishing.

Mehlhorn, H. (2016). *Animal Parasites*.

Mehlhorn, H. *Human Parasites*. DOI: 10.1007/978-3-319-32802-7

Pérez de León, A. A., Mitchell, R. D., & Watson, D. W. (2020). *Ectoparasites of Cattle*.

Raef, A. M., El-Ashram, A. M. M., & El-Lateif, A. E. A. (2002). Morphological studies on *Argulus* (Crustacea: Branchiura) infesting ornamental fish with chemotherapeutic control.

Raef, A. M., & El-Ashram, A. M. M. (2004). Observations on the morphological characters of metacercariae and adults of *Posthodiplostomum cuticula* (Trematoda: Diplostomatidae) in cultured *Oreochromis niloticus*.
Beni-Suef Veterinary Medical Journal, 14(1), 39–49.

Raef, A. M., El-Ashram, A. M. M., & El-Sayed, N. M. (2000). Crustacean parasites of some cultured freshwater fish and their control in Sharkia, Egypt. *Zagazig Veterinary Journal*, 28(2), 180–191.

Selim, K. M. (2002). *Studies on some factors affecting health and survival of ornamental fish* (M.V.Sc. thesis).

Simon. (2005). *Handbook on Poultry Diseases* (2nd ed.).

Skelly, R. *MCQs in Tropical Medicine.*

Thienpont, D., Rochette, F., & Vanparijs, O. F. J. (2003). *Diagnosing Helminthiasis by Coprological Examination.*

University of Trinidad & Tobago. (2010). *Alternate Examinations.*

Urquhart, G. M., Armour, J., Duncan, J. L., Dunn, A. M., & Jennings, F. W. *Veterinary Parasitology* (2nd ed.). Blackwell Science.

Wise, L. N., Kappmeyer, L. S., Mealey, R. H., & Knowles, D. P. (2013). Review of equine piroplasmosis.
Journal of Veterinary Internal Medicine, 27, 1334–1346.

Zafran, Roza, D., Johnny, F., Koesharyani, I., & Yuasa, K. (2000). *Diagnosis and Treatments for Parasitic Diseases in Humpback Grouper (Cromileptes altivelis) Broodstock.* Gondol Research Station for Coastal Fisheries & JICA, Indonesia, 8 p.

FSC
www.fsc.org
MIX
Papier | Fördert gute Waldnutzung
FSC® C083411

Kolibri 360 GmbH
Ferdinand-Jühlke-Straße 7
99095 Erfurt, Deutschland
produktsicherheit@kolibri360.de

Druck:
CPI Druckdienstleistungen GmbH
im Auftrag der
Kolibri 360 GmbH
Ferdinand-Jühlke-Str. 7
99095 Erfurt